Matthew Hollis is the author of *Ground Water,* shortlisted for the Whitbread Prize for Poetry, the *Guardian* First Book Award and the Forward Prize for Best First Collection. *Now All Roads Lead to France* is his first prose book.

Praise for *Now All Roads Lead to France*:

'Finally gives the poet's poet among the dead of the Great War the measured and moving biographical treatment he deserves.' Jonathan Bate, *Sunday Telegraph* Books of the Year

'With calm grace and candid respect, Hollis gives contemporary relevance to the last powerful works of [Edward Thomas].' Iain Finlayson, *The Times* Books of the Year

'Hollis's great achievement is to use the odd shape of Thomas's verse life as a way to explore the state of British poetry on the eve of the Great War, poised between Georgian lyricism and stark modernism. He triumphantly demonstrates how, far from being a baggy or moribund genre, biography can be a sharp tool of literary criticism.' Kathryn Hughes, *Guardian* Books of the Year

'One of the year's most engrossing biographies . . . sensitively recounted the growth-spurt in Thomas's art.' Boyd Tonkin, *Independent* Books of the Year

'The best book about poetry . . . moving and insightful . . . nothing I have come across before has got so well the feeling of how that complex symbiosis worked and how the parting of Thomas and Frost was as significant in its way as their first encounter. By its end the book is the perfect setting for Thomas's perfect poems.' Bernard O'Donoghue, *TLS* Books of the Year

'Brilliant and superbly written.' Nigel Jones, *Sunday Telegraph* Book of the Week

'Extremely readable ... Thomas is well served by Hollis's clear-eyed sympathy.' Sean O'Brien, *Independent* Book of the Week

'Exceptionally fine ... perhaps, above all, a gentle reminder that poetry can be almost as essential to the human spirit as breathing.' Craig Brown, *Mail on Sunday* Book of the Week

'Like Edward Thomas's poetry, *Now All Roads Lead to France* is a work of careful, unobtrusive excellence, subtle insight and great emotional power. It tells the story of a compelling figure from a half-forgotten England whose influence on contemporary writing seems to grow and grow.' Adam Foulds

'Matthew Hollis's superb biography focuses on what transformed a talented journalist into one of the most highly regarded nature poets of the twentieth century.' Sameer Rahim, *Daily Telegraph*

'My favourite biography of 2011 is Matthew Hollis's eloquently perceptive *Now All Roads Lead to France*, an atmospheric study of poet Edward Thomas, his life and times, and particularly his friendship with Robert Frost which led him to nature poetry and ultimately to powerful lyrics shaped by war.' Eileen Battersby

'Thoughtful and scrupulous ... A bravura critical performance.' John Carey, *Sunday Times*

'Elegant and insightful ... A brilliant, even inspiring biography.' Hugh MacDonald, *Herald*

'Excellent and highly readable ... Hollis writes a fascinating and knowledgeable study of England and Englishness of the era.' Gerald Dawe, *Irish Times*

'Wonderful ... Hollis tells this tale with a sigh – but also with dry wit, deep compassion and a poet's eye for evocative detail.' Paul Carter, *Daily Mail*

'Hollis writes with great sensitivity and understanding . . . The enormous strength of Hollis's study is the way in which it portrays the different influences that suddenly converged to produce a great poet.' Mark Bostridge, *Literary Review*

'This biography is a marvel.' Thomas McCarthy, *Irish Examiner*

'An evocation of a lost England that Thomas himself elegised so movingly in the nature poems that have found an enduring place in the canon of British literature.' Jason Cowley, *Financial Times*

'Compelling.' Paul Dunn, *The Times*

'[Thomas's] discovery of his own considerable talent and place in the world – as that world was in the process of falling apart – is almost unbearably poignant . . . Wonderful.' Wayne Gooderham, *Time Out*

'*Now All Roads Lead to France* tells a story so delicate, tragic and inevitable, and which contains examples of such searingly perfect poetry, that all I can say is that this is a beautiful book. Read it.' Robert Giddings, *Tribune*

'Compelling . . . Among the most fascinating aspects of Hollis's book is showing how Thomas transformed the contents of his past notebooks into powerful and haunting verse.' Hugh Cecil, *Spectator*

'Hollis, a poet himself, is at his best in examining this extraordinary creative friendship with Frost . . . Riveting.' James Fergusson, *Country Life*

by the same author

poetry
GROUND WATER

as editor
STRONG WORDS: MODERN POETS ON MODERN POETRY
(with W. N. Herbert)
101 POEMS AGAINST WAR
(with Paul Keegan)
EDWARD THOMAS: SELECTED POEMS

NOW ALL ROADS LEAD
TO FRANCE

The Last Years of Edward Thomas

Matthew Hollis

W. W. Norton & Company
New York • London

First published in 2011 by Faber and Faber Ltd under the title
Now All Roads Lead to France: The Last Years of Edward Thomas

For information about permission to reproduce selections from this book,
write to Permissions, W. W. Norton & Company, Inc.,
500 Fifth Avenue, New York, NY 10110

For information about special discounts for bulk purchases, please contact
W. W. Norton Special Sales at specialsales@wwnorton.com or 800-233-4830

Manufacturing by RR Donnelley, Harrisonburg, VA
Production manager:Anna Oler

Library of Congress Cataloging-in-Publication Data

Hollis, Matthew.
Now all roads lead to France : a life of
Edward Thomas / Matthew Hollis. — 1st American ed.
p. cm.
Includes bibliographical references and index.
ISBN 978-0-393-08907-3 (hardcover)
1. Thomas, Edward, 1878–1917. 2. Frost, Robert, 1874–1963.
3. Poets, English—20th century—Biography.
4. British—France—Biography. I. Title.
PR6039.H55Z736 2012
821'.912—dc23
[B]
2012015784

W. W. Norton & Company, Inc.
500 Fifth Avenue, New York, N.Y. 10110
www.wwnorton.com

W. W. Norton & Company Ltd.
Castle House, 75/76 Wells Street, London W1T 3QT

1 2 3 4 5 6 7 8 9 0

for Mum

and I rose up, and knew that I was tired, and continued my journey
EDWARD THOMAS, *Light and Twilight*

Contents

Illustrations

Maps

Edward Thomas spent the day before he died under particularly heavy bombardment. The shell that fell two yards from where he stood should have killed him, but instead it was a rare dud. Back at billet, the men teased him on his lucky escape; someone remarked that a fellow with Thomas's luck should be safe wherever he went. The next morning was the first of the Arras offensive. Easter Monday dawned cold and wintry. The infantry in the trenches fixed their bayonets and tightened their grip around their rifles; behind them, the artillery made their final preparations to the loading and the fusing of the shells. Thomas had started late to the Observation Post; he had not rung through his arrival when the bombardment began. The Allied assault was so immense that some Germans were captured half-dressed; others did not have time to put on their boots and fled barefoot through the mud and snow. British troops sang and danced in what only a few hours before had been no-man's-land. Edward Thomas left the dugout behind his post and leaned into the opening to take a moment to fill his pipe. A shell passed so close to him that the blast of air stopped his heart. He fell without a mark on his body.

I

STEEP

1913

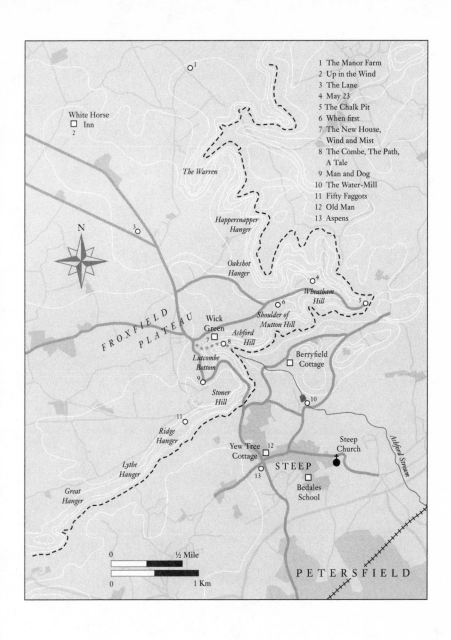

1 The Manor Farm
2 Up in the Wind
3 The Lane
4 May 23
5 The Chalk Pit
6 When first
7 The New House,
  Wind and Mist
8 The Combe, The Path,
  A Tale
9 Man and Dog
10 The Water-Mill
11 Fifty Faggots
12 Old Man
13 Aspens

White Horse
☐ Inn
2

N

The Warren

*Happersnapper
Hanger*

*Oakshot
Hanger*

*Wheatham
Hill*

FROXFIELD PLATEAU

Wick
Green
☐
7

*Ashford
Hill*

8

*Shoulder of
Mutton Hill*

6

4

5

Berryfield
☐ Cottage

*Lutcombe
Bottom*

9

*Stoner
Hill*

10

11

*Ridge
Hanger*

*Lythe
Hanger*

Yew Tree
Cottage ☐ 12

Steep
Church
●

Ashford Stream

STEEP

13

*Great
Hanger*

Bedales
School

0   ½ Mile

0   1 Km

PETERSFIELD

Winter

There has been opened at 35, Devonshire-street, Theobalds-road, a 'Poetry Bookshop', where you can see any and every volume of modern poetry. It will be an impressive and, perhaps, an instructive sight.

EDWARD THOMAS, *Daily Chronicle*, 14 January 1913

At the cramped premises off Theobald's Road in Bloomsbury, Harold Monro was preparing for the opening of his new bookshop. Before the turn of the year, Monro had announced that on 1 January 1913 he would open a poetry bookshop 'in the heart of London, five minutes' walk from the British Museum'. It would be devoted to the sale of verse in all its forms – books, pamphlets, rhyme sheets and magazines – and would be both a venue for poetry readings and the base for an intrepid publishing programme. 'Let us hope that we shall succeed in reviving, at least, the best traits and qualities of so estimable an institution as the pleasant and intimate bookshop of the past.' To Monro that revival meant something particular: wooden settles, a coal fire, unvarnished oak bookcases, a selection of literary reviews lain out on the shop table and, completing the scene, Monro's cat Pinknose curled up beside the hearth.[1]

The premises stood on a poorly lit, narrow street between the faded charm of the eighteenth-century Queen Square and the din of the tramways thundering up Theobald's Road. The shop occupied a small ground-floor room, twelve feet across and lit from the street by a fine five-panelled window; in the back was an office from where Monro ran his publishing empire. Upstairs was a dignified drawing room where the twice-weekly poetry

[5]

readings were initially held, and two floors of bedrooms lay above, available to guests at a price of 'a sonnet and a shilling' – or three and sixpence a week in hard cash. Much of the surrounding area had been slum-cleared at the turn of the century when Kingsway was carved through from Bloomsbury Square to the Strand, but not Devonshire Street, which survived in squalor, cluttered by dustbins and vaulting cats. Public houses pinned the street at either end, while along its modest 150 yards traded two undertakers and, by report, a brothel. Many of the buildings were served by a single outside tap, and it was not unknown for passers-by to be hit with fish bones and other scraps cast out from an upstairs window, or chased down the street by boys with catapults. This was the setting for the Poetry Bookshop, in the heart of what one visitor called a 'murderous slum'.[2]

On 8 January 1913, a week later than planned, the Bookshop officially opened its doors. Poets, journalists, critics, readers, patrons: they came in their dozens, until barely a foot of standing room was left unclaimed. That afternoon and the one that followed, three hundred people crammed into the little shop, filling the staircase and the first-floor drawing room; for the capital's poets it was an occasion not to be missed. Wilfrid Gibson, the most popular young poet of the decade, was already resident in the attic rooms and had only to walk downstairs, while the wooden-legged, self-declared 'super-tramp', W. H. Davies, had hobbled in all the way from Kent. Lascelles ('he said it like tassels') Abercrombie had been invited to open the proceedings, but speculated that to ask a man of his years might seem tactless to the elders (he was about to turn thirty-two); W. B. Yeats diplomatically suggested that perhaps the honour should not befall a poet of any description. But Monro was adamant, and turned to the fifty-year-old Henry Newbolt, then Chair of Poetry at the Royal Society of Literature, to perform the ceremony. At Newbolt's side was Edward Marsh, Secretary to the First Lord of the Admiralty Winston Churchill and editor of an anthology launched that day that would become one of the best-selling poetry series of the century. Among its contributors was the twenty-five-year-old Rupert Brooke, who was in Cornwall that afternoon recovering from the strain of his fraught personal life but who would give a reading at the Bookshop before the month was out. F. S. Flint, a dynamic young civil servant and poet who spoke nine languages, took a place on the busy staircase and told the stranger beside him that he could tell by his shoes that he was an American. The shoes belonged to Robert Frost, newly arrived in London, who confessed that he should not have been there at all:

One dark morning, early in the New Year, or maybe it was late in December, I found myself passing before the window of a shop where a clerk was arranging volumes of current poetry. A notice announced the opening, that night, of Harold Monro's Poetry Bookshop. I went in and asked if I might return for the evening. The assistant told me the guests were 'Invited'. But I might try.[3]

Frost, aged thirty-eight, was a literary unknown without a book to his name and he had come to England to see that changed. Through the Poetry Bookshop he would make an introduction with another American who had achieved the very thing that Frost desired. Ezra Pound was a precocious young poet and editor who, at twenty-seven, had published four collections of his own; he would become closely involved in Frost's drive to publication and would make many appearances in the Bookshop himself. In the time ahead, almost every poet worth their salt would become part of the story of the Poetry Bookshop. T. S. Eliot would be a caller, Wilfred Owen a tenant in the attic rooms. Robert Graves, Charlotte Mew, Frances Cornford, Richard Aldington and Eleanor Farjeon would have books published under the shop's imprint. Others saw print through the shop's journal, *Poetry and Drama*: Thomas Hardy, D. H. Lawrence, Robert Bridges, Rabindranath Tagore, Amy Lowell, F. T. Marinetti and Walter de la Mare among them. Others again gave public readings: Yeats recited to a sell-out audience, Wilfrid Gibson performed in a droning monotone; W. H. Davies suffered nerves (cured when he was encouraged to think of the whisky afterwards), Sturge Moore forgot his lines; Ford Madox Hueffer read hurriedly, Rupert Brooke inaudibly, and Ralph Hodgson, who could not tolerate so much as a mention of his own work, simply refused to read at all, while simply no one could silence the actorly John Drinkwater.

The Poetry Bookshop would withstand all weathers: poor sales, infighting, alcoholism, a world war, competition, relocation, expansion and contraction, even romance between the poets and employees. 'All the poets have joined together to hire a big house near the British Museum,' reported the visiting sculptor Gaudier-Brzeska, 'where they live and work, and have underneath it a shop where they sell poetry by the pound.' For the next two decades, the Bookshop would be exactly what Rupert Brooke pronounced it to be when it opened that January in 1913: the centre of the New Poetry.[4]

In 1913, a new direction in poetry was desperately needed. The heyday of Victorian poetry was long over. Matthew Arnold had died in 1888, Robert Browning a year later, and the Laureate Alfred, Lord Tennyson had followed three years after that; the brother and sister Rossettis either side of this eminent trio. Swinburne and Meredith lived on but their best work was behind them, while the curtain had fallen on the risqué *fin-de-siècle* and their leading lights: Aubrey Beardsley, Oscar Wilde and Ernest Dowson had all died as the century turned. The Edwardian decade that followed had left behind a strandline of conservative imperialist verse: Henry Newbolt likening the Englishman at war to a public school-boy at cricket ('Play up! Play up! And play the game!'), while Rudyard Kipling wrote of the Empire's inheritance as 'the white man's burden'. It was 'tub-thumping stuff', Siegfried Sassoon told Rupert Brooke, offensive to some, plain silly to others. But the poet who most typified the inadequacy of the age was the laureate Alfred Austin, a poet considered so terrible that he was better loved for the parodies of his verse rather than anything he wrote. In a hasty ode to the botched 1896 Jameson Raid in the Transvaal (a raid so shambolic that instead of cutting the telegraph wires to mask their position Jameson's company cut a wire fence by mistake), Austin attempted to honour his subject with a dignity reminiscent of Tennyson's 'The Charge of the Light Brigade', but instead he managed only this:

> So we forded and galloped forward
>   As hard as our beasts could pelt,
> First eastward, then trending nor'ward,
>   Right over the rolling veldt,

Bad as they were, these verses might have been quietly forgotten had it not been for an unkind satirist who parodied them yet more succinctly – 'They went across the veldt, | As hard as they could pelt' – a couplet that stuck in the public's craw, forever attributed to Austin, though he never actually wrote it. The mockery of the laureate might have been vindictive (it would worsen), but it was not without purpose; as Ezra Pound put it, 'Parody is, I suppose, the best criticism – it sifts the durable from the apparent.' The treatment doled out to Austin characterised a wider discrediting of Edwardian literature, and when Henry James said of H. G. Wells that he had 'so much talent with so little art' he said as much about Edwardian fiction in general as he did about Wells himself. Expectations were high for a promising new generation of novelists. Katherine Mansfield had recently published her debut *In a German Pension*, while Virginia Woolf was finishing hers (*The Voyage Out*) and James Joyce was preparing *Dubliners*. D. H. Lawrence, whose *Sons and Lovers* would publish that year, said much about the moment when he likened it to an awakening from a night of oppressive dreams:

And now our lungs are full of new air, and our eyes see it is morning, but we have not forgotten the terror of the night. We dreamed we were falling through space into nothingness, and the anguish of it leaves us rather eager. But we are awake again, our lungs are full of new air, our eyes of morning.[5]

These were unsettling times in England. The cost of living was soaring, and trade union membership had rocketed in recent years; the political left anticipated strikes, even riots as the Liberal government and the conservative courts undermined the legal standing and protection of the unions. Suffragettes were taking up direct action, breaking shop windows, starting letterbox fires, defacing public artworks, chaining themselves to railings; some went on hunger strike in prison and were subjected to brutal force-feeding. Women did not have the vote, nor did men who were without property. Irish Home Rule dominated debate at Westminster: the predominantly Catholic South urgently wanted to see it implemented, while the mainly Protestant North just as vehemently wished to block any measure of independence. Civil war loomed across the water, the British army feared mutiny, while the unofficial and rival armies of the Irish Volunteers and the Ulster Volunteer Force were now drilling and gun running. The agricultural labour force was demoralised and impoverished, and England's 'green and pleasant lands' were rarely seen by the industrial classes locked into long and dangerous hours in the factories; the venerated 'all red line' of telegraph cables that linked Britain's Empire across the globe seemed a profitable market only for the rich. So did the telephone, the aeroplane, the radio, the motor car, the electric light bulb, the high-speed train, the cinema and other recent developments. The United States and the newly unified Germany had overtaken Britain as industrial powers. These were difficult days for Britain, uncertain hours for a fading empire, watching nervously the growing danger of Germany's own imperial aims.

At the end of the Edwardian era, literary attitudes were also in revolt. According to the *Times Literary Supplement*, 'public taste decreed that you should attend Fabian summer schools with vegetarians and suffragettes, and sit at the feet of Nietzsche, Ibsen, and Mr Bernard Shaw'. True enough, many of the poets who emerged from university at the turn of the century did so with leanings that were Fabian, Socialist or Liberal; but more importantly, they were writing in new ways, downplaying Victorian rhetoric and laying claim to anything, however 'unpoetic', that might lend their work realism. By 1911 that search for realism had introduced a coarseness which resonated with public taste but not with the gatekeepers of English literature. When Rupert Brooke published *Poems* that year (the only collection that appeared in his lifetime), its graphic treatment of a seasick, love-sick 'Channel Passage' included the lines, 'Retchings twist and tie me, | Old meat, good meals, brown gobbets, up I throw', which were generally considered vulgar, below decency or, at best, what the *Times Literary Supplement* described as 'swagger and brutality'. But it was John Masefield's poem *The Everlasting Mercy*, published first in the *English Review* in 1911, that had the greatest effect of all. The 1,700-line poem recounted the exploits of a bawdy, boozy village poacher; a braggart who boasts, 'I drunk, I fought, I poached, I whored, | I did despite unto the Lord', and who is confronted setting a trap:

> Now when he sees me set my snare,
> He tells me 'Get to hell from there.
> This field is mine,' he says, 'by right;
> If you poach here, there'll be a fight.
> Out now,' he says, 'and leave your wire;
> It's mine.'
>   'It ain't.'
>   'You put.'
>   'You liar.'
>
> 'You closhy put.'
>   'You bloody liar.'[6]

Modest as it might seem by today's standards, this was far from polite Edwardian fare and the poem thrilled the new audiences; as Edmund Blunden later reflected, it 'energised poetry and the reading of it, no matter what extremes of feeling it then aroused or now fails to arouse'. Gutsy, galloping, vernacular, here was verse story-telling that readers hungered for – as Harold Monro put it, 'that the general public could appreciate without straining its intelligence'.[7]

If Masefield and Brooke were the figureheads of this poetic revival, they were not yet the poets' poets. That distinction fell to two men: Thomas Hardy and W. B. Yeats. But they were an older generation and of secure reputation with a dozen volumes of verse between them, whose passions were seen by some to lie elsewhere. Hardy was by then in his seventies, and it was his novels that the public seemed likely to remember. Irishman William Butler Yeats was still in his forties, but his work with the Abbey Theatre was considered by many in the poetry world as a waste of his considerable talents, while his aloof manner by common agreement made him unapproachable. Neither man seemed likely to direct a revolution in verse; that challenge would fall to a younger division of writers, 'the two newest and most forward movements in English poetry', said Harold Monro: the Georgians and the Imagists.[8]

In the summer of 1911, with George V newly enthroned, Harold Monro addressed his friend Arthur Sabin over lunch with uncharacteristic excitement. 'We are living in a new Georgian era – and, by Jove, Arthur, we are the new Georgian poets'. Within eighteen months, he would publish a book from his Devonshire Street headquarters that captured the new mood exactly; but the idea for it would not come from him.[9]

Rupert Brooke was a frequent guest at Edward Marsh's apartments in Gray's Inn, London, and one night in September 1912 he and Marsh sat up late, discussing how best to shake the public of their ignorance of contemporary poetry. There and then, they counted a dozen poets worth publishing, and put the idea of an anthology to Monro. Five hundred copies were printed: half received on 16 December 1912, the remainder on Christmas Eve; all were sold by Christmas Day. A reprint was hurried through, then another and another. By the end of its first year, the book was in its ninth printing and was on its way to 15,000 sales. The name of this remarkable anthology was *Georgian Poetry*.

At its simplest, the Georgian Poets were those who appeared in the five volumes that Edward Marsh would edit over the next decade; but these writers were brethren by more than publication alone. The Georgians looked to the local, the commonplace and the day-to-day, mistrusting grandiosity, philosophical enquiry or spiritual cant. Many held an attachment to the traditions of English Romantic verse; they looked to Wordsworth in their connection to the land rather than to John Donne and the Metaphysical pursuit of the soul. The style was innocent, intimate and direct; lyric in form, rhythmic in drive, it dovetailed short sketches of the natural world with longer meditations on the condition of the human heart. It was not a poetry of public politics and represented no particular ideology or constituency, but attempted instead to convey rapture in the modest miracles of life: in a daffodil, a bird's song or the breeze that stroked the branches of an oak tree. It employed whimsy in place of calculation, charm rather than conviction, and attempted the lightness of a pianist playing with one hand; its subject matter would be as everyday as a country lane or a village fence post.

To its critics, this was an approach that could only equate to 'minor' verse and 'littleness', and some thought them in love with littleness; Richard Aldington: 'They took a little trip for a weekend to a little cottage where they wrote a little poem on a little scheme'; Robert Graves: 'Georgianism became principally concerned with Nature and love and leisure and old age and childhood and animals and sleep and other uncontroversial subjects.'

Sentiment came easily to the Georgian poets, rigour less so. Their rhythm could be flip, their diction vague, their imagery imprecise. 'Unless a man write with his whole nature concentrated upon his subject he is unlikely to take hold of another man,' wrote Edward Thomas in a book published in 1913; and the Georgians did not concentrate nearly hard enough. The desire for realism lost intensity, becoming homely, hearthside and lazily affectionate. What in the mouth of John Masefield or Rupert Brooke had in 1911 seemed like the gritty tang of a rough cider became instead the comfort of a hot drink at bedtime; T. S. Eliot: 'The Georgians caress everything that they touch.' More likely than not, the Georgian poem about a songbird or a wild animal would embalm the little creature that it had intended to 'free' in the imagination of the reader; worse still, what it captured was rarely some essence of the animal but more frequently the poet's dubious decoration. But still they ventured, using their notebooks as butterfly nets to capture and take home their subjects for examination. 'We go to it as would-be poets or as solitaries, vagabonds, lovers,' wrote Edward Thomas temporarily adopting a Georgian guise, 'to escape foul air, noise, hard hats, black uniforms, multitudes, confusion, incompleteness, elaborate means without clear ends – to escape ourselves.'[10]

'We are at the beginning of another "Georgian period",' wrote Edward Marsh proudly in 1912, 'which may take rank in due time with the several great poetic ages of the past.' Humbug, thought Ezra Pound, who was busily ensuring that the Georgians were not going to have the new dawn entirely to themselves. Under his direction there would be an alternative to these country verses that was more angular, more radical, more revolutionary: Imagism.[11]

It was in a tea shop in Kensington in 1912 that Pound first informed Richard Aldington and Hilda Doolittle that they were 'Imagists', which entailed agreement upon three principles:

1 Direct treatment of the 'thing', whether subjective or objective.
2 To use absolutely no word that does not contribute to the presentation.
3 As regarding rhythm: to compose in the sequence of the musical phrase, not in sequence of a metronome.

Direct treatment, a pared language, a relatively free verse: these were sharp distinctions from the gentle Georgians. No sing-song rhythms or cloying subject matter, no abstractions, no ornament, no superfluous word; this was language stripped down to the bone, harder and saner, 'austere, direct, free from emotional slither.' Pound's two-line 'In a Station of the Metro' from 1913:

> The apparition   of these faces   in the crowd :
> Petals   on a wet, black   bough .[12]

Modern, forward-facing, trim, these were poems for their age, influenced by French Symbolism and pictorial Cubism, in which a single, carefully chosen image could do more, it was proposed, than any detailed description that the Georgians might concoct. If the Georgians were to be regional in their outlook, Imagists would be citizens of the world, Aldington explained, and they chose their meeting place accordingly, gathering in a restaurant called The Eiffel Tower in London's Soho under the watchful direction of a young Cambridge graduate, T. E. Hulme, and the fiery, Idaho-born Ezra Pound. A roving talent scout, Pound sent off the work of Aldington, Doolittle (whom he rechristened 'H.D.') and others to Harriet Monroe (no connection to Harold Monro) for her Chicago-based magazine *Poetry*, and he would counter *Georgian Poetry* with the most declamatory anthology of its kind for the Poetry Bookshop in 1914, *Des Imagistes*.

It seems unthinkable that Ezra Pound could ever have cast in his lot with the rustic Georgians, but it almost happened. In 1912 Edward Marsh wrote to Pound to ask if he could include two of his pieces in the first *Georgian Poetry*, but Pound declined.

He declined not out of an aversion to Georgianism: he withheld one poem because he felt it did not represent any modern trend and the other because it was due out imminently in a book of his own. Was there anything among his earlier works that Marsh might take, asked Pound. There was not, but they agreed to have the question revisited if the anthology went into a second volume. By the time it came to assembling the next edition a feud had opened between the bitterly opposed camps of Georgians and Imagists.

These were intoxicating days in the capital. London was, wrote Ford Madox Hueffer, 'unrivalled in its powers of assimilation – the great, easy-going, tolerant, lovable, old dressing-gown of a place that it was then, but was never more to be'. For poets, the Bookshop on Devonshire Street would be at the centre of operations, and on its opening on 8 January 1913 many of the era's shaping forces were making their introductions. Robert Frost may not have been invited but he had found his way to the right place at the right time. 'I was only too childishly happy in being allowed . . . for a moment in a company in which I hadn't to be ashamed of having written verse,' he recalled. But there was someone else in the Poetry Bookshop that day who was not known to the American. This person would open more doors for him than F. S. Flint, be a more influential critic than Ezra Pound and be a better friend than Wilfrid Gibson; he would influence the reputation of almost every writer present and would become, in Frost's words, 'the only brother I ever had'.[13]

Though they did not meet that day, also in the room was Edward Thomas.

Edward Thomas had travelled to the Poetry Bookshop from his parents' home in Balham, London. He had spent the past two months living in East Grinstead, West Sussex, completing the only novel he would finish. But Sussex was not his family home: that lay fifty miles to the west at Steep in Hampshire, and he had come away to escape it. His spirits were desperately low. Thirty-four years of age, a married father of three, Thomas was, in his mind, little more than a literary hack, writing all the hours that he could manage to bring home a modest income. The relentless, ungratifying work left him exhausted and bitter, while the din of family life served only to worsen his mood. In poor spirits he treated his family cruelly, scolding the children and reprimanding his wife, and the more he did so, the worse his spirits became. The only way he knew to break the cycle was to leave; sometimes his absences lasted days, at other times he would be gone for months. At these moments, even to drag himself home for a weekend was more than he could manage, and though the children missed him and his wife yearned, he convinced himself that they could only be happy without him. Away from his family he could begin to lift himself again and carry on.

However turbulent his home life, Thomas's literary work could not afford to skip a beat. In weekly visits to London he would petition editors for commissions and take the opportunity to catch up with friends, among them Harold Monro, who had been a guest at the family home that autumn when Thomas had teased that although Monro sold poets he was really no better than a poet himself. Thomas rarely spoke or wrote in a style that brought his audience to outright laughter, but he had a subtle wit that was so dry it could be mistaken for waspishness. He could sting, certainly, and was frequently stung, but only rarely would he allow a poison to creep into his comments, and even then only out of desperation. He was rarely motivated by jealousy or egotism, he lacked vanity and was spared the arrogance of some of his peers, so when Thomas told Monro that he would attend the opening of his bookshop on the condition that he was guaranteed protection against assault by any of the poets, Monro knew precisely how to take the remark. The guarantee was sought only partly in jest, for Thomas was a professional reviewer of verse and his brilliant, uncompromising articles were the making of many young reputations and the breaking of others; as a letter in *The Times* put it, 'He was the man with the keys to the Paradise of English Poetry', and those he damned could be unforgiving. A fortnight after he died in 1917, de la Mare wrote:

Edward Thomas must have been a critic of rhymes in his nursery. How much generous help and encouragement many living poets owe to his counsel only themselves could say. To his candour, too. For the true cause, he believed, is better served by an uncompromising 'Trespassers will be prosecuted' than by an amiable 'All are welcome'.

Trespassers came in many forms – the pompous, the incompetent, the insincere, the unskilled, the tone-deaf – and those he suspected of inadequacy he pursued without mercy. Thomas despised the substandard wherever he encountered it: in the anointed, in his peers, but most especially he despised it in himself. For when he was not sharpening his mind on the reviewing he did for a living, he was blunting it again through the commissions that were beneath his talents: endless and often aimless prose measured out by the page to fulfil his contractual obligations. The homes of the writers, lepidoptery, superstitions, civic guides, topography, lumbering biographies, histories of castles: these were just some of the efforts that he put his name to, work that left him empty and exhausted, and bitter at the abuse of his powers.[14]

By 1913 Edward Thomas had published twenty prose books under his own name and had edited or introduced a dozen more. Over seventy of his articles had been printed in periodicals and well in excess of 1,500 signed book reviews while many more were published anonymously. In 1912–13 he had published three biographies, a gathering of Norse tales and almost fifty signed reviews of works ranging from Chaucer to his contemporaries. He was working on a travel book tracing the Icknield Way, a country tale told by a townsman, an autobiographical novel and several smaller pieces for the literary journals. For all this, Thomas might expect to earn up to £250 a year, a salary a little over that of a schoolmaster's. Financially, he was comfortable enough to feed a family of five in a rented cottage; sometimes there was a little left over to hire some help about the home, at other times he took in paying guests to subsidise the household income. But he always honoured his promises, whether or not he was paid for keeping them.[15]

Thomas left the opening of the Poetry Bookshop that evening to meet Mervyn, his twelve-year-old son, at Victoria station and catch the seven o'clock train back to his parents' house in Balham. Bronwen, his ten-year-old daughter, waited for him there, but his youngest, Myfanwy, aged just two and a half, was carrying a cold and a boil and remained at East Grinstead, where the family had joined Edward for Christmas, cared for by Helen, the woman he had married thirteen years ago, who loved him with a passion that he could no longer return.

By all accounts Edward Thomas was a striking man who turned heads wherever he went. At six foot he was tall for the times, slim, loose-limbed and vigorous. He had thick, rather long fair hair, lightened by his time spent outdoors, a narrow face with strong cheekbones, rounding at a firm chin, and steady grey-blue eyes so sharp that he once observed the difference in the two eyes of a dog from a moving bus. His expression was grave and detached, but his smile, when it came, could be coy, whimsical or proud. He rarely laughed. A short clay pipe was never far from his lips or the palm of his left hand. He spoke in a clear baritone, though often he kept his own counsel, and preferred the company of an individual to a group. He had a countryman's stride, and never put his long legs under a table but always sat square on. He dressed in a suit of tawny tweed, which was old, sunned and slightly loose, and which, he liked to say, smelt of dog whenever it was damp. His jacket pockets were impossibly deep, and from these he would pull maps, apples and clay pipes in a procession as apparently endless as the scarves from a magician's hand. It was said that the melancholy that was stamped upon him seemed only to make his beauty more apparent.[16]

Thomas had been plagued by depression from before his university days at Oxford. There, he fought to shake it out of himself: he tried drink and opium, took up rowing and rowdiness, but could not hold the bleak moods back. When the dark thoughts overran him, he told himself that he valued life too much to take it away, or that he was too sedentary to go through with ending it; but in recent years he had become harder to console. In advertising his sorrows, as he put it, he had punished his family, decimated his friends and broken down his self-respect. 'Things have been very wrong,' he told his old friend Jesse Berridge in February 1913. 'My health is now definitely bad – not mere depression – and I don't know how it will develop.'[17]

Towards his wife Helen he was cruel at these times. Hard silences, harsh words, quiet fury, despair. She learned not to pursue him into his agony but to leave him be, and continue with her daily chores. She would chatter across the silences until she ran out of chatter or he of patience, and either the silence resumed or it would be broken by his angry departure from the house. She became expert at identifying his mood from his demeanour returning home: his hundred-yard stare, his pale and haggard expression, his hunch at the shoulders, his lips tightly shut as if to hold in an unkind word. Often he worked or walked late in the evening and if she waited up with his supper he would rage at her for doing so. He hated her fussing and her pretence that all was well, but the loathing he felt toward his own cowardice was stronger. Unable to do what he believed he should and put an end to his suffering, he was left to berate himself bitterly: 'I'm the man who always comes home to his supper.' Mealtimes could pass in silence: the children too frightened to talk, Thomas grief-stricken by his effect upon them. He would provoke them and they would cry and he would depart again, leaving Helen afraid that he might not return, and afraid of his mood when he did.[18]

Some years before, at Berryfield Cottage in Steep, Thomas had written this:

I sat thinking about ways of killing myself. My revolver has only one bullet left. I couldn't hang myself: and though I imagined myself cutting my throat with a razor on Wheatham I had not the energy to go. Then I went out and thought what effects my suicide would have. I don't think I mind them. My acquaintances – I no longer have friends – would talk a day or two (when they met) and try to explain and of course see suggestions in the past. W. H. Davies would suffer a little; Helen and the children – less in reality than they do now, from my accursed tempers and moodiness. It is dislike of the effort to kill myself and fear that I could not carry it through if I half did it that keeps me alive. Only that. For I hate my work, my reviewing: my best I feel is negligible: I have no vitality, no originality, no love. I do harm. Love is dead and lust almost dead.[19]

In the winter of 1908 he made an attempt on his life that he documented in a short story, which, layered against Helen's account, his diary and his notes, forms a picture of events on that November day. He had turned on Bronwen because she dared disturb his melancholy; and now she was wailing, and her cries struck him to the core; he could stand it no longer. He went to the drawer where he kept an old revolver, the barrel of which was brown with rust and whose chambers had become so stiff that they would not turn without the encouragement of both hands. Time was when he had thought of throwing the gun away; but now he was grateful for it and the one remaining ball cartridge which would still, he fancied, force its way along the rusty barrel. He turned toward the front door. His wife had watched him at the drawer; she knew what he kept there. Desperate to distract him, she pleaded that he might take his daughter along; but he rebuked them both. He felt sure of what he was to do: he said he felt 'called to death'. He crossed the wheat fields in front of the house and began to climb Shoulder of Mutton Hill. Hurriedly, Helen gathered the children and led them away from the cottage down to the stream so that they could paddle and push their boats on the water without needing her attentions; she was out of her mind with worry. From the hill he stared at the house, hoping perhaps to see his daughter run into the garden and compel him to go back. He gazed down upon the elder hedgerow that flanked the house, and then lifted his eyes to the Downs and the hazy sun, searching to find a reason to turn around. Nothing responded to him and he responded to nothing. He wished for a place to hide, away from family and self-disgust, somewhere far off enough that the sound of a gunshot would not travel home, and finally he found it, surrounded by beech trees, cut off from the path and flanked by the hill. He pushed the cartridge home and turned the chamber into place, and took a final glance across the woods. Someone was walking in the hills above him, calling a name that he could not determine. He felt a sudden sense of shame, and raised the gun quickly to his chest. His finger fluttered on the trigger; too lightly to fire. He closed his eyes and imagined that he had succeeded, imagined his discovery by the walker, who would marvel at the calm confidence of the act. He opened his eyes. He was shaking with cold. He turned for home. Neither husband nor wife would speak of the episode, though both would write of it. 'Shall I make the tea?' said Helen as he took off his boots. 'Please,' is what he said.[20]

'How nice it would be to be dead if only we could know we were dead,' he had written to Gordon Bottomley in the weeks before the attempt. 'That is what I hate, the not being able to turn around in the grave & say It is over.'[21]

Helen Noble first laid eyes on Edward Thomas in the summer of 1894 when the sixteen-year-old youth began calling on her father at their home near Wandsworth Common. James Ashcroft Noble mentored Thomas and helped in finding him a publisher for the book he published at the age of eighteen, *The Woodland Life*. Thomas was by then already a precocious essayist, but was still impressionable enough to be guided by Mr Noble in his discovery of Keats and Shelley. But Mrs Noble took less kindly to Thomas's appearances at their Wandsworth home and less kindly still to her husband's attempts to encourage a friendship with their daughter. Not that the bohemian Helen needed any encouragement in the company of the athletic, handsome young man who climbed high into elm trees to steal her a heron's egg and who sent her a chaffinch's nest prised from an apple tree because she said she had never before seen one. A year older than Edward, Helen was a confident, even forward girl who took it upon herself to call on the Thomas household while Edward was out in order to introduce herself to his parents. The move incensed Helen's mother, who felt that her daughter's behaviour was wholly unbecoming, and when Mr Noble died in 1896 she forbade Helen any sight of Edward. In the bitter fights that followed, Helen left home for a post as a nursery governess in Broadstairs, Kent, where she looked after a young girl called Hope Webb and from where she wrote long, affectionate letters to Edward. By the time he went up to Lincoln College, Oxford, in the autumn of 1897 they had become lovers. Helen was still a governess but now in London, and it was here that the young couple would meet for walks on Wandsworth Common or to browse the salacious paperbacks on the booksellers' row at Holywell Street.[22]

When Helen fell pregnant while Edward was an undergraduate their relationship underwent a sea-change. It became one of temperance, described by Thomas as a happiness 'so mild and cool' that it resembled a 'saintliness'. They married secretly at Fulham Register Office on 19 June 1899 and kept their union from their parents. Mrs Noble's discovery of their secret brought about the final estrangement in the turbulent relationship between mother and daughter, though Helen was at least now welcomed in the household of Mr and Mrs Thomas and allowed to move in there while Edward completed his degree.[23]

Philip Mervyn Thomas was born while Edward was still at university. The prospect of having to earn a living for his new family put a strain on the young man which he would never fully overcome. Distracted and depressed, Edward missed out on the First in History for which he was headed, thereby ruling out the academic career that he had seen as the answer to his financial plight. He desired a literary life for himself but feared the poverty it would inflict upon his family. His father pushed him towards what he saw as a more reputable career in the civil service; but Edward instead began a series of speculative calls upon London's literary editors, among them Henry Nevinson of the *Daily Chronicle*, who remembered their unlikely interview.

He was tall, absurdly thin, and a face of attractive distinction and ultra refinement was sicklied over with nervous melancholy and the ill condition of bad food or hunger. Almost too shy to speak, he sat down proudly and asked if I could give him work. I enquired what work he could do and he said 'None' ... I asked whether he would like some reviewing on any subject, and on what. He replied that he knew nothing of any subject, and was quite sure he could not write, but certainly he did want work of some sort.[24]

From the *Chronicle* and the other papers for which he toiled he earned a meagre £52 in the twelve months after leaving Oxford University; he doubled that income the following year, but it was not nearly enough: he owed Lincoln College £60, and was summoned before the Oxford County Courts.

Helen and Edward's first home together in Earlsfield's Atheldene Road was a squalid south London terrace; it lasted them only four months. Then came rooms off Nightingale Lane in Balham for 11s. a week; they endured those for just eight months. Teaching posts promising £120 a year came and went but Thomas did not apply for a single one of them. The fights with his father worsened, and Edward forbade him to make job enquiries at Whitehall on his behalf even though the young couple were living hand to mouth. The penury, the squalor, the sleepless nights around the baby became too much to bear. Edward turned against city living. Day after day he took a bicycle or a train out of the capital to look for a country home. From one such journey he returned to tell Helen that he had found them a functional red-brick cottage a mile from Bearsted in Kent, not a pretty house and not cheap, but at least not London. From Kent, Edward earned what he could from his pen: calling on or corresponding with the London editors as he would do throughout his life, at times begging his way into work. His total savings in 1902 were 1s. 8½d., about enough to rent his cottage for a day. He suffered long fits of melancholy, and took extended walks in an attempt to keep his mood away from the cottage. But he could not save Helen from his anger. One morning she returned from the post office to report that no letters offering work had arrived for him that day. 'Why tell me what is written on your pale wretched face?' he lashed out at her. 'I am cursed, and you are cursed because of me. I hate the tears I see you've been crying. Your sympathy and your love are both hateful to me. Hate me, but for God's sake don't stand there, pale and suffering. Leave me, I tell you; get out and leave me.' For the only time in their life together, the unsinkable Helen lost her ability to cope. Pregnant for a second time, she wrote distressingly to her best friend, Janet Hooton, 'This alone is terrible as no one wants the wee thing; no one looks forward to its coming, and I least of anyone.'

You ask why we don't want it? Because we are very poor; because it means more anxiety for Edward and more work for him. Home will become unendurable to him. Even now poverty, anxiety, physical weakness, disappointments and discouragements are making him bitter, hard and impatient, quick to violent anger, and subject to long fits of depression . . . He is selling some of his dearest books to pay for baby clothes and doctors, etc. and as he packs them up I know how he is rebelling at fate, how hard life seems to him, how he regrets it all . . . He cannot love, Janet, he cannot respond to my love. How can he when all is so dark, and I, I have deprived him of it all, the joys of life and love and success. If he would only begin life again without me my heart would rejoice. I should be very happy, for his happiness is all I care for . . . I have prayed that I and my babe may die, but we shall not, tho this would free Edward.[25]

Helen's sister Irene could not bear to see her sibling in such despair, and for the only time in his life, Edward found himself openly challenged about his matrimonial behaviour. 'My spirit burned within me,' Irene recorded, 'and I felt I *must* say what was in my heart. I shall never forget how he took it, – admitting everything, extenuating nothing. His humility melted me, and I felt drawn to him in a way I had never before.' Edward's callous behaviour had once again slipped retribution.[26]

It was the commission of a book on Oxford that rescued them both; that, and a legacy that had come to Helen. The contract from A. & C. Black came with a £100 advance, £20 on signature: it was Thomas's first commission and it was a lifeline. Rachel Mary Bronwen was born in 1902, and the family, now four strong, moved closer into Bearsted village itself, to a half-timbered tall and narrow house on the village green. For a while the new setting and the new work helped to lift the family's spirits. Thomas even participated in village life. He learned to improve his woodworking skills from the neighbouring wheelwright, who taught him how to make a simple spade handle out of ash and the different uses to which a plane could be put. Thomas would in time take what he was learning to carve the furniture around which they would live. But he was also stealing yet more time away from domestic company he found harder and harder to abide. 'No one knows how difficult I find it to live with Helen,' he wrote in his diary in 1903, 'though I admire her, like her, perhaps love her.' Helen consoled herself that through a longer struggle they would win out. 'Deep in my heart I knew that he depended on me, and would need me when his horrible suffering was over.' She loved him as a wife and with 'the pride of a mother', and bided her time, and devoted herself to her children.[27]

At eighteen months, young Bronwen developed pneumonia and almost died; the house on the green was deemed insanitary and brought a move to a farmhouse in the Weald of Kent, a few miles south of Sevenoaks. Elses Farm was surrounded by oast houses, hayricks, stables and an orchard; nightingales flocked in the hedgerows. For the first time, Thomas came to watch the year's seasons in completion: to watch the team of horses turning the plough before seeding, or the raking of the bush harrows or the reaping of the crops. He rented a study-cottage a mile or more from the farm, and wore a footpath through the copse trekking back and forth; other times he took off for London. With two children to attend to on her own, his absences confined Helen to an isolated life, indoors away from the friends she had made in Bearsted. Once more she found herself writing long, aching letters after him; his replies were sometimes warm, sometimes brusque, but mostly businesslike in their call on her to cash cheques or send whatever items or clothing he needed.[28]

By 1906, earning £250 a year, the poverty that Edward and Helen had known in their early years together seemed to be behind them at last, but it had come at a price to their relationship. 'What I really ought to do is live alone,' he told Jesse Berridge. 'But I can't find the courage to do the many things necessary for taking that step. It is really the kind H. and the children who make life almost *impossible*.'[29] Somehow they adapted to the outbursts and the absences. The wretchedness at home rose and tempered and rose again; the absences became longer. Edward was away when their third child, Helen Elizabeth Myfanwy

('Baba') was born, some eight years after Bronwen. By the time Edward Thomas met Robert Frost, it was clear to the American that he was all but living alone.[30]

The absences were crippling to Helen. She was warm and impulsive, a product of her father's free-thinking influence, but her untidy spontaneity made her a hopeless housekeeper and a poor cook to Edward's irritation. She felt acutely aware that she was not conventionally pretty – she wore round glasses on a round and rosy face – and was mortified by a sense that Edward's friends must have wondered what he saw in her, a woman who was neither as brilliant nor as beautiful as he; she believed that he kept her apart from his London life as though she were someone to be ashamed of. But she took pride in her body and her physicality, and lacked the sexual prudery of the time and was indifferent to the opinion of others, outraging her closest friend by her premarital intimacy with Edward. She said she 'hated' the idea of the legal contract of marriage and saw herself as a semi-wild child of nature, 'a part of the stirring earth'; she looked to Edward to teach her the nouns for it all. It was her bohemianism that allowed her to 'manage' his disappearances emotionally; but it was these same unconventional attitudes that left her isolated and wounded when he left.[31]

Edward Thomas's doctors diagnosed him with neurasthenia, a term largely discredited today, but widely used then to describe any number of ill-defined conditions, including anxiety, lassitude, listlessness or a general emotional disturbance characterised by fatigue or irritability. For years his physicians prescribed one abstinence after another: from tobacco, from alcohol, a sugar-free diet. They tried brown bread and vegetarianism, even a prescription of fifteen minutes' daily exercise with dumb-bells for a man who would think nothing of walking twenty miles a day. But instead of helping in his recovery, Thomas felt that these doctors were merely 'unmaking' him. 'I have somehow lost my balance,' he confessed to a friend in 1911, 'and can never recover it by diet or rule or any deliberate means, but only by some miracles from within or without.' Exhaustion overtook him; he had written seven books that year and could no longer keep his despair at bay. Helen feared he was once again suicidal, and in desperation turned to his friends for help. But their response was not always sympathetic. W. H. Hudson, the naturalist whom Thomas admired more than any living writer, said idly: 'I am sorry to hear that Thomas has broken down again – why will he work so incessantly and so furiously?'[32]

Psychology in England was in its primitive stages before the war, with psychosomatic disorders little understood. Thomas himself was not uncritical of his own condition, nor was he unappreciative of the energies that it produced within him. Aware that the depression was also a source of creativity, he had in the past been ambivalent about attempts to purge it. 'I wonder whether for a person like myself whose most intense moments were those of depression a cure that destroys the depression may not destroy the intensity,' he wrote in 1908, adding ' – a *desperate* remedy?' But in 1912 he had finally met an individual who could help with a subtler understanding of his suffering.[33]

Godwin Baynes was every bit a new man for a new century. Tall, charismatic and athletic, he had studied medicine at Trinity College, Cambridge (where he had been a 'blue' for the university as a swimmer and oarsman), before training at Barts and at La Salpêtrière in Paris. Baynes was a war hero before the Great War, decorated by Enver Pasha for his work to establish a hospital for Balkan refugees in 1912; he had returned to England to open a practice for the poor in Bethnal Green, where many of Baynes's first clients were suffering from starvation and had little to offer by way of payment. The surgery attracted a constant stream of social visitors, both in and out of hours, and evening gatherings would include poetry readings or musical recitals. Baynes was at the centre of a whirl of leisured young socialites who liked nothing more than to spend their time on tennis courts, inventing parlour games or attending the theatre. His popularity would eventually exhaust him, and when it did he moved with his wife from London to Wisbech, Cambridgeshire, in the winter of 1913 in search of a quieter life. When the town council learned of his impending arrival, they met him from the train with a brass band.[34]

Godwin Baynes would study under Carl Jung and was a pioneer of an early form of psychoanalysis in England, and with Edward Thomas he made an experimental foray into the discipline. Their first session took place in April 1912, when Thomas spent ten days in Baynes's company at Broughton Gifford in Wiltshire. There the men walked and talked, and Thomas reported enthusiastically, 'The doctor is working magic with my disordered intellect.' Helen witnessed the progress from a distance; Baynes was indeed a magician, it seemed to her, and she implored Edward to grasp the opportunity given him. Thomas would stay with Baynes in the Bethnal Green surgery for a few days at a time, talking formally on a daily basis for an 'analytic hour' for a payment that was likely to have been 2s. 6d. a session (about the price of a poetry book). But of equal importance was the time spent together out of surgery, when Baynes had the foresight to treat Thomas as a friend and not only as a patient.[35]

No medical notes survive of their sessions together, but a notebook exists that Baynes kept while studying under Jung in 1920. In it he records a dream in which Thomas appeared before him.

The delicate poet who was killed in the war. He was my friend. In my early, eager innocence I tried amateurishly to cure his Neurasthenia by suggestion. I often reproached myself for taking a fee for my childish effort for of course I did not cure him.

He was a generous, witty comrade and in his soul he was saintly. He saw deeply into the hearts and souls of men for he too had known the clutch of the erotic complex and this was the source of his neurosis.

His face was Christ-like and it is his link with Christ the Lover of Man that brings his sorrowful, pitiful soul into his eyes.[36]

Baynes never expanded upon his insight into Thomas's neurosis, but possibly he alluded to a belief that since childhood Thomas had relied too deeply upon other people, notably his mother, to lift the gloom of unhappiness.

To find self-reliance, to determine his own path: these were the drives that Thomas took from his sessions with Baynes. How was he to live without paining others? Could he cast his own fortune after these lengthy years or would he continue down the same tormented path? And if he could effect a change, where should he look to in order to make it happen? Should he live without dependence upon others as the sessions with the doctor seemed to suggest, or should he hold out for the help of a rescuing hand? It was a question that was forming into the central and tumultuous struggle of his life. In 1906 Thomas had prophesied that amid his despondency an individual would one day emerge as his rescuer. 'I feel sure that my salvation depends on a person and that person cannot be Helen because she has come to resemble me too much.'[37]

Early in 1913 it seemed to Thomas that the prophecy might prove true, and that the long-hoped-for saviour could be the gifted, kindly Godwin Baynes.

Such a person would indeed emerge to help Edward Thomas out of his despair that year; but he would not be a doctor.

As the SS *Parisian* skirted the dark headlands of Donegal and Antrim, Robert and Elinor Frost and their four children must have wondered what this new episode in their lives would bring. They had sailed from Boston nine days before, barely a fortnight after making a decision to sail at all. Seasick and wearied, landfall had been a welcome sight, and at sunrise on 2 September 1912 the *Parisian* – which months before had sailed to the aid of the stricken *Titanic* – entered the Clyde estuary and brought its tired passengers safely to disembarkation at Glasgow docks. In Frost's pocket was $1,100 raised, after mortgage, from the sale of the family's simple, two-storey white clapboard farmhouse and thirty acres of land outside of the small New Hampshire town of Derry. In addition, he was due an annual annuity of $800 from his grandfather's estate, minus the $120 they had spent on their passage: it would be enough to last them a year or even two, but they had no home in New England to which they could return and the gamble simply had to pay off. 'We could risk it,' said Frost.[38]

Robert Frost felt he had made little of his life up until then. A failed poultry farmer and poet who had been all but ignored by American editors, he chose now to be as far away as possible from his prying relatives in Lawrence, Massachusetts, and out of the grasp of his teaching job at Plymouth, New Hampshire, which was making too much use of his time, he thought. In the summer of 1912 the family gathered in the kitchen of their Derry farm to discuss a change of scene: west, across a continent to Vancouver where Frost's friend and lifelong correspondent John Bartlett was living, or east, across an ocean to England, where Frost's wife Elinor had long spoken of a wish to live 'under thatch'. Frost's daughter, Lesley, recorded the moment.

We were standing around my mother who was ironing in the kitchen when my father said, 'Well, let's toss for it,' and he took a nickel from his pocket. 'Heads England, tails Vancouver.' Heads it was! All that had been contemplated was fresh scenery, peace to write, the excitement of change.[39]

A fortnight later, on 23 August 1912, the Frosts were sailing to England. But England was not, contrary to the advice he had been given, cheaper than America, and an exchange rate of almost five dollars to the pound ensured that Frost would have to look beyond London and its expensive rents for a home. To do so he walked not into a property agent as might be expected, but into the offices of the popular journal *T.P.'s Weekly* after reading a column on country walks, which to Frost's mind suggested a knowledge of neighbouring rural locations. The column's editor, a retired policeman, not only advised the American of several possibilities but went so far as to guide him personally, accompanying him on the twenty-one-mile train ride north-west of London to Beaconsfield, where the Frosts would find their first English home in a new-built bungalow. Frost bought second-hand furniture locally, and from London he made arrangements for the delivery of the family's possessions: the rugs, some kitchenware, his typewriter and, for reassembly, Elinor's rocking chair and his stout, adjustable Morris chair on which he wrote by laying a wooden board across its stout arms. It would be, as he informed a friend, 'a lesson to you in plain living', homely enough for now, although little more, he would reflect, than camping. For the time being, Beaconsfield seemed a suitably literary stop for Frost's ambitions. G. K. Chesterton lived just four streets away, but he was merely the most recent of many esteemed residents that had also included Thomas Gray, buried at nearby Stoke Poges, and most alluring of all, the cottage in nearby Chalfont St Giles where Milton finished *Paradise Lost*. Frost had found himself a home amid what he called 'the great tradition of English lyric poetry'.[40]

Shorter and stockier than Thomas, and almost as physically restless, Frost had fair hair which the wind would blow into untidy tufts. His blue eyes lit up when he was teasing his friends. He spoke with a New England drawl, and was frequently blunt and quick to anger, an anger that unlike Thomas's could become physical. But his humour pervaded all his talk, sarcastic one moment, kindly another. Goader, teaser, talker, thinker, Frost was cubbish, mischievous and driven. He once said that he would like his epitaph to read that he had a lover's quarrel with the world.[41]

Frost's father, William Frost, had married the Scottish-born mathematics teacher Isabelle Moodie in 1874, who bore him a son and a daughter. But William Frost was no family man: a gambler and drinker who carried a revolver on San Francisco's semi-feral streets: in his son's words, 'a bad boy who never stopped being one'. William Frost died of tuberculosis when Robert was just eleven and his mother Isabelle moved the children back to the ancestral family home of Lawrence, Massachusetts. It was in high school that the shy seventeen-year-old Frost met the equally retiring Elinor White, the woman he would marry. By then he had begun writing his first poems, publishing a handful of verses and articles in the high-school bulletin for which he was chief editor. (He published Elinor's poetry too, though it has been suggested that she stopped writing when this stoked jealousy in Robert.) He entered Dartmouth College and Harvard University but failed to stay the course at either; he suffered from a mysterious recurring illness (he feared tuberculosis), and when Elinor became pregnant with their second child he saw no virtue in continuing his study. First born had been a boy, Elliot, who became a constant companion as soon as he was able to walk, following Frost about the farm as he saw to his daily chores. But Elliot was overcome by fever in the summer of 1900, and was prescribed ineffectual homeopathic treatment by Isabelle's doctor. As their son's condition worsened, Robert and Elinor called in their own doctor, who examined the boy and gravely announced that he had been summoned too late: Elliot had an acute case of cholera infantum and would not survive the night. Elliot died that evening; he had not reached his fourth birthday. A wild grief came between the parents. Frost reproached himself for failing to summon help sooner, saying first that his neglect was tantamount to murder, then crying out that this was a wrathful God's vengeance upon him; but to Eleanor his was merely the selfish and hubristic anguish of a man unable to see that the loss was not his own but Elliot's.[42]

A farm in west Derry, New Hampshire, offered a fresh start for Robert, Elinor and their surviving daughter, Lesley. The family moved in October 1900, and grew to include a son, Carol, and two more daughters. But the trials were not behind them. In 1907, Robert caught pneumonia, possibly brought on by a drunken night lost in snowy woods, and Elinor nursed him to recovery while heavily pregnant with their sixth and, as it would turn out, final child: a baby girl who died the day after she was born. The pain of Elliot's death had been enormous, but to lose a second child was unthinkable and unbearable, and strain entered the marriage like never before. Robert succumbed to bouts of severe depression, Elinor to exhaustion. Lesley Frost recalled one terrible night when she was woken by her father and told to follow him down through the cold house to the kitchen. There she found her mother, weeping with her head in hands, and noticed for the first time that her father was holding a revolver. Robert told the distraught child to choose between them, a mother or a father, as only one of them would make it through to morning.[43]

No wonder the Frosts sought a change in fortunes, and though the probity of Lesley's recollection has been questioned, it nonetheless marked a turning point in the family story. In the autumn of 1906 Frost began teaching in Derry and was by all accounts an effective if rather indolent teacher. ('Anything here anyone wants to keep?' he asked his class of the assignment they had just given in, and when they shook their heads in unison, Frost binned the lot, saying that if they did not value them enough to keep then he did not value them enough to read.) Teaching was a financial necessity in those Derry years, for Frost admitted that any one of his apple trees earned more a year standing stock-still with its roots in the ground than he did uprooted and rushing around, and he vowed to write better verse and find an audience for it. Although he was already writing the poems that would fill his first two books, he had published only a handful of them. By the winter of 1911 he was focussed on the idea of a literary career, and told a friend that 'the forward movement is to begin next year'. In 1912 he made the commitment to his poetry that he had long put off. 'I am going to be justified of my poetry before the end,' he commented. 'I have hung off long enough. I wasn't going to pass forty without having it out with myself on this score.'[44]

From his study 700 feet up on the East Hampshire Hangers, Thomas could make out sixty miles of South Downs at one glance. Beneath him, the hillside dropped southward into a dark coombe of beech and yew trees; along the ridge lay the Shoulder of Mutton, so called for the lamb-chop shape of its grassy clearing amid the yew line. To the north lay the hangers of Oakshott, Happersnapper, Roundhills, Reston and the Warren, each descending rapidly north-east from the plateau into farmland. To the south and west, Ashford Hill and Lutcombe Bottom pinned a second, curling ridge that passed through Strawberry Hanger, Lythe Hanger, Great Hanger and Cold Hill. Thick, broad-leafed woods plunged down from the plateau, more beech and yew, some small-leafed limes, some larch wound with clematis or ivy and carpeted with wild garlic and the celandines that prospered in the wetter lands each February. Woodpeckers drummed through the canopy, roe deer and fox ran the floor below. The village at the foot of the scarp was named Steep (Old English *stēap* or steep place) after the sheer escarpment at the western end of the Weald (OE *weald*, woodland); the clay and flint plateau above it was Froxfield (the frogs' field or stream). Connecting the two was Stoner Hill, a cart road impassable in heavy weather, in places sinking fifteen feet below the fields under the pounding of the carriers and the rain. While trade men trekked this hard hill, Thomas and his children followed a cut through the woods down through Ashford Hanger along a path that led to school.[45]

Thomas's heart would quicken whenever he looked upon Shoulder of Mutton Hill, but it would not quicken for the house that lay on top of it. Wick Green on Cockshott Lane should have been a dream home, but it never became so. Since 1906 the Thomases had rented at Berryfield Cottage a mile along the Ashford stream from Steep, but when the estate was broken up for sale Thomas had no means of purchasing the cottage there. In September 1908 a friend came to the rescue: a William Morris disciple named Geoffrey Lupton offered to build the Thomases a house at the head of Ashford Gorge to the highest standards: hand-made bricks and tiles, solid oak doors and timbers and floors, finished with wrought-iron fittings cast from Lupton's own smithy and a recessed terrace that Helen had petitioned for. Nothing could fault its aspect or those sixty miles of South Downs views, but the house was hard, cold even in summer and frequently enveloped in the foggy mists that would crawl out of the coombe below and swallow everything about them. Worse than the mist and the cold was the wind, which roared over the hills or rushed up from the valley with a terrible moan. On some days it seemed to govern the house and its inhabitants, and Thomas readily submitted to its rule, feeling that it bound together somehow his past and the past of the world within it. He said that it carried upon its back old griefs and new griefs yet to come, foretold of terrible times and made a new house old. On the high slope, the wind was his subject and his master; it seemed to bully at his spirits and was locked into the house with him on the day he first closed the front door. It was in the gable room beneath this wind that Myfanwy was born, and he did not know which sound caused in him the more despair: her cries or the wind's howl. All around were the hard, stone soils, and the flint that was 'the one crop that never failed'. It was a cold, biting, bitten-at place. The grey mind of the wind, he wrote, looked down upon his own grey mind.[46]

The day after the opening of the Poetry Bookshop in January, Thomas had returned to Steep, where a New Year's greetings card lay in wait. It was an introductory correspondence with a young, naive socialite who would become his confidante. This was Eleanor Farjeon, thirty-one years of age, who had sent him a goodwill message emblazoned with a sailing ship, which he took, teasingly, as an invitation from her to what he called 'lessons in navigation' at their upcoming social gathering in Broughton Gifford, Wiltshire. It was a coquettish, even flirtatious response by Thomas: he was familiar with the social set and hardly needed any help in negotiating the subtleties that accompanied these occasions. Yet beneath his surface he yearned for all the navigation he could get. Edward and Eleanor had met at a tea gathering before Christmas, and he would not have mistaken her for anything other than an impressionable character. She was a quiet, shy, bespectacled woman, her dark hair fixed carelessly in a bun, who thought herself unnoticeably plain and who, in her own description, was as emotionally immature as a girl of eighteen. From an early age she felt more at home in a library than in polite society and as a child she retreated into familial relationships and a passion for books. Her father was a Jewish Victorian novelist who had escaped East End impoverishment, her mother the daughter of an actor, and she had a trio of talented brothers; but Eleanor would be outdone by none of them. From the age of seven she was pounding out stories on her father's typewriter; by the time she met Thomas she had already published two volumes of poems. It was said of her that when she wrote she smiled; and it would not be long before she would fall in love with Edward Thomas, the writer and the man.[47]

*

On 14 January, a warm if mischievous review of *Georgian Poetry* appeared in the *Daily Chronicle*, written by Edward Thomas, in which he praised the initiative of a bookshop that, he believed, promised not only a new access to readers but discernment in an age in which anyone with five pounds to spare could have a book of poems printed. 'It brings out with great cleverness many sides of the modern love of the simple and primitive, as seen in children, peasants, savages, early men, animals, and Nature in general.' Thomas wove an acerbic wit through many of his reviews. He wrote once to Monro, 'I can't pretend to take myself seriously as a writer about poetry when even the ½d. news-papers are forsaking me. And your Review does seem certain to give that false appearance of seriousness to what I might say.' He enjoyed playing with false appearances in his articles, and in his praising of the primitive love of children, peasants, savages and early men he was giving a gentle send-up to Georgian sensibil-ities. In a second review of the anthology, the same mocking tone appeared when he suggested that the volume was an exem-plary selection of poetry from the years 1911 and 1912: 'Compare it with a similar book of poetry from 1901 and 1902 and its novelty is apparent,' – adding, 'There is, by the way, no anthol-ogy of 1901 and 1902.' But his humour did not always come across entirely as he intended, and on this occasion he wrote to Monro to explain: 'I was alarmed to see how chilly my notice of the Georgian Anthology appeared in the Chronicle. But I had to ask the editor to cut out the passage where I made a mistaken reference to Poetry and Drama and he cut out too much.' Dry or chilly, his review at least carried the stamp of independence that would mark his work throughout his life; by contrast, a notice in *Poetry and Drama* (published at the Bookshop) by Henry New-bolt (guest of honour at the Bookshop) would stake the unlikely claim that these poems would astonish and delight the reader in equal measure and 'prove the coming of a new breath of poetic emotion'.[48]

Thomas had long since refused unpaid review work, and had once declined an invitation from Monro to review '*con amore*', in part fearing the journal in question, *Poetry Review*, would become 'a sort of home for incurables'. But in January 1913 he had made an exception to help launch the new journal from the Bookshop, *Poetry and Drama*, and his first contribution would cause a sensation. Ella Wheeler Wilcox was probably the most widely read poet of the day; her *One Hundred Poems*, just published in London by Gay and Hancock, would breeze through 100,000 sales in only a decade and a half. Wilcox employed a popular rather than literary language, a homespun, hearthside philosophy, and a wobbly sense of rhythm ribboned with a chiming end-rhyme. Those familiar with Thomas's incisive reviews could not have expected him to like Wilcox's work, and sure enough he did not; but what made such an impact upon readers of the piece was not his consternation but the tone that he employed in communicating that consternation. Thomas wrote the review ironically. In a meticulous sacking, he feigned praise in order to make a series of irresponsible claims that he knew Wilcox's poetry could not hope to meet. He lauded, for example, her subtle appreciation of the Japanese people and then quoted her description of 'Brave little people of large aims.' Of her stance towards life he asked, 'How many times does she repeat the lesson contained in this? "Don't look for the flam as you go through life." Well she knows that you cannot have too much of a good thing.' Wilcox said familiar things cheerily and repeatedly, Thomas wrote, and what was her greatest triumph? To possess a talent that the common man or woman could aspire to. 'Her glory is the more bright that it has been attained with the help only of a metrical skill commonly possessed by minor poets, a light sympathy with all sorts of ideas, and without principle or sense of beauty.'[49]

A light sympathy with all sorts of ideas; it was a piece of critical surgery as withering as it was precise, and at London's literary gatherings Thomas's review was hailed triumphantly. Not only had he exposed the most popular poet of the day as an impostor, said his peers, but more importantly he had landed a blow against the kind of popular Victorian literature that had come to swamp contemporary bookshelves. It was an achievement of which Thomas himself was unusually pleased. Rarely before had he congratulated himself on his work, but now he referred to himself proudly as 'the poisoner of Wilcox'. But for all the guile, for all the dry and witty pen strokes, the risk of adopting irony was self-evident: not everybody may pick up on the tone. Wilcox herself came to consider Thomas a great admirer, and her American publishers appeared to have been similarly caught out; so delighted were they by the review that they supplied Thomas with a complete set of her books. It was not the present, surely, the reviewer would have hoped for; but perhaps the publishers understood the article's tone full-well and were simply returning serve.[50]

Godwin Baynes had encouraged in Edward Thomas a process of self-interrogation, and in 1913 Thomas began to use his life story as subject for his writing more expressly than before. Towards the end of January, a short account of his early years appeared in the journal *T.P.'s Weekly* under the title 'How I Began'. At the same time he was completing an autobiographical novel, and would later that year begin work on a childhood memoir. Thomas had frequently projected himself onto his countryside characters, but not until now had he expressly made himself the subject of his writing in the first person, and for the first time, readers were offered an insight into his childhood.[51]

On what is now Lansdowne Gardens, nestled between London's South Lambeth and Wandsworth Roads, stands an imposing, four-storey, semi-detached Victorian villa that was the first London home to Philip Henry and Mary Elizabeth Thomas. It is built on the northern spoke of a fine residential circus completed by local builder John Snell in the middle of the nineteenth century. By the time Mr and Mrs Thomas rented their rooms, South Lambeth had become heavily built-up on the back of a wave of 1860s terraces that had filled in around the expansive villas of twenty years earlier. Residential building had swept over smallholdings, market gardens and farms along the line of the London and South Western Railway, and had recently overrun the isolation of Battersea and Clapham villages. It was here among these urbanising boroughs that on 3 March 1878 Edward Philip Thomas was born.[52]

Philip Henry Thomas had distinguished himself in the Civil Service Examination and been posted to the Board of Trade on a staff clerkship for light rail and tramways. He had moved to London in 1873 from Swindon, having left his home town in Tredegar, Ebbw Vale, thirty miles north of Cardiff. A self-made man, and the first from his family to make the social climb from skilled manual labour into the middle classes, he was a Welsh speaker whose preparation for the Civil Service Examination had given him command of French, German and Latin besides. He was a staunch liberal committed to free trade and Home Rule for Ireland, and an ardent follower of David Lloyd George, with whom he would walk across the park from the underground station at Westminster most mornings. At the Battersea Parliament he honed his skills in public speaking and was invited by the Liberal Party to stand as their candidate in the Clapham Division of the 1918 General Election where, according to a local newspaper, he 'put up a strong fight against odds' despite losing. To his family he was known as 'The Public Man' for the lectures he gave each Sunday in the nearby town hall for the Battersea Ethical Society. Baptised Anglican and brought up Methodist, Philip Thomas became an atheist after exploring many denominations, eventually settling in Positivist circles, where he spoke from the pulpit at the Church of Humanity in Holborn. Edward remembered his father taking him along to the hustings at Washington Music Hall in Battersea on Sunday evenings to hear Keir Hardie talk about the formation of an Independent Labour Party and Michael Davitt on the pressing need for Irish Home Rule.

I have only one clear early glimpse of my father – darting out of the house in his slippers and chasing and catching a big boy who had bullied me. He was eloquent, confident, black-haired, brown-eyed, all that my mother was not. By glimpses I learnt with awe and astonishment that he had once been of my age.[53]

To his surprise, Edward learned that his father knew more about marbles than the best players at Edward's school. He would tell and retell the story of the Wiltshire moonrakers hanging in a chain over a bridge to fetch the moon out and had a repertoire of songs and comic speeches that would delight his children, together with a library of several hundred books in which young Edward had his formative literary encounters. But he was a stern and aspirational man who pushed the young Edward relentlessly: first toward evening classes in Physics and Latin, later for St Paul's School in Hammersmith, and later still a career alongside him in the civil service. Years of pushing and badgering and bloody-mindedness left the relationship between father and son fraught and fractious; it deteriorated irrevocably when Edward, at university, found himself accused by his father of being a bad debtor, reading libidinous materials, drinking and smoking to excess. An 'open break' occurred, in Helen's words, fuelled by Philip Thomas's disgust at what he saw as a kind of dandyism in his son: an aesthetic whim to pursue literary dead-ends rather than provide as a husband and father should provide. When Edward finally found his way to writing verse, he would record his feelings for his father in contemptuous terms. 'I may come near loving you | When you are dead,' he wrote. 'But not so long as you live | Can I love you at all.'[54]

Of his mother, Edward could recall even less, although what he remembered he did so in idealised terms:

She is plainest to me not quite dressed, in white bodice and petti-coat, her arms and shoulders rounded and creamy smooth . . . I liked the scent of her fresh warm skin and supposed it unique. Her straight nose and chin made a profile that for years formed my standard. No hair was so beautiful to me as hers was, light golden brown hair, long and rippling. Her singing at fall of night, especially if we were alone together, soothed and fascinated me, as though it had been divine, at once the mightiest and the softest sound in the world.[55]

As a physical description, these words would not have seemed out of place if Edward Thomas was writing of a lover, and certainly she appeared to offer him a perfection that he never found in Helen. Towards his mother's sister, Edward expressed a similar physical attraction, and it was in watching her sitting less than half dressed on a chair that he developed what he called his first 'conscious liking for the female body'. Mary Thomas dressed in long skirts with mysterious hidden pockets, and a wide black belt into which she tucked a half-hunter watch on a long gold chain. She made and mended Edward's clothes, cooked and comforted, and may have been prone to the melancholia that would wreak havoc upon him, as hinted at in Edward's description of her as 'diffident and sad and not clever', and Helen's as 'very retiring and shy and sad'. One of Edward's earliest memories was witnessing her rise distraught from the dining table to cry out, 'I am going to die', before her husband took her on his knee to soothe her. In her son's letters and prose, she remains a ghostly, sallow figure, attractive and remote, comforting yet forlorn, someone towards whom Thomas felt protection and love.[56]

When Edward was two, the Thomases moved to a late-Victorian end-of-terrace house just off Bolingbroke Grove, fifty yards from Wandsworth Common. The house was more modest than the last, but unlike their restrictive rooms in Lambeth, the family had its entire run. Edward lived here until the age of ten; his brothers Ernest, Theodore and Reginald were all born there. The family moved again, four streets to the north to a larger house at Shelgate Road where Edward's fourth and fifth brothers, Oscar and Julian, were born. This was the house that would remain the family home throughout Edward's time at university.[57]

Thomas liked best of all the map-making sessions at his Wandsworth board school, poring over the intricacies of the western coastline of the British Isles, or inking the mountainous uplands with a herring-bone marking. It was the journey to school rather than anything that happened within its walls that captured the young Edward's imagination: spinning tops or marbling or trading small objects with the other boys in the streets. Walking back in cold weather he would strike sparks from his iron-shod heels against the kerbstone. But it was the Common that was the principal site of Edward's childhood games. Though divided by a railway track and bordered on all sides by houses, it was a wild and inexhaustible place to Edward, with its hawthorn and gorse thickets, its towering elms and roaming foxes, its tumbledown slopes and irregular-shaped ponds. He fished with a worm and a cotton line, dropping sticklebacks and anything else he caught into a jam jar. Other times he would go further afield still, to Wimbledon Common, to gaze at the caged animals outside the corn chandler's, or to study the hapless fishermen on the River Wandle. The smell of the local paper mill caught on the evening breeze and stirred in the young boy 'a quiet sort of poetic delight'; it was the first time he had witnessed the allure of bright running water.[58]

At ten, his father moved him to a local private school, where he now studied alongside the sons of tradesmen. At eleven, he won a place at Battersea Grammar School, and he found he could learn quickly and easily, taking pleasure in coming top of his class. He took to Byron more than he took to his classmates, though more than either he took to keeping pigeons after watching a neighbouring boy's mastery of the birds. At the clap of this boy's hands they would ascend half a mile into the sky, returning at the lure of his carefully tuned whistle; Edward learned the boy's whistle, but was never able to gain such height from his own flock. He kept a dozen different breeds: homers, tumblers, dragoons and, pride of the roost, a pair of red-ruffled Jacobins from Wales. Endlessly he watched for signs of offspring; but no young ever came from the few eggs and he took away the duds to blow.

Philip Thomas's peripatetic search through different chapels and preachers took an early toll on Edward. He loathed Sunday school, and made no friends at the chapels, instead cultivating what he called a 'drug of boredom' that saw him through the sermons, largely oblivious to their teachings. But worse than this were the stiff Sunday clothes that set him apart from the other boys playing on the street. Edward longed for a sudden gust that would blow his hat clean from his head and into some puddle. He called it his 'Upastree', in a reference to the evergreen that was said to destroy all life for a fifteen-mile radius. Chapel and Sunday school became 'cruel ceremonious punishments' for the freedom of weekends; he retained what he called a 'profound quiet detestation' of Sunday for the rest of his life.[59]

At twelve, Thomas moved school again, to another private school in Wandsworth at his father's direction, where intense attention was given to manners and etiquette. Thomas's early interest in books dissipated, and he found encounters with Virgil and Shakespeare 'obscure and tedious'. He became engaged in party politics for the only time in his life, and stood as a Liberal candidate in his school elections (a Tory landslide): 'poetry was nothing to me compared with Home Rule'. Greater success lay in his athletic pursuits, for while Edward was no runner, he could out-walk any boy in the school. On sports day, it seemed he would leave his peers in his wake on the mile-walking race; but as he approached the finish line in the lead, he believed he could hear one of the boys running behind him, cheating surely, but closing on him nonetheless. He hated the feeling of being hunted down, and could not abide the prospect of being over-taken so close to the line, and so with a hundred yards to go, convinced that victory would be stolen away, he pulled up. It was better to throw the race than to be beaten; but his father did not agree, and accused him of cowardice and of lacking the courage to see the race home. He would carry the charge of cowardice throughout his life: it would haunt his friendship with Robert Frost and would even influence his thinking about the war.[60]

St Paul's in Hammersmith, at the age of fifteen, was an alto-gether different experience. Never before had he encountered boys like this, who discussed Maupassant's stories knowledge-ably or had already secured a scholarship for Oxbridge. Lunch-times he kept his own company, reading Richard Jefferies and not easily making friends. In broken Latin, he wrote in his Alge-bra book 'I love birds more than books', and was ridiculed by the boy next to him, not for his sentimentality but for the short-coming of his Latin. 'I felt unimportant, isolated, out of place, and only not despised because I was utterly unnoticed.' School reports painted a distant child, unengaged in the school com-munity. 'I wish he seemed to take more interest in life generally' (July 1894). 'I wish he were a more sociable person' (Decem-ber 1894). Eventually Mr Thomas became discouraged: Edward failed to win a scholarship to ease the crippling school fees, and in the Easter of 1895 he withdrew his son from the school.[61]

But of all images from his school days that stayed with him most deeply, it was perhaps the gift of his first school prize, a book called *The Key of Knowledge*, which to Thomas's eternal anguish, he lost.

It disappeared, I never had any idea how, before I had read far into it, and I never saw it again. From time to time down to the present day I have recalled the loss, and tried to recover first of all the book, later on the thread of its story, something that would dissipate from its charm the utter darkness of mystery. For example, fifteen years ago in Wiltshire, two strangers passed me and I heard one of them, a big public schoolboy, say to the other, a gamekeeper, 'What do you think is the key of knowledge?' and back came the old loss, the old regret and yearning, faint indeed, but real. There were times when I fancied that the book held the key to an otherwise inaccessible wisdom and happiness, and the robbery appeared satanically sinister.[62]

Spring

In the spring of 1913 *The Icknield Way* appeared. Handsomely published by Constable at 7s. 6d. in green ribbed cloth with gilt edges, a folding map and illustrated endpapers, it was a book that promised a great deal of its author. 'Much has been written of travel, far less of the road': these were the enigmatic words with which Edward Thomas opened, so announcing the book's true subject – neither the departure nor the arrival nor even, in the familiar adage, the journey itself, but the *road*, 'the rough, tussocky sheaf of cartways', the lanes riddled with rabbit burrows, the ancient chalk path lined with pewits, stone curlews and wheatears.[1]

On a hot, dry summer's day in 1911, Thomas had joined the old highway at Thetford in Norfolk, crossing the chestnut-shaded clear water of the Thet, through a field of buttercups to the heavier waters of the Ouse, over the Nuns' Bridges and out in the Brecklands. The hard, straight lands of Cambridgeshire lay before him, then the hillier country of Hertfordshire, over the old Ermine Street at Royston, through Bedfordshire, climbing steeply over Telegraph Hill, and descending to cross the third of the ancient roads, Watling Street, beneath the Downs at Dunstable. There at dusk he fell in with a man who appeared to be following the same path, a man who might easily be mistaken for Thomas himself: 'a lean, indefinite man; half his life lay behind him like a corpse, so he said, and half was before him like a ghost'. Jealous of youth, disrespectful of seniority, the man, whom he called simply 'the philosopher', could not decide whether to feel happiness or melancholy at the sight of the Downs at dusk, and turned to his past in order to decide the matter, recounting an occasion when he had been digging all day in heavy flint soils like those of the Froxfield plateau. He said he had been turning clay at the very limit of his strength at just such a dusk as the men witnessed now when he overheard a woman singing through the woods on the hill road above him. Her song had been captivating: full of wild love and youthful spirit, marked by melody and a bewitching silence, hanging and swooping in the air as a kestrel might in flight, and it roused 'the philosopher' to lyricism.

Oh, for a horse to ride furiously, for a ship to sail, for the wings of an eagle, for the lance of a warrior or a standard streaming to conquest, for a man's strength to dare and endure, for a woman's beauty to surrender, for a singer's fountain of precious tones, for a poet's pen!

Thomas listened to the man's lament, himself uncertain whether to attribute the encounter half to happiness or half to melancholy, but never confessing to the reader that the other man was his own alter ago, in search of his own poet's pen. It was not the first time that Thomas had carved an image of himself into his writing, but from that moment on the other would become a doppelgänger to haunt his writing, and would loom larger and more sinister in works still to come.[2]

Thomas should have excelled in his subject along the Icknield Way: an expert map reader with a hawk's eye for detail and an innate internal compass, he ought to have loved his tracing of the old chalk highway that ran from East Anglia to the South West. But Thomas had been mentally and emotionally exhausted when he prepared the book in 1911, and it showed in the weight of his prose, in thick, heavy passages that at times threatened to congeal around the reader. So feverish was his need to produce work that year, and so feverish his moods, that he barely gave himself time enough to navigate the route, covering most of the ground in two cycle rides and an extended stint of research at the British Museum. A book that was to have been a delight became simply, in his words, 'another of those books made out of books founded on other books', and the critics agreed with him: 'The ordinary reader may gain the impression of a tired man struggling with blistered feet over hot, dusty roads, with so many miles a day to walk in order to write a book so many words in length, rather than a writer fresh and eager, entering upon his task with zest. A tired author too soon fatigues his reader.'³

One night of rain on his journey, recorded in three overbearing pages, the darkness overwhelmed him. That evening, Thomas had ridden downhill under a train of Lombardy poplars and ash into the Berkshire village of East Hendred. The rain that had been building all day began to thunder down in long, soaking strokes. He sheltered at the village inn and lay awake listening to the rain on the roof. Louder and louder it fell, hammering the gutters, roaring in the trees, flattening and pounding and exhausting. It was a terrible rain, he wrote, endless and somehow judgemental, extinguishing the flame of summer, a rain that would still be falling on him when he was in his grave, and that spoke to him now like 'a ghostly double'. He lifted his face to the window to counter the bitter words, but there was nothing out there but the darkness and the thick black rain. Briefly, the unremitting sound was broken by the call of a bird in the downpour, but the cry seemed so content that it served only to distance him further from nature. He was not a part of nature. The wonder of the world was drowning and returning to the darkness; the rain was taking away the gift of life he had never truly grasped. 'Blessed are the dead that the rain rains on.'⁴

On 15 March 1913 the first issue of Harold Monro's *Poetry and Drama* appeared, priced at 2s. 6d. and bearing an engraving of the Poetry Bookshop on its front cover with a map showing the shop's location on the back. Among its announcements was the award of a prize for the best poem of 1912, to Rupert Brooke's 'The Old Vicarage, Grantchester'. Edward Thomas had been among the judges, but he did not vote for Brooke. 'I have found it very hard to choose among your poets,' he admitted to Monro. 'I should like to give four names instead of one, but as I must not I have come to the conclusion I ought to name "The Stone" by W. W. Gibson.' If this were a surprise to Monro, it was a far greater one to Thomas, who had written disparaging reviews of Gibson for years, but he had admired this effort in long, looping iambic tetrameter in which a stonemason is asked by the woman he loves to cut a memorial for her dead lover. Brooke, who took the £30 prize by 'a decided majority of the votes', was becoming a familiar name in the Poetry Bookshop. On 28 January he had become the first poet other than Monro to give a reading there, and had been harangued en route by the children of Devonshire Street on account of his long hair. For Brooke to have recited his own poetry would have seemed vulgar in those early days at the Bookshop, when the style of the day was the theatrical recitation of others' work. Anthologies and handbooks taught the student poet how to deport himself with an essential complement of twenty-six basic emotions, contempt, fear, pride, mirth, indecision, self-esteem, love and gratitude among them, or this communiqué on how to enact 'sorrow':

Sometimes the face is buried in the hands; sometimes the hands will be firmly pressed together; often the whole body will lie prostrate, and sobs that are almost convulsive, will shake it. Sometimes the hands will be pressed to the forehead, or they may be extended in front of the body.

Brooke kept to passages from Donne and Swinburne and reported that thousands of devout women were present, 'and some clergymen'. But he was sending himself up; his audience that night had been six people.[5]

Edward Thomas had contributed not only his article on Ella Wheeler Wilcox to that first number but a review of W. B. Yeats, who had just issued a revised edition of his *Poems* of 1895. Faced with a new edition of older work, some reviewers might have taken the opportunity to make a summary assessment of a career to date, but not Thomas, who made instead a careful inspection of Yeats's corrections down to his hyphens, and found the Irishman's revisions wanting. To Thomas the alterations that Yeats had made over the intervening years seemed overworked, inappropriate and even 'limp'; Thomas concluded that, 'He seems to have been revising in cold blood what was written in a mood now inaccessible.'[6]

That Thomas could be stern with Yeats was due in part to his admiration for a poet whose reputation he rightly felt was 'not only assured, but pre-eminent among the distinguished poets still in their prime'. Thomas was tough on the writers he most admired, partly to maintain his critical independence but partly also out of the disappointment he experienced when he believed a genuine talent was underachieving. Between 1902 and 1913, Thomas appraised the Irishman's work in fourteen signed reviews; in many he found Yeats's choice of subject matter lazily convenient – especially when it came to the fashionable Celtic revival – and once condemned him for 'moving about in a world where perfect dreams are as cheap as evening papers'.[7]

Yeats's craft as a writer, however, overcame reservations that Thomas held about his subject matter. His use of speech rhythms in particular caught Thomas's imagination from his earliest reviews. Quoting lines from 'The King's Threshold', Thomas observed that '"Speech delighted with its own music" is the best definition of Mr Yeats's verse.' Just as he would Frost's, Thomas could not praise highly enough Yeats's use of blank verse for the way it could communicate spoken language. 'We are now more than ever struck by the beauty of the ordinary speeches which, in their naturalness and real poetry, prove as much as Wordsworth's preface that the speech of poetry can be that of life.' It seems likely that Thomas and Yeats would have met in the small world of London poetry, but there is no evidence to that; yet even without a personal relationship Yeats bestowed upon Thomas a great gift. In reading Yeats, said Thomas, 'I seem to find, with astonishment, that verse is the natural speech of men, as singing is of birds'. That verse could be natural speech would become central to the beliefs and friendship that Edward Thomas would share with Robert Frost in 1914; but Thomas had made his comment on Yeats in 1904.[8]

Robert Frost had marked his arrival in England with a pale lyric about the pleasures of experiencing the English maritime ('For the breeze was a watery English breeze | Always fresh from one of the seas'), but it was the need to find a publisher for his existing poems that motivated him more than the new work. Over several evenings in the autumn of 1912, after the family had gone to bed each night, Frost began to lay out on the living-room floor in front of the fireplace what he called his 'stack' of loose manuscript poems brought over in his suitcase to Beaconsfield. He had begun with a hundred or more, three times the number that he would need for a book; and bit by bit, he filleted the manuscript, crumpling up the rejects and casting them onto the fire, until he was left with an assembly of thirty-two poems.

I have never written poetry every day as you know. It was just every so often that I would weed out this pile or do something to a poem. One evening I found myself sitting on the floor by the fireplace, burning what I could spare. These were poems of youth, written separately, between 1892–1912, not in a design to be together. They were all of the period when I thought I preferred nature to people, quite at the mercy of myself, not always happy. They represented a sort of clinical curve. I put the [unburned] poems in my pocket, and next day realized that they had a unity, could be a book.

The 'unity' was an account of five of his years on the Derry farm, and was what he called 'the unforced expression of a life I was forced to live'. He titled the manuscript after a line of Longfellow's, *A Boy's Will*, and set Lesley, his eldest, the task of typing a fair copy on the family's elderly Blickensderfer machine. Before the end of October, less than two months after setting foot in the country, Robert Frost had found a publisher willing to take him on.[9]

David Nutt's offices were at 6 Bloomsbury Street, on a bustling corner near the British Museum; but it was Marie Nutt who greeted Frost, an 'erratic, erotic, exotic' French widow, 'dressed all in black, as if she had just risen from the sea'. A novelist and suffragette who had been a vice-president of the National Political League since 1910, Mrs Nutt was a formidable character and wily businesswoman who offered to publish Frost provided that he subsidised the printing, an arrangement that was commonplace at the time. Frost refused to contribute, but signed a contract in which he waived his rights to the royalty of the first 250 copies thereby ensuring that he would donate his first £3 2s. of earnings straight back to the publisher. Moreover, the tie-in clause insisted that the next three books should also come to David Nutt and should do so 'on the same terms'. It was, as Frost would later reflect, 'a fool's contract' that would cause considerable irritation to his future American publisher, Henry Holt & Co., but for now he was anxious not to let the opportunity for publication pass.[10]

Early in March 1913, a week before the planned publication of his debut *A Boy's Will*, Frost took a train from Beaconsfield into London for an appointment with Ezra Pound, who had given him his calling card addressed 10 Church Walk, Kensington, to which he added in hand 'at home sometimes'. (Frost: 'I didn't like that very well.') Pound received his guest in a purple silk gown, and asked to inspect a copy of Frost's book. Frost confessed that he was waiting to see a copy himself, but would gladly send one on when they arrived from the publisher. Patience was not one of Pound's known virtues and he insisted that the two of them pay a visit right then and there to the offices of David Nutt. On arrival, they were offered a single advance copy between them, which Pound snapped up; Frost, it is said, did not so much as manage to hold the book in his hands that day. The two men returned to Pound's Kensington flat, where Frost was told to pick a book for himself while his host settled into his reading. 'You don't mind OUR liking this, do you?' asked Pound. 'Oh no – ' Frost said, 'go ahead and like it.' Pound shooed his guest from his home and began work on a review. 'Have just discovered another Amur'kn'', he noted proudly to Harriet Monroe in Chicago. 'We should print this notice at once as we ought to be first and some of the reviewers here are sure to make fuss enough to get quoted in N.Y.'[11]

Ezra Pound had come to London in 1908, aged twenty-two, with £3 in his pocket and knowing no one, but with one introduction particularly in mind: 'I thought Yeats knew more about poetry than anybody else.' He succeeded in gaining an invitation to Yeats's Monday salons at 18 Woburn Buildings, off Russell Square. 'This queer creature Ezra Pound, who has become really a great authority on the troubadours, has I think got closer to the right sort of music for poetry,' wrote Yeats to Lady Gregory at the time. 'However, he cannot sing, as he has no voice. It is like something on a very bad phonograph.' Yeats adopted Pound in a quasi-secretarial fashion, while Pound taught Yeats to fence, a moment recorded heroically by the Irishman ('I thought no more was needed | Youth to prolong | Than dumb-bell and foil | To keep the body young'), and mockingly by the American ('He would thrash around with the foils like a whale'). But strains in the relationship began to show when Pound exceeded his station in attempting silent 'improvements' to those poems by Yeats that he was preparing to send to *Poetry* in Chicago. By 1913, Pound had taken Yeats firmly in hand and did not shy from giving a few home truths. 'Although he is the greatest of living poets,' said Pound, '. . . his art has not broadened much in scope during the past decade.' Yeats knew it to be the case, and in January 1913 confessed to 'a fortnight of gloom over my work – I felt something was wrong with it. However on Monday night I got Sturge Moore in and last night Ezra Pound and we went at it line by line and now I know what is wrong and am in good spirits.' Yeats let it be known that between Sturge Moore and Pound, it was the latter who was the more insightful critic of the two (Pound: 'I should *hope* so!!!'), admitting that the young American had him return to 'the definite and concrete'. But he remained cautious in his opinion of Pound's own writing and told Lady Gregory, 'he is very uncertain, often very bad though very interesting sometimes. He spoils himself by too many experiments and has more sound principles than taste.' He found Pound's rhythms erratic ('devil's metres') and he took a dwindling interest in the American's verse. Pound responded in kind, downgrading his respect for the Irishman, saying Yeats was 'a bit woolly at the edges', then that 'Yeats on VERY rare occasions would make an intelligent remark', and finally that he had become 'merely celtic'.[12]

Pound, in Frost's eyes, was ever 'the stormy petrel', but he was also the gatekeeper for the introduction that Frost wanted more than any other, to Yeats himself, and at the end of March 1913 the invitation he so badly sought finally arrived. Yeats's Monday gatherings had been a fixture for almost twenty years when Frost joined the circle, and were remembered affectionately by some, scathingly by others. John Masefield had been among the guests charmed by the gothic candles (electricity was shunned), a flickering coal fire, the Jack Yeats paintings, the Blake etchings and the wooden lectern where the works of Chaucer lay casually but deliberately open. But to others, the effect was artificial and even facile. Douglas Goldring, an editor from the *English Review*, recalled an evening where a young poet curled at Yeats's feet pressed him to sing one of his lyrics to a traditional Irish air. Yeats, who despite his comments on Pound was himself tone-deaf, duly obliged, and what followed was, in Goldring's memory, 'a sort of dirge-like incantation, calculated to send any unhappy giggler into hysterics'. As the tuneless wail gathered strength, the young editor tried to stifle his mirth, but eventually the settle on which he was seated began to shake under his merriment until Yeats flashed him a look from behind his pince-nez that brought all laughter to an end.[13]

Frost's first evening at Woburn Buildings was wearing on without him having made any noticeable impression upon his host. During a lull in conversation, he seized his opportunity and proposed that in reading any poem he could always tell whether it had come quickly to the author or whether it had been a product of labour. Yeats was dubious, but Frost now had his attention and pressed on, saying that he could tell, for example, that Yeats's own 'The Song of Wandering Aengus' was very clearly the act of a single, fluent burst of inspiration. Not so, said Yeats, he had agonised over the poem, an agony which those present understood to refer to Maud Gonne; and as Yeats went on, ever deeper into his personal stories, Frost knew that the moment had passed and he left that first evening with the sense of opportunity squandered.

Elinor Frost despaired at Yeats's refusal to help forward her husband's career. She watched the frustration build in Robert, aware of the significance that a good word from Yeats could bring. He had in fact praised Frost's work in conversation with Pound; 'If only he would say so publicly,' Elinor bemoaned to a friend, 'but he won't, he is too taken up with his own greatness.' When no endorsement came, Frost took matters into his own hands, informing one publisher that 'Ezra Pound acclaimed me publicly. Yeats has said in private that the book is the best thing American for some time.' The public endorsement never came and Frost would tire of Yeats, though not before he would tire of Ezra Pound.[14]

Frost's friendship with Pound lasted a mere four months.

Pound would press him to join his exploration of *vers libre* (Frost: 'writing free verse is like playing tennis with the net down'), and in order to make his point rewrote a poem of Frost's, saying, 'You've done it in fifty words. I've shortened it to forty-eight.' 'And spoiled my metre, my idiom and my idea,' Frost protested. The tension spilled into knockabout comedy in the middle of the London restaurant in which the two men had lunch in 1913. Pound was then taking lessons in judo and insisted on demonstrating a hold upon his lunch date. Frost was told to rise from his chair, whereupon Pound grasped his wrist and proceeded to throw him over his back and on to the restaurant floor, where he lay dazed, surrounded by the surprised glances of restaurant onlookers. 'Wasn't ready for him at all,' said Frost. 'I was just as strong as he was.' Along with T. S. Eliot, Frost would one day help secure Pound's release from St Elizabeth's Hospital for the criminally insane, but for the time being their friendship was done. 'An incredible ass', wrote Frost of Pound in autumn of 1913, 'he hurts more than he helps the person he praises'.[15]

In the spring of 1913 Edward Thomas may not yet have known about Robert Frost but already he knew all he ever wanted to about Ezra Pound. When Thomas reviewed Pound's debut collection *Personae* in 1909, the young American was 'only just getting under sail', in Thomas's words, and he chose, as often he would with debutants, to ease the passage of that journey. 'He has very great things in him,' Thomas told his friend Gordon Bottomley before taking his support public. In the first of two reviews, Thomas described how the work 'bursts upon the mind' and offered an astute summary of verses that were not seduced by melody, golden words, fashion, rhetoric or Celticism. 'It is the old miracle that cannot be defined, nothing more than a subtle entanglement of words, so that they rise out of their graves and sing.' In a second notice in the *English Review* Thomas praised the promise of this 'admirable poet' who would, he believed, eventually be exposed as a 'great soul'. Edward Thomas should not have been alone in identifying the precocious talent on display in that book, but so contrary did his opinions run to prevailing tastes that his reviews got him into difficulties with London's literary circles.[16]

The Square Club was one of the many literary cliques that met in the capital in those pre-war years. One regular attendee was the adventure writer Edgar Jepson, and it is to him that we owe the colourful account of the moment when Square Club read with horror Thomas's reviews of Pound. 'You could not be a poet in those days unless they discovered and made you,' Jepson explained. 'They would not allow it.'

Then E. T. fairly tore it: in a review *he praised the verse of Ezra Pound!*
I shall never forget the meeting of the Square Club a few days after that monstrous action: the pale, shocked, contorted faces of the poet-makers, the men who discovered and made John Freeman; the nervous leaping into corners; the choked whispers; the jerky gestures; even between the courses the harsh sound of grinding teeth.
Poor Edward Thomas! He did look so hot and bothered. His protest that he had acted in good faith, that at the time of the writing of the review he had really fancied that he liked the verse of Ezra Pound, drew from his colleagues only horrid rumblings. How *could* he have liked the verse of a man whom none of them had discovered, much less made? Why, none of them even knew him! The thoughtlessness! The betrayal! The shattering blow to English Literature.[17]

Never before had Edward Thomas suffered the bad opinion of his peers, and the effect on him was distressing. With his literary reputation under scrutiny, for the only time in his career Thomas renounced his opinion. 'Oh I do humble myself over Ezra Pound,' he wrote to Gordon Bottomley a few days later. 'He is & cannot ever be very good. Certainly he is not what I mesmerized myself – out of pure love of praising new poetry! – into saying he was & I am very much ashamed & only hope I shall never meet the man.' Alas, Thomas would not have his way on this either, and in September 1909 found himself seated beside Pound at a Square Club dinner. Pound's flamboyance and Thomas's introspection found no meeting point as the evening wore on, and Pound took little from the encounter except to say in a letter home that he had met the man who reviewed him to his advantage. Thomas, on the other hand, prickled with dislike for Pound. His literary opinion of the work had already been turned on its heels in private, and in a review of Pound's second book, *Exultations*, later the same year he would clarify his error in public. In it Thomas admitted to have been duped by Pound's pyrotechnics and suggested that behind the poems' dazzling façade there existed 'very nearly nothing at all': no expression from the heart, no memorable phrasing, in fact much that he had said about *Personae* but without the benefit of the doubt that he gave to a first book. Pound's style was obscure, thought Thomas, and pestered by variousness: 'still interesting – perhaps promising – certainly distressing'.[18]

In truth, the difference in Thomas's public attitude toward Pound's two books was not considerable, but the change in his private views was pronounced. Edward Thomas had let Pound get under his skin and it provoked in him a brutal self-examination. 'Ezra Pound's second book was a miserable thing and I was guilty of a savage recantation after meeting the man at a dinner,' he told Bottomley. 'It was very treacherous and my severity was due to self-contempt as much as to dislike of his work.' Thomas's response to Pound had been wildly temperamental: in the space of only a few months he had first admired the work then said that he had been mistaken, a mistake that he initially described as literary, then personal and then, finally, one born of self-contempt. There may be no truth in the suggestion that the writers of the Square Club influenced his change of mind, but there can be no doubt that Ezra Pound effected in Thomas a crisis of his own convictions. Thomas's erratic treatment of Pound is a clouding episode in a critical career of otherwise incorruptible value: a man who knew his own literary mind inside-out and was never afraid to tell it straight to his very closest friends.[19]

Pound had no notion of the anxieties he had stirred within Edward Thomas, but his dismissal of the man was absolute. 'He was a mild fellow with no vinegar in his veins.'[20]

A wild south-westerly brought thunder and downpour to London on Good Friday 1913. Thomas waited for the worst of it to pass before setting out on his bicycle from his parents' house in Balham at ten that morning. He headed south-west, weaving between puddles a yard wide and three inches deep through a city that seemed to him to be expanding hungrily. The fields that surrounded Garratt Green in his youth were being filled in by allotments and new houses, though here and there was evidence of the low clearings he remembered as a child. Watercress beds were still worked in the River Wandle, though the mudbanks at the old Copper Mill no longer marked the town boundary that he recalled from childhood. His commission was a simple one: to take a bicycle ride from London to the Quantocks and write a 300-page account of the journey. Thomas's route would take him from Nightingale Lane in Balham, under the North Downs to Guildford, along the Hog's Back to Farnham towards Winchester, over Salisbury Plain and the Mendips to Glastonbury, before Bridgwater, the Quantocks and down to the sea. He would set out with one purpose in mind, to look for the arrival of spring in an early martin, some larch green or blackthorn white, a chiffchaff: any sign to show him that the new season had arrived, and he would complete the journey in a week.

The rain fell harder as he crossed the rail bridge at Haydons Road station, harder still as he turned onto Merton Road, until finally he was forced to take shelter from the downpour under the awning of a cheerless pet shop. Another traveller sheltered there, and with no sign of the weather relenting, Thomas watched as the other man, for want of something better to do, entered the shop for a scrawny cock chaffinch that hung in the window; he emerged awkwardly a few moments later with a paper bag in which the small bird was pounding away. As the rain subsided, the man mounted his bicycle but had not advanced more than a few hundred yards before he pulled to the side of the carriageway, and released the dingy bird, which flew straight up and into the lavender of a neighbouring garden. To the watching Thomas, the man performed this task with a self-conscious air, 'as if he knew how many great men had done it before'. It was the first of many unsettling encounters with this strange character that Thomas would have en route.[21]

Somewhere beyond Morden, he caught up with him once more, sketching a gilt weathervane that had captured his attention and being jeered by a band of young men. In Salisbury he met him again, this time in a hotel lobby, with a growing ambivalence toward their encounters.

This Other Man, as I shall call him, ate his supper in silence, and then adjusted himself in the armchair, stretching himself out so that all of him was horizontal except his head. He was smoking a cigarette dejectedly, for he had left his pipe behind at Romsey.

Wherever he went, Thomas browsed the tobacconists for the perfect pipe. He chose plain, bone-like clays, unglazed and uncoloured, short and straight, and liked to keep two or three about his person at all times. Most that he acquired were indifferent; many cracked at sudden exposure to the flame, others heated too quickly and could stick on the lip, or broke when tapping out the fur. But one or two survived the process by a heat gradually applied, and these became toughened and sweetened and aged with a fine old ivory hue. But the Other Man's eyes had glazed as Thomas explained all this to him, and when he had finished he asked instead whether Thomas had seen the weathervanes and pub signs at Albury, Butts Green, Dorking, Shalford, Leatherhead. Some Thomas had seen, certainly, though from the conversation they shared it was apparent that the two men had independently been travelling the very same route.[22]

Each day, Thomas travelled onward towards Somerset; each day, the Other Man caught up with him. The bells of George Herbert's Bemerton church were calling worshippers to prayer as Thomas cycled past in a rare moment of communion from which he was shaken by the sudden appearance of the Other Man, who overtook him on the road and turned to recite in an exaggerated fashion Herbert's sonnet 'Sin', followed by some improvised lines of his own, 'Good Lord, or whatever Gods there be, deliver us.' Thomas was disgusted at the Other Man's tone, which he found mocking and self-congratulatory, and was pleased to lose him at the next village.[23]

Again and again came the encounters with the Other Man, at by-roads, weirsides and village inns. Thomas scorned him for his aimless anecdotes, his health-food snacks of monkey nuts and brown bread (once his own diet), and took delight at seeing him bettered in an argument; it was some time before it dawned on Thomas that his companion might be a travel writer like himself. 'You are lucky to get money for doing what you like,' said Thomas:

'What I like!' he muttered, pushing his bicycle back uphill, past the goats by the ruin, and up the steps between walls that were lovely with humid moneywort, and saxifrage like filigree, and ivy-leaved toad-flax. Apparently the effort loosened his tongue. He rambled on and on about himself, his past, his writing, his digestion; his main point being that he did not like writing. He had been attempting the impossible task of reducing undigested notes about all sorts of details to a grammatical, continuous narrative. He abused notebooks violently. He said that they blinded him to nearly everything that would not go into the form of notes . . . 'Good God!' said he. But luckily we were by this time on the level. I mounted. He followed.[24]

Catkins wagged in the poplars on the narrow lane down to Kilve church, where Thomas approached the culmination of his journey. There, he had one final encounter with the Other Man, who explained he had come to establish whether Wordsworth was correct in suggesting that the church had no weathercock; Wordsworth was, and the Other Man departed, laughing as he rode. Thomas sat on the pebbles of Kilve beach, watching smoke from a fire on the Quantocks roll down toward the sea. A meadow pipit hauled itself twenty or thirty feet skyward, and swung down and away with a sweet blast of song. The next day he climbed the north slope of Cothelstone Hill in the Quantocks, and there he discovered on 28 March the first bluebells and cowslips that told him that he had found spring.[25]

'You mustn't give away the fact that the Other Man is rather a lie,' said Thomas to Jesse Berridge presenting him a copy of *In Pursuit of Spring*. (Berridge had ridden with Thomas on part of the journey, as had his brother Julian.) But the Other Man was not a lie, he was a projection of Thomas's alter ego, just as the figure of 'the philosopher' and the 'ghostly double' of the rain had been in *The Icknield Way*. Under the tutelage of his doctor Godwin Baynes, Thomas was drawing even deeper into his inner matter, dredging up disturbance, doubt and even despair for what his publisher had expected to be a work of mild-mannered travel literature.[26]

Thomas worked hard in writing up *In Pursuit of Spring* from his parents' house in Balham and from Martin Freeman's in Maida Vale. He was pleased with his progress: his rhythm was fluent and for several weeks he wrote exhaustively, typing 4,000 words a day. On 6 May he felt he had progressed sufficiently to return home to Wick Green at Steep. His time in London had brought no review work, but he had at least secured a small commission from B. T. Batsford on the subject of 'ecstasy'. It seemed strange that Thomas should choose a moment of extended depression to address a rapturous subject, but it was not without reason. He hinted at his thinking when he told Gordon Bottomley that he was interested in any stories which communicated 'man's belief at various times that something can clear things up for him without immediate help of the intellect.' Thomas wanted the work to be a piece of personal salvage and naively hoped that in exposing himself to the subject matter he might somehow discover a cure for his own condition. But he found the work heavy going and could not settle to the task. By the end of July he was still struggling for a way into the material, and finally set it aside in the autumn. He would explain to Eleanor Farjeon at the time, 'I did a third, then soberly and finally decided it was mostly muck and so ill-arranged that it could not be rewritten.' His attempt to jump-start his prose into rapture had been a failure.[27]

Robert Frost may have been a novice on the publishing scene, but he was in no doubt as to what it was that sold books. For all the efforts of the Poetry Bookshop, works like Frost's were not sold through browsing but through the notices they received in the newspapers. So when a fortnight had passed since publication of *A Boy's Will* without any sign of attention, Frost became anxious. 'I am in mortal fear now, lest the reviewers should fail to take any notice of it.' When the notices did come they were not what he hoped. The first, in the *Athenaeum*, set the tone. 'Many of his verses do not rise above the ordinary, though here or there a happy line or phrase lingers gratefully in the memory.' The second, a round-up shared with no fewer than sixty-two titles in the *Times Literary Supplement*, was barely better. 'The writer is not afraid to voice the simplest of his thoughts and fancies . . . though the thought may be feebly or obscurely expressed.' More agitating still were two reviews from Pound which praised Frost's lack of pretension but went on to describe the poems as infelicitous and 'a little raw', referring sceptically to their 'utter sincerity' as if that were something to be suspicious of. Worse followed when Pound provocatively announced that Frost had 'been long scorned by "the great American editors"' (a phrase dripping with sarcasm from Pound's pen): 'It is the old story.' Frost winced to see his book being used as an object with which to beat his country's editors, and was furious with Pound for usurping the review. Better notices followed, but few seemed to get beneath the skin of the poems, and fewer still were moved to outright praise.[28]

The book's reception was proving to be a struggle for Frost, who was feeling his first pangs for America. 'We are very, very homesick in this English mud. We can't hope to be happy long out of New England. I never knew how much of a Yankee I was till I had been out of New Hampshire a few months.' And yet perhaps all too aware of the bind of his contract with David Nutt, he noted ruefully, 'I seem in a fair way to become an Englishman.'[29]

Rupert Brooke also wished himself away from England. Distress in his romantic life had forced upon him the desire to be anywhere else, and by mid-May, he had finalised his plans for a voyage to the United States and the South Seas that would keep him abroad for more than a year. He had planned to visit Edward Thomas in Steep before sailing, but London's tireless social whirl gripped him too firmly once again. 'I'm sorry,' he wrote to Thomas. 'I wish I'd been able to come. Now, I'm off to America. I sail next Thursday. I shall stay – I don't know how long. Perhaps next March's primroses'll fetch me back.' The night before his departure, Brooke threw a party for himself in a dingy club off Regent's Street; Wilfrid Gibson came to see off his friend, as did the critic John Middleton Murry. 'You might charge me with some message for the continent of America and for Ella Wheeler,' Brooke told Thomas. 'And I could leave the muses of England in your keeping – I do that anyhow. Feed the brutes.'[30]

Thomas and Brooke had been on friendly terms since the summer of 1910, when Brooke was courting a pupil at Bedales School in the village of Steep. Thomas discreetly abetted the young couple by issuing invitations for them to rendezvous at Wick Green, but Brooke's attention wandered and he embarked on other relationships that led to misery, a stillborn child, an elopement to Germany and ultimately a nervous breakdown. Athletic, intelligent, mischievous and labelled by W. B. Yeats as 'the handsomest young man in England' (Winston Churchill concurred), Rupert Brooke captivated those whom he met throughout his short life. Thomas was not so easily seduced, though he enjoyed Brooke's company when he returned to stay later the same autumn, this time while Helen was away, leaving the two men to fend chaotically but cheerily for themselves in the kitchen. Between courses and breaks for tobacco, Brooke shared his poems with his host and left Hampshire recharged, setting all else aside to work on them. In age, the men were nine years apart, in temperament even further, and though Thomas grew to mistrust Brooke's flamboyance, he liked his early work well enough.

Poems, issued by Sidgwick & Jackson in December 1911, was the only collection that Brooke saw published. Gravelly and gutsy, it was a book that gave the equivalent of literary indigestion to many reviewers, some of whom felt that Brooke was wilfully out to shock and even repulse. Most did not hide their revulsion, focussing their rage upon 'A Channel Passage' and asking, as did the *Morning Post*, 'what possible excuse is there for a sonnet describing a rough Channel crossing with gusto worthy of a medical dictionary?' Reviewers lined up to agree: 'The appalling narrative of a cross-Channel voyage should never have been included in the volume' (*New Age*); 'His disgusting sonnet on love and sea-sickness ought never to have been printed' (*Times Literary Supplement*); 'better left unprinted, nay unwritten' (Dublin *Express*). Not for the first time, it would take Edward Thomas in a review for the *Daily Chronicle* to change the literary weather. Unlike his more conservative colleagues, Thomas understood Brooke's particular brand of revolt as 'a symptomatic quintessence of the rebellious attitude today'. Brooke was new, and he was representative, Thomas realised, and though he could identify naivety in the preparation of the work (Brooke had lazily reused the same image in three places, he pointed out), he knew that such mistakes were corrected with practice as a poet's artistry grew. And grow it surely would, Thomas announced, for Brooke would not be an inconsiderable poet; and in a brilliant and witty swipe at the critics, Thomas signed off in this way: 'Copies should be bought by everyone over forty who has never been under forty.'[31]

Summer

The English newspapers carried accounts of renewed troubles in the distant Balkans that June. With the ink barely dry on the first treaty, a second Balkan War had broken out that would take the death toll to 150,000 in the region. Austria–Hungary looked nervously on at her quarrelling neighbours, and in particular at Serbia, which had grown strong under the patronage of Russia. But the events seemed a long, long way from England. In 1913, nobody could foresee the distance these sparks would carry; certainly not Edward Thomas, who at that moment could barely see beyond his writing desk. He had written, rewritten and typed *In Pursuit of Spring* and might have felt some joy at finishing his most coherent prose book yet, but instead he was exhausted and felt himself at a crossroads, feeling that home was the worst place for him to be and yet unable to decide whether or not to decamp. Helen tried to keep out of his way, but the strain was terrible and she sparked his temper in remarking that he looked tired. 'Tired is not what I am,' he snapped. 'I'm sick of the whole of life – of myself chiefly, of you and the children . . . I despise myself for not putting an end to it.' He set off on a bicycle tour, but tiredness overtook him and forced him to turn back. Days later he tried again, this time reaching friends in Broughton Gifford. He felt no anger toward Helen and the children, only a need to be apart. He kept in touch with her and asked what she might like for her birthday, but his tone was considerate rather than affectionate, familiar rather than intimate. At nearby Dillybrook Farm, a white cock and a turkey cock were fighting in the yard when Thomas arrived. The white cock puffed out his neck feathers and jumped at the larger bird, but could not see him off, conceding ground until eventually the turkey began to tread him down and the white cock escaped only by clambering beneath him. Round and round the white cock circled before it retreated. The victorious turkey dragged his outstretched wing tips through the dirt, his breast feathers exaggerated to a dark sporran. It was a brutal display, but Thomas was not about to intervene in a conflict that did not concern him.[1]

To write even a page of anything new attempted the impossible, wearying both himself and the family, and he told Eleanor Farjeon of his 'little yet endless' tale. 'The point is I have to help myself and have been steadily spoiling myself for the job for I don't know how long,' he wrote.

You see the central evil is selfconsciousness carried so far beyond selfishness as selfishness is beyond self denial, (not very scientific comparison) and now amounting to a disease, and all I have got to fight it with is the knowledge that in truth I am not the isolated selfconsidering brain which I have come to seem – the *knowledge* that I am something more, but not the belief that I can reopen the connection between that brain and the rest.[2]

Thomas had to help himself more; and part of that help lay in a restoration of a long-standing partnership with his literary agent in Covent Garden, Charles Francis Cazenove. Thomas had grown impatient at his agent's inability to place the books he was having ideas for and had announced a parting of company the previous autumn. 'I must see what a change will do, if anything can be done at all,' he told Cazenove at the time. 'The combination between us was ceasing to be anything but a friendly one.' But Thomas was not entirely doing justice to a combination that had produced, in Cazenove's words, 'quite a respectable number of books through our intermediary', and the agent tactfully explained the difficulty. 'You want to write books of a certain kind, and to have a commission in each case before you write. As what you want to say is not of the obvious kind which publishers can grasp at once, and as you prefer not to write first and sell the book afterwards, your agent's work is necessarily – please don't think I'm grumbling at all – rather more difficult than is the case with most of the men for whom one acts.' Cazenove took his ten per cent share of the fees he negotiated, but often he would secure an offer from a publisher that Thomas would turn down, leaving him unpaid for his efforts. He was a shrewd and even-tempered agent, canny enough to attempt to charge Martin Secker £10 for the mere privilege of viewing Thomas's first 15,000 words (non-refundable if Secker did not take the book). Thomas's proposals to Cazenove could be wild or untimely: he once put forward a boxing anthology ('with a good title it might be attractive, don't you think?') and an anthology of 'worst poems', while he turned down offers for books on Wordsworth and Tennyson and Shelley (because of unacceptable terms) and blew the most lucrative deal he had ever been offered when he dithered and disappointed over a proposal on Shakespeare. Now, less than a year after its dissolution, the partnership of Cazenove and Thomas was reinstated, and the agent busied himself on his client's behalf, beginning negotiation with Methuen for a book following in the footsteps of English authors that would posthumously become *A Literary Pilgrim in England.*[3]

The summer days of 1913 were not happy ones for Robert Frost. 'This getting reviewed for poetry over here is all sorts of a game,' he wrote. The early reception of *A Boy's Will* had been undeniably disappointing, and had confirmed his fear that the sophistication of his work might not be understood. He wrote to a colleague in America, 'At least I am sure I can count on you to give me credit for knowing what I am about. You are not going to make the mistake Pound makes of assuming that my simplicity is that of the untutored child. I am not undesigning.' That summer, driven by a desire to give weight to his design, Frost immersed himself more deeply than ever before in a study of prosody. From the mid-1890s he had mentioned ideas about speech and about sound, but he had yet to connect them. It had taken the sting of those early reviews and their charge of 'simplicity' to stir him into outlining a theory of his poetry. He would call it 'the sound of sense'.

I alone of English writers have consciously set myself to make music out of what I may call the sound of sense. Now it is possible to have sense without the sound of sense (as in much prose that is supposed to pass muster but makes very dull reading) and the sound of sense without sense (as in Alice in Wonderland which makes anything but dull reading). The best place to get the abstract sound of sense is from voices behind a door that cuts off the words.[4]

Simply stated, Frost's belief was this: cadence is a natural part of human speech – it gives the speaking voice its intonation, its modulation and its rhythm. We use cadence to indicate and understand meaning in a way that goes deeper than the content of individual words into the arena of moods and atmospheres. So when, in Frost's favourite example, we hear voices behind a closed door we can broadly make out sense even if the words themselves are not clear. We can detect anger, affection, happiness and so forth because the cadence gives us a kind of sonic blueprint for the meaning and carries a communicative charge all of its own. This is the basis of 'the sound of sense' and its importance to poetry lies in the understanding that a line of verse can communicate tonally as well as through the literal definition of words. Patterns of sound and rhythm establish a tone or mood that the poem must work towards – or against – but to which it must never be indifferent. As Frost wrote, it is entirely possible to separate sense from the *sound* of sense: 'Jabberwocky', in his example, is full of the *sound* of sense without containing any real sense at all, whereas a set of travel directions, conversely, may be full of sense without anything resembling the sound of sense.

Eleanor Farjeon was walking with Frost and Thomas in

Gloucestershire in 1914 when they encountered the idea in practice. Standing atop a cart two fields off, they saw a farmhand lifting up some kind of load with his pitchfork. Frost stopped and
hollered a question to the man, 'What are you doing there, this
fine afternoon?' The farmhand was too far away to have heard
Frost's precise words, but he straightened up and hollered an
answer that in turn was too distant for the individual words to
be audible – and yet the meaning of the exchange was precisely
clear. Frost turned to Thomas, Eleanor recalled: 'That's what I
mean,' he said.[5]

Once the poet has grasped the sound of sense, Frost believed,
the next task was to stretch the irregular rhythms of speech
across the regulated rhythms of poetry:

if one is to be a poet he must learn to get cadences by skillfully breaking the sounds of sense with all their irregularity of accent across the
regular beat of the metre. Verse in which there is nothing but the beat
of the metre furnished by the accents of the polysyllabic words we call
doggerel. Verse is not that. Neither is it the sound of sense alone. It is
a resultant from those two.[6]

Frost's beliefs had been forged in a culture that was quite different from that of his English peers. He had grown up with a
sense that his country's history was being written by his contemporaries and was not simply handed down from forefathers
or ancient textbooks. It was disparate, contested, dramatic and
changing by the day in ways that seemed distinct from the tales
of the Old World. The idea of the frontier was something that
many Americans had experienced in the nineteenth century,
and the isolation, self-determination and the pioneering sense
of individualism that accompanied it. Frost may have paid little
homage to Walt Whitman, but he shared his predecessor's manifest interest in the destiny of a new people. The British were
not a new people: they had traditions, rules, they had things to
lose; Americans, in contrast, had everything to gain. True, there

were literary and moral influences that had travelled from England: the Romantics' sense of quest and their investment in the landscape had made a profound impact on Frost and his fellow American poets; so too had certain Puritan values based on self-reliance. But Frost and many of his countrymen would employ a language of progress that valued conversation above rhetoric in its drive to speak plainly: to communicate across vast distances, to be national through the personal. Like so many in his generation, Frost pursued what Whitman called the 'song of myself': an epic of individualism, self-discovery and ceaseless adventure. Writing when he did and from where he did, Frost stood at the confluence of two streams, traditional and modern: a meeting of English craft with American idioms and ideas, or what he once called, 'the old-fashioned way to be new'.[7]

That language should carry a sonic meaning was not a new idea: Frost understood that something in the vocal gesture of primitive humans conveyed a meaning long before the development of a framework of language. He was aware too that the idea had its antecedents in poetry and liked to paraphrase Carlyle's instruction to poets from 1840: 'See deep enough, and you see musically.' And he acknowledged the sonic skill of his contemporary, the poet Edwin Arlington Robinson whose plain address and musicality had not gone unnoticed by Frost ('we two were close akin up to a certain point of thinking'). What made Frost's approach different was that he believed that it was the rhythms of *speech* – as opposed to music or traditional metre – that should guide our ear when employing the sound of sense. It was a view entirely counter to the times in England – counter to the ornate Victorians and the minimalist Imagists, counter also to the musical Georgians – and was born out of a trenchant belief that 'words exist in the mouth, not in books'. Shakespeare, John Clare or William Wordsworth may have extolled similar practices before him, as had Longfellow or even Robinson, but Frost felt certain that his register was lower, more communal and ultimately more natural, stating, 'I dropped to an everyday level of diction that even Wordsworth kept above.'[8]

But in one claim at least Frost was mistaken: that he alone of English writers had consciously set out to make music from the sound of sense. As he was soon to discover, Edward Thomas had been thinking along the very same lines.

Behind his loquacity and sometimes bluff manner, Frost's assurance was fragile and prone to doubt. He confessed to F. S. Flint that he was suffering from a sense of uncertainty both towards his poems and his ability, even to feeling foolish. But his outward crisis did not appear to tamper with the writer within, as between the winter and summer of 1913 Frost was writing many of the finest poems he would ever write.[9]

The meditative 'After Apple-Picking', with Frost's long two-pointed ladder sticking through a tree toward heaven, was probably underway before Frost came to England, but he had finished it in Beaconsfield earlier in the winter. The harrowing 'Home Burial', in which an estranged couple struggle to overcome the death of a child, was written over this time; Frost said that he based it upon grieving friends in Epping, New Hampshire, but it seemed unmistakable in its reflection of the Frosts' own tragedy with Elliot and even repeated the words that Elinor used at the time, 'the world's evil'. 'Mending Wall' would be written that summer after the drystone walls of Fife reminded him of those that hemmed his old farm at Derry. And he wrote the masterful 'Birches' tramping through the muddy front garden at Beaconsfield Bungalow. Like other pieces from that time, the composition was English but the setting was distinctly American, and recalled his childhood riding birch trees, taught to his own children. Frost's daughter Lesley, then aged six, wrote at the time of an outing into the woods to collect chestnuts: 'We started home and on the way home i climbed up a hi birch and came down with it and i stopped in the air about three feet and papa cout me.' (Frost went out of his way to have it known that every one of his poems from this period onward were 'based on actual experience'.) 'Birches' showed the complete grasp that Frost had on his art. It demonstrated his belief that the individual line was a unit of sense tied by 'sentence sounds', and showed the unerring skill with which he varied his rhythm to avoid monotony and maintain surprise. His exquisite use of image (bent tree trunks like girls who had thrown their hair forwards), his hearthside wit ('Earth's the right place for love: | I don't know where it's likely to go better') and the unshakeable strength of his opening and closing phrases were on as powerful display in this poem as they ever would be.[10]

Pinpointing the composition of these poems is not without its difficulty. Frost did not date his work, nor did he like to preserve drafts. ('A poet never takes notes. You never take notes in a love affair.') He maintained that there were very few drafts, in fact, and that the poems came naturally, as Keats once said, or not at all. 'I wrote whole poems of two hundred lines at a sitting,' he claimed: 'I believe I was not over two hours with "Home Burial". It stands in print as it was in the first draft.' Frost wished his work to be seen as the offerings of a natural and unforced writer, and took care not to present himself as 'writerly'. In part, he was manufacturing an image for himself, but he was also protecting a vital ingredient in his art. Frost was a great believer in surprise. He believed a poem required surprise in order for it to operate at its full potential, and wrote of the need for the poet to succumb to this. 'No tears in the writer, no tears in the reader. No surprise for the writer, no surprise for the reader.' He said that he never started a poem whose ending he already knew, for to have done so would, he believed, deny a fundamental purpose in poetry: that writing was an act of discovery. 'I write to find out what I didn't know I knew.' Other times he phrased the idea slightly differently, but always the same basic premise: surprise leading to discovery. It was a thrilling and courageous approach to poetry, and one that might suppose a high number of discarded drafts as the poet came to 'find out' what it is that their poem had to say. But not Frost, or so he maintained.[11]

In fact it was rarely wise to take at face value any story about Frost that was rendered by the man himself. He was, for example, a keeper of notebooks (forty-eight that we know about), and was not always effective in covering his tracks. Of 'Stopping by Woods on a Snowy Evening', he said that he was working late into the night and crossed to the window seeing that dawn had arrived, whereupon the poem 'just came': all he needed to do was cross the floor and write it down. But inspection of his surviving manuscripts tells a different story. Though much of the poem did indeed come swiftly to him, the second stanza nearly defeated him altogether: he made four passes at its first line before leaving it incomplete. This cubbish, and at times dissembling, writer understood full well the value of being the storyteller. He was at pains to point out that he was not, unlike his peers, contributing a penny toward the publication of his book, when in fact he was underwriting it through his royalties. He chose to present himself as a farmer, when really he had struggled even to keep chickens. In political language, Frost was a 'spinner' who took great care to put across the image of himself that he thought did his work the best service. 'You want to watch me,' he advised knowingly toward the end of his life. 'Check up on me some.'[12]

On 3 July 1913 W. B. Yeats read for the first time for Harold Monro's Poetry Bookshop. The event was a sell-out, the shop's first, and forty disappointed people had to be turned from the door. A shop assistant remembered the moment when Yeats took to the stage. 'A ripple of excitement ran through the packed audience, then a deep expectant hush as the poet stood silent for a moment framed in the candlelight against the dark curtain, a tall dark romantic figure with a dreamy inward look on his pale face.

He began softly, almost chanting, "The Hosting of the Sidhe", his silvery voice gradually swelling up to the solemn finale. No one moved.' Edward Thomas did not attend. He was in Steep making the final arrangements for the move to the newly built workman's cottage yards from Bedales School in the village. For five years the Thomases had lived at Wick Green on the top of the Froxfield plateau but he prepared for the move to a smaller house by selling his books and gathering 'a vast collection of manuscripts' and letters for burning; he saved little. Yew Tree Cottage was made available for a minuscule rent of three shillings a week. The living room and kitchen were one room, and with no study for Thomas to work in, he arranged with Geoffrey Lupton to retain the Bee House in the garden at Wick Green indefinitely for a shilling a week. Thomas climbed the hill every day to the study, descending for lunch at noon before walking in the early afternoon via a route which would take him back to the study for the rest of the day until supper at half past eight. When he was not walking, Thomas took pleasure in attending to the garden in the shadow of the ancient yew after which the cottage was named. He planted herbs by the door: rosemary, lavender, thyme and old man, propagated from cuttings given by Gordon Bottomley or carried with them from their cottages in Kent. Damson trees were trained over the brickwork, honeysuckle and traveller's joy woven about the trunks. He built a modest porch over the entrance and encouraged jasmine to climb freely. He wrote to Bottomley, 'We have moved & are now fairly fitted into our narrow quarters to everyone's satisfaction.' Not least to Helen's, who wrote to Janet Hooton,

We are in our cottage now, and we love it. It's awfully cosy and pretty and I love doing all the work . . . It is I who am making a home for Edward, the only time I've had it all in my own hands, and I believe it's going to be the happiest home we've had. I know I shall do my best, and my dear old boy is trying too . . . He's tried hard during these last two years to kill my love for him but it's just the same as it always was, it's my great treasure, the thing that keeps me going, that is my life, that and the children. In my heart I have memories so splendid that I am rich in happiness tho' I spend so very many days of utter misery. Sometimes I think he does not love me any more, and my soul gets into a panic of terror, and then out of the darkness comes some wonderful gleam that gives me new hope, new life, new being and I start again. And now in this cottage it's all going to be easier.[13]

The school holidays arrived, and Helen left for Switzerland with her sister Irene and the girls and Thomas took up an offer from Eleanor Farjeon for Mervyn and he to join her and friends aboard a houseboat on the Norfolk Broads. The holiday was a postponement from the previous year when the great floods of August 1912 had devastated the Anglian waterways, humbling bridges and washing away the roads that could bring help. Then, quanters and marshmen had rowed over the waterlogged fields and herded tonne bullocks into swimming downriver to safety, but now Ranworth Broad was a happy haven as the company assembled on a small houseboat called *The Fawn*. Slow meals were cooked and enjoyed on deck under the summer sunshine. Thomas was contented: he sang Welsh songs as he washed up after dinner, and larked around with dinner plates over his head in the position of a halo: 'Let us be Saints!' He talked easily on daily walks with Eleanor, chatting breezily with a passing carrier and filling his impossibly large pockets with the season's first apples. Mervyn slept on the cabin floor, and won a full bed when Eleanor's friends left a day early, giving the three of them a contented familial last day together on the water. With Mervyn present, Helen would have had no reason to fear the intimate living arrangements, and could she have seen the manner in which her husband relaxed into Eleanor's company she would have been pleased. In her absence, the friendship that was building between Edward and Eleanor was gaining strength: kindly, playful and for each of them liberating. But it would be, said Eleanor, the last week of happiness that Thomas experienced that year. The buoyancy of those summer weeks was only short lived and when the holiday was over she said the gloom that descended on him 'weighed him down till the end of the year'.[14]

Early in August, from the offices of the Poetry Bookshop, Robert Frost received an inviting postcard from Wilfrid Gibson. 'I'll be here at 7:30 on Wednesday evening and delighted to see you. Bring some poems.' Gibson had taken a room in the upper storey of the Bookshop, and it was here that he received Frost on the evening of 6 August. After W. B. Yeats and John Masefield, Wilfrid Gibson was the most popular poet of his day. He was an affable character, cherished for his kindness and his warmth (D. H. Lawrence: 'I think Gibson is one of the clearest and most lovable personalities I know'), and Frost took to his unpretentious style instantly. 'He's just one of the plain folks with none of the marks of the literary poseur about him – none of the wrongheadedness of the professional literary man.' The two became such fast friends that by November Frost had announced Gibson as the closest of his peers in England, and a finer poet than the man he had briefly befriended, Ezra Pound. But Gibson had a streak of vanity that would soon undo him in Frost's eyes, and he would later imply that the American had called unannounced to push his work upon him. Frost would come to detect a superior tone in Wilfrid Gibson that would later enrage him, but in the immediate months ahead their friendship would blossom.[15]

Frost saw in Gibson's mature poetry a mirror of his own: the verse of a 'people's poet' who concerned himself with the lives of working folk and who, in Elkin Mathews, had found himself a publisher of repute from the start. Yet Gibson's first verses, published in his early twenties, had been cruelly exposed when he sent them out into the sharp-toothed world of literary London, where a young Edward Thomas, just six months older than Gibson and busily making his own name as a critic, lay in wait.

'He seems to us to be nearly a perfect minor poet – without

the intellectual equipment for originality,' wrote Thomas in a damning first review in 1902. 'Minor' was not the insult that it might be mistaken for today (Thomas himself had once stated that the future of poetry was minor; adding, 'Anything, however small, may make a poem; nothing, however great, is certain to'), but in case there was any doubt about Gibson's particular kind of minority Thomas would clear up the matter in a later review: 'He is essentially a minor poet in the bad sense, for he is continually treating subjects poetically, writing about things instead of creating them.' Harsh though this sounds, Thomas had made a crucial point about not only Gibson's verse but all poetry: namely, that bad poems make the mistake of confusing poetic writing *about* a subject with the skill of making good poetry. Thomas would frequently charge Gibson with the crime of distorting subject matter to meet the needs of poetry and of possessing a wobbly sense of craft: 'It is utterly cheap senseless rhythm, and lack of value in words no artist would pass by.'[16]

Poor Wilfrid Gibson. By his own admission, he was never a master craftsman; he once told an assembly of Chicago professors that he did not know one form of versification from another. By the time he was producing his best verse Thomas had all but written him off. Gibson learned to strip back the ostentation that had bedevilled his earlier books, and while Thomas conceded this he nonetheless thought that Gibson was somehow in the wrong business. 'At the end of this book we have the feeling that after all, he has merely been embellishing what would have been more effective as pieces of rough prose, extracts from a diary, or even a newspaper. The verse has added nothing except unreality, perhaps, not even brevity.'[17]

Not everyone agreed with Thomas in his opinion of Gibson. In certain circles, Gibson was seen as a star in the making, if not one already made: a popular new writer giving voice to experiences and to people outside of the recent realm of poetry. A poet's standing will rarely stay fixed across time, but Gibson's has plummeted to such a degree as to make it seem incredible to modern readers just how popular he was in the years before and during the war. Yeats and Hardy were more widely read than Gibson, but they were of older generations, and among his own only John Masefield, in the wake of his vastly successful *The Everlasting Mercy*, enjoyed more popularity. In one single week in January 1913, 20,000 people saw Gibson's poetic-drama *Womenkind* performed in Glasgow, while a whirlwind reading tour of the north of England saw him feted at literary receptions and society dinners. Such was Gibson's elevation as a poet that when Frost and Thomas called unexpectedly one day in 1914, they were turned away by Geraldine Gibson because the great man was at work in his study and should not be disturbed. She was not alone in her assessment of her husband's talents: Robert Bridges told Marsh that he considered Gibson's work in *Georgian Poetry* to be 'very remarkable', to which Marsh responded 'I think he is the most careful artist of them all.' Few poets at that time had troubled to enquire into working lives as Gibson was doing then. His interest in the women's movement (his sister Elizabeth was active with the Women's Social and Political Union) undoubtedly influenced *Womenkind*, and saw two of his poems published by Sylvia Pankhurst's paper, *The Woman's Dreadnought*. It is curious that Thomas should be so ruthless with him; Thomas who, after all, was frequently found giving voice to people working across the landscape that he himself knew: the watercress man, the fieldhand, the landlady at the inn, the farmer, the alienated urban worker. He may have sensed an attempt to court popularity in Gibson that he mistrusted, even suspected a distasteful appropriation of their lives, real or imagined, for the purposes of poetry. Neither would have been traits of which Thomas would have approved, but nor would he have believed that they constituted cardinal sins. So what was at the root of Thomas's disdain?[18]

Gibson's lack of precision, and his lack of an inner editor, made for moments of laziness or generalisation that Thomas would not have been able to tolerate. His failure to deliver memorable speech in writing, his failure to fix an irresistible rhythm, his inability to communicate tonally, was to Thomas an unconscionable breach of his promise as a poet: without cadence, a poem could only act upon the intellect and could therefore only ever be partially successful. Gibson was an example of the noble failure that Thomas perceived in his own prose and would seek to rectify when given his chance in verse. Gibson's work had been a platform on which Thomas had honed the beliefs that would lead him to the deepest development of his own art. He had no title quite so neat as Frost's, and never would, but what he was expressing was the sound of sense.

Autumn

Edward Thomas idled away the last of the school holiday with Mervyn at London Zoo, where he watched the vultures flap lamely down from their perches after being stirred up by the keeper. He longed to be away from family life, far away, and explained to his agent that he felt he must consider an extended visit to Australia, New Zealand or Canada if he could find a publisher to underwrite the move: 'I am quite prepared to go.' Cazenove was quick to dissuade him that there would be a market for such a book, and the moment would pass, but a seed had been planted in Thomas's mind and in the months to come he would think very seriously about leaving England. Helen returned from Switzerland at the end of August, and shared just a few days with Edward in Steep before he headed to Bethnal Green to stay with Godwin Baynes. It would be his last visit to his doctor. Following such a promising start, Thomas had come to doubt the effectiveness of his treatment. His spirits were no longer improving and the charm of Baynes's attention was wearing thin; he was ready to dispense with the doctor's services. 'Godwin can't really help me,' he confessed to Eleanor Farjeon. 'When he first came to see me he made me feel that I was the most important person in the world to him. As I came to know his world I found he gave the same impression to everybody – and I don't like being one of a crowd.' It was a petulant but characteristic remark of Thomas's: as a child he had not liked the crowd of five brothers, as an adult he abhorred the scrum of Clapham Junction. His doctor treated him as an individual and as a friend, but he did the same with everyone he treated. Godwin Baynes, it seemed, would not after all be the 'saviour' of Edward Thomas.[1]

Thomas left Bethnal Green and crossed to London's Victoria station, where he took a train to the home of Vivian Locke Ellis at East Grinstead for a week's stay; by now, Eleanor noted, the grey mood had thoroughly set in. He had come to suspect that he might be suffering from the initial stages of diabetes, though he was never formally diagnosed. His mind was bitter and furtive, and began to disturb his sleep. Even with a good book and lighted candle at his bedside, Thomas struggled to stay awake for more than a few minutes after turning in, but lately he had taken to waking before dawn, restless and disturbed. 'Any memory can now decompose me,' he wrote, 'any face, any word, any event, out of the past has to be entertained for a minute or an hour, according to its will, not mine.' In this semi-waking condition, his senses would harangue him and cause him to distort his surroundings. The rain-soaked poplars at the window crackled with a sound like fire. A robin's song in the fir copse behind the house seemed to be a relentless and dreadful form of hypnotism. He lay trying to understand the significance of the discord – the flat birdsong and the quiet moan of the wind in the fir trees – and as he lay in the darkness, to his surprise, the moment began to cast itself in his mind in verse form, rhymed in order to help preserve it in his memory.

I was resolved not to omit the date; and so much so that the first line had to be 'The seventh of September,' nor could I escape from this necessity. Then September was to be rhymed with. The word 'ember' occurred and stayed; no other would respond to all my calling. The third and fourth lines, it seemed, were bound to be something like –

> The sere and the ember
> Of the year and of me.

This gave me no satisfaction, but I was under a very strong compulsion. I could do no more; not a line would add itself to the wretched three; nor did they cease to return again and again to my head.

Gradually the lines dimmed in his head and the moan of the fir trees and the robin's song returned, and Thomas slipped back into sleep.[2]

Later that day, Thomas wrote to Walter de la Mare. 'In sleepless hours this morning I found myself (for the first time) trying hard to *rhyme* my mood and failing very badly indeed, in fact comically so, as I could not complete the first verse or get beyond the rhyme of ember and September. This must explain any future lenience towards the mob of gentlemen that rhyme with ease.' In time to come, Thomas would tell a friend that his poems had all been written since November 1914 ('I had done no verses before and did not expect to'); yet the three abandoned lines from that September night in 1913 show that Thomas was tuning in to the possibility of recording his experiences in verse before then.[3]

In fact Thomas had written verse in his late teens. His notebooks record a number of efforts through the spring and early summer of 1896, aged eighteen, which squeeze ornate words or insensible phrases into uncomfortable shapes, such as this triplet:

> I love thee thou'rt my own in hue
> I love thee oh the word was hard
> And thou wert very fair and good.

The language of these early lines was literary and already archaic for the times, and sat proudly beside his more natural prose entry of the same date:

> Happy whitethroats – singing ever and flitting
> thro' the brake together in sun and shadow[4]

Poems, as opposed to disembodied verses, begin to appear in his notebooks in 1897, when Thomas was a first-year undergraduate at Oxford, but these had ceased by 1898 after his inner editor found them pale, unmusical and imitative. They remained dormant until he was preparing his prose book *Beautiful Wales* in 1905 when, under cover of an anonymous translation ('reduced to its lowest terms by a translator'), he slipped in an effort of his own.

> She is dead, Eluned,
> Who was part of Spring,
> And of blue summer and red Autumn,
> And made the Winter beloved;
> She is dead, and these things come not again.

Even to his close friends the 'translation' had not been an obvious trick. When Gordon Bottomley had enquired after the original in Welsh, Thomas had looked sorrowfully at him and asked if he would be disappointed to learn there was no original in Welsh. Then who wrote it, Bottomley had asked, only to see in Thomas's kindly smile that the piece was clearly his own. Bottomley urged further such efforts of his friend, but Thomas had said then, 'I do not know how to do the trick again.' Yet the instinct to versify did not remain completely buried in Thomas. Under a deluge of book reviews, he wrote to Bottomley in 1905 that he dreamed of 'original writing', as he called it, 'but never get so far as to get out paper and pen for it'. In 1907, again to Bottomley, he admitted to interruptions in his thought that tantalisingly escaped him: 'things occur to me and I think for about the length of a lyric and then down and blank and something new – '. Thoughts 'the length of a lyric' then had been bubbling for many years before his night of insomnia at East Grinstead, but these thoughts came and went without ever being captured in poetry. For the time being at least, the 'trick' of announcing himself in verse form continued to elude Thomas.[5]

Frost had been waiting at Beaconsfield station for the train to London when he noticed some lines of verse in a discarded newspaper at his feet. 'Eve, with her basket, was | Deep in the bells and grass, | Wading in bells and grass | Up to her knees'. It had an appealing rhythm, dactylic and driven, and the American read on. 'Picking a dish of sweet | Berries and plums to eat, | Down in the bells and grass | Under the trees.' The poem was 'Eve', a lyric by the poet and Fleet Street veteran Ralph Hodgson. Frost tore it out and put in his pocket, and asked Gibson for an introduction; and in the second week of September the poets met. Frost gave Hodgson his verse in typescript, to which Hodgson responded, 'it is like nothing I have seen from your country, and I foresee a welcome for it in ours.' It was a warm and supportive introduction from Hodgson, but more important still would be a second introduction that he set up a few weeks later.

My dear Frost,
Shall you by chance be in town on Tuesday? If so you might turn up at St George's Restaurant, next to the Coliseum in St Martin's Lane close by Trafalgar Square – at about 4. Edward Thomas will be up and I think you'd both like to know each other.

Thomas and Frost were now within touching distance.[6]

Thomas returned to Steep from East Grinstead, and wrote to a friend about his financial anxieties in the new cottage. 'It is cheaper here, not cheap enough though for my income, to use a euphemism. Am I just to wait and do work I can in a quietly dispirited state? I get wonderfully near deciding I shall not go on indefinitely, tho I don't see how to round it off.' His spirits seemed as fractious now as they had ever been. It pained Helen terribly to see him this way, and she felt helpless in the face of it. As an untrammelled spirit, she believed that Edward was entitled to his moods, even to his harrowing behaviour towards her and the children; but there were moments when his despair seemed to pass into something deeper, and these were the times that she became truly frightened, as now, when he left once more stating business in London. On Sunday 5 October, en route to Walter de la Mare's, Thomas penned a hasty note to Eleanor Farjeon about their meeting the next day.

Will you forgive me if I do not turn up tomorrow? I have an appointment of uncertain aim with an American just before and may not be able to come. In any case it would be 4.30 before I could come. So if it suits you you will wait there: if you dislike the uncertainty don't come but forgive me. You understand: I might not come at all.

The American was Robert Frost, but Thomas almost did not make it there at all.[7]

When Thomas arrived at de la Mare's south London home, his host found him wildly out of sorts, fitful and despairing. For the only time in his life, Thomas spoke openly to his friend of his desire for suicide. De la Mare listened to Thomas's anguish and did everything he could to talk his friend around; but he could not have been entirely confident of his success, for no sooner had Thomas left than de la Mare felt the need to write to his friend, no doubt repeating the advice and friendship he had given in company. The letter was waiting for Thomas at his parents' the next morning. By then a desperate Thomas had been out early to make what he ominously called 'a certain purchase'; but as he read de la Mare's kindly, caring letter a change was effected in him. His hand was shaking, his writing uncharacteristically scrawny as he scribbled a hurried reply.

My dear de la Mare

I don't know how much I have to thank you before and can't nicely distinguish between post and propter but certain it is that this morning I hadn't more of my original design left than to make (I think largely for form's sake) a certain purchase. I wish I could have seen you again. I was a nuisance, I know. But I can at any rate write something better now than 'The Attempt'. Your letter when I found it here at 7 finally disarmed me. I feel a fool, a sort of wise fool, – not one of your best creations, – with not a shred of peacock about me, – but such as it is, it thanks you for its existence.

'The Attempt' was the name Thomas gave to the short story he had published in 1911 based upon the day he took his revolver into the woods at Steep, and now he told de la Mare that he had something better to write about. But as the morning progressed, Thomas's nerves began to steady and later that same day he wrote for a second time. 'Thank you for what you said last night. I think I have now changed my mind though I have the Saviour in my pocket. The final argument was my mother who has received nearly all the other blows possible. I very much hope you did not take me quite as seriously as I did myself.'[8]

A certain purchase . . . the Saviour in my pocket, chilling words that seem likely to have meant one of two things: that about his person Thomas was carrying a weapon or he was carrying a poison, either one of which he intended to put to a terminal application. Thomas already owned a gun, but that lay in a drawer back in Steep with Helen. To have acquired another would not have taken a great deal of effort, though thankfully it would have required at least some. In 1913, a licence was necessary for the purchase of a pistol but that licence was readily available from any post office and needed only the payment of a fee; no licence was required at all for anyone intending to keep the pistol solely in their home. But the picture of Thomas queuing in a post office for what was in effect a suicide permit seems incredible, given his manic frame of mind. More likely, he had gone out for a toxin that he could self-administer. Horticultural poisons, a number of which carried arsenic in potentially fatal doses, were readily available over the counter in 1913 and required no permit, nor even special labelling if they were sold for agricultural use in such products as sheep-dip. From his years of medicinal use, Thomas also knew how to obtain opium in sufficient doses to poison himself that way if he wished to. Whatever the 'Saviour' – bullet or poison – it was in his pocket when he went on to meet the American in St George's Café at four o'clock that day.

*

Robert Frost recalled clearly the St George's Café at which Edward Thomas held court each Tuesday. He remembered its curious access off St Martin's Lane, 'through a little side door to the right, up two flights of brass-lined stairs, through a door with "Smoking" on it, to the chess room, where he presided over another gathering at tea.' So regular were Thomas's appearances there that he acquired from his peers the nickname 'The Iambic'. The room on the first floor was light yet cosy, with white overmantels to the fireplaces and an oak clock ticking from the papered wall; but mostly the poets met on the floor above that in a room that mingled the scent of coffee with, as one guest remembered, 'the reek of half a hundred pipes'. A dining guide from 1899 told that the clientele had changed very little over the years, describing 'a fair sprinkling of men, neither obtrusively smart nor obtrusively shabby', which might well have described Thomas's crowd when he made it his regular haunt sometime around 1906. 'Chessmen, draughts, and dominoes in action. A hum of men's talk,' recorded one visitor: a place where the actors gathered and nodded their recognition to the writers, the painters, the handful of travelling paper merchants that made the vegetarian café their home. Davies, de la Mare, Hodgson and the two Freemans, John and Martin, were Thomas's regulars; others including Edward Garnett and Harold Monro came and went. The informal conversation of the circle was captured by another visitor, who unbeknown to Thomas kept notes of their conversations at the café and other meeting spots in London in 1908–9. In what is in effect the only interview that Thomas ever gave (albeit unwittingly), he emerges as fluent and relaxed in his conversation in the café, and moves smoothly between discussions on reviewing, on critics, on Oxford and Wales, and on his contemporary generation of poets. Thomas banters good-naturedly with Walter de la Mare, who says he does not think Masefield a genius; Thomas disagrees, and de la Mare says that every reviewer who used the word 'genius' ought to be fined for the benefit of a literary fund. Harry Hooton interrupts to say that he had seen a viper in Minsmere; a sure sign of spring, replies Thomas, and asks had Hooton pinched its tail and let it go, for that was the way to ensure that future generations were frightened of men. De la Mare confesses that he could not distinguish between a viper and an adder, but Thomas assures him, 'They are one and the same.' Thomas and de la Mare had met at the St George's Café most weeks since being introduced in 1907. It was at such moments in the company of de la Mare and in the reviewing of his poems that some of Thomas's formative theories on poetry had been forged. But the friendship would be gently demoted by Thomas in favour of the American's; by 1916 he would say of de la Mare, 'We rather fence with one another now, remembering we once got on very well.'[9]

Curiously, nothing at all survives of a meeting that was to mark the beginning of the most important friendship either Frost or Thomas would ever have. A few days later, Eleanor surprised Thomas with a singularly direct question. 'Haven't you ever written poetry, Edward?' Thomas let out a self-deprecating laugh. 'Me?' he said, 'I couldn't write a poem to save my life.'[10]

In October, Martin Secker published Thomas's critical biography of Walter Pater at 7s. 6d., with its dedication to Joseph Conrad. Twenty-one years his senior, Conrad was one of the very few people who ever overawed Thomas, making him prone to an uncharacteristic form of babbling. Time and again in Conrad's company he found he would blurt out commentaries that he instantly wished he could retract in case Conrad believed that he had meant them. Thomas's visits to Conrad in Kent were not infrequent: he was there when Myfanwy was born in Steep in August 1910 and he brought Mervyn with him on other occasions. Once, Conrad came across his son Boris fishing with Thomas using a line without a hook in a pond which had no fish in it. 'Thomas smiled with a shadowy irony, but he sat on, fishing.'[11]

Conrad was a great stylist, Thomas believed, more so than Walter Pater, who privileged the eye over the ear and suffered from a catastrophic failure of rhythm. As failures go, a lack of sound and rhythm might seem a curious charge to lay at the door of a prose writer, whose readers might reasonably look to other qualities besides. But Thomas was stating something more than the qualities of Walter Pater; he was beginning to make a statement about himself. In writing the book, Thomas had understood more clearly than before that the engine of writing should, he believed, first and foremost, be rhythm. 'An exquisite naturalness is hard to attain, when the writing, disturbed by protuberant words, has no continuous rhythm to give it movement and coherence.' From the eye to the ear using naturally expressive rhythm: Thomas was naming the qualities he would look for from now on, and they were qualities that he would find only in verse.[12]

Following four months of wrangling, Cazenove finally delivered a deal with Methuen for *A Literary Pilgrim in England* that Thomas felt he could sign. At £80, it was a substantial advance and it would need to be, as it was among the last and the most grinding of the prose books that Thomas would write. Virginia Woolf would say that the book brought 'the very look of the fields and the roads before us', but hers was a lone voice of praise. The book turned out to be a lethargic ramble through the locales of twenty-nine of his favourite writers, infused with the weariness that he experienced when writing it, and conveying, in the words of a review at the time, a 'waywardness of direction'. His moods were very bad, full of anxiety and gloom, and he likened his spirits to a dull flat shore that no longer expected the tide to return. He felt entirely unprepared for a return to life in Steep with Helen and the children. 'The less I see the better of anyone who can't ignore that there is something there,' he told Eleanor. How the family were expected to ignore the depressive 'something there' was beyond any of them. For years Helen had absorbed the brutality of his moods rather than impose boundaries on his behaviour; she would recoil from his words white and wounded, refusing to rise to the shouting match that he appeared to seek. He told her once that these occasions were moments of 'dreadful playacting' that overcame him, and he wanted her to know that the truer condition was one of love. She clung to those words every time he raised his voice at her, adamant that the 'real' Edward was the man who loved her and not the man of cruelty. But as she had done the previous winter, she now had to watch him pack his bag once more as he began to make arrangements to repair to East Grinstead, where the Ellises had once again made available to him 'the long small room' that was the stone outbuilding in their garden.[13]

Thomas left for East Grinstead early in November. Once again, he had seen to it that the atmosphere at Yew Tree Cottage was one of misery. 'We have been having a rotten time,' he confessed to a friend. 'I had a very persistent attack of depression which a series of quite tangible if not really enormous misfortunes seemed to be confirming beyond anything I had known before. This made me unbearable at home. In fact the sense of being the cause of so much worry and pain to Helen and the children made me daily worse (both to them and myself). So I decided to get away.' Family life had not always been like this. In the past, when the depression was at bay, Thomas at times had taken pleasure in domesticity. Picnics on the South Downs, walks together through the Hangers, descents of the Shoulder of Mutton with one or other of the children on his shoulders, songs at bath time in front of the fire: such moments were not unknown. But they had not been a feature of family life lately. For the next two and a half months Thomas would keep his distance and recover his nerves. But the children missed their father, no matter what his spirits. 'I hope you are feeling better and happier,' wrote Bronwen from Steep. 'I must say good bye yet I do not want to, I wish I could be sent by post to you but I cannot. Good by Daddy

Boy'; it had been her eleventh birthday just over a week before. For Thomas at least, the change in circumstance began to pay dividend, as almost overnight his volatile moods improved. He worked steadily on a study of John Keats, sitting down at his desk from half past six in the morning until five at night, though he found the work trying and mechanical, and doubted if he would muster the strength for any insight into the poems.[14]

On Tuesdays he continued to make his weekly visits to London, taking trains into town to catch up with friends at St George's Café or occasionally to meet with Helen. Two thousand copies of his 1911 book *Celtic Stories* had been ordered by the Australian government for their schools, and here at last was some literary news which cheered him. But not everyone was so receptive of his work: the critics had not been kind to *Walter Pater*, and Thomas revealed candidly that he feared for its chances. 'Pater will be a complete failure,' he forecast. 'It is universally condemned by the Patricians who have been whipped up as reviewers.' But he had at least finally completed the twenty-four 'proverbs' for younger readers, as he called them, which he posted to Cazenove, even though they lacked a title. 'I think they are mostly intelligible to quite young children but hope adults will want to look over the children's shoulders.' An expansion of popular sayings into miniature fictions, the 'proverbs' were Thomas's first and only venture into children's books, written across a decade but completed in a year when he was frequently away from his own children. Cazenove had been touting a proposal around the publishing houses for months, and had finally had them accepted by Heinemann in October. But it would be knocked back a few weeks later, after Thomas had unwisely begun to harangue the publisher and they returned the draft manuscript as a result. It would be a further two years before the book saw light of day, and only then paid for with a measly £10 from Gerald Duckworth; by this time it had found itself a name as *Four-and-Twenty Blackbirds*, and a dedication, to Eleanor Farjeon.[15]

In November Duckworth published the only novel that Thomas would complete, *The Happy-Go-Lucky Morgans*, priced at 6s. and dedicated to his parents. A semi-autobiographic tale about a Balham family of Welsh ancestry ('more Welsh than Balhamitish'), its story stretched across the commons of south London and the landscapes of Wiltshire and South Wales that Thomas experienced as a boy. It would not be a success. The novel won few readers and fewer plaudits for its thin plot and polite style. Thomas's friend W. H. Hudson went so far as to consider the book a mistake. 'I believe he has taken the wrong path and is wandering lost in the vast wilderness,' he wrote. 'He is essentially a poet, one would say of the Celtic variety ... I should say that in his nature books and fiction he leaves all there's best and greatest in him unexpressed . . . I believe that if Thomas had the courage or the opportunity to follow his own genius he could do better things.' But the novel had fulfilled a purpose: it had been a staging post in a remarkable year of self-examining prose that Godwin Baynes had inspired.[16]

The Italian Futurist Filippo Marinetti gave a recital for the Poetry Bookshop in November, impersonating the sound of a machine gun in order to express the violence of modernity. 'London is vaguely alarmed and wondering whether to laugh or not,' reported Richard Aldington. Marinetti was so noisy that Yeats had to ask him to stop after his neighbours banged on the party walls during a private audience at Woburn Buildings. But Harold Monro at least was swept up by the possibility of adapting some tenets of his own and wrote in an editorial:

The first principles of *our* Futurism are:

  i. To forget God, Heaven, Hell, Personal Immortality, and to remember, always the earth.

  ii. To lift the eyes from a sentimental contemplation of the past, and though dwelling in the present, nevertheless, always to *live* in the future of the earth.

There was barely a poet in Imagist or Georgian circles who would not have concurred with Monro's first principle in 1913: contemporary poets were more likely to inspect the ground beneath them than they were to look up at the heavens. But the second principle would not only separate the Georgians from the Imagists but, when he began to write verse himself, from Edward Thomas as well. Monro's second tenet would be a challenge that few, if any, Georgian poets would succeed in truly passing; but when Edward Thomas eventually turned to verse his best poems would have precisely that eerie feel of having been written in the present while living in the future of the earth.[17]

For all the unintended comedy of Marinetti's delivery, Futurism did have a watchful eye fixed upon developments in Europe. In the autumn of 1913, with parts of south-eastern Europe already at war, disputes between the fractious poets in London eerily echoed those concerns that were in debate nationally and internationally. Modernity, technology, rapid-fire, confrontation: this was Futurism; preservation, contemplation, timeless methods of communication: this was Georgianism. Across the continent, European economies were embracing new technologies and mechanised powers; many, including Germany, were taking full advantage of these developments to arm militarily against their neighbours. Britain may have held naval superiority but her standing army was barely a quarter the size of Germany's. The British government put her faith in her navy and in older emblems of national character and traditional methods of governance and trade, believing that its greatest enemies lay not on the European mainland but at home. Strikers, unionists, suffragettes, Irish republicans and the unemployed were just some of the rebellious groups that Westminster strove to quell, and may very well have failed to suppress had war not broken out in 1914.

Winter was moving in. Cold winds were bringing showers from the south-west as Robert Frost sat up late in Beaconsfield reflecting on his next move. In letters back to the States he was busily shaping his thoughts about the audience he wished to have for his work, and it was not the literary coterie that he sought. 'There is a kind of success called "of esteem",' he wrote, 'and it butters no parsnips.' That form of success meant approval by the critical few, he reasoned, and Frost yearned to reach beyond that.

I want to be a poet for all sorts and kinds. I could never make a merit of being caviare to the crowd the way my quasi-friend Pound does. I want to reach out, and would if it were a thing I could do by taking thought.

But Frost did not yet have the literary platform beneath him that he needed, and what he sought, consciously now, was a reputation that he could carry back to America, one that would help him persuade publishers there that he could be a poet 'for all sorts and kinds' of readers. Only that way did a literary income lie, he reasoned. But he knew there was more still to do. Though homesick, he prepared to dig in for a little longer:

Of course no amount of success can keep us here more than another year after this. My dream would be to get the thing started in London and then do the rest of it from a farm in New England where I could live cheap and get Yankier and Yankier. We may decide to go home this year.[18]

Winter

Thomas would stay at East Grinstead until 15 January. There he had made what he called a 'cloistered tranquillity', in which he could work provided that he received no news from home. He had visited Steep at the end of November and found the stresses intolerable; he felt in no hurry to return. His work on a childhood memoir was underway in earnest, a book which he intended as an attempt to put on paper what he saw when he thought of himself up to the age of seventeen. And he was preparing a second autobiographical novel that, he promised Eleanor, would feature people 'totally unlike himself' – a gentle joke about the introspection in which he was now engaged.[1]

Thomas's spirits were improving with every day he spent away from Steep, and he found himself in receptive mood by the time W. H. Davies came to stay in December. Wherever Davies went and whoever he stayed with he was guaranteed to leave behind plenty for his hosts to talk about. Since the publication of *The Autobiography of a Super-Tramp* in 1908, he had been a curiosity to literary London, a much-courted accessory to any social function for his shocking travelling tales of vagrancy and prostitution. To Davies, such attentions were a flattery that both baffled and overwhelmed, but it also brought him a square meal which, at times, could not otherwise readily be relied upon. His friends worried that he was little more to these society hosts than a semi-exotic bird, caged for their pleasure, and some petitioned the government for financial help on his behalf to aid his independence, none more so than his closest literary friend, Edward Thomas, whom he met in 1905.

W. H. Davies was Welsh born, older than Thomas by seven

years, and he lived a peripatetic, hand-to-mouth existence that his friend quietly admired. Thomas was drawn to the carefree existence that he associated with a tramp's life and as a boy had marvelled at a man he met on a Wiltshire riverbank, David 'Dad' Uzzell, for his knowledge of safe havens, sources of food and places to bed down for the night. By Davies's standards, 'Dad' was no tramp (he lived in a Victorian town house that he shared with his wife), but his freedom to obey his own hours and follow only nature's rules had been an intoxicating embodiment of a spirit that the teenage Thomas had found in the pages of Richard Jefferies. The homeless, roaming countryman would be a frequent visitor to Thomas's prose, as eventually to his verse, and was always a character of application and know-how, having a relationship to his earthy surroundings that Thomas could not help but envy. Davies's experience of destitution was a little different. He rarely slept in open fields and was more familiar with hostelries, missionaries, park benches and whorehouses. His right foot had been severed at the ankle when he went under the wheels of a railcar he had illegally jumped in Ottawa, and although dogs would sink their teeth into the wooden leg he had been given, he remained cheerful, explaining that all dogs had that prejudice and you could not blame them for it. Nor were children averse to having their fun: Bronwen, Thomas's eldest daughter, once teased poor Davies after he was barely mobile enough to escape an oncoming wooden cart: 'It would not matter if it ran over you, would it Sweet William, because you are made of wood!' On one occasion the leg did become broken, and Davies pressed upon Thomas the need to be discreet about obtaining a replacement. Thomas duly sketched a design for the local wheelwright without giving away its purpose, and received in return a bill for 'Curiosity Cricket Bat 5s. od.'.[2]

Davies published a debut volume that, thanks to an unscrupulous printer, cost him his life savings of £19 (it should have cost him £5, said Thomas); he sent it to literary reviewers asking for the price of the book or its return. Thomas reviewed it positively (Davies was destined for fame, he wrote) and encouraged him to write of his wild North American experiences, which he duly did, although a manuscript of *The Autobiography of a Super-Tramp* was rejected by publishers until A. C. Fifield said he would take it on if it were accompanied by an introduction from a known writer. It was Thomas who secured the foreword from George Bernard Shaw that all but guaranteed the book would sell.[3]

In Kent in 1905–6, Thomas offered Davies the tiny study-cottage he had taken a mile from his home at Elses Farm. Some days the two worked side by side, but Thomas soon gave over the space entirely to Davies, paid his rent and provided furniture and every comfort he could afford his friend. When the Thomases moved to Hampshire in 1906, Davies was encouraged to stay on subsidised by Thomas, but he seemed lonesome without his ally and chose to give up the cottage to move first to Sevenoaks and then back to London. Helen wrote asking if the furniture they had provided might be passed on to a maid of hers; Davies replied that, not having known what to do with the furniture, he had chopped it up and burned it, and not knowing what to do with the tin utensils given to him he had buried them. He moved to London above a grocer's shop in Great Russell Street, and busied himself with furnishing it in the design that he thought would befit a metropolitan poet. He had heard that literary men burned peat, and he turned to Thomas for his advice on where he should store it within the confines of his cramped flat: Thomas suggested that if he burned a few books then there might be space on the vacated shelf to stack the peat as bookends. Davies never quite knew when he was being teased but he ordered the peat nonetheless and stored it in the only place he could think to accommodate it, on the hearth in front of the fire. He returned home one day to find a crowd had gathered around the grocer's shop and firemen dousing flames from the upstairs room where a spark from the fire had set the peat alight.[4]

Davies won friends quickly (Frost, December 1913: 'Davies is lovely') but lost them just as quickly (Frost, May 1914: 'simply assinine' [sic]). But for all his naivety, Davies was no simpleton, recalled Helen Thomas. He knew well enough what people took him for, and was a shrewd judge of character, neither duped by flattery nor humbled by those who thought themselves above him. Davies was a professional misfit who earned what he could from adopting the part of a shocked and shocking traveller in life's experiences. But his attempts at sensation remained always modest: he was so naturally shy that when he attended a party he rarely moved from the seat he first occupied in case he drew too much attention to himself in the process.[5]

The December issue of Harold Monro's *Poetry and Drama* showed that the journal was now more than finding its feet, attracting contributions from Thomas Hardy and Robert Bridges, who had become Poet Laureate following the death of Alfred Austin that summer. Frost sent a copy of the journal to a friend in the States, annotating it with humorous and biting descriptions of his peers, including his assessment of Monro as 'the gloomy spirit that edits this'. Never a professional critic, Frost was spared the potential embarrassment of having to comment openly on others' work; not so Edward Thomas, who when not in the invidious position of reviewing acquaintances in public was frequently pressed for his private comments by friends. Whatever the work and wherever it came from, Thomas was principled in his opinion. Literary criticism was at a low ebb in those years before the war, and was a profession characterised, he felt, by 'secondhand words and paralysed, inelectric phrases'. Reviews appeared regularly in the tabloid as well as broadsheet press, but informed insight was comparatively rare. 'There seem to be four principal kinds of reviews –', Thomas would announce in 1914, 'the interesting and good; the interesting, but bad; the uninteresting, but good; the uninteresting and bad. Most are of the last kind.' Thomas's ability – and crucially his willingness – to write frankly as well as incisively in his reviews made for reading that was both interesting and good, but it caused him considerable anguish. He once asked Jesse Berridge to forgive his 'diabolical frankness' after advising his friend that sonnets were not his strong suit at the very moment that Berridge was planning to publish a collection of them. He told Harold Monro that he might be wise sticking to prose as his verse-form was so decorous as to become an obstacle between his ideas and the reader. And poor Jack Haines would find out bluntly and simply that 'you do not express yourself in verse'. In all his critical dealings Thomas remained resolute to his commitment to use, 'as the trees and birds did, | A language not to be betrayed'.[6]

Eleanor Farjeon may not have been aware of quite how uncompromising Thomas could be when she sent him the fantasy novel that she had had privately bound. Though not yet an accomplished poet, she was no novice by 1913 with two full-length volumes under her belt, the first with the respectable Elkin Mathews. If Thomas felt a special affection for Eleanor he would not let it intrude upon the opinion that he gave of her *The Soul of Kol Nikon*, informing her that he had failed to finish the work after stumbling over her prose. '[I] am wondering if I ought to go on after the sentence where he "sank his hand in the moon-ray and drew forth a silver horn and offered it to Kol". For I find myself trying in vain to see or in some way to apprehend the action.' Thomas made clear that he found the work inauthentic, believing that Farjeon had suffocated her material by imposing too many authorial aspirations, while failing to draw out any artistic expression. 'Is this brutal?' he asked her. 'Much reviewing prevents me from seeing books as men walking. I hit them and get quite a shock when I find I have hit a man: yet go on hitting books all the same. However I know that you don't want me to tell lies even to save my own soul and it's doubtful if I could do so by being a polite saint in the matter of

Kol Nikon.' Though she put on a brave face, Thomas's dissec-
tion of her book could only have been devastating from a writer
she admired, a critic she respected, and a man with whom she
had now fallen in love.[7]

As Thomas completed his book on Keats early in December he
saw it as the closing of another short chapter in his own life.
He was beginning to feel that he was intruding upon his hosts
in East Grinstead and would, in the new year, need to move on
once more, though whether this meant to Hampshire was not yet
clear. With work on *A Literary Pilgrim in England* having stalled
he was thinking of new projects he might undertake and gave
his agent a familiar sounding list of subjects: 'Shelley; next the
Shakespeare, next the Living Poets'. None of these would come
to pass. Thomas's moods had been lightening at East Grinstead,
but as the prospect of departure approached he began to slump
back into his usual patterns, and he wrote of 'a very persistent
attack of depression'. His confidence in his writing was low, and
he felt he was not earning enough to support his family. For the
first time since university he thought seriously about an alternative career. He secured testimonials from his friends to help with
his references before applying for a teaching job with London
County Council. But no sooner had he submitted the application than he withdrew it, explaining that he would rather face a
gamekeeper than stand before any class of students.[8]

   With Edward more or less permanently away, Helen turned to
Eleanor Farjeon for companionship that winter. As they sat up
late at night, Eleanor unburdened her feelings for Edward. 'You
know what I feel for him, don't you,' she asked tentatively, 'you
know I love him?' 'Yes, Eleanor, I do.' Eleanor delicately offered to
withdraw from the Thomases' lives altogether, but Helen would
have none of it. She chose instead to see Eleanor's feelings as a
mirror of her own, a confirmation of herself at a time of abandon-
ment. 'If having you could make him any happier, I'd give him to

you gladly,' said Helen. Her comments were kindly meant, but she would never have 'given' Edward to Eleanor or anyone else. For Helen had made a calculation: that so long as she retained Edward's fidelity then she would, she believed, retain him along with it. She felt sure that he would not develop a sexual attraction for Eleanor; that being so, Eleanor would be not only an ally to her but an asset, providing something that Helen could not: Eleanor would, in effect, look out for Edward when he was away in London, just as Helen did when he was in Steep.[9]

Helen and the children joined Thomas and the Ellises at East Grinstead that Christmas as they had the year before. For once, Thomas seemed comfortable surrounded by his family and friends. The children were delighted to be with their father, and Edward was able to take pleasure in their company. He managed even to be kindly toward Helen in the few days she stayed before taking the children to her sister in Chiswick. On Boxing Day Thomas told Eleanor of the 'cheerfulness' of the Christmas they had all spent together. His head throbbed from the mulled wine of the day before, but his spirits seemed bright, even coquettish, as he thanked her for the hamper she had sent from London. 'If only you could have included some of yourselves in the box! For excellent as the elements are – Ellises, Coxes & Thomases – still, somehow, I don't know.' Thomas's comments must have seemed like a dalliance to the impressionable Eleanor, a flirtation of the kind that he had made during their week together on the Norfolk Broads and one that she found alluring and flattering. These were confusing times for Eleanor: she had admitted her love to Helen and herself, but she was far from breathing a word of it to Edward.[10]

Dear Frost (if you don't mind),

I shall be glad to see you again and Flint for the first time on Monday next at St George's at 4. You remember the place in St Martin's

Lane where we first met. Top floor. I think Davies and Hodgson will
be there.

    Yours sincerely

    E Thomas.[11]

Three days before Christmas, Thomas and Frost met again at St
George's Café. The meeting must have gone well, for Thomas
would begin to invite Frost to stay with him at Balham whenever
he was in London. Among their conversations that day would have
been the news that Frost's friend Wilfrid Gibson had moved out
of the Poetry Bookshop for a cottage in Gloucestershire. Gibson
had married Harold Monro's assistant Geraldine Townsend on 9
December, and Monro was not in the least bit pleased. In a momen-
tary loss of perspective, he accused Gibson of wooing Geraldine
in order to make use of her editorial experience in a publishing
venture that Gibson was planning with Lascelles Abercrombie.
Gibson was furious and he blasted his former landlord to anyone who would listen. 'Monro is a swine!' he told Edward Marsh.
'He's shown himself up in his true colours.' The newly-weds left
London under a cloud and moved to a half-timbered rosy brick
cottage at Greenway Cross in Dymock, Gloucestershire, less than
two miles from the Abercrombies. It was known as the Old Nail-
Shop after the trade that was once plied there, and it stood on a
low track close to the course of the River Leadon. Robert Frost
learned with interest of Gibson's new venture: he had never lived
in a community of poets and now the calling seemed irresistible.
'There was the urge to be with those who spoke our language
and understood our thoughts.' Gibson's enthusiasm for his new
surroundings penetrated deep into Frost's homesickness for the
life he had given up in New England. He took no pleasure from
suburban Beaconsfield, while all the time his frustration with the
narrow-mindedness of London's literary society was mounting.

I should have thought to escape such nonsense in the capital of the
world. It is not a question with them of how much native poetry there

is in you or of how much you get down on paper, but of what method you have declared for. Your method must be their method or they won't accept you as a poet.

Frost would follow Gibson to Gloucestershire in 1914 and in so doing draw Edward Thomas with him. But he was not the only one preparing to turn his back on the city. Godwin Baynes had exchanged his practice in Bethnal Green for a new start in Wisbech. Though they had become all but estranged, the departure of his former doctor took from Thomas the one man who had tried to take a deeper interest in him. In his friendship and counsel, Baynes had not uncovered a cure for Thomas's chronic depression but he had opened the way for a more self-examined life. The bounty of autobiographical writings that Baynes had triggered were in full flow and would aid Thomas in his movement toward the most expressive output of his life, the poems. It was the closing of the only formal chapter of psychoanalysis that Edward Thomas would undergo, but the self-reflexive processes that it had triggered would emerge fully formed in the extraordinary year ahead.[12]

II

DYMOCK

1914

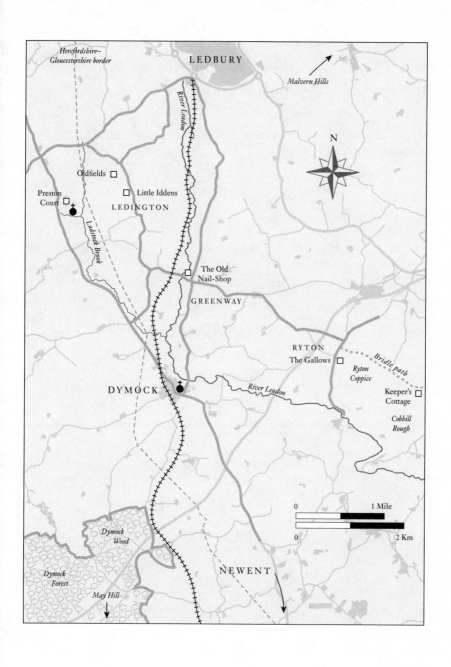

LEDBURY

Malvern Hills

N

River Leadon

Oldfields □

Preston
Court □ ✝

LEDINGTON

Little Iddens □

Ludstock Brook

The Old
Nail-Shop □

GREENWAY

RYTON

The Gallows □

Bridle Path

Ryton
Coppice

DYMOCK ✝

River Leadon

Keeper's
Cottage □

Cobhill
Rough

Dymock
Wood

NEWENT

Dymock
Forest

May Hill

0   1 Mile

0   2 Km

Winter

The Gallows in Ryton, east of Dymock, Gloucestershire, was perishingly cold as Lascelles Abercrombie put the finishing touches to a new dramatic poem. Ground frost lay for two weeks around the house that had no electricity, and sitting still to write five hundred lines of verse was no way to stay warm. But the work, a grand poem with a grand title, had fired his energies over the chill winter and brought almost daily enquiries from his neighbour, Wilfrid Gibson. 'The Olympians' was to be the crowning contribution to a publishing venture that the two men had planned since the later spring of 1913. Stirred by the success of *Georgian Poetry* and by Abercrombie's recent and profitable self-publication, Gibson had been persuaded that the home-produced anthology was a viable route to market if the content were good enough. He urged Rupert Brooke to come in on the project (Brooke: 'I'll "come in", right in, without knocking'), John Drinkwater too, and agreed with Abercrombie that the four-handed journal would promote the work of these men and no others. They settled on a title for their Gloucestershire venture, *New Numbers*.[1]

'I foresee the average number will read as follows,' wrote Brooke in an affectionate send-up of his partners in print:

1 Lascelles Abercrombie: 'Haman and Mordecai' pp. 1–78
2 John Drinkwater: 'The Sonority of God: An Ode' pp. 79–143
3 W. W. Gibson: 'Poor Bloody Bill: A Tale' pp. 144–87
4 Rupert Brooke: 'Oh, Dear! oh, Dear! A Sonnet' p. 188
5 Lascelles Abercrombie: 'Asshur-Bani-Pal and Og King of Bashan' pp. 189–254

6 John Drinkwater: 'William Morris: an Appreciation in verse' pp. 255–377
7 W. W. Gibson: 'Gas Stoves: No. 1. A Brave Poor Thing' pp. 377–594[2]

Brooke's spoof was entirely benign – of Abercrombie for his light pomposity, of Drinkwater's worthiness, of Gibson for his try-hard humility and a dig at his own histrionic style for good measure – although as it turned out, it would eerily resemble the contents of the first issue proper. Announced for January publication, *New Numbers* was quite literally a cottage industry: Abercrombie and Gibson steered the editorial work from the Gallows, while Catherine Abercrombie addressed the envelopes with a child on her knee and Wilfrid made himself pale by licking too many stamps. The journal was printed locally at the Crypt House Press in Gloucester, and mailed to subscribers from the post office in Dymock and initially to local booksellers as well, although this was stopped after Geraldine Gibson explained that the beastly bookshops 'take copies in sale or return and generally send them back rather the worse for wear'. To the editorial team's delight, the printing of five hundred copies had to be repeated when it sold out faster than anticipated.[3]

While Harold Monro noted 'the bad commercial organisation' of the journal, others gave the new imprint a helping hand. Writing anonymously in the *Times Literary Supplement*, Walter de la Mare was fulsome in his praise: 'so fine, so individual, and so various'. Edward Thomas, who in general was kinder to new projects than to repeat offenders, wrote in uncharacteristically glowing notices for the *New Weekly* and *Daily Chronicle* that the journal showed 'much that is best and newest in poetry': Brooke at his most brilliant, Drinkwater at his most lucid, and Abercrombie and Gibson at their most vivacious. Thomas would not be so forgiving of later issues, which in printing Brooke's 'The Soldier' would publish the war's most popular poem, but for now *New Numbers* was off to an undeniably good start.[4]

The journal was the seal on a literary community that Abercrombie had long sought. He had attempted to woo John Drinkwater to the area before he persuaded Wilfrid Gibson; Gordon Bottomley had once been targeted too. Yet it would be many years before the botanist and poet Jack Haines gave a collective name to the individuals who gathered in Gloucestershire in the year before the war. Abercrombie, Gibson, Drinkwater, Brooke, Frost and Thomas: christened 'the Dymock Poets' after the parish which, for a time in 1914, became a part of each of their lives.[5]

Dymock lay to the north-west corner of Gloucestershire, in an enclave that spilled untidily into Herefordshire a few miles from the market town of Ledbury. The vale took its name from the Leadon or 'broad stream' which winds south and east through Dymock before tumbling into the Severn west of Gloucester. The valley is bounded to the north by the ancient Malvern Hills which rise for eight northerly miles toward the Iron Age fort at British Camp and their peak at Worcestershire Beacon. To the south of the valley lies a landmark more distinctive still, the whaleback Silurian sandstone dome of May Hill, with its crown of pine trees, its grassland slopes of birch and oak.

By the time the poets came to the region, Dymock was no longer the rich wool community that it once had been. Cider and perry were still produced from the red-loamed orchards, while the pressing of wild daffodils for hessian cloth brought a migrant labour force by rail each spring; but much else besides was in change or decline. Six blacksmiths and three wheelwrights had once made fittings for the railway and for the carriages and carts that serviced the rail tracks and fields; none survived by 1914, though the station continued as a well-kept branch line with neatly tended flower beds and horse-drawn carriages waiting outside. Labourers and mechanical reapers now worked alongside one another, the horse-drawn machines cutting the bulk of the corn while men took sickles and scythes to the field edge, working their take into string-bound stooks to dry. Threshing of the corn continued long into the winter months, sometimes for a hundred days without break, and took a team of six or seven men: two pitching the sheaves onto the threshing box, another feeding it into the drum, a fourth man bagging the grain as it was cast down the rear chute of the machine, while two or three others carried the filled bags to the granary. In this way a bay of sheaves, some eight yards by five yards and twenty feet high, could be threshed in a single day.

The poets who came to Dymock in those pre-war years were drawn to such ways of living. They came from the cities for an elemental life, for the earth beneath their boots or the breeze that stirred the wheat fields. They came to walk, to write, to cultivate a few crops for their kitchen table; they were moderately poor but not as poor as the labourers around them, and the little they earned from their pens was enough to keep themselves and their families.

First to arrive had been Lascelles Abercrombie, an articulate and kindly man, a dreamer who worked for his dream, whose buoyant spirits became subdued in later life by a sense of literary underachievement. He was a shy man, who laughed well, said Rupert Brooke, but it was the generosity of character that most stayed in the memory of his friends, as it did in Thomas's, who days before his own death in Arras wrote, 'I do not know his equal for keenness and warmth'. Abercrombie's instincts were typically Georgian in spirit: a move from the industrial north to the southern countryside to pursue an artistic life based on self-sufficiency on the land. In truth neither Abercrombie nor any of the Georgian poets could depend upon their farming skills to survive; with the exception of Ralph Hodgson, who later farmed in the United States, the most any of them could hope to cultivate was a modest vegetable patch. But it was the ideal that was important, and when the Abercrombies secured a cottage in Ryton, east of Dymock village, in April 1911, Lascelles believed his utopian dream could be realised.[6]

The Gallows were a pair of adjoining cottages connected by a narrow passageway which took their name from the site where, centuries before, a poacher by the name of Jock of Dymock had been hanged for stealing the King's deer. (Jock, a pagan, strapped the antlers to his back and would charge at passers-by from the underground tunnels that joined the old Priest's House in the village with Wintour's Green and the Harrow where he lived.) The cottages stood above the lane, reached by sheer stone steps, sheltered by elms and flanked by a cherry orchard, close to the Redmarley hills and their dense covering of larch conifers. The smaller and older of the two cottages, where Abercrombie liked to work, was known as The Study. This side of the red-brick house was plastered and whitewashed, and had a rye-thatched roof three hundred years old in places, so steep, noted Frost (himself a future tenant), that the eaves descended to brush the sleeves of passers-by. Abercrombie worked in the downstairs room, while upstairs was the bedroom he shared with his wife Catherine and beside that, the children's room. The larger, newer cottage at the end of the passageway was built of red sandstone and connected to a kitchen, a pantry, a shed and three upstairs bedrooms.

Wilfrid Gibson would be among the first guests. 'This is a fairy-tale house,' he told Edward Marsh, who would make his own visit and describe, in turn to Rupert Brooke, a 'most delicious little house' with crimson ramblers and a stone courtyard where Abercrombie had rigged up a cold-water shower. Brooke travelled to see the cottage for himself, and it impressed him no less than it had the others. 'Abercrombie's is the most beautiful you can imagine: black-beamed & rose-covered. And a porch where one drinks great mugs of cider, & looks at fields of poppies in the corn. A life that makes London a foolish affair.' But it was the lifestyle as much as the Gallows that appealed to the Abercrombies and their visitors. Under an awning permanently pitched beneath the elms they came to call the Seven Sisters, the Abercrombies cooked dinner in a cast-iron pot slung over an open fire in the company of Gibson or Drinkwater, reciting their latest poems in draft. 'I lay on a stoop of hay and listened,' Catherine Abercrombie remembered, 'and watched the stars wander through the elms, and thought I had found the why and wherefore of life.' Lascelles Abercrombie had found his measure in Gloucestershire. He found fulfilment writing by day, stepping out in the evening to take the air or to hear owls hooing in the woods.

Here I am in a cottage in Gloucestershire, living the life (or very nearly) I have always wanted to live! – How did that happen? I scarcely know ... the opening came, and without stopping to think, I broke away and ran.

These were happy days for Abercrombie, and Gibson, ever quick to chronicle events, mopped up the atmosphere in a poem dedicated to Lascelles and set beneath his elms beside a back-garden campfire. 'As, under the shelter of that ageless tree | In a rapt and dreaming circle we lay around | The crackling faggots, listening to the sound | Of old words moving in new harmony.'[7]

Abercrombie was an insightful and conscientious critic, who spent slavish hours at his copy. Thomas feared that the effort would one day break his spirit ('how long can he stand it?'), but Abercrombie, who published few prose books, had little choice as he depended upon his reviews almost exclusively for his living. By 1914 his financial predicament was causing concern among friends; once £200 a year, his income would tail off dramatically in 1914. A worried Catherine Abercrombie suggested her husband take harvesting work, but the situation was temporarily relieved when Edward Thomas and Walter de la Mare, supported by Edward Marsh and Robert Bridges, successfully appealed for the award of a relief bursary for struggling writers.[8]

Abercrombie's verse was held in high regard in 1914. It was often florid in design and grand in execution: long, sweeping monologues and dialogues which devoured politics, philosophy and the classics alike. For sheer intelligence alone, it cut a swathe through middlebrow Edwardian verse, not least in its ambitious desire to unite philosophy and drama en route to a new kind of dramatic verse. The staging of his poetry – part theatrical, part page – was comparatively experimental for the time, as was the blank verse in which Abercrombie trusted. But he, like many of his peers, suffered from a lack of editorial conversation. The Georgians were not pushed nearly hard enough by one another or by their publishers, who were in effect little more than paid printers; worse, they were not pushed hard enough by themselves. They settled too readily for comfort and consolatory tropes, and almost to an individual failed to develop fully their inner editor. They formed a coterie of gentlemen who cared for polite manners and polite verse, which helped them to work collegially and generously to secure financial assistance for one another; by the same creed, they thought it ungallant to comment upon one another's work or were too grand to seek advice themselves. It would be no wonder when the quiet, respectful, straining-to-hear Georgians were blown clear by the deafening war.

Thomas had been among the first in his reviews to identify Abercrombie's promise. In 1908 he applauded the freshness of the irregular rhythms, the drama of the delivery and the ambition of the themes: inspection of any half-dozen lines, he wrote in an early review, 'would prove him a new poet, not a mere melodious gentle spirit'. By the time Abercrombie published his second book of poems in 1911, he was writing, thought Thomas, a 'tremendous unflagging rhapsody' of a kind that had not been seen since Shelley and Marlowe. By now he and Thomas had become friends. Thomas was three years older than Abercrombie and kept a benevolent eye on him; but friendship, with Thomas, was no guarantee of critical favour and as Thomas grew disappointed in Abercrombie's lack of advancement, their relationship would come under strain. Abercrombie had no ear for his verse and frequently wrote with 'no cumulative value', said Thomas. A long poem, 'Mary and the Bramble', had 'few charms', he declared, while Abercrombie's dramatic verse marked a squandering of talent that by 1914 Thomas felt the need to describe as 'intolerable'. Robert Frost did not share Thomas's disenchantment: 'Abercrombie (whom I mustn't praise too much for he is in the house with me) leaves them all behind in the sublime imaginative sort of thing,' he wrote. But Thomas could not agree and let it be known in the way he always did: publicly, and in print. For Catherine Abercrombie, the reviews of her husband could be too much, and Thomas learned to keep his distance from Ryton at these times: '[I] shall hardly venture there as Mrs Abercrombie is a little hostile because I sometimes criticize Lascelles.'[9]

Edward Thomas had left East Grinstead for a month-long stay in a friend's town house in Hammersmith that January. He spent a weekend in Balham with Helen and the children, who stepped around him as delicately as they knew how, but the strain of reuniting in front of Edward's disapproving father was not easy on anyone. Edward had invited Frost to be a regular guest at the St George's gatherings, and in those early weeks of 1914 it seems likely from the sudden informality of their letters that Frost joined Thomas and others at one of the weekly four o'clock gatherings. Frost sent the first of many poems he would show Thomas over the time ahead (possibly 'The Housekeeper') about which Thomas commented that he liked the poem considerably except for the final line. But a critical commentary was not Thomas's only motivation for writing to Frost. Uncertain of a return to Steep, but certain that he would not be able to withstand London for long, he was on the hunt for another study and enquired of Frost whether he knew of cheap lodgings in

Beaconsfield. Progress on the childhood memoir was haphazard, his drafting chaotic. He had slept under half a dozen different roofs in as many weeks, and had grown tired of the travelling, beginning, or so he feared, to treat his friends as little more than innkeepers. After three and a half months of living apart from his family, Thomas decided that there was nowhere else to turn but Steep.[10]

Never had the continuing marriage of Edward and Helen Thomas been in such doubt as it was that winter. In his earliest conversations with Frost, Thomas had been reminded of a partnership's commitments. Frost had experienced his own moments of doubt in the past: in depression or anger, or amid the recriminations that followed the loss of two children; but nothing now could turn the American from his family or his marriage, and it was, he felt, up to Thomas to reflect the same belief in his own situation. A union that had survived fourteen and a half years now appeared to be on the line. 'I set about trying to reconcile them,' said Frost.[11]

'I wish you were nearer so that we could see one another easily and our children,' Thomas confessed to Frost in February. He had eyed the distances on the map: it was a day's cycle ride from Steep to Beaconsfield, not entirely discouraging, but not as near as he would like. He had enjoyed reading 'The Code' in the journal that Frost had sent him ('your poem was really the only thing in "Poetry" I was glad to read'), and set about planning a visit for the following month. Frost enclosed some photographs from New England, and Thomas responded to the pictures by saying that he wished he could be sure that he might see the American's homeland with his own eyes: 'But you know already how I waver and on what wavering things I depend.'[12]

One of those waverings was money, and in the winter of 1913–14 it was reasonably tight. For Thomas, the business of publishing books had long become a financial necessity as he struggled to earn a living wage. He had proposed studies on Conrad and Masefield, to which his agent had tested the market and replied in disparaging terms that made Thomas's anger boil. Not for the first time he lost patience with his agent: '[£]37.10 for 60,000 words is impossible for a writer who can't serialise and is not immensely prolific,' he told Cazenove. 'It isn't merely that the money is so little but that to work at that price means to do bad work and that means that my reputation and my price get worse and worse.' It was a familiar trap, and it was closing around Thomas. He felt his writing was downwardly mobile, worthy of decreasing respect, and it was torturing him. The relief was palpable when, on 26 February, he was able to break the news to de la Mare that he was to receive a grant of £150 from the Royal Literary Fund, lobbied for in part by de la Mare himself.[13]

Spring

Eleanor Farjeon was in Steep in March to join Helen in the celebration of Edward's thirty-sixth birthday; she gave him a gift of an apple tree. Getting to her feet at the end of the evening, she kissed Helen goodnight, and then Edward, before ascending the stairs to bed. It was a small gesture, but it was the first time Eleanor had openly displayed her affection for the man she felt so much for. As she began to undress in her bedroom, Helen entered quietly and embraced her as if she had given them both something more important than any fruit tree. It took courage to slip Edward's defences, Eleanor admitted, but through her courage she would leave behind her an atmosphere more tranquil than before. Edward and Helen busied themselves in the garden after she departed, sowing peas and beans, and digging in the potatoes, the artichokes and the apple tree. As they toiled, a harmony seemed to exist between them that had not been apparent in years.[1]

Frost celebrated his fortieth birthday on 26 March. Thomas had been at the Bungalow in Beaconsfield with him the day before: it was Thomas's first visit and it would be his last, for the Frosts were days away from moving. But closer as the men were drawing, they were not as yet the intense friends they would become. For the moment, that distinction belonged to the man who had tempted Frost to Gloucestershire, and the day after Thomas's departure Frost wrote, 'I have no friend here like Wilfrid Gibson'.[2]

Gibson wrote to say that he had found a cottage a mile and a half up the lane from his, in Ledington; to Frost, this sounded like the very move the family needed and he quickly closed out his arrangements. By the end of March the family had packed and were ready to leave, but first a birthday treat was in order. Having sold some poems to Harold Monro for *Poetry and Drama*, Frost cashed his payment in the form of a week's accommodation at the Poetry Bookshop, and moved the family into two rooms on Devonshire Street, across the landing from Jacob Epstein, as a base for the family's sightseeing. 'We mean to do the city for the youngsters', he reported, which meant the Tower of London and – well, for the moment he could not think of another sight that London might have to offer but he bought himself a guidebook and the family took in what they could, including the Albert Memorial in Hyde Park, whose bronze animals he would later say sparked his poem, 'The Cow in Apple Time'. Elinor and the children revelled in their week in London; Frost too, though his thoughts were squarely on Gloucestershire. 'I am going to be with my friends Gibson and Abercrombie, the English poets,' he wrote cheerily, and although the family had not yet seen the place that would become their most famous English home, they did at least have a name. Little Iddens.[3]

Wild daffodils were thick in the meadows when the Frosts arrived at their new cottage. The neighbouring fields were busy with lambing, and nearby in the elm trees a cuckoo sang throughout that first month. Little Iddens was just two miles from Gibson's cottage on a road without motor cars, and the rent was cheap – at around 4s. a week, a fraction of the sum paid at Beaconsfield, although it was smaller than the Bungalow and was perishingly cold. The sixteenth-century frame of the cottage must have seemed to the Frosts every bit the quaint ideal of English rural living they had longed for. Though the roof was tiled and not 'under thatch', as Elinor had dreamed of, its exterior of whitewashed brick and dark timbers had buckled over the years, adding characterful protrusions to the brickwork above the latticed porch. A black wrought-iron wood stove offered little heat to the two downstairs rooms, while two bedrooms and a recessed alcove just large enough to take an overnight guest were to be found up a tight, sheer staircase.[4]

The cottage faced southward toward May Hill and opened onto a vegetable garden, shaded in places by a weeping ash and a bay tree. At its back was a walnut tree in a yard of cobbles that opened onto grass; from there a hand-pump supplied the water. A yew shaded the house on the roadside, an orchard flanked it on the other. Mealtimes (and bedtimes too, recalled Eleanor Farjeon) were at no particular fixed time and were simple affairs, usually cold rice, bread and fruit from the pantry. The children were told to help themselves whenever they felt hungry, just as they were told to go to bed whenever they felt tired. Gibson and Abercrombie were daily callers in those first weeks, and would gamely round up the Frosts for picnics; but they were far from the only guests. Jack Haines travelled from Gloucester to try and meet the American he had heard so much about, though apparently not what he looked like, by chance stopping Frost the better part of the way up from Greenway to Little Iddens to ask if he knew where the American poet lived. Haines was a solicitor by profession, but a poet by vocation, and his love for botany gave the two men much common ground for their walks into the Malvern Hills. It was Frost who urged Haines to make the acquaintance of Edward Thomas: 'You are to meet him when he is here for the month of August – and a mighty fine fellow you'll say he is.' But Thomas did not wait until then.[5]

Frost had been settled for just three weeks when Thomas made his first visit to Little Iddens. With Mervyn and Bronwen in tow (Helen remained in Steep with Myfanwy), Edward had spent ten days cycling in Wales, and the children were tired as they stowed their bicycles aboard the train that brought them to Dymock. The Frosts' cottage was too small to accommodate the three of them and Thomas rented rooms at the neighbouring farm, Oldfields. On the morning of 27 April he called on Frost just after seven thirty, before setting out to cross Ludstock Brook for Preston Church, in the first of what would be many such walks together in Gloucestershire that year. 'We can go almost anywhere we wish on wavering footpaths through the fields,' reported Frost. 'The fields are so small and the trees so numerous along the hedges that, as my friend Thomas says in the loveliest book on spring in England, you may think from a little distance that the country was solid woods.' *In Pursuit of Spring* had been published for only a fortnight when Thomas brought along a copy for Frost. The American was delighted with his gift and would go on, in a tale that has been frequently retold (though much misquoted), to thumb through the book and urge his friend to revisit his prose and write it out in verse form using just the same cadence; but that moment was still to come.[6]

In his notebooks Thomas recorded warm days beside the River Leadon, but few of the marvels that he and Frost were uncovering in the countryside. The daffodil fields, the woods of Dymock Forest, the Leadon Valley, the Malverns, May Hill, the medieval tempera and frescos at St Mary's, Kempley: all of these were as new to Thomas as they were to Frost. The more they walked the more their friendship deepened: Frost chuckling as Thomas havered over which route to take, Thomas grinning at another enquiry from Frost as to whether they had much further to go. 'I think Edward blamed most my laziness,' Frost told Haines. 'He would have liked me better if I had walked farther with him.' But walk they did, at times as many as twenty-five miles, though usually, for Frost's benefit, considerably fewer. They would spend days together in this way: walking and talking, about verse, about their home life or their peers, stopping now and again to examine the flora in the hedgerow, or to lean on a stile or gate. Frost delighted in his friend's knowledge of wild flowers and bird calls, while Thomas could listen all day to his companion speak about verse; and they found a meeting of minds on their ideas about poetry: on speech rhythms and sound-sense, on uncluttered diction, on cadence and the ear. To Frost, the thoroughness and insight of Thomas's knowledge was second to none; to Thomas, Frost's instincts were sharper and truer than any he had met. Writer to reader, poet to critic, or at least that is how Thomas understood those first talks; but Frost had already seen a poet in Thomas and would set about convincing his friend that they were talking writer to writer. It was in this good-humoured and affectionate manner that their friendship found its spirit-level.[7]

That week in April Thomas made a call on Lascelles Abercrombie in Ryton, and if Thomas's reviews had created a tense atmosphere in the past it was temporarily forgotten. But not so at the Old Nail-Shop, where Thomas's years of pounding had been neither forgotten nor forgiven. 'Gibson and I are too conscious of what we used to think of one another,' Thomas confided on his return to Steep. 'I like his later work, but temperamentally.'[8]

Thomas had returned to Hampshire by the time W. H. Davies paid his 'respects' to Dymock in May. He booked himself in with Gibson at the Old Nail-Shop and in little time at all disgraced himself as only Davies could. Once there, he had volunteered conversation about the prostitutes it had been his good fortune to know, going so far as to reveal some prices that he had paid in the past fortnight, and according to Frost 'entirely disgusted the Gibsons with whom he was visiting'. Davies's hosts would take an unkindly form of revenge on a later visit. Under a heavy rainstorm, the Gibsons attempted to hurry Davies on his wooden leg the best part of two miles down to Ryton, cajoling him onward until he was breaking out in sweats. The reward for his endeavour, said Gibson as they strode, was an appointment with Abercrombie, the greatest poet in England. 'Huh,' puffed Davies, 'a good thing it's the greatest poet in England.' Gibson let the sarcasm in Davies's tone pass and hurried in on arrival to tell Abercrombie the news that Davies thought him the nation's greatest poet. 'But that's what Davies thinks he is himself,' said Frost, when he heard the story.

'And that is what Gibson, or Gibson's wife, thinks Gibson is.' Already the poets were squabbling in their new Eden and Frost's displeasure was beginning to rise, no doubt increased by Davies's visits to Little Iddens, where the grateful Gibsons deposited him daily. There Davies appointed himself a tutor on nature to Lesley Frost who, at fifteen, was more than a match for the Welshman. *See now*, he said, gesturing, *That little green bird, what is it?* Lesley struggled to keep a straight face. *A sparrow*, she said, *And it isn't green, is it?* 'He really doesn't know nature at all,' Frost remarked dismissively of a poet whom he had initially admired. Nor was Davies found to be a better conversationalist when it came to prosody. 'Absolutely uncritical untechnical untheoretical', said Frost: the very qualities that Frost himself had been accused of.[9]

Davies's visit to Gloucestershire may not have been a success, but Thomas's had been. 'He and I tired the sun down with talking on the footpaths and stiles of Ledington and Ryton,' recalled Frost. It would be the first of many occasions of what the American liked to call their 'talks–walking'. 'The important thing to us is that we are near Gibson,' Frost had written in May, but by June the Frosts' personal compass was turning toward Thomas. 'Rob and I think everything of him,' wrote Elinor Frost. 'He is quite the most admirable and lovable man we have ever known.'[10]

The meadows may have been flush with spring, but in those first weeks in Dymock Robert Frost witnessed another aspect of rural life that lurked out of sight of the casual visitor. On his walks, he observed a poverty in the English fields that was quite unlike anything he had seen at home. In Gloucestershire, mothers cleared stones ahead of the plough for a shilling a day; he watched them work through a downpour, carrying flints the size of their fists in their aprons. Children worked as soon as they were physically able to bring in an extra sixpence a day. Families survived on a pound a week, some on as little as half that. But worse even than the physical and financial hardship, what riled Frost in particular was the sight of the English class system in action, where the fieldhand was at the lowest rung of a social structure that demanded cap-tipping and kowtowing. Bullied by farmers, hounded by gamekeepers, the rural worker's life was one where even a minor transgression could put you out of work or worse. It was humiliating and dehumanising, Frost thought. 'These people are allowed to call only a small part of their soul their own.'[11]

Agricultural workers were as poor in 1914 as they had been in 1880 when Thomas Hardy portrayed their hardship. To manage a household on one pound a week, in the words of a social study of the time, took 'wisdom and loving-kindness, and after that as much cleanliness and order as can be squeezed in'. Rent would comprise a third of spending, then clothing and finally food. Diets were poor. Bread formed the bulk of any spending on food, a few potatoes and a little meat or fish in the cities, a little cheese and bacon on the land. Whatever protein there was in the household went to keeping the breadwinner fit, as his ill health could leave the family destitute. An allotment of any kind could entirely change a family's fortune, for if you could grow potatoes then you could keep chickens on the skin peelings, which in turn brought you eggs. But mostly such smallholdings were fought off by ruthless landowners, fearing that allotments would not only drain energy but increase the independence of their farmhands. There was one other outlay without which no work could be undertaken, and that was boots. Footwear was an item that had to withstand all conditions: mud, flint, sun, walking, rain and frost. In the towns, careful families saved through a boot club to replace worn shoes, but rural workers had no insurance and no organisation that could have provided it. Their population was scattered, hard to unionise, poorly educated, and living entirely in tied cottages at the mercy of the farmer for their job, their wage and their home. At the Census of 1911, a teacher earned annually just over £175, an agricultural labourer under £50.[12]

*

Thomas had returned from Little Iddens with Bronwen and Mervyn to Steep on 2 May. He and Helen had spent most of April apart, and though they had seemed to be getting along better already he was preparing for another absence. The dry heat of April had given way to ten days of May rain, and on the 11th Thomas returned to Gloucestershire, this time to join Eleanor Farjeon at an ancient (they suspected haunted) farmhouse at Kingham in the Cotswolds, which had been loaned to her for the month, accompanied by her brother Bertie and the woman that he would marry in October, Joan Thornycroft. Thomas worked on *A Literary Pilgrim in England* from 5 to 7.30 each morning before relaxing in the company of his friends, walking amiably with Eleanor, smoking endlessly with Bertie and casting admiringly after Joan Thornycroft, whom Eleanor believed was Thomas's very ideal of femininity. It must have troubled Eleanor to see Thomas look after another woman in that way, yet if she was uncertain of her place in his complex affections, then she might have taken comfort in the outcome of a parlour game they played one evening after dinner. Under the rules of the game, each player was asked to liken their mutual friends to a list of towns or flowers or other criteria that was similarly pleasant or benign. But Thomas interpreted the rules rather differently, awarding or withholding marks based on his friends' personal qualities: positive scores for such attributes as grit, minuses for vanity or similar. Eleanor scored highly among the eleven names rated by Thomas, though, tellingly, it was Godwin Baynes who outshone all others (he did not include his new friend Robert Frost or any of the poets known only to him). But tucked away in the middle of his list was something more revealing still: namely, what appeared to be Thomas's self-scorecard of his own qualities and failures. In it, he rated himself as highly adaptable and lacking in vanity or ostentation, but cursed with little fire or *joie de vivre*; and he described himself as one part Christian to nine parts Pagan.[13]

By the time he left Kingham, Thomas was planning a return to Gloucestershire provided he could sublet Yew Tree Cottage. This time he would bring Helen and the entire family with him for a month of living beside the Frosts. The summer was beginning to be mapped out, and August 1914, their date of choosing, looked set to be an unforgettable month.[14]

On 15 May 1914, little more than a year after the first, David Nutt published the second book of verse from Robert Frost. It had been advertised in their company catalogue as *Farm Servants and Other People*, but Frost had abandoned this in favour of the more generic *New Englanders*, then *New England Hill Folk*, until he remembered the property page of his old newspaper that carried the section-heading 'North of Boston', which gave the collection its title. One thousand octavo sheets were printed, as they had for *A Boy's Will*, with 350 or so copies bound in coarse green linen for distribution.[15]

Frost said that *North of Boston* took up the themes where *A Boy's Will* laid them down; but it was more confident, more firmly defined, darker and more gripping than its predecessor, and certainly more assured in its footfall. The beginnings of the book were made in Derry, where three of its poems were written; 'All the rest of North of Boston I wrote in England,' said Frost, 'on an inspiration compounded of homesickness and the delight of new friendships.'[16]

'Something there is that doesn't love a wall.' The book opened with a first line of intrigue and guile, in a loose, variable blank verse that would send a pulse rippling through the collection. 'The Death of the Hired Man', 'Home Burial', 'After Apple-Picking' would follow in a volume bookended by two short lyrics, each set in italics to distinguish them from the main works. The first of these lyrics was an octave that would ever after be set as the preliminary verse of his *Collected Poems*, beginning 'I'm going out to clean the pasture spring,' and concluding 'I sha'n't be gone long. – You come too.' Inclusive, informal, inviting: Frost was making good on his promise to be a 'a poet for all sorts and kinds'.[17]

When Thomas wrote to Frost on 19 May, *North of Boston* had been out for four days although Thomas had yet to see it. Nonetheless, his mind was focussed on the discussions about prosody that the two men had shared that spring, and he gave Frost a friendly warning: 'You really should start doing a book on speech and literature, or you will find me mistaking your ideas for mine and doing it myself. You can't prevent me from making use of them: I do so daily & want to begin over again with them & wring all the necks of my rhetoric – the geese. However, my "Pater" would show you I had got onto the scent already.' Indeed he had. Walter Pater was once a stylist much admired by Thomas, but now found hard to read. In explaining Pater's limitation, as he saw it, Thomas summoned phrases that would define his very approach to writing, in tones he would subsequently find echoed in Frost. Of Pater, Thomas observed –

When his prose sounds well it is with a pure sonority of words that is seldom related to sense.

– in other words, it was the *sound* that powered and defined the sentence and not only the definition that might be found in a dictionary. Thomas had not met Frost when he wrote this in 1912, still less heard the phrase 'sound of sense', yet already he was employing the vocabulary of sounds, sonority of words and sense. Earlier still, in 1910, Thomas wrote of Robert Burns's verse, 'It is as near to the music as nonsense could be, and yet it is perfect sense.' It was a statement that entirely foreshadowed the beliefs that he shared with Frost.[18]

In fact Thomas had been mining this seam for many years. As early as 1901 he had written, 'The best lyrics seem to be the poet's natural speech', and in 1907 championed Sidney Lanier's comment that verse comprises 'such sounds and silences as can be co-ordinated by the ear ... and exists by virtue of the simple time-relations between the units of sound'. Over a number of years he paid tributes to Yeats's deployment of speech rhythms; on occasion he even employed the same language as Frost, complaining in 1912 that Lafcadio Hearn lacked 'any natural sweet cadence', while admitting that there were powers at work in Swinburne's verse beyond his explanation, except to say that 'the sound and the sense of the first line seem to prepare for it all'.[19]

But it was with Walter Pater that Thomas had made his case most clearly, a writer, he said, who was incapable of hearing the rhythms of speech.

His very words are to be seen, not read aloud; for if read aloud they betray their artificiality by a lack of natural expressive rhythm.

And he continued,

Nothing so much as the writer's rhythm can give that intimate effect 'as if he had been talking'. Rhythm is of the essence of a sincere expressive style.

Natural expressive rhythm: in other words, cadence; *as if he had been talking*: speech sounds. And now Thomas combined them to lay down a charge and a challenge for living literature:

It has to make words of such a spirit, and arrange them in such a manner, that they will do all that a speaker can do by innumerable gestures and their innumerable shades, by tone and pitch of voice, by speed, by pauses, by all that he is and all that he will become.[20]

Writing *Walter Pater* had allowed Thomas to identify the values he most admired in writing, but it had also illuminated the shortcomings in his own method. In the spring of 1912 he saw for the first time that his own processes of note-taking were destroying his natural expressive rhythm: 'Criticising Pater has helped the discovery. But it is too late now, in these anxious and busy times, to set about trying to write better than perhaps I was born to.'

From his prose criticism of Walter Pater it seemed clear now that, consciously or not, Thomas was preparing a run at poetry. And now, in May 1914, he put to Frost the most important question he would ever lay before his friend: could he, Edward Thomas, possibly write poetry?

I wonder whether you can imagine me taking to verse. If you can I might get over the feeling that it is impossible – which at once obliges your good nature to say 'I can'. In any case I must have my 'writer's melancholy' though I can quite agree with you that I might spare some of it to the deficient. On the other hand even with registered post, telegraph &c & all modern conveniences I doubt if I could transmit it.

Frost could certainly imagine his friend taking to verse and had no doubts about his ability to transmit it; he told him so.

Edward Thomas had about lost patience with the minor poetry it was his business to review. It took me to tell him what his trouble was. He was suffering from a life of subordination to his inferiors. Right at that moment he was writing as good a poetry as anybody alive but in prose form where it didnt declare itself and gain him recognition. I referred to the paragraphs here and there in such a book as The Pursuit of Spring and pointed them out. Let him write them in verse form in exactly the same cadence and we would see. Thats all there was to it. His poetry declared itself in verse form and in the year before he died he took his place where he belonged among the English poets.[21]

The declaration of Thomas's verse was now less than six months away, but it was not the only event that occupied his mind in the spring of 1914. Since their earliest meetings, Frost had spoken about New England with a passion that had stirred Thomas. The American had not hidden his desire to return home and in February had encouraged Thomas to think about joining him. Thomas had considered such a move once before when, in the spring of April 1912, in some despair, he had written to his agent lamenting the lack of work and speculated on a change of career and a relocation to the United States. Cazenove had talked him out of that voyage as he had the trip to Australia, but in the spring of 1914 Thomas and Frost were beginning to talk with increasing seriousness about a move by both of their families. The two would farm together, said Frost, and if farming did not work for any reason then there would always be the possibility of teaching. Thomas knew he was no farmer and had not struggled to see behind Frost's pretence to be one, and he doubted that he could ever be capable of teaching. But perhaps he might find a literary living in New England more or less as he did in the 'old' country. By the spring they had made an agreement that whenever Frost sailed back home he would take Mervyn with him in an advance party on the expectation that the rest of the Thomases would follow.[22]

North of Boston received an anonymous mention that May in the *Times Literary Supplement* in a disappointing notice that spoke of Frost's 'naïve individuality' and his 'little pictures from ordinary life'. To Frost it must have seemed that the pattern that had accompanied *A Boy's Will* looked likely to repeat itself. He was on his guard for what might follow, but he took comfort from the knowledge that his neighbours Lascelles Abercrombie and Wilfrid Gibson were also preparing reviews: friends, he reasoned, who had been party to his discussions on the sound of sense and could surely be relied upon to deepen readers' understanding of his art. Ezra Pound had also declared his intention to produce a review, but that worrying news was more than compensated by the knowledge that Edward Thomas was also to write about the book. From their week together in April, Frost knew that Thomas understood his thinking better than anyone and had shared in Frost's despair at the unsigned *TLS* review. Thomas suspected he knew its author to be Walter de la Mare, and he told Frost as much. Though he had yet to meet him, Frost now decided that he supposed de la Mare to be 'a bit of a British snob'.[23]

[135]

Summer

The prospect of further commissioned work must have filled Thomas with dread that first week in June. He was bone tired and working ever longer hours to meet his deadlines. The manuscript of *A Literary Pilgrim in England* dragged on, and he slaved away at criticism for the usual journals about books about which he did not care one jot. Half a dozen of his reviews and two articles were printed in June alone, and still he tried for further commissions. 'I am so plagued with work,' he confessed to Frost, 'burning my candle at 3 ends.' All the while the one book he did wish to write about was still to make an appearance through his letterbox. With no sign of a review copy of *North of Boston* from the publisher and no personal copy sent by Frost, Thomas contented himself in re-reading in typescript the poems that his friend had sent him, and told Gordon Bottomley eagerly, 'His getting back to pure speech rhythms is going to do good.' He bided his time by continuing his correspondence with Frost on sound-sense. 'Yes I quite see about using the "naked tones", not the mere words, of certain profoundly characteristic instinctive rhythms,' he concurred. 'And No, you don't bore me. Only I feel a fraud in that I have unconsciously rather imitated your interest in the matter.' There was no imitation, only a convergence of minds, but it was typical of Thomas's graceful manner to offer Frost the stronger hand.[1]

When Thomas left for London on 8 June *North of Boston* had just arrived. He devoured the book on the train, revisiting the familiar poems 'Home Burial' and 'The Housekeeper', and encountering for the first time the newer pieces that he had not seen in typescript. By the time he met up with Walter de la Mare

on 9 June he had made up his mind about the singular importance of the work and he prepared to argue out the point with
his friend. To Thomas's surprise de la Mare had not seen the
book, which told him that he had been wrong to suppose his
friend the author of the disparaging *TLS* review. He told Frost
of his mistake, but the American's mind was made up about this
Englishman who considered himself superior.

'There is not a bad one among them, not one I haven't enjoyed
very much', Thomas wrote in a letter to Frost '– only the last line of
each of those two leaves me with a shade of dissatisfaction. Which
is a foolish thing for me to say without saying a great deal more.'
Thomas would say more, a great deal more, and over the next few
weeks he began to prepare the copy for the reviews that would do
more than any other to influence the reception of Frost's book.[2]

It was not unusual at the time for professional critics to write
more than one review of an individual book. When a second
commission occurred, a less scrupulous writer might respond by
reconstituting their original ideas in an unsigned notice; but not
Thomas. When he reviewed a book a second time, he was fas-
tidious in breaking new ground. Each review should be a development from the last, he believed, so that if he had discussed a
writer's rhythm in one review, for example, he might address
their use of rhyme in another, or if prosody first then influences
next, and so on. With imagination and diligence, he kept his
copy fresh: it was not easy to distil your thoughts into one piece
of writing only to be asked to do it again; but for *North of Boston*,
Thomas chose to write three.

As Thomas prepared his copy, he set off to see Gordon
Bottomley in his new home, The Sheiling at Silverdale, in
Lancashire. He found his friend laid up by another in a line of
crippling illnesses that had incapacitated him since childhood,
wishing for a break in the sultry weather and yet, despite it all,
uncomplaining and seemingly 'one of the happiest people in the
world'. Thomas was ashamed of his own petulance in the face of

such stoicism. In the past, they had taken a steamer boat on Lake Windermere (Thomas had refused to pause at Wordsworth's grave at St Oswald's Church), but with Bottomley now immobile, they sat together and watched the weather rumble in over Morecambe Bay. 'This has been a year of years for weather,' he wrote to Helen. 'I wish things were coming right. Still I have contrived to get more pleasure than almost ever before out of the weather. We have been happier too, in spite of all.'[3]

Bottomley had listened as Thomas recounted in detail his conversations with Frost about sound-sense. What Thomas told Bottomley that day stayed with his friend and would enter into his own writing practice. Bottomley summarised Thomas's words:

[W]hen a man writes verse so attentively and of custom that his skill becomes instinct and carries him beyond the domination of verse-mechanism, his own speech-tunes and phrasings in daily life will control his use of metrical pattern. The latter will become a constant, felt rather than exhibited, and the actual words will go over it like a counterpoint: in the end the poet's own speaking voice and cadences will be heard, through his personal vocal rhythms.[4]

Thunder broke on 10 June; a torrential downpour followed. The cool nights gave way to hot days, which by the month's end were rocketing into the eighties. In the roasting heat, London was enjoying a musical summer like no other. The Grand Russian Season at the Royal Theatre, Drury Lane, was the talk of the town: the self-taught Russian bass Fyodor Chaliapin enthralled opera-goers with his performances of Mussorgsky, Prokofiev and Borodin. But it was the Diaghilev Ballet that truly won the capital's hearts thanks to the performances of its stars, Vaslav Nijinsky and Tamara Karsavina. On the night of 23 June, Richard Strauss's *The Legend of Joseph* had its English premiere conducted by the composer himself. Edward, Helen and Joan Thornycroft squeezed into the packed and stifling auditorium, and heard the audience give the performance an outstanding reception, although the *New York Times* in a cable dispatch reported the grumbling of the critics. Thomas too was doubtful, and referred to the evening as 'hot air', and not only in deference to the unseasonably fierce temperature.[5]

The next morning he rose early at his parents' house in Balham. The weather was glorious from 4.20 a.m., and by ten o'clock tiers of thin white cloud stepped high into the morning sky. Helen and he hurried to be away, leaving the children with Edward's parents, and crossed London to Paddington in time to catch the 10.20 train to Malvern. At 11.44 the train drew up at Oxford; haymakers toiled beneath the hot sun; it was eighty degrees in the shade that day.

Then we stopped at Adlestrop, thro the willows cd be heard a chain of blackbirds songs at 12.45 & one thrush & no man seen, only a hiss of engine letting off steam. Stopping outside Campden by banks of long grass willow herb & meadowsweet, extraordinary silence between the two periods of travel – looking out on grey dry stones between metals & the shiny metals & over it all the elms willows & long grass – one man clears his throat – and a greater rustic silence. No house in view[.] Stop only for a minute till signal is up.[6]

It was midsummer. The weather in Dymock was hot and rainless; wild roses flowered in the hedgerow, and somewhere distant a blackcap sang. With the early evening sun at their shoulder, Edward and Helen and Robert and Elinor left Little Iddens and headed down the lane toward the Old Nail-Shop. Helen was meeting these new friends for the first time, and that evening there was a gathering that would do much to define the Gloucestershire poets. Rupert Brooke had returned to England from the South Seas on 6 June and was staying with the Gibsons, looking 'browner and older and better looking after his tour', thought Thomas; Abercrombie and Catherine made the short walk from the Gallows. Never before or again would so many of the poets gather in Gloucestershire: only John Drinkwater was missing of the six who would one day be known as the Dymock Poets. Gibson recorded the moment in metric prose.

> Do you remember the still summer evening
> When, in the cosy cream-washed living-room
> Of The Old Nailshop, we all talked and laughed –
> Our neighbours from The Gallows, Catherine
> And Lascelles Abercrombie; Rupert Brooke;
> Elinor and Robert Frost, living a while
> At Little Iddens, who'd brought over with them
> Helen and Edward Thomas? In the lamplight
> We talked and laughed; but, for the most part, listened
> While Robert Frost kept on and on and on,
> In his slow New England fashion, for our delight,
> Holding us with shrewd turns and racy quips,
> And the rare twinkle of his grave blue eyes?
>
> We sat there in the lamplight, while the day
> Died from rose-latticed casements, and the plovers
> Called over the low meadows, till the owls
> Answered them from the elms, we sat and talked –
> Now, a quick flash from Abercrombie; now,
> A murmured dry half-heard aside from Thomas;
> Now, a clear laughing word from Brooke; and then
> Again Frost's rich and ripe philosophy,
> That had the body and tang of good draught-cider,
> And poured as clear a stream.

For once Gibson's craft is not on trial: we are simply grateful for his documentation. No other testimony allows us to imagine how these poets interacted: Frost, holding court, the tireless raconteur, Abercrombie's sharp interjections, Thomas's arid undercuts, Brooke irresistible in his wit and merriment; even Gibson himself is mirrored in the observational, workmanlike reportage. If ever these poets had a moment of unity it was at the Old Nail-Shop that evening of 24 June; and among the conversational topics that united them that evening might well have been a letter which would bring them closer still.[7]

When Thomas called at the Gallows two days later, he was shown a letter that Abercrombie had just received from Ezra Pound who, even by his irascible standards, had written in unusual temper. For reasons that were clear to neither Abercrombie nor Thomas, Pound's patience with the former had snapped, and now he demanded public satisfaction. 'Ezra Pound has tried to honour himself by challenging Abercrombie to a duel,' Thomas recounted. 'Pound merely said something like "Your stupidity now amounts to a public insult" and "My seconds will wait on you." Whether Abercrombie had trounced the Imagists I don't know but I fancy not. Ezra has long been antipathetic to his betters.' Pound's summons does not survive, although Thomas's recollection of its contents is confirmed by two others who also saw it. Privately, Pound had been scathing about *Georgian Poetry*, but he had at least reserved judgement on Abercrombie himself, whose work, he felt up until then, had risen above the decrepitude of the other contributions. But Abercrombie had subsequently drawn Pound's ire for reasons that escaped him. According to one version of the story, Abercrombie had called on young poets to return to Wordsworth and Milton; in another, he had publicly taken a veiled swipe at Imagism. Most likely, Pound's pique was stoked by little more than Abercrombie being the most identifiable figure of the Georgian school of poets, which was excuse enough for a quarrel. (Pound would remove a line of Eliot's from *The Waste Land* with the damning inscription, 'georgian'.) Imagists laughed that, hearing of Pound's skill with a rapier, Abercrombie had cold-called on Yeats to ask him to intervene only to have the front door answered by Pound himself and to flee terrified into the London streets. Georgians joked that Abercrombie had the upper hand because he had invoked his right as the challenged party to nominate the weapon of combat, and had wittily picked unsold copies of their respective books. No duel was ever fought, and whether or not Pound was serious about the encounter, he would not lower his sights from the Georgians. Abercrombie, once respectable in Pound's eyes, was singled out for ridicule as one of the 'literary hen-coops', and the Georgians 'the stupidest set of Blockheads to be found in any country'. Thomas had once praised the potential of Abercrombie and Pound evenly, but he no longer felt need to be impartial. 'What imbeciles the Imagists are,' he said.[8]

Eighteen months previously there had been no 'Georgians' and no 'Imagists', only individual poets writing individual poems. In the days before such sharp lines were drawn, Pound might have found his way into Edward Marsh's *Georgian Poetry*. Yet Harold Monro's decision to give each of these competing clans their own anthology under the imprint of the Poetry Bookshop appeared not, as he might have hoped, to have fostered diversity, but merely to have heightened intransigence.

After lunch on 27 June, Thomas left the literary squabble behind and took the train with Helen for Coventry to see the friends with whom their son would later lodge. As they returned home two days later, the papers carried news of an assassination in Sarajevo. The heir to the Austro-Hungarian throne had visited the Bosnian province; seven conspirators, Serbian nationalists, had lain in wait along the route. The first lost his nerve and let the royal car pass, a second threw a grenade that bounced off its target and detonated further down the street. As the cortège re-routed the attackers' moment appeared to have gone. Gavrilo Princip had abandoned his attempt, and had stopped on the corner of Franzjosefstrasse to buy a sandwich when the royal car came unexpectedly into view. The driver had taken a wrong turning; in trying to reverse, the engine stalled. Princip could not believe his luck. At nineteen, he was barely old enough to call himself a man, yet the shots he fired that day would trigger the greatest slaughter the world had ever known.

*

Heavy rains fell in July. Thomas spent the month at Steep behind his typewriter working on *A Literary Pilgrim in England* and assembling a flora anthology that publishers T. C. & E. C. Jack had agreed to commission. He asked Frost whether he might include 'A Tuft of Flowers', and by 17 July the anthology was finished. 'I like him more and more,' he told Bottomley, 'which is as it should be if I am to till New Hampshire at his side which appears more and more likely.' Frost came to Yew Tree Cottage for the weekend of 18–19 July: it was his first visit to Steep, and it gave the friends the chance to talk over the idea of America further. Thomas longed to be rid of the endless literary criticism; he had been covering twenty pages a day writing about sub-standard books and felt that he could not go on. 'I hate it all and find it more than difficult to keep up,' he told Eleanor Farjeon. 'So I am beginning to think of New Hampshire as the only possibility though really not thinking of it as quite possible either.' The only-possible-and-yet-impossible road: how often had Thomas found himself there, without options or self-determination, following a path that he did not fully understand but which at a deep level he believed to be inevitable. He was wavering in a way that Frost had already begun to mock; even so, the American's friendship was gratefully received: 'His wanting me is some encouragement,' said Thomas.[9]

Thomas published the first of two round-up reviews of John Drinkwater in which the most he could manage by way of compliment was to praise the writer's 'enthusiasm and eagerness'. In 1911 he had accused Drinkwater of facility, quipping that he dispensed with 'a fluency of words that leaves no more behind it than a five-minute shower on a hot day'. Drinkwater may have been the least accomplished of the Dymock poets ('Bell daffodils that are aglow | In Ryton Woods now, where they go | Who are my friends and makes good rhymes'), but his work for the Birmingham Repertory Theatre was the envy of Abercrombie and Gibson. He was a polite, polished and determined character who needed no invitation to share his work, as Catherine Abercrombie remembered of his arrival at Ryton, where 'he read some of his poems to us straight away, and how I wished he would not, as he turned himself into a fashionable parson, voice and all, and eyes to the ceiling, to do it –'. Thomas and Drinkwater never met, though Thomas had established all he thought he needed to know about the man from his writing. 'I had always heard ill of Drinkwater and rated him by his verses which was pretty hard on him.'[10]

Rupert Brooke was relishing his return to London. He dined at 10 Downing Street and at the Savoy, brushed up on the Russian Ballet season, breakfasted with Siegfried Sassoon, Paul Nash and W. H. Davies, lunched with D. H. Lawrence and with Henry James, and supped with W. B. Yeats, Bernard Shaw, J. M. Barrie and G. K. Chesterton: a not untypical week in the life of Rupert Brooke. On 28 July he read for the second and, as it turned out, last time at the Poetry Bookshop, reciting from his own work to an audience of sixty-five. He was nervous and confessed privately to one member of the audience how he dreaded the thought of having to perform. He sat on the corner of one of the Bookshop's oak tables, swinging a leg to and fro as he listened to the admirers who had gathered around him, 'beautiful as an annunciating angel' said one, but not to the American poet and critic Amy Lowell, who happened to be in town that night:

I toiled up the narrow stairs of a little outhouse behind the Poetry Bookshop, and in an atmosphere of overwhelming sentimentality, listened to Mr Rupert Brooke whispering his poems. To himself, it seemed, as nobody else could hear him. It was all artificial and precious. One longed to shout, to chuck up one's hat in the street when one got outside.

Throughout the reading, an elderly lady in the front row raised and lowered her ear trumpet, straining to make out his voice until eventually she could take no more. 'Speak up, young man!' she hollered."

Austrian authorities in Sarajevo responded brutally to the Archduke's assassination. Two hundred Bosnian Serbs were rounded up and hanged in the city's prisons, while authorities were believed to be turning a blind eye to a wave of pogroms in the countryside. But the ripples from Princip's shots had not yet carried beyond the region. The royal funeral in Vienna would focus weeks of internal manoeuvres among the country's political and military leaders. An Austrian invasion of Serbia needed the support of Germany if Russia were to be kept at bay. It registered little with the poets of London and Gloucestershire when at twelve noon on the day of Brooke's reading Austria declared war on Serbia.

It was Jack Haines who sent Robert Frost the unsigned notice in *The Nation* of *North of Boston* that both men recognised as the work of Abercrombie. The review was both warm and astute, and had applauded the attempt by Frost 'to capture and hold within metrical patterns the very tones of speech'. In making a direct reference to the sound of sense, Abercrombie scored a notable first (though rather ungallantly Frost said that he had provided Abercrombie his 'catchwords'). A second, anonymous write-up in the *Pall Mall Gazette* had noted 'the woof of familiar metres crossed constantly by the warp of instinctive cadences' in what was a perceptive analogy for the overlaying of variable speech rhythms upon the strictures of conventional blank verse. Other reviews were less fulsome, but at least Frost had an endorsement to look forward to from the second of his Gloucestershire neighbours, Wilfrid Gibson. Or so he thought; but the review in *The Bookman* that July was not at all what Frost had been hoping for. Gibson's opening remarks affected praise, but in acknowledging that some readers might entertain such descriptions as 'unsophisticated', 'simplicity' and 'artlessness' he cast an ambiguity that could not fail to get up Frost's hackles. In company with Gibson, as with Abercrombie, Frost had spent many hours talking about the sound of sense and Gibson was well aware of the sophistication of the American's prosody. But the tone of the review worsened.

I am inclined to wonder at times if, in his determination to avoid artifice, Mr Frost has not discarded too much. There are legitimate excitements, as well as illegitimate, in the enjoyment of verse; and in reading some of these poems I have missed the exhilaration of an impelling and controlling rhythm.

Gibson may have felt many things about *North of Boston*, but it seems unthinkable that he could have missed an impelling rhythm in this most skilfully rhythmic of books. Thomas, in his reviews of Gibson, repeatedly accused him of lacking any metrical art himself, which might go a little way to explain Gibson's remark, but to Frost the commentary from his friend must have seemed bizarre. What was Gibson up to? Was he trying to put Frost somehow in his place? Was he envious? Until that moment, Frost had declared Gibson his closest friend, but now that friendship would begin to deteriorate. In 1916 Frost said of Gibson that, 'No sooner had I got down into the country near him than I began defining my position with regard to him – and you know what that means. It means sheering off from him.'[12]

Frost believed that a good showing in England was essential to help him find publication at home. He now feared that after everything he had tried – uprooting his family from New Hampshire, the year in Beaconsfield, the move to Gloucestershire, the fruitless efforts to procure the favour of Pound and Yeats and lately Gibson – after all of that, his literary venture in England might still result in failure.

But his fortunes were about to change.

'This is one of the most revolutionary books of modern times,' Edward Thomas declared, 'but one of the quietest and least aggressive.' It was a bold and intriguing claim with which to open the review that appeared in the *Daily News* on 22 July: could a book really be both revolutionary *and* quiet? Thomas prepared to explain.

These poems are revolutionary because they lack the exaggeration of rhetoric, and even at first sight appear to lack the poetic intensity of which rhetoric is an imitation. Their language is free from the poetical words and forms that are the chief material of secondary poets. The metre avoids not only the old-fashioned pomp and sweetness, but the later fashion also of discord and fuss. In fact, the medium is common speech.

For old-fashioned pomp read the Edwardian elders; for discord and fuss read the Imagists: even Thomas, it appeared, was not above mud slinging in the wake of recent events. But the comparison was not merely personal, for Thomas was making yet another statement about the kind of writing that he valued: neither the old florid styles nor the fashion for new artificialities, but simple common speech.[13]

The poems of *North of Boston* depended not upon objects of conventional beauty and yet they were beautiful, he wrote. The language rarely relied on rhetoric and yet it was memorable speech. And the style was as 'low' as the characters who spoke it, as unembellished as the blank verse that conducted it; it had the unpretentiousness of prose but was not prose; tellingly, said Thomas, 'It is poetry because it is better than prose.'

The book was not without failures, Thomas conceded. What began in mystery in places ended in obscurity, and here and there the accents required for reading seemed to remain just out of reach of the reader. But the successes such as 'The Death of the Hired Man' lifted Frost to a place of his own, 'above all other writers of verse in America'. Ezra Pound could not have liked that, not one little bit; but finally, here was a statement in which Frost could delight and could take back to his native country. 'It speaks,' wrote Thomas, 'and it is poetry.'

It is poetry because it is better than prose. It speaks, and it is poetry.
Two phrases that stand out as much for what they tell us of
Thomas as Frost.

In the summer of 1914 Thomas was still a prose writer and
not yet a poet. For almost his entire adult life he had earned
his living from prose, but clearly now, in this review and elsewhere, Thomas was retuning his ear toward a form of writing
that is cadenced and memorable and that propels itself using
the rhythms of speech.

In a second notice, for the monthly *English Review*, Thomas
praised Frost's refusal to be seduced by the modern fashion for
'glory' words. Frost's book stood out from the crowd, he wrote,
in its ability to make poetry without being poetical, which was
an experiment reminiscent of Wordsworth's but with an important difference. Where Wordsworth contemplated, Frost sympathised, exposing fewer of his own feelings and more of his
subjects', so allowing him to write a form of eclogue that was
both homely and racy, lyric and dramatic. In places the results
were 'masterpieces of deep and mysterious tenderness': plain-
spoken verse that might appear akin to prose in places, until
spoken aloud when the emotion of the work rises out through
the unmistakable rhythm of the poetry.[14]

A third review was to follow in the *New Weekly*, and Thomas
found a still sharper way to focus his ideas about speech.

Mr Frost has, in fact, gone back, as Whitman and as Wordsworth went
back, through the paraphernalia of poetry into poetry again. With a
confidence like genius, he has trusted his conviction that a man will
not easily write better than he speaks when some matter has touched
him deeply.

Thomas had isolated precisely what it was that allowed Frost's
work to stand apart from the pack.[15]

In the space of three short reviews, Edward Thomas had
concisely introduced and evaluated the importance of this new

writer. In not one of the three reviews did he baffle the reader with discussions of prosody or technique, he did not even employ the words 'cadence', 'tone' or 'sound' that Frost himself used so much. Thomas had said simply that Frost was revolutionary because he wove everyday speech rhythms and common dictions across blank verse, and in so doing had taken readers much closer to the genuine matter of poetry than just about anyone before him. Frost was delighted by what he read. At last he felt understood, endorsed by a man whom other men listened to, and believed for the first time that his work might, after all, begin to earn him the reputation that he yearned for. Frost was in no doubt of the gift that Thomas had bestowed upon him, and would never lose sight of it. 'He gave me standing as a poet –', Frost acknowledged in 1921, 'he more than anyone else.'[16]

It was a debt that Frost feared he could never repay.

But he had already begun to repay it.

On 1 August the Thomases were in Steep making their final arrangements for their month's holiday in Gloucestershire. The family would travel in two parties: Edward and Mervyn would set off by bicycle on the 3rd, breaking the journey en route, while Helen and the two girls would leave Steep a day later by train. Peter Mrosovski, a pupil at Bedales who was boarding at Yew Tree Cottage, was put on the train to London for his summer holiday return home to Russia, leaving the Thomases to finalise their plans. But as 1 August wore on, something unexpected happened: Peter reappeared on their doorstep. The boy explained that he had got as far as Millwall docks to be told that Germany had declared war on Russia, and that there was no longer a safe passage home for him. Helen and Edward discussed the new situation: there would be room for Peter in Gloucestershire, and the boy could travel with Helen if he could find no alternative route home. For the time being Thomas appeared more interested in the glorious weather than in the escalation of war, baking skies which he speculated idly might form 'a minor poem in prose'. He had that day delivered the typescript of *A Literary Pilgrim in England* to Cazenove and admitted to Eleanor Farjeon to feeling at a loose end. 'Who will want the thing now? I may as well write poetry. Did anyone ever begin at 36 in the shade?' The previous September he had begun but abandoned a poem in his waking hours at Ellis's East Grinstead house. Then, in May, he had asked Frost whether he could ever imagine him taking to verse. And now, on the eve of his holiday with Frost he was again prospecting for poetry.[17]

On 3 August, Edward and Mervyn set off from Steep in breezy, showering weather. They rode north-west, breaking their journey in Wiltshire as planned, and may well have learned the news that Germany had that day declared war on France. They were away early the next morning, into a headwind, and were quickly on the outskirts of Swindon. As a boy, Thomas had spent many of his holidays here and was familiar with the Great Western Railway's engineering works that dominated the town: some of his relatives had been employed there. Many times as a boy he had heard the factory hooter calling its workers. Each morning it hailed at 6.45, then again with a shorter blast at 7.20 and again at 7.25; if you were not in the factory by the fourth blast, you were late for work. But on the evening of 4 August, the twin brass domes of the hooter let out ten extended bellows that carried for miles.

Britain was at war.

Germany had violated Belgian borders early in the morning of 4 August. Twelve forts around Liège guarded the gateway to the Belgian plain; under heavy barrage, all of them would fall by 16 August. The Germans torched towns as they went, pushing a human wall of refugees ahead to protect them from retreating infantry fire. Six thousand five hundred Belgian and French civilians were mown down or massacred in the first month alone. The push toward Paris would end in a French stand at the Marne river in September. Germany pulled back to higher ground and dug in, the French followed suit, and so began the building of trenched fortifications that would eventually stretch five hundred miles from the English Channel to the border of Switzerland.

Thomas and Frost were sitting together on an orchard stile near Little Iddens when word came that the firing had started. They wondered whether they might be able to hear the guns from their corner of Gloucestershire.[18]

In London, Harold Monro had no doubts about the right course of action. A call from the War Office for motorcycle volunteers had appeared in that morning's *Daily Mirror* and he responded, only to be turned away on account of the difficulty of finding spare parts for his American motorcycle. When he returned the next day on a British-built bike, he was told that the vacancy had been filled.[19]

At Cley-next-the-Sea on the north coast of Norfolk, Rupert Brooke woke from a nightmare about impending war to find that it had begun. To his hosts, the Cornfords, he uttered not a word all day, but that evening Frances asked, 'But Rupert, *you* won't have to fight?' Said Brooke, 'We shall *all* have to fight.'[20]

At a teachers' conference in Stratford-upon-Avon, Lascelles Abercrombie and John Drinkwater were extolling the importance of Shakespeare when they learned the news. Godwin Baynes and his wife Rosalind were idling in a rowing boat on the River Ouse at St Ives; they tethered their boat and rushed to buy in food supplies.[21]

Rosalind's first cousin, Siegfried Sassoon, had walked into the Drill Hall at Lewes and enlisted the day before.[22]

Robert Graves, aged nineteen, was in his family's holiday home in North Wales; within days he would volunteer for the Royal Welch Fusiliers.

In Bagnères-de-Bigorre, in the south of France, a twenty-year-old man who would train alongside Edward Thomas was teaching when France was invaded; he climbed to the top of a hill and gazed both north to where he supposed the fighting might be, and south over the Pyrenees to the safety of Spain, wondering in which direction his future lay. His name was Wilfred Owen.[23]

'GREAT BRITAIN DECLARES WAR ON GERMANY', read the banner of the country's most popular paper, the *Daily Mirror*. The *Daily Telegraph* reported the deployment of 'enthusiastic troops', and *The Times* looked to a poem from Henry Newbolt to rally the national mood. By the following morning, the tone of the national press had become determined. 'England expects that every man will do his duty', wrote *Daily Express* while the *Daily Telegraph* urged upon its readers 'tears of pride' for the strength of the nation's stance. But the Manchester *Guardian*, which had hoped Britain would not be drawn into the conflict, warned that the country was facing 'the greatest calamity that anyone living has known'.[24]

Thomas loathed what he was reading in the newspapers: jingoistic clichés and nationalistic nonsense about the brave Brits and the evil Germans. How one nation could be painted so honourably and another so diabolically bewildered him: the Germans and Britons were not so different, men were men and felt fear equally whatever their uniform if you pointed a gun at them. He neither hated Germans nor loved Englishmen and wanted nothing to do with this campaign. 'I should like to avoid too much of this strain because it is not the strain of the men who are fighting or going to fight, but rather of morbid people in whom their balance and fusion of mind and body is impossible, and who admire frantically what is impossible to themselves.'[25]

The language of the press was provocative if not incendiary, but in Dymock, where Thomas was headed, the war seemed less immediate. Robert Frost had gone into Ledbury to stock up on tins of biscuits, boxes of soap, packets of cereal: preparations that seemed oddly siege-like and that did not go unnoticed in the town. Later that afternoon, Edward and Mervyn arrived along the Gloucester road having covered the 120 miles from Hampshire without difficulty, but Helen's journey had been anything but straightforward. When she set off that morning, with the two girls and Peter Mrosovski in tow, the transport systems were already in chaos, and her train from Petersfield stopped at Oxford and would not continue any further. Laden with suitcases and children, and the pet dog Rags, Helen had prepared for a night on the station platform when finally a train arrived that would take them as far as Malvern. The taxi that took them onward stopped to ask directions from a policeman in Ledbury, who questioned them suspiciously about the late hour of their travel and the presence of a foreigner, though just a boy. There was a harvest moon above the Malvern Hills when the car pulled up at Oldfields; Edward was waiting for them at the gate and greeted them with his signature call, *Coo-ee.*[26]

Helen's midnight journey and Frost's conspicuous stock-up in Ledbury had attracted local attention. Stranger still, the Gibsons had staying with them a curious, thickly bearded poet from the Netherlands called van Doorn and the volume of unfamiliar accents aroused mistrust in the parish reminiscent of that which greeted Coleridge and Wordsworth in Nether Stowey during the Napoleonic War. Until then, the denizens of Dymock had been tolerated, if not welcomed, in the lanes and inns, as Thomas explained, 'But once it got about, in a certain part of Gloucestershire, that a Dutchman had been staying in one house, that an American family lived in another, that a party (including a Russian boy) had arrived by motor-car at a third in the middle of the night, all sorts of people joined in the hunt – the policeman, the retired clergyman, acting on the principle that "you never know what these naturalised Americans are," and the illiterate anonymous senders of reports that we sat up late at night.' A policeman came calling to follow up reports of those late-night sightings, even that Frost had been heard singing Germanic songs from the cellar at Little Iddens. Gibson was pressed over his Dutch visitor, and even Abercrombie, well known locally by now, came under suspicion for entertaining an artist with a rare physical disability. Thomas laughed off the intrusion as country gossip, Gibson too, but Frost did not; it riled him and according to Helen announced that if the policeman cared to call again then he, Frost, would personally shoot him. It would not be the last time that Frost had a run-in with the local constabulary.[27]

In the days that followed, calm was restored in the parish. Thomas and Frost renewed their talks—walking. Oldfields and Little Iddens were separated by three meadows, a gate, a brook and two stiles, so close that on a clear evening when the wind was low, it was possible to hear the voices of the children ringing from one place to the other. Each day, several times a day, Thomas walked between the cottages, through the rolling meadow beside Oldfields where a bay colt and an old mare ambled, down the sloping middle meadow and a tiny brook, there over a stile and up into the rougher grass of the Iddens meadow.[28]

Sometimes they tended to the garden, or took their families for a picnic outing. But best of all, they liked to slip the reins and walk out together on the Dymock fields. Scant rain fell to break the heat, but the rains of July had swelled the corn and the rooks cawed while the wheat fields were harvested beneath them. Wherever the men walked, half-attentive to footpaths, among the windfalls that the wasps had undermined, they moved in an instinctive sympathy. Their talk ranged over marriage and friendship, wildlife and the war. Sometimes there was no talk and a silence gathered about them; but often at a gate or stile it started up again or was prompted by the meeting of a stranger in the lanes: a word or two and they were off once more. Where they went they went without a map, setting their course by the sun or by the distant arc of May Hill crowning the view to the south; at dusk, the towering elms and Lombardy poplars or the light of a part-glimpsed cottage saw them home.[29]

On 6 August a full moon rose on an evening of heavy precipitation. The two friends were descending the Malverns when a rare lunar rising occurred, what Frost recorded as 'A very small moon-made prismatic bow'. What they witnessed, judging by Frost's description, was a moonbow that as it rose in the night sky became a lunar corona. Frost wrote of it later:

> A wonder! Bow and rainbow as it bent,
> Instead of moving with us as we went,
> (To keep the pots of gold from being found)
> It lifted from its dewy pediment
> Its two mote-swimming many-colored ends,
> And gathered them together in a ring.
> And we stood in it softly circled round
> From all division time or foe can bring
> In a relation of elected friends.

To Thomas, it seemed like the first rainbow that ever was.[30]

The moods indoors were less agreeable. Helen found the conditions in Oldfields cramped and was less than taken by the company of her American neighbours. About Elinor Frost she was scathing: she found her careworn and defeated, a hopeless housekeeper who peeled potatoes in a dry bucket, and whose personality was nebulous and lacked the vigour of her husband's. Around Robert, Helen was uneasy, and found him erratic, bossy, given to illiberal and offensive remarks. The Thomas children became bored and Myfanwy injured herself falling from a swing, while Edward heard from Cazenove that *A Literary Pilgrim in England* was under-length by 10,000 words and would need enhancing. 'One thing and another leaves me very irritable indeed,' Edward told Eleanor Farjeon. To make matters worse, Mr Chandler, the owner of Oldfields, was called into service in Hereford, and Thomas suspected he and Frost might be left to complete the farmer's harvest. Worse still, with the country at war Thomas was aware that literary work of the kind that he depended on was certain to dry up. He told his old friend John Freeman that he felt more secluded than ever from the realities of events. 'I am working as much as I can by finding jobs for myself when even an unpatriotic person can't imagine it is of the least importance or money value,' he wrote. 'I get no work and discover no likelihood. Otherwise little is changed except in the newspapers. The harvest comes in.' Even with his landlord called into service, the war remained remote to Edward Thomas, and ten days after the outbreak of hostilities he admitted that he had not given first thought to serving his country.[31]

Eleanor Farjeon herself joined the party on 20 August, and settled in quickly at neighbouring Glyn Iddens as the guest of an elderly, kindly couple called Farmer, from where she recorded two of the more characterful episodes of those summer weeks. Mr Farmer's chuckling manners met Mrs Farmer's matronly ways ('Mother!' was his name for her, 'Father!' hers for him), and one evening they invited the poets to a lavish dinner replete with vats of the Farmers' home-made cider. When the moment in the evening came for the poets to rise to their feet, they found they had no legs beneath them. They attempted to rise and sank again, grinned and rose again in supportive pairs – Thomas and Frost, Abercrombie and Gibson – before weaving their ways home. On another occasion, an afternoon of stirring heat, Frost eyed his potato patch and announced that it was ready for digging; Thomas tugged his forelock mischievously and said yes sir, he would be about it the very next day. Sure enough when the morning came Thomas was at the vegetable patch; he was joined by Eleanor and, for a while at least, Frost's twelve-year-old son

Carol. Under a hot sun, the 'hired' help rolled their sleeves and worked their rows in toil and sweat while Frost moved among them, directing here, smoking there. 'Wot abaht that little bit, mister,' said Thomas, a glint in his eye, straightening on his fork before turning back to the patch in hand.[32]

A new moon rose over Dymock on 21 August. In the days that followed, Frost and Thomas continued their pattern of talks–walking, and as they did so, something seemed to be shifting in Thomas's mind. On 26 August the friends found themselves walking through the afternoon into the night. Thomas jotted in his notebook: 'a sky of dark rough horizontal masses in N.W. with a 1/3 moon bright and almost orange low down clear of cloud and I thought of men east-ward seeing it at the same moment. It seems foolish to have loved England up to now without knowing it could perhaps be ravaged and I could and perhaps would do nothing to prevent it.' A new sensibility was emerging in Edward Thomas. The war was three weeks old and for the first time he was imagining his countrymen abroad, sharing the same moon as he. He had no care for the politics of the conflict, but his mood was troubled by a different kind of awareness. He was weighing the worth of the land beneath his feet and the way of life that it supported. What would he do, if called upon, to protect it? Would he do anything at all?[33]

The walks with Frost had inspired Thomas to suggest a new line of work to his agent back in London. On 19 August, Thomas had asked Cazenove whether he could place a series of articles that recorded the impact of the war upon the working people he was meeting in the fields of Gloucestershire and Herefordshire. From conversations happened upon with labourers or drovers at a stile or gate or country inn, the pieces would form a foot-worn, first-hand, non-combatant's view of the campaign; they might even allow Thomas to feel that he was doing something for the war effort. Cazenove understood that the country was in the grip of patriotism, and felt that any such pieces would require careful handling. He passed on Thomas's proposal to Austin Harrison at the *English Review*, who echoed the agent's anxiety. 'Nothing must be said which will stop recruiting,' Harrison had warned: this was his belief and that of his peers in the press, and no journal would risk appearing unpatriotic at the present time. Thomas was summoned to London on 27 August to give Harrison his assurances in person. He felt confident that he could strike a tone that did not seem unpatriotic, and made a gentleman's agreement with Harrison to that effect. Thomas would write three articles to appear over nine months and in return Harrison would offer £25 for 5,000 words. At a time when his livelihood looked doubtful, Thomas's proposal was a financial masterstroke.[34]

Thomas was not alone in struggling to find a satisfactory response to the war. Frost felt himself on similarly uncertain ground, if anything more persuaded than Thomas of the patriotic cause while knowing it not to be his own. 'You must think I have been and gone to war for the country that made me a poet,' he wrote to a friend in America on 20 August. 'My obligation is not quite as deep as that.' Nevertheless, were he younger, he said, and not the father of four then he might well make the cause his own. 'American or no American, I might decide that I ought to fight the Germans simply because I know I should be afraid to.' But in truth, what troubled him deep down was not the prospect of action or even the suffering of others but his own immediate prospects in literature. 'The war is an ill wind to me,' he admitted. 'It ends for the time being the thought of publishing any more books. Our game is up.'[35]

In 1913, the number of books published was just one tenth of the output of today, but it was then a growth economy that had boomed by 25 per cent in five years. The war would have a devastating impact on the industry – a shortage of resources, labour and income would ensure that by 1918 the production of new editions was only a third of the number before the war; it would be the mid-1920s before the industry recovered. Overnight, editors were no longer commissioning book reviews, only articles that were expressly concerned with the conflict, and for Abercrombie and Thomas this posed a practical crisis. Abercrombie admitted to Marsh that his earnings to date were about half those of previous years, while expectations for the rest of 1914 were 'about £10'. At the same moment Thomas told Bottomley, 'I have of course no prospect of earning any sort of living while the war lasts.' Gibson did not rely upon review work and his income was less threatened: earnings from his verse alone matched Abercrombie's entire annual income. Publishers were swift to cut back on their commissioning and also on their staff, as Walter de la Mare found when he was released from his role as Reader at Heinemann. Frost did no such work, but he could see the ceiling being lowered on his *North of Boston*.[36]

If Frost could not see past his next publication, Rupert Brooke was experiencing a more physical response to the war. Something had shifted within him that August. To Gibson, he appeared listless and distracted, and confessed to his friend of feeling tearful and depressed. All he could focus on was the war. Part of him wanted to be left alone, quite alone, to live his life and follow his writing in peace: had he wished to be a soldier he would have been one long ago. But the unrest within him grew until he came to understand the war as potentially the most important experience of his lifetime. 'Well, if Armageddon's *on*,' he said, 'I suppose one should be there.' Being there, he imagined at first, might mean accepting a placement as an international correspondent – many of his writer friends had put themselves down for that. But to go to war in that capacity was merely to offer curiosity when decent people were offering their lives, he believed: gesture was not enough. He wanted to feel that he might use his brain somehow, felt certain his skills must be needed in intelligence work; but so did many of the literary young men up and down the country and wherever he looked, Brooke found only waiting lists. Bitterly despondent, unable to vent his feelings, his moods became tortured and destructive. 'Half my heart is of England,' he wrote, 'the rest is looking for some home I haven't yet found.'[37]

The war, it was widely said, would be over by Christmas, and everywhere young men were rushing to do their bit in time. But doing your bit was harder than Brooke had supposed in those early days of the war. The professional army was well equipped for the needs of the short campaign that was believed to lie ahead; officers were not required, and applicants could be rejected on such irrelevancies as the condition of their teeth. Brooke explained: 'It's not so easy as you think – for a person who has no military training or knowledge, save the faint, almost prenatal, remembrance of some khaki drilling at Rugby – to get to the "front". I'm one of a band who have been offering themselves, with a vague persistence, to their country, in various quarters of London for some days, and being continually refused.'[38]

For Edward Thomas the summer in Dymock was over. On 2 September, the family packed their bags and left Oldfields. He told Gordon Bottomley that he had seen too little of Abercrombie, too much of Gibson and Frost daily. His three articles for the *English Review* had given him a watering hole in a commissioning desert, but he knew beyond those any further prospects for work were remote. For all his adult life he had lived by his prose but now he could see his livelihood disappearing. Perverse as it seemed to him, he would now entertain the thought of volunteering for financial reasons alone. A private earned only 1s. a day in 1915, but officers considerably more: a corporal upwards of 2s. 6d. daily, a sergeant in excess of 3s., a sergeant major 4s., with separation allowances of 12s. 6d. paid weekly to spouses (a family with four children would receive as much again), and responsibility allowances on top of that. It was nothing like the income that Thomas's writing had once generated, but it was more than it could generate now. Owlishly, Thomas watched the movements of his friends for the slightest guide. 'Hodgson is guarding Chelsea Gas Works. Rupert Brooke I hear has joined the army. The Blast poets I hear have not. If this war goes on I believe I shall find myself a sort of Englishman, tho neither poet nor soldier. If I could earn anything worthwhile as a soldier I think I should go.'[39]

Thomas had once felt an ambivalence toward his 'Englishness'. 'I am 5/8 Welsh,' he had said when pressed by a Welshman on the subject in 1908, continuing, 'I have some Spanish blood and some blood from Wiltshire in my veins.' Thomas never spoke or understood Welsh and never lived in Wales, but from the age of four he holidayed with great-aunts in Newport, Caerleon and Swansea. At ten, he would sing the Irish nationalist song 'The Minstrel Boy', believing it to be about Wales, 'and as I sang the song I melted and trembled with a kind of gloomy pleasure in being about to die for Wales'. At twenty-one, he wrote of the country as a calling: 'It is like a homesickness, but stronger than any homesickness I ever felt – stronger than any passion.' For much of his life, perhaps until the war, Wales held an almost mystical draw for him, 'In spite of my accidentally Cockney nativity'. But as the summer of 1914 moved into autumn, Thomas had reached into a corner of himself that he had been barely aware of. The man who did not consider himself a patriot, who loathed nationalism, who believed his countrymen were the birds, was cultivating a new skin.[40]

On 3 September 1914 he put it this way to Jesse Berridge: 'I am slowly growing into a conscious Englishman.'[41]

Autumn

The temperature was eighty degrees in the shade as Mervyn Thomas and Peter Mrosovski set off from Dymock back to Steep at the beginning of September. Peter had stayed with the Thomases throughout their month in Gloucestershire, and as Edward headed north by train to begin his commission for the *English Review*, his bicycle was ridden home by the young Russian. The boys made good progress until Mervyn took a nail in his front tyre outside Swindon. They broke their journey at the Central Hotel in Swindon, sharing a bed to save money, and next morning carried the bikes on the train in a journey interrupted by troop manoeuvres on Salisbury Plain and a mass of soldiers at Winchester station. They made it home an hour before Helen and the girls at five o'clock on 3 September.[1]

Edward Thomas meanwhile was on his way north, recording the conversations of the people he met en route about the war. For a week he sought the views of working people in railway compartments and station platforms, in taverns and on trams, and in between took pleasure in the sights encountered along the way: a shipless sea north of Hartlepool, the bridges onto Newcastle's riverside streets below. But introducing himself to the British public was not the most comfortable of activities for this man who once described social intercourse as an intense form of solitude. He found his own conversation unnatural, his questions forced, stultifying to any spontaneity on the part of those he interviewed; even so the portrait he captured was filled with character.[2]

In the West Midlands, people poured into Birmingham library to learn more about the war. In the East Midlands, a thin man with a duck-bill nose berated another too overweight to serve: 'When the Kaiser reaches Coventry he'll see a lot like you.' At Sheffield, a Saturday football crowd were donating part of their wages. A young man, homesick for his Northumberland village, walked twenty-six miles into Newcastle to enlist. Elsewhere, people talked without inhibition. The Irish had responded manfully, said one man looking up from reading the *British Weekly*, and now it was for the English to follow suit. This unfortunate business had bound people together as nothing else could, said another. One man took a swing at someone who had called him German in his looks, but mostly the atmosphere was calm, the mood stoic and reflective.

Many were talking as much of work as war. Companies cut wages or lengthened their hours; some laid off their young unmarried men, knowing they had recourse to enlist: in Birmingham, these were jewellers whose labour was now less in demand, at Newcastle, the men of the collier ships whose markets had been Prussian. But elsewhere firms did well: bootmakers in Leicester, saddlers in Walsall, manufacturers of explosives at Elswick; the war firms prospered. Recruitment bands played cheerily in the streets with campaign tunes that carried across the rooftops. Publicans were busier than ever, and a man in khaki did not need to buy drinks. The roasting summer sun had produced a bumper harvest, and warmed the labourers and the recruits sleeping out of doors; park keepers struggled to keep control of their crowded parks.

Paris would fall, German communications would be cut, an Allied advance would send them back to where they came from: such was the talk of the taverns and the parks and the streets in the towns up and down England. The Germans were a savage lot, killers of children and of pensioners, and those who had settled in England should be turned out and those on the continent should be moved on. And as for the Kaiser himself, the mad bull, which English man or woman did not seek just five minutes alone with him, he who not so long ago was only too happy to kiss the cheek of King Edward? People struggled to explain the early German advances; some said the retreating Allies were luring them into a trap, some that the Germans must be good soldiers. The working classes were suffering disproportionately, said one man, but he was shouted down with cries of 'Socialist!' Someone in Coventry spoke against the grain to say, as Thomas would to his appalled father, that a German was not so very different from an Englishman, no better and no worse. Girls said the men should get themselves off the street corner and fight: it is not in our nature to fight, says one. It is in all our natures to fight, says another.[3]

In the countryside, the war seemed less tangible. Stories of German casualties or sinkings at sea were passed by word of mouth without any real means of confirming their accuracy. The town had its newspapers and its cheek-by-jowl talk, but the countryside was dispersed and isolated. The war was often most noticeable by the absences it created: many fieldhands had left their work and gone into the towns to enlist. On the coast, the fishermen had met many Germans and now plotted their country's defence, but inland some had never met one and had no idea how to react if they did: was it true that the Germans would cut off the hands of those they captured?[4]

Thomas wondered what all of this might pose for England. He asked what did it mean at a time like this to have a love of one's country, and met a man who seemed to provide an answer. To that man, wrote Thomas, 'England was a place where "one isn't forbidden to do what one wants to do or forced to do what somebody else wants", and that in spite of gamekeepers, for whoever met a landowner in a wood? I take this to be the foundation of patriotism.' It was significant that Thomas should invoke the symbol of the gamekeeper at a time of war. Since his youth, the gamekeeper had represented the privatisation of nature, to him, the possession of the living ground and the animals to which it gave a home, the miracle of the earth patrolled for the benefit of the few: 'Pride, stupidity, servility'. One who loves the world outside the gamekeeper's patrol, who loves tolerance and permission, who engages with the living land, that person might reasonably be considered a patriot. But other forms of patriotism were not so benign. Thomas condemned the kind of patriot who, out of ignorance or prejudice alone, scorned the lifestyles that he had not experienced for himself, the man who belittled the cultures of foreign lands or even of neighbouring counties. The Wiltshire man who said Hampshire was the place where they held the pig aloft to see the band go by; the Hampshire man who said that in Wiltshire they buried the donkey with its feet out of the ground so as to polish its shoes. These were neighbours who quarrelled at their every difference only to turn as one upon the outsider who interferes. 'A happy nation luxuriates in its differences and distinctions,' he wrote; the greater the differences, the greater the affection for those differences. There may be places that we find more pleasant, but there can be no word that stirs the emotion quite like that of 'home'. In a line that reads peculiarly modern, he concluded, 'England is a system of vast circumferences circling round the minute neighbouring points of home.'[5]

'The thing is going pretty well,' Brooke had said on the eve of the publication of the third *New Numbers* in July, 'about seven or eight hundred of each number, which pays expenses very easily, and leaves a good bit for division.' But that was before the outbreak of war, and surely the Dymock journal would now struggle to survive. In truth, the harmony of *New Numbers* had always been deceptive. Despite Drinkwater's insistence on a mutual appreciation of each other's work, Gibson and Abercrombie had shared an uneasiness toward his and Brooke's contributions to the journal, suspecting that Drinkwater might use it as a vehicle to print the work that he could not get published elsewhere while Brooke's offerings seemed wildly variable. 'They're very poor, aren't they?' Gibson lamented to Edward Marsh of Brooke's poems; Abercrombie agreed. D. H. Lawrence had poured scorn on the second issue that spring, and in particular on the two-act play in blank verse that Abercrombie had set in a country pub. 'Why, why, in God's name, is Abercrombie messing about with Yokels and Cider and runaway wives?' he demanded. 'I loathe his rather nasty efforts at cruelty . . . What is the matter with the man? – there's something wrong with his soul.' Thomas had let that issue pass uncontested, but about the third number he would not be restrained. Abercrombie's efforts were journalistic, Gibson's mercantile, Brooke was going to war anyway, while 'Drinkwater must be hopeless in this incarnation and I haven't heard of another.' Thomas's patience with these writers had finally run out, but his reservations were slight in comparison to the more personal attack launched by Robert Frost, who on 21 September wrote to Jack Haines.

All Drinkwater is is a soaker. All one reads him for is to find out who he has been soaking in lately. Neither is Brooke worth bothering with (in this phase – if he ever was in any) . . . Abercrombie doesnt quite persuade me to accept his [?]convention that it doesnt matter if his people say unlikely things provided they say poetic things. And Gibson is sometimes so [?]even he makes me nervous.

Abercrombie confirmed privately that the next issue of the journal would be its last.[6]

In travelling the country for his *English Review* articles, Thomas had been given his first exposure to the impact of war. Times were as hard and they were uncertain, and he was no less affected than the men he had spoken to on his travels. 'I don't quite know what will happen,' he admitted to Jesse Berridge. 'The obvious thing is to join the Territorials but I can't leave other people to keep my family till I know I can't do it myself.' To Bottomley and to Farjeon he said the same. His thoughts began to loop in those first days of September. 'I don't know what may turn up.' 'My own plans are more uncertain.' It would be a good time for trying America, he told Bottomley, if only he could leave Helen and the children: but he could not. A good time for the Territorials, but he could not go there either. The walks with Frost in Gloucestershire had brought him a friendship like no other as well as a desire to protect the country he walked; he felt pushed in two sharply contrasting directions: to America with Frost or to the war in Europe. He returned to Steep on 10 September and set to work writing up the first of the three articles for the *English Review*. 'When it is done,' he said, 'I shall find out what sort of soldier they still want at Petersfield.'[7]

Frost had considered that the game was up for the publishing of his poetry in England. But on 2 September, the publishing house of Henry Holt in New York wrote to the London offices of David Nutt to say that a copy of *North of Boston* had been enthusiastically pressed upon them by Florence Holt, the wife of the company president, and that the poems were 'uncommonly interesting'. In fact Mrs Holt had written directly to Frost in August from her home on Four Winds Farm, in Stowe, Vermont, taking care not to commit her husband's press, and yet still hoping that, even from Gloucestershire, the American might recognise the publishing name behind her letter ('you will not be displeased to know of our interest'). But Frost mistook the letter for that of an unknown New England farmer's wife and offered no reply. The opportunity might so easily have passed had Mrs Holt not tried again, this time through her husband's company. The Holt editors were cautious, and informed Mrs Nutt that 'we cannot see a paying market here for this particular volume', though they would be glad to inspect any next book that Frost produced. Mrs Nutt was not impressed: 'We consider that under present political circumstances American publishers ought to show some willingness to help English publishers who have had sufficient daring and intelligence to recognise the talent of one of their countrymen.' In the event, Mrs Nutt's letter crossed with a follow-up from Holt, who had written again to advise that they were prepared after all to gamble on a modest 150 copies of the sheets for binding in the US market. Between the efforts of two women, Mrs Holt and Mrs Nutt, Robert Frost was finally to be published in America.[8]

Back in London, yet another new character was about to become entangled in the story of the Poetry Bookshop. On 7 July, a twenty-five-year-old Harvard graduate, T. S. Eliot, had passed through London en route to summer school in Germany, only to find himself stranded when the course in Marburg was cancelled in the wake of the declaration of war. In the ensuing lock-down, students were told they could not leave the country for a fortnight, and it was not until 21 August that the American arrived back in London. Uncertain of his next move, he took rooms on Bedford Place not far from the Bookshop and was struck by the little corner of bohemia he had discovered. 'Shady Bloomsbury, the noisiest place in the world, a neighbourhood at present given over to artists, musicians, hackwriters, Americans, Russians, French, Belgians, Italians, Spaniards, and Japanese, formerly Germans also . . . a delightfully seedy part of town.' He swiftly won himself a scholarship to study at Oxford and went up to Merton College that autumn. But this bright young student was also a gifted poet whose first poems were about to reach the desk of Harold Monro.[9]

Like Pound and Frost, Eliot was a literary unknown when he arrived in London. A Harvard friend, Conrad Aiken, was living in the capital at the time and offered to circulate his friend's work ahead of his arrival. Eliot agreed and gave him a poem written in the summer of 1911 that had yet to see the light of day, 'The Love Song of J. Alfred Prufrock'. But Monro was not in the least interested in taking the poem for

Poetry and Drama and according to Aiken returned to him saying that it was 'absolutely insane'. Undeterred, Aiken found a second occasion to present Eliot's work to the editor, possibly at a party following Brooke's Bookshop reading of 28 July, when he happened to have with him a copy of 'La Figlia Che Piange' (Eliot: 'the first poem of mine that was ever put in to any respectable anthology and therefore must be completely inoffensive'). Monro gave this second piece similarly short shrift, handing it back to Aiken, remarking, 'O I can't be bothered with this'; but as Aiken walked home, he became concerned that Monro might have mistakenly thought that he had thrust his own work upon him, and wrote the next day to clear up any confusion, sending Eliot's poem together with an address at which to reach the American. 'Of course that too was rejected,' Aiken reported.[10]

Edward Thomas knew nothing of the unpublished T. S. Eliot, but he did know Conrad Aiken, who had just sent him his work. 'I am reading the third bard who wants my opinion since September,' he told Eleanor wearily that October. 'The first 2 I spoke the truth to and they didn't thank me. This one will be the same I fear.' Aiken was an unashamed self-promoter, something which would not have gone unnoted by Harold Monro and may well have contributed to the editor's reluctance to look properly at the material before him; even so, said Aiken, Monro passed over the work three times. 'I doubt if he ever received an idea clean at first go,' said Pound dismissively, 'or ever gripped it at once by the handle,' and he took from Eliot a copy of 'Prufrock' when they met for the first time that September. By the following summer, Pound had succeeded in getting the poem published in Harriet Monroe's *Poetry*. Eliot made the best of an awkward situation and attended his first event at the Bookshop that month ('lectures at 5 p.m. with wax candles'), but he was not settling well to literary London. His sympathies about the war were complicated by his time in Germany, and he found incredible the decision of an

American friend at Oxford to become naturalised in order to seek a war commission. ('I certainly shall not go to that length.') There were few signs that autumn in 1914 that Eliot's residence would be a permanent one. 'I don't think that I should ever feel at home in England,' he wrote.[11]

Thomas had spent much of September travelling but longing to be back at home; yet no sooner was he in Steep than he felt ready to leave once again. On 5 October, he set off by bicycle for Wales, passing through Avebury, then Bristol and Swansea, the Brecon Beacons, arriving in Gloucestershire on the 14th after rainfall and punctures had hampered his journey. His destination was not Little Iddens for once but the Gallows, where the Frosts had moved early in September after their landlord asked for the cottage to be vacated for hired help and the Abercrombies had taken them in. The Frosts had stayed only five months on Ledington Hill, but now, with the move to Ryton, Elinor could at last fulfil her dream of living under thatch. Lascelles, Catherine and the Abercrombie children would live in one of the adjoining cottages, the Frosts in the other, though with Catherine pregnant with her third child, the Abercrombies spent much of the winter away, leaving the Frosts the run of the entire property. Frost would draft or set a clutch of poems at the Gallows, among them some lines to the elms behind the cottage, 'The Sound of Trees'; but by far the most important of the poems he would begin there was a piece that for the time being carried the working title 'Two Roads', which was to become 'The Road Not Taken'. Thomas found the Frosts off colour during that October visit: Elinor was tired, Robert nervy and barely eating. 'I don't know how the Frosts will get through the winter,' he told Eleanor Farjeon. 'He isn't a bit well and she is too hardworked.' They idled and talked under languid weather, and Thomas for once found himself longing to be not with Frost but at home. He told Helen he was sorry to be extending his time away, but was finding comfort from the soft still days, rising ahead of his hosts each morning to light the fires before heading out to pick apples from beneath a bent old tree in the fodder field. Thomas walked up into the woods above the path at Ryton; along the Leadon the trees carried yellow and ruddy leaves, and only the silver willows and the dark green elms held on to their summer colours. He wrote to Cazenove to propose an anthology 'about England, English places and English life', but his agent was doubtful, replying that the market was saturated with such books; five had been published in the past week alone. 'What I want to write,' Thomas persisted, 'is an account of the name of England and its meaning, especially its emotional meaning . . . to show what is meant when a man speaks of England and especially since the war.' It seemed that nothing now, not a week in Wales or talk with Frost about New Hampshire, could distract Thomas from the topic that truly captivated him in the autumn of 1914: England. He jotted in his notebook: 'The war national but as yet dark and chaotic in brain'. Poets had further to go, he thought, before the experience of war would find a valuable translation into poetry.[12]

A gloomy letter from Frost was awaiting Thomas when he returned to Steep. Ill health and poor spirits had gotten the better of the American. 'When I wrote like that you replied that you wished I were near enough to be kicked,' wrote Thomas. 'Well, I wish you were near enough to kick you, but have no faith in that kind of school.' It was the first time that Thomas was able to dictate the emotional temperature of their relationship, and it would not be the last; but for now, Thomas had anxieties of his own that he wished to share. 'I have just made myself ill with thinking hard for an hour, – going up to my study and sitting there, – that I ought to enlist next week in town.'[13]

As Thomas began six months of dithering about the probity of enlisting, Rupert Brooke was having his application fast tracked.

Having failed to get into the army, he pressed Edward Marsh to exercise his influence with Winston Churchill, and was found an opening in a new naval unit, a volunteer reserve attached to HMS *Victory*. The company would be an assembly of 'more or less trained men' – 'more' being the Royal Marines, 'less' being Brooke, who had received only the most preliminary of drills. But as a naval reservist, he had the chance to circumvent months of training camp. On 15 September he completed his application for a commission, and by the 27th he left Charing Cross for camp on the Kent coast. On the night of 4 October, Brooke sailed from Dover in a convoy escorted by two destroyers, and by morning lay off the coast of Dunkirk, waiting for the tide to turn. They were heading for Antwerp and reached the outskirts of the city to find that it had been pounded almost to rubble by German shells. The Brigade's own station was heavily bombarded, and Brooke lost his spare clothes and some unfinished draft manuscripts in scrambling to safety. On 9 October, the city fell and a British retreat was ordered.

I marched through Antwerp, deserted, shelled, and burning, one night, and saw ruined houses, dead men and horses: and railway-trains with their lines taken up and twisted and flung down as if a child had been playing with a toy. And the whole heaven and earth was lit up by the glare from the great lakes and rivers of burning petrol, hills and spires of flame. That was like Hell, a Dantesque Hell, terrible.

But the Hell for the refugees was worse: hundreds of thousands, stricken and crying, moving into the night in two endless columns. What he witnessed would only harden his resolve about his decision to fight, and back in London he reported the slaughter directly to Winston Churchill. Friends found him harrowed and traumatised, quite changed with his cropped military haircut from the man they once knew. In July when he read at the Poetry Bookshop he had been called angelic, but now when he called on Monro the proprietor described him as 'haggard and discouraged, and talking almost entirely about the war'. Within ten days, Brooke was back with his unit and waiting redeployment, but he was exhausted and succumbed to flu. As he made his recovery, he began a run of five sonnets, among which was one that would enter the national consciousness for what it appeared to say about self-sacrifice.

> If I should die, think only this of me:
> That there's some corner of a foreign field
> That is for ever England . . .

He gave the poem and the other four pieces to Wilfrid Gibson for *New Numbers*, but it was to be *The Times* that would make the sonnet famous when it reprinted the poem after his death. He wrote to Walter de la Mare of his horror at the thought of England invaded 'as of some virginity violated'; but beneath the bravado, Brooke was privately concerned at the scale of catastrophe the war implied. A letter in November hinted at his turmoil. 'It's a great life, fighting, while it lasts. The eye grows clearer and the heart. But it's a bloody thing, half the youth of Europe blown through pain to nothingness, in the incessant mechanical slaughter of these modern battles.'[14]

At the St George's Café, Edward Thomas was about to extend his quarrel with the war. Late in October, he took tea with Ralph Hodgson, who a year before had introduced Thomas to Frost in the very same space. Hodgson had been among the first of their circle to enlist in August, and was serving as a warden at the Chelsea Gas Works when Thomas expressed his hesitations about the conflict. He would not believe that the German was a worse fellow than the Englishman, or that one countryman felt any less fearful about the war than the other. These were controversial views for Thomas to be exposing at this moment. The 'rape' of Belgium, as it was coming to be known, had stirred public anger, and Hodgson rounded on Thomas. Every

Englishman had a duty to be patriotic and to do their bit, he said, and Thomas's views were an abomination. Hodgson became angrier, until he branded Thomas a 'Teuton', rose hastily and knocked aside a nearby chair before storming out of the Café in a fury, his British bulldog Mooster trotting loyally after him. Thomas was shaken by the exchange: rows with his father on the subject had been one thing, but this assault by a friend so rattled him that he wrote to Harold Monro to say that Hodgson's remarks had almost made him join up. 'Hodgson flung off today labelling me pro-German. I almost enlisted afterwards in repentance. I could almost face bayonets to bring him round, but not quite, tho I fear it would be the only measure.' The dispute had become so heated and so painful to each man they concluded it inadvisable to be in one another's company for the time being. 'He and I are not meeting till the war is over,' Thomas told Bottomley. 'I am not patriotic enough for his exuberant taste.' Edward Thomas and Ralph Hodgson would never speak again.[15]

Between 25 and 30 November, Edward Thomas returned to see Robert Frost at the Gallows, his sixth visit to Gloucestershire since April, and the last trip he would make there. En route, he took a train to London to collect volunteering papers from the Parliamentary Recruiting Committee. He was a long way from a decision to join up, but he knew that he would rather conduct any enlistment on his own terms than risk being 'pitchforked', as he put it, into service. It was curious that Thomas should think he might be pressed in that way: in November 1914 there was no conscription and would not be for another year and more. When Prime Minister Asquith introduced it in January 1916, married men continued to be exempt; it would not be until April 1916 that service was made universal for men under the age of forty-one, by which time Thomas had long since been at war. For the time being, it was not at all apparent how a course of action might become clearer to him: he lacked the impulse to fight that had pulled in

'When first I came here I had hope': Edward Thomas at Steep, 1914

'It is really the kind H. and the children who make life almost *impossible*': conditions at home were frequently under strain. Clockwise: Helen (1914), Mervyn (1912), Myfanwy (1914) and Bronwen (1910)

'the centre of the New Poetry': the Poetry Bookshop, 35 Devonshire Street
WC1, February 1913
'A young Apollo, golden-haired': Rupert Brooke, 1913
Dymock Poets, Birmingham Repertory Theatre, May 1914, left to right: John
Drinkwater, Wilfrid Gibson, Edward Marsh, Lascelles Abercrombie, Geral-
dine Gibson, Catherine Abercrombie

'pre-eminent among the distinguished poets still in their prime': W. B. Yeats, 1911 (left)

'the stormy petrel': Pound (right), 1913, was never far from the centre of the controversy

'Nights of storm, days of mist, without end': Wick Green was an unloved family home 1909–13, though Thomas retained happier memories of the Bee House in the garden which he kept on as a study until 1916

'greater friends than almost any two ever were practising the same art': Robert
Frost and Edward Thomas forged a seemingly unbreakable friendship only
for the war to tear it apart

'Fast beat | My heart at sight of the tall slope.' View from the Shoulder
of Mutton Hill, Steep, nearby Thomas's study at Wick Green. Berryfield
Cottage, the family's first Hampshire home, lies to the right hidden by yew
trees; the stone in the foreground is a memorial to Thomas, erected in 1937

'I have come to the borders of sleep': Thomas chose to keep his verse secret from his army colleagues by disguising it as prose: he used capital letters to indicate new lines and paragraph breaks to mark stanzas ('Lights Out', Royal Artillery Barracks, Trowbridge, November 1916)

Thomas was loved not only by Helen, but by Eleanor Farjeon (above, 1913) and Edna Clarke Hall (below, c.1894)

'I'm bound away for ever': a harrowed-looking Thomas, one month before his departure for France, by Mervyn Thomas, High Beech, 1917

Rupert Brooke and other men and realised that thinking endlessly as he had been doing was unlikely to produce an answer. On the train to London he had shared his dilemma with a young soldier sitting opposite him, and the men agreed that 'no man could face war if he could foresee his own part in the fighting. The difference between people is that they try or do not try in various degrees – often against their will – to foresee it.' He collected his volunteer's papers, though they would remain unsigned for now.[16]

Thomas arrived at the Gallows to find that the Abercrombies were still away, leaving the Frosts the continued run of the two cottages and Thomas the chance to settle in for a few days. As before, he would rise early to light the house fires in what would have been his working hours, but now he had no work, and this November visit was intended to be pure leisure. He and Frost would head out to walk as far as the weather would allow. Some days they swept south and west toward May Hill, others east to Ketford Mill, but wherever they walked they were frequently the guests of William Lygon, the seventh Earl Beauchamp. Lord Beauchamp's seat was the Madresfield Court at Malvern that Evelyn Waugh would make the setting for Brideshead, although his holdings extended to a thousand acres of wooded land that surrounded and included the Gallows. Abercrombie and select locals (possibly including Wilfrid Gibson) were granted access to the preserve – and to the neighbouring land owned by an industrialist, George Stacey Albright – for walking, picnics or blackberry picking; but unaccompanied children were not permitted and if caught were terrified into dumping their punnets by the surly head gamekeeper, a man named Bott who reported to Albright at Bromsberrow Place north-east of the Gallows, and may also have reported to Lord Beauchamp. Rarely without his shotgun, Bott was a prowler and a bully, and was not averse to waving his weapon at any adults he suspected to be trespassing.

One morning in late November, Thomas and Frost were strolling in the woods when they were intercepted by the keeper, who challenged their presence and told the men bluntly to clear out. As a resident of the Gallows, Frost believed he was extended the same courtesy as Abercrombie and so entitled to roam wherever he wished, and he told the keeper as much. Bott was unimpressed and some sharp words were exchanged, and when the poets emerged onto the road they were challenged once more by the keeper who, according to a notebook source, had lain in wait, 'snooping in the hedge, glowering'. Tempers flared and Bott called Frost 'a damned cottager' before raising his shotgun at the two men. Incensed, Frost was on the verge of accosting the man, but hesitated when he saw Thomas back off. Heated words continued to be had, with the adversaries goading then finally parting and the poets talking heatedly of the incident as they walked. Thomas said that the keeper's aggression was unacceptable and that something should be done. Frost's ire peaked as he listened to Thomas: something would indeed be done and done right now and if Thomas wanted to follow him he could see it being done. The men turned back, Frost angrily, Thomas hesitantly, but the gamekeeper was no longer on the road. His temper wild, Frost insisted on tracking the man down, which they did, to a small cottage at the edge of Grove Coppice along the bridle path that linked the Old Smithy at Ryton to Redmarley D'Abitot. Frost beat on the door, and left the startled keeper in no doubt as to what would befall him were he ever to threaten Frost or his children or bar them access to the preserve. Satisfied that the force of his point had been made, Frost repeated his warning for good measure, turned on his heel and prepared to leave. What happened next would be a defining moment in the friendship of Robert Frost and Edward Thomas, and would plague Thomas to his dying days.[7]

The keeper, recovering his wits, reached above the door for his twelve-bore shotgun and came outside, this time heading straight for Thomas, who until then had not been the keeper's target. The gun was raised again; instinctively Thomas backed off, and the gamekeeper saw the men from his property and back onto the bridle path, where they left under the keeper's watchful aim.

Unknown to the poets, there was a witness to the incident. Ted Hill, a boy of twelve, had been 'going down fro' grandmother's' in Ketford Mill and was on the way to nearby Gamage Hall to pick hops when he stopped in to see 'ole Bott', as he knew him. The boy was inside the cottage when the poets rapped on the door. Through the open doorway, he saw the whole exchange from beginning to end and remembered Frost's words for the rest of his life. 'He said "Come out over the fence," he said, "and I'll teach you a lesson". He said, "Come on, put 'em up."' When the keeper put up not his fists but his shotgun, the poets did not stay to complete the lesson: they 'went off a bit smartish like', said Hill.[18]

For Ted Hill the incident had little to do with notions of 'gentry', as Frost would claim, and everything to do with 'spying'. The countryside was rife with suspicion towards anything and anyone out of the ordinary. The post office at nearby Bromsberrow Heath, he said, was run by a blind man, German, a 'perfeck stranger', who was thought to be a spy. And that was the concern about Frost and Thomas, Hill recalled: they had arrived in the area at about the same time and on the eve of war, and they lived close by one another, and Frost spoke English strangely. They were suspicious all right and the keeper was doing his job as would have been expected, thought Hill; in fact, the strangers were very lucky not to have been filled with lead shot that day.

The poets walked back along the bridle path to the Gallows, Frost's anger cooling into a satisfaction with his own response; but not Thomas's, who wished that the incident had never arisen and that his mettle had not been tested in the presence of his friend. The next day the constable from Ryton arrived at the Gallows to inform Frost that a complaint had been made against him of threatening the keeper with bodily harm, and explained that while he was sure that it was nothing he was nonetheless obliged to investigate all such complaints, and issued the American with a summons to appear before the local magistrate. With Abercrombie still away, Frost turned for help to Wilfrid Gibson, but to the American's horror his neighbour refused to side with him against the gamekeeper. Like the Gallows, Gibson's cottage at Greenway Cross was in the gift of the Beauchamp estate, and he was not about to risk his tenancy over a dispute with a gamekeeper who, after all, was Albright's – and possibly also Lord Beauchamp's – man. Frost's fury would now turn on Gibson, but thankfully Abercrombie at least did come to his friend's aid, calling on Jack Haines in his role as a solicitor for legal guidance on how they might respond.

My dear Haines,

Frost, I hope, has by this [time] put before you his trouble with Albright's keeper. I am trying to get at Albright personally, but don't yet know what the result will be. And if he won't keep his keeper in order, I am determined to bring the law in if it *can* come in. As to the affair in the wood, we can, of course, do nothing; but when the keeper takes to threatening Frost *in the road*, the affair is obviously intolerable and must be put a stop to. Preferably, as I say, by getting directly at Albright; for I still think there must be some misunderstanding. But I should like to know now whether the fellow's brutal behaviour does make him liable to a summons. I understand Frost has Thomas as a witness. Sorry to trouble you!

Yours in haste

Lascelles Abercrombie.[19]

Abercrombie understood well the different implications between an encounter in private woodland and one on the public highway, where neither Albright's nor Lord Beauchamp's jurisdiction extended. Haines must have urged caution and calm, and while his reply is lost, his advice effects a change in attitude from Abercrombie, who writes again a few days later.

My dear Haines,

Many thanks for your most sensible letter. My sole reason for writing to you was on account of the alleged insult in the road, which, if true, was clearly intolerable and to be put a stop to somehow or other. Thomas's description of it, however, scarcely bears out Frost's, and I now believe he had rather exaggerated the incident in a way which he is a trifle inclined to: I mean he is peculiarly sensitive to anything remotely resembling insult or deliberate annoyance to himself. This is not the first time he has been aggrieved. – As to the wood incident, he had, of course, no right there. I have permission, but that does not imply permission to my friends. The strange thing was that the keeper, knowing where Frost was staying (so Frost says) should have been so unpleasant. If you can see Frost it would be a great advantage. I believe the secret of the whole thing is that Frost does not know how to talk to such folks as keepers. We are all very well and hope you and your family are too.

Yours sincerely

Lascelles Abercrombie

[*margin*] I have asked my sister to interview Albright.[20]

Abercrombie skilfully persuaded the landowner not only to drop the case against Frost, but may also have succeeded in having the gamekeeper re-educated in his ways. In Frost's re-telling, Lord Beauchamp sent him no less than a personal apology, accompanied by an instruction to the gamekeeper that if he wanted so much to fight he had better enlist.[21]

In the days that followed, Thomas and Frost did their best to make light of the incident. Frost wrote to Monro at the Poetry Bookshop in ebullient terms:

Think of me as engaged in a little war of my own down here with a bad game keeper who attacked me for going where he allowed the Gibsons to go as gentry. Me he called a 'damned cottager'. *Now* who will have the better claim of the title of People's Poet? Thomas says it is the best testimonial I have had and I must get my publisher to use the game keeper in advertising me – that is, if I survive my war with the brute – and even if I don't.[22]

But the mood at the Gallows had become more uncertain. Frost was unaware of the degree to which Abercrombie and Haines and even Thomas mistrusted his handling of the episode. Whatever the motives for Gibson's behaviour, he understood, as Thomas did, the rules that governed English country affairs, and it was apparent to all that Frost did not. But Frost would not forgive Gibson for his lack of support, and made no effort to conceal it. 'I can't help looking on him as the worst snob I met in England and I can't help blaming the snob he is for the most unpleasant memory I carried away from England: I mean my humiliating fight with the gamekeeper. Gibson is a coward and a snob not to have saved me from that.' Frost's feelings for Gibson would never recover.[23]

Back at the Gallows, Thomas watched a storm picking up in the trees; he imagined he could hear the clothes on the line crackle like a wood fire rising. He turned over the day's events in his head. Had he acted cowardly? He felt certain of it and suspected Frost of thinking the same. Not once but twice had he failed to hold his ground, while his friend had no such difficulty standing his. Many times as a boy he had run the gauntlet of gamekeepers, sometimes slipping them, other times not and so taking their punishment; but they had never held any fear for him. Something had changed in him; something that amused him as a child now frightened him. The worst punishment that had befallen him as a boy had been to be dragged before his father; this time, with his father nowhere to answer for him, he had let Frost speak instead. His courage had been found wanting, at a time when men such as Rupert Brooke had found it in themselves to face genuine dangers.[24]

In the years that followed, Myfanwy Thomas would suggest that Frost was near to calling her father a coward for not squaring up to the gamekeeper. But Frost made no such suggestion; even had he believed it to be the case he would not have needed to express it. He knew that Thomas's profound self-examination would make that unnecessary. More likely the incident fuelled Frost's tendency to tease his friend for a timidity that he found 'funny and fascinating'. Thomas would not take a teasing well, and his feelings on the episode turned characteristically inward. 'I've thrown away a chance to fight a gamekeeper,' he would reflect, 'And I less often trespass.'[25]

The incident with the gamekeeper symbolised all that was rotten in the state of England's fields for Robert Frost.

We found that like as not the gamekeeper had his eye on us, squinting out from under his cap. One had to show a birth certificate to prove he wasn't a poacher and avoid arrest; and because one didn't have on knee breeches and a red coat they suspected the worse.

But it was an incident that Frost would overcome. In time, he would embrace it anecdotally, retelling the story with aplomb and making it fully his own as he would so many of the challenging episodes in his life, cheerily likening his treatment by Bott to that doled out by his English publisher. But for Edward Thomas, the encounter would leave him haunted. He would relive the moment again and again. In his verse and in his letters to Frost – in the week when he left for France, even in the week of his death – Thomas felt hunted by the fear and cowardice he had experienced in that stand-off with the gamekeeper. He felt mocked by events and probably by the most important friend of his life, and he vowed that he would never again let himself be faced down. When the call came again he would hold his nerve and face the gunmen.[26]

'That's why he went to war,' said Frost.[27]

The friends parted company at Newent station; Thomas returned to Steep a troubled man. But he was also a changed man. In the days that immediately followed his visit to Ryton, he would tackle the task of which Frost thought him wholly capable, if 'afeared'. A movement of gigantic, personal significance was underway. It had been surfacing before he met Frost, but it had taken the year's friendship for it to boil over. It would lift his spirits, deepen his tolerance, satisfy his life-long need to find self-worth. Never again would his chronic depression overwhelm him so utterly, never again would he think of himself as a mere hack. Not a different man, said Eleanor Farjeon, but the same man in another key.[28]

Edward Thomas was about to become a poet.

Winter

Early in November 1914, sometime in the weeks before visiting Frost at the Gallows, Edward Thomas had called at the White Horse inn on the Froxfield plateau above Wick Green, known as the pub with no name ever since its sign went missing from the frame that leaned from the blackthorn hedgerow into the road. The inn was a regular haunt for Thomas, his favourite of those which surrounded Steep, standing on higher ground than any in Hampshire. It was set back from the road in a ring of beech trees, surrounded by gorse in which stone curlews made their home. Thomas liked to sit in the low-ceilinged tap room after walking, writing his notes or listening to the cadence of conversations in the bar. In May he had told Frost of the new start he intended to make in his writing, to 'wring all the necks of my rhetoric – the geese', and on that November day he echoed that same phrase in a few hasty notes scribbled down in his notebook, beside an entry dated 2 November 1914.[1]

> I could wring the old girl's neck
> That put it here
> A public house! (Charcoal burner)
> by bringing up and quite outdoing
> The idea of London
> Two woods around and never a road in sight
> Trees roaring like a train without an end
> But she's dead long ago
> Only a motorist from far away
> Or marketers in carts once a fortnight
> Or a few fresh tramps ignorant
> of the house turning.

Thomas was a perennial note taker: he depended on his notebooks to refresh the details that would vitalise his prose. In them he recorded the landscape that he was moving through, a crook in a river, a cottage gable, the variety of birds in the hedgerow, whether the trees were elm or beech or yew, the direction of weather. But on this day, the jottings had a more conversational tone than usual, phrases that resembled less his topographic style and something more like the patterns of speech. *I could wring the old girl's neck | That put it here | A public house!* . . . twelve thin, disjointed lines quickly scribbled down. Thomas did not return to these notes immediately: he had commitments to fulfil to the *English Review* and *Poetry and Drama*. But on 16 November he did return, and began to craft a 1,200-word prose sketch in an exercise book to which he gave the title 'The White Horse'. The sketch began:

Tall beeches overhang the inn, dwarfing and half hiding it, for it lies back a field's breadth from the by road. The field is divided from the road by a hedge and only a path from one corner and a cart track from the other which meet under the beeches connect the inn with the road. But for a signboard or rather the post and empty iron frame of a signboard close to the road behind the hedge a traveller could not guess at an inn. The low dirty white building looks like a farmhouse, with a lean-to, a rick and a shed of black boarding at one side . . .

The prose continued to describe the situation of the inn on the high plateau, and it introduced what it now became apparent was an individual speaker of the lines jotted in the field notebook: a girl who had been born in the isolated inn, but had departed and returned to find it an exposed, forsaken place, where the wind howled through the trees.

'I should like to wring the old girl's neck for coming away here.' So said the woman who fetched my beer when I found myself at the inn first. She was a daughter of the house, fresh from a long absence in service in London, a bright wildish slattern with a cockney accent

and her hair half down. She spoke angrily. If she did not get away
before long, she said, she would go mad with loneliness. She looked
out sharply: all she could see there was nothing but the beeches and
the tiny pond beneath them and the calves standing in it drinking,
alternately grazing the water here and there thinking, and at last
going out and standing still on the bank thinking.[2]

There is no reason to suppose that the piece was intended
to be anything other than a short prose piece; but sometime
between concluding the draft on 16 November and returning in
early December from his visit to Frost, Thomas did something
extraordinary that he had not systematically attempted in years.
He began a poem.

> 'I cd wring the old thing's neck that put it here!
> A public house! it may be public for
> Squirrels and such like and ghosts of charcoal burners
> Or highwaymen . . .'

The poem had opened with stride, confidence and a command of
tone. Instinctively it had found its form in variable blank verse,
in a loose iambic pentameter that moved the poem calmly but
surely forward: I could *wring* the *old* thing's *neck* that *put* it *here!* |
A *pub*lic *house* it *may* be *pub*lic *for* . . . Thomas continued,

> . . . 'But I call it a hermitage

He paused; this was possibly the first wrong step. The hermit-
age was not necessary to the story of the poem, he realised,
or at least not necessary at this point in the tale; he should
let the speaker – and more importantly, the reader – pause
for breath. Thomas took his pen and struck out the line. He
continued.

> . . . The wild girl laughed.

(or maybe simply 'She' laughed? No, the former had the better
scansion)

                                        ... 'But I
        Loathe it ~~and sort~~ since I came back from Kennington
        And 'twas to see it. And for nothing else

no, not that,

                                ... since I came back from Kennington
        And gave my place up.'

not quite. Again,

        ... gave up a good place.'

Yes, that was it. From the top, then, Thomas read back:

        'I could wring the old thing's neck that put it here!
        A public house! it may be public for
        Squirrels and such like and ghosts of charcoal burners
        Or highwaymen.' The wild girl laughed. 'But I
        Loathe it since I came back from Kennington
        And gave up a good place.'

With these five and a half lines, the poem had its opening. He
continued:

                                ... Her Cockney accent only

no, not *only*, that was an unwanted extra couple of syllables,

                                ... Her Cockney accent
        Made her seem wilder
        Made her and the place seem wilder as she shrieked at me

too long, too harsh. He tried again, but found only wrong
turnings:

                                ... seem wilder by calling up
            ~~Through tassled tumbled hair~~
            ~~Pausing~~ there in her ~~scrubbing~~
            ~~And then subduing quite the idea of~~
            To be subdued immediately by wildness
            Only to be subdued at once by wildness

The idea of London here in this forest parlour.
~~shade~~
~~Under the beech murmurs~~
~~beech tree mur~~
~~Under the~~

Maddeningly, the poem was getting away from him. The start had been assured, but now he was becoming disoriented by the many possible paths that were opening up before him. Over the next few hours the draft moved both forward and backward. He would strike through every third or fourth line, but still he made rapid progress, filling four pages of the exercise book with 100 lines and more of the poem with all the speed that his training in journalism had lent him.[3]

Some sections snapped quickly into place; others were more of a struggle. Three simple lines about the ploughing up of charcoal took him a dozen attempts to find his way, but find his way he eventually did, until the draft began to peter once more, this time toward the end, where it finished on an inconsequential note.

Once upon a time 'twas plain the inn and smithy
    on
Stood merely ~~over~~ the border of a waste
~~Through which the road meandered~~
  horse or   ~~take~~
Where ~~ever~~ cart could ~~make its~~ pick its own new course
~~Paths come on all sides to the inn~~
On all sides, then as now, paths ran to the inn
But not one road. And a farmtrack from a gate

As an ending this was hopeless and Thomas knew it. Instinctively he moved these lines into the first third of the poem, which left the draft to conclude with the serving girl stating that despite her complaining she intended to remain at the inn.

You won't catch me going back to Kennington.

I reckon I shall stay, ~~now the signs gone~~. But I do wish
Twasn't so lonely and the wind wouldn't ~~roar~~ sound so.

This was better, but an ending was required that was more suggestive and more resonant still: something that might deepen or elevate the experience, that might open out the possibilities of the poem. To find it, Thomas would do something that was entirely his own: he went back to the initial prose draft, to the calves grazing around the pond. In so doing he gave a clear illustration of how his mind was working at that moment: to use his prose as a well into which he might dip for poetry.

A second handwritten draft followed immediately, tidying up the sprawl of the first, and on Thursday 3 December, Thomas typed up the 115-line poem, making final amendments as he went. Here is the poem's opening and its closing:

UP IN THE WIND

'I could wring the old thing's neck that put it here!
A public-house! it may be public for birds,
Squirrels and such-like, ghosts of charcoal-burners
And highwaymen.' The wild girl laughed. 'But I
Hate it since I came back from Kennington.
I gave up a good place.' Her Cockney accent
Made her and the house seem wilder by calling up –
Only to be subdued at once by wildness –
The idea of London, there in that forest parlour,
Low and small among the towering beeches
And the one bulging butt that's like a font.
. . .
                    Between the open door
And the trees two calves were wading in the pond,
Grazing the water here and there and thinking,
Sipping and thinking, both happily, neither long.
The water wrinkled, but they sipped and thought,
As careless of the wind as it of us.
'Look at those calves. Hark at the trees again.'[4]

If the opening owed something to his friend Robert Frost in their conversational eclogue, these final lines were utterly Thomas's. In laying them down he had demonstrated to himself a key notion: that his poem should use only words that his speaker, the girl, might use, and should find rhythms in the poem that rightly reflected her rhythms of speech. Rigid iambic pentameter would have sounded unnatural in the mouth of this wild-eyed girl, but blank verse – extending or contracting a line where need be – was the right expression for the mixture of casual gossip and dramatic energy with which the poem spoke.

His first poem had emerged in an unwieldy manner from his prose, but it was, in an important sense, better than his prose. The prose had done everything asked of it: polite, unshowy lines pitched at the level of a quietly spoken conversation; but the poem had that and more besides: it had cadence and it had drama. It was an extraordinary first effort, full of character and good phrasing; tonally, perhaps, it borrowed from his friend Robert Frost, and by the standards of poetry it carried a prosaic bagginess that he would have to shake off; but in places it soared with an energy and confidence that showed glimpses of the promise to come.

Thomas left his study at Wick Green and descended through the December darkness of the Hangers to Yew Tree Cottage. The most severe of self-critics, he remained dissatisfied with the poem he had written and would omit it when the time came to prepare his book. But his lack of satisfaction would simply drive him on, and he would return to his study the following morning and make a start on an entirely new poem.

For the next four days Thomas climbed through the hanger woods to his study to begin a new poem with each new day. 'November', his second, was, like his first, developed from a rough prose paragraph that he had jotted down in his notebook days before, but it was a piece quite unlike the first in every other way. It emerged not in the blank verse of 'Up in the Wind', but was instead clasped in rhyming couplets, using a song phrasing of Thomas's own that overlaid a more familiar medieval calendric rhyme, 'Thirty days hath September'. With its fascination with the seasons and the weather, the poem signalled a subject matter that would become a hallmark of Thomas's verse.

> November's days are thirty:
> November's earth is dirty,
> Those thirty days, from first to last;
> And the prettiest things on ground are the paths . . .

It was an uncomplicated piece of natural observation, never entirely comfortable in its skin; 'a shade sententious', thought Thomas, and owing a debt to Shelley that few but Thomas would have noticed had he not pointed it out. At so early a stage in his verse, Thomas had an eye for detail that was stronger than his sense of the poem, and this one swung unevenly in and out of its guiding rhyme and metre; but he posted it nonetheless to Ryton to draw Frost's comments. The draft had included phrasings that seemed either too precious or too trivial to the American, and Thomas was grateful for the 'kick' to set him straight. 'The foot's seal and the wing's light word', Thomas had written frothily until Frost advised against it, and helped him settle upon a phrasing that was altogether sturdier. 'I am glad that you spotted "wing's light word",' wrote Thomas appreciatively. 'I knew it was wrong and also that many would like it.' Knowing that many would like it and yet that it was wrong: in only his second poem, Thomas had tackled a challenge that all poets must address some time in their development – namely, that popularity may need to be conceded for the sake of a better poem. It can take years for a young poet to learn the importance of that sacrifice, but it had taken Thomas just two poems in two days.[5]

Next morning, 5 December, Thomas climbed up through Ashford Hanger once again to the Bee House and settled in to compose a companion piece to 'November' which he called 'March'.

> Now I know that Spring will come again,
> Perhaps tomorrow: however late I've patience
> After this night following on such a day.

If Frost's hand was apparent in the conversational tone of 'Up in the Wind', and in the revised lines of 'November', in 'March' it took a more inspirational touch still. Thomas's search for a true spring had been the subject of the prose book he gave to Frost, *In Pursuit of Spring*, and now these first three lines seemed to reflect Frost's urging for Thomas to revisit those lines of prose, and to write them, as Frost put it, 'in verse form in exactly the same cadence'. In prose:

All the thrushes of England sang at that hour, and against that background of myriads I heard two or three singing their frank, clear notes in a mad eagerness to have all done before dark; for already the blackbirds were chinking and shifting places along the hedgerows.

In verse:

> What did the thrushes know? Rain, snow, sleet, hail,
> Had kept them quiet as the primroses.
> They had but an hour to sing. On boughs they sang,
> On gates, on ground; they sang while they changed perches
> And while they fought, if they remembered to fight:
> So earnest were they to pack into that hour
> Their unwilling hoard of song . . .

What did the thrushes know? There, in those five words, is a phrasing that is already and entirely Thomas's own. The questioning, doubtful tone, the restless enquiry, the fallibility of a poet's voice: these were already instinctively, distinctively, the voice of Edward Thomas. Some Georgian poets might promise to understand a bird and 'translate' it for the reader's benefit; others might even claim to become the bird itself and live the experience on behalf of the reader. But Edward Thomas was altogether more equivocal in his promise, knowing that as a human being he must always remain outside of the experience of the animal, as if knowledge itself was uncertain, guessed at, and yet still possible to catch for the careful listener, at least in the moment of birdsong. 'Something they knew – I also, while they sang': as close to the animal as we are ever likely to get, a vague sharing of we know not what through song – these were marks of Thomas.[6]

But if the ideology was tentative and subtle, the craft was gaining in confidence. Thomas had finished three of the final nine lines with the word 'silence': a bold use of repetition in a form where each word counts for so much. It was a courageous move that might be expected of a veteran poet; but Thomas was accelerating his apprenticeship. The past three days had brought impressive results, but on the fourth day Thomas would achieve something spectacular.

In the same exercise book in which he wrote his short prose 'The White Horse' is another from 17 November 1914, called 'Old Man's Beard'. The title may have been a rare slip from Thomas, for the plant he wrote of in the piece was not Old Man's Beard but old man, a southernwood shrub sometimes known as Lad's Love. The plant was a gift from Gordon Bottomley upon moving into Wick Green in December 1909; by April 1910 it had grown to become 'a beautiful great bush' at Thomas's study window. When the family moved down the hill and into the cramped Yew Tree Cottage in 1913, Thomas took a cutting from the bush and planted it beside the front door of the new home.[7]

On 11 November 1914 Thomas had scribbled in his field note-book: '*Old Man* scent, I smell again and again not really liking it but venerating it because it holds the secret of something very long ago which I feel it may someday recall, but I have got no idea what.' The thought of writing about the redolent smell had been with him for some time (at least since a story from the summer of 1909 called 'The Old House'), but in November 1914 a prose draft followed the inscriptions in his notebook, just as it had with 'Up in the Wind'. 'Old Man's Beard' was less than 300 words in length and carried the feel of an accomplished prose poem, beginning with an image of Myfanwy taking in the scent, and concluding,

No garden comes back to me, no hedge or path, no grey green bush called old man's beard or lad's love, no figure of mother or father or playmate, only a dark avenue without an end.

A little less than three weeks later, and Thomas roughed out a draft in verse.

> Old Man or Lad's Love. – in the name there's nothing
> To one that knows not Lad's Love or Old Man.

The first two lines had snapped cleanly into place, but when it came to describe the herb itself Thomas unexpectedly fumbled his lines. Three or four times he went about the plant's description, finding the line and then losing it again. But mostly he moved forward with little correction. The intense crossing-out that had characterised the first poems, the transposing of sections, the striking-through of ideas: mostly these were absent now as the act of drafting itself was rapidly becoming more assured. Where the first three poems had laboured and lurched, 'Old Man' had grown into itself very quickly, demonstrating Thomas's growing confidence with blank verse, unafraid to swell or contract the line by two or three syllables where necessary. No sooner had he finished than Thomas brushed down the poem in a second, cleaner draft that was almost without correction. With 'Up in the Wind' he had struggled for an ending, but here it was largely in place from the outset, nudged gently into position with each working draft:

> ... only a dark avenue without an end. [prose]
> Only a dark avenue: without end or name. [first draft]

Only an avenue dark without end or name. [second draft]
Only an avenue, dark, nameless, without end. [final draft][8]

'Old Man' was a poem of which Thomas was rightly proud, and one that caught the attention of editors. When in February 1917 Harriet Monroe took three of Thomas's poems for her Chicago *Poetry*, it was the piece she led off with, and when, a month later, Thomas was anthologised for the first time in England, this would be the first of eighteen poems printed in *An Annual of New Poetry*. It had taken a mere four poems for Thomas to find his voice.

On Monday 7 December, Thomas began his fifth poem in five days, 'The Signpost', which found a traveller standing at a junction unable to choose the path to take. Thomas had spoken of his indecision so often to his friends that to some – especially Frost – it had become an almost comic attribute of his character. But Thomas himself was less amused, and frequently felt anxiety towards the decisions he faced about his home life, about the way he earned his living and, recently, about the war. And now he was giving himself something else about which to decide: poetry. And the self-analysis was bursting through.

> I read the sign. Which way shall I go?
> A voice says: You would not have doubted so
> At twenty. Another voice gentle with scorn
> Says: At twenty you wished you had never been born.[9]

Once again, Thomas drew upon the method he had employed all week: beginning with a reaching back into his notebooks or his prose, then producing an incomplete first draft by hand in his exercise book, followed by a second in which he effectively completed the poem, then a third draft, typed, in which minor changes of tense or phrase would be made as he tidied up the poem for presentation. The time frame from the first draft to the typed poem was usually a single day. The opening of this poem gave him more difficulties than he had experienced earlier in the week, and the fit of the form was not at all obvious to him: first he used rhyming couplets, then quatrains, then back to couplets. The first draft brought him eighteen lines, the second a further twelve, and by the end of the afternoon he had an accomplished draft.[10]

Throughout Thomas's prose are figures at a crossroads uncertain of their path ahead; here, in his verse, the speaker of the poem is left standing at the signpost paralysed by indecision. The need to make decisions and the fear of doing so would be an emblem of Thomas's thinking and writing over the next six months as he wavered about the war. And something else too: Thomas would send the poem to Frost the following week, and it would reinforce in Frost the line of thinking about his friend that resulted in the American's most famous poem of all, 'The Road Not Taken'. But that poem was still a year and a half away, and for now it was Thomas not Frost who was experiencing a creative explosion in a remarkable week of poetry.

'My works come pouring in on you now,' Thomas told Frost on 15 December. 'Tell me all you dare about them.' Less than a fortnight after completing his first poem, Thomas had not only sent his friend a batch of verses in Ryton, but had had a reply and had written in response to that reply. Thomas's industry was frantic, even manic: poems and letters about poems and replies to those letters about poems. There was little room for family or for worrying about money: the experience was all consuming. He confessed to Frost of feeling 'uncommonly cheerful mostly', pleased with some of the pieces, but something else besides. 'I find myself engrossed and conscious of a possible perfection as I never was in prose,' he said. 'Still, I won't begin thanking you just yet, tho if you like I will put it down now that you are the only begetter right enough.'[11]

In that first week of poetry, Thomas had established most of the themes that would characterise his verse in the two years ahead: the rhythms of speech and thought and song, the variable blank verse form, the use of country characters who would conduct his narratives, the elemental conditions of the weather and the seasons, the spaces in which the human and the natural worlds intersect, the power of memory and of childhood, the hesitation and doubt that he found so disabling in his own life. His writing would get clearer, more focussed and more memorable, but there would be few new themes introduced after that first week. One such new theme, however, would arrive in the next few days. It was a feature that had touched his prose in recent years and had been guided to the surface by Godwin Baynes; now it would feature in his verse. It saw Thomas at his most schizophrenic, at his darkest and most interesting: it was the projection of his alter ego upon his writing.

'The Other', probably from the second week of December 1914, was one of four poems written that week for which no manuscripts survive; only a single typescript, retained by Robert Frost, ensured that the poem was preserved at all. Like 'March', 'The Other' seemed to take a helping hand from Frost's directive to look back at his prose such as *In Pursuit of Spring* and write it again in verse cadence. The 'Other Man' then had ridden with Thomas along his trail from London to Somerset, and it is likely that his appearance in that book recalled in Frost an episode in the American's past, when he encountered his own double on a snowy wood road in New Hampshire and 'felt as though I was going to meet my own image in a slanting mirror'. More chilling, more energised and more disturbing than any of its appearances in prose, 'The Other' had a distinct formal structure: ten stanzas of ten lines (Thomas added an eleventh verse in his note to Frost), in loose iambic tetrameter and a novel but rigid rhyme scheme which pinched and pushed at the reader's senses. Thomas knew instinctively how rhyme eased the transmission

of a poem, but here he deliberately stacked the rhymes vertigin-
ously in a way that made them tense and clipped, hunched at
the shoulders of the poem, and so setting the reader's nerves
jangling.[12]

'The forest ended,' the poem began, in the most beguiling
of the openings that Thomas had found to date. Out into the
clearing the 'I' emerges glad of the light, glad of the smell of
mint and grass, and finds before him an inn. There, he is mistaken for another man, a double, identical in every way, who
had slept there the night before. The 'I' is gripped by a sense of
fear and yet, urged on by some unarticulated desire, he chooses
to pursue the man in the hope to 'outrun that other', with no
clear notion of what he would do were he to catch him. Days
pass without a sighting, the 'I' ever more driven to confrontation. In a tap room in a roadside inn, where the 'I' is taking rest,
he hears above the pub chatter the voice of the Other Man asking for him, telling the bartender of a figure he knew had been
following him, oppressing him, chasing him down; and with the
tables turned suddenly, the once-persecuted now-persecuting
'I' slips silently from the inn. The 'I' continues to follow the
'Other', but at distance, careful not to be detected. And so it
would go on: the 'Other' pursued, unable to rest; the 'I' pursu-
ing, unable to give up the chase.

In 1911, in a pit of despair, Thomas had written to a friend
about his doctors' decision to prescribe him a vegetarian diet. 'I
hope it will cure my head, which is almost always wrong now –
a sort of conspiracy going on in it which leaves me only a joint
tenancy and a perpetual scare of the other tenant and wonder
what he will do.' The 'joint tenancy' had been crippling at times
for Thomas. More often than not, it took the form of a critical or mocking voice from within: an inner judge who was not
afraid to voice his contempt of Thomas's behaviour, his decisions
or his talents. Thomas had met him in *The South Country*, 'a tall,
spare, shock-headed man' escaping the life of a town clerk for

the country. He had met him again on the Icknield Way, 'a lean, indefinite man' lamenting a raft of lost opportunities. He had been a projection in *The Happy-Go-Lucky Morgans*, and elsewhere, in a short story, 'a poet of a kind, who made a living out of prose'. He was the voice who mocked him in 'The Signpost', and now it appeared that he would be pursued into the realm of his verse.[13]

Thomas had sent his fortnight's work to Frost, but his friend was not the only recipient of his poems. With some boldness, he sent them also to Harold Monro at the Poetry Bookshop. 'I enclose some poems which I should like you to look at,' wrote Thomas on 15 December. 'If you think anything of them the writer, who wishes to be very strictly anonymous, would like to see a small book of these and others. I deliver myself into your hands.' That Thomas felt able to send his work to the leading poetry journal of the day a mere two weeks into his apprenticeship said much for the self-belief he had attained.[14]

After ten poems in two weeks, Thomas took a few days' break from writing verse. Christmas came and went, the family all together for once and enjoying one another's company ('in the modified Thomas style', he said). But even amid the opening of presents and the washing up of dinner plates, Thomas did not neglect his poetry for long. Set at the Elizabethan house at Prior's Dean on the Froxfield plateau north of Steep, 'The Manor Farm' was a transitional poem for Thomas that carried cadences of Frost's (Thomas: 'But earth would have her sleep out, spite of the sun'; Frost: 'But they would have the rabbit out of hiding'). But it contained moments in which Thomas was using a syntax that was quite his own: 'The air raised not a straw,' he wrote, knowing that no other wording would work so precisely as this; a dignified, respectful syntax, mild in its formality, iambic for the memory's aid. There were false notes too: an awkward elision 'But 'twas not Winter', in no way needed for the metre, seemed an elevated, poetic stroke. But he was confident of his ending when challenged by a friend: 'I rather think I will stick to it,' he wrote, adding sagely, 'If one can feel what one has written and not what one *meant* . . .'[15]

On Christmas Day, Thomas wrote a song based on a traditional ballad, 'The Lincolnshire Poacher', which he now adapted to reflect his encounter with 'ole Bott' at Ryton only a month before:

> Since then I've thrown away a chance to fight a gamekeeper;
> And I less often trespass, and what I see or hear
> Is mostly from the road or path by day: yet still I sing:
> 'Oh, 'tis my delight of a shiny night in the season of the year.'

From an early age, Thomas had loved the song form; given the opportunity in adult life he readily compiled an anthology of his favourite selections in *The Pocket Book of Poems and Songs for the Open Air*. He liked to sing to himself as he walked across the south country or to Myfanwy as she sat on his knee before bed. Thomas was a fine singer with a musical ear and a drive to explore musical phrasings that would distinguish him from Frost. His friend had a gift for hearing the speaking voice and for casting it into speech rhythms, but he was no musician; and while the poems that Thomas wrote in song form may not have been among his finest efforts, he would frequently use the measures and the line breaks of ballad and of song form to vary his natural leaning towards blank verse.[16]

Two shorter poems followed, set in the coppice that surrounded the narrow Ashford stream at Lutcombe in Steep, each skilful in its use of repetition to tune the reader's ear to the circumstance of the poem. 'The Combe' was the more powerful of the two with its tone of foreboding and its harking back to the older, Celtic woodlands, and the badger, 'That most ancient Briton of English beasts', dug out and given to the hounds. Thomas had finished fifteen poems in the month of December – eclogues, blank verse, ballads, poems short and long – roughly one quarter of the number that he would need to compile a collection for the Poetry Bookshop. But on that front his verse now received its first setback. Harold Monro wrote to say that he did not have time to consider Thomas's work. Thomas – who had contributed, unpaid, the best of the articles that *Poetry and Drama* had published over the past two years, the figure whom many thought the leading critic of his day and the greatest catch that Monro had made for the journal, a man who had just broken into verse – for him, inexplicably, Monro could not spare the time to read his first poems. Thomas was stunned. 'I sent what I had to Monro asking for secrecy. He kept it 4 days and then said he hadn't had time to read it, so I took it back rather crestfallen, tho it is quite possible that he meant he hadn't been able to get anyone to help him to an opinion.'[17]

It would be only the first of a series of setbacks that Thomas would receive on the long road to the publication of his verse.

As December deepened, it became increasingly apparent to the British public that the war would not be over by Christmas. Edward Thomas was no more decided than before about enlistment and at the beginning of the month had even written to his literary agent to seek his thoughts. 'You startle me by saying you are not sure whether or not you should enlist,' Cazenove had replied. 'That is a matter which every man must settle with himself, but I should have thought your calls were elsewhere.' London was teeming with soldiers in the run-up to Christmas, and it startled Robert Frost to find several of them in the Poetry Bookshop when he called in one morning. A young man in uniform eyed him for a short while before approaching him and opening a discussion that kept the men engaged for some time. The soldier was Robert Graves, still only nineteen, who listened patiently as Frost mused briefly on whether or not he, as an American, should enlist in the British Army, before turning to the reception of his work by publishers in the United States.

'They say the germans [sic] have made the whole Atlantic unsafe', Frost had written that month. 'This raises questions for me.'

1) Do I dare to go home now?
2) Won't it be more dangerous to go every day we delay?
3) Won't it be impossible to get money across to live on pretty soon?
4) Do I dare to stay?

The letter caught Frost's dilemma on the horns. And yet it was not everything that it appeared to be. In a letter from earlier that month, now lost, Robert Frost had written to Thomas to tell him of his 'few remaining weeks here', and though he did not yet have a timetable for a departure, the course of action was at least decided upon. When he left, Mervyn would go with him; this too was now decided upon. Thomas let his thoughts turn to his fourteen-year-old son and the life he would now experience on the other side of the Atlantic. 'I thought it might be god's idea to get Mervyn away from me for ever.'[18]

On New Year's Day 1915, Edward Thomas settled into a poem in which a man leaning on a rake was mistaken from a distance as possessing a third leg. Though the man in the poem was not of serving age, the image of maimed or paraplegic men on crutches was becoming a more familiar sight in the cities, one which Thomas would have seen in his visits to London and which seemed now to have entered his verse. The man wished the new year would come soon, as the public had wished for Christmas, but his words were muffled by the roar of the wind through the trees. Thomas would write many poems over the next two years in which the events of the war took place obliquely in the margins of the page: the missing cast of characters who had been killed in France, the unattended garden tools, the rusty harrow, the older men missing their mates, the bereft wives. But he would never write of or from the trenches. In his poems of early January, the source of a river would be found 'drowning the sound of earth', a brook 'roaring with black hollow voices', while another, written on 8 January, found him asking himself whether the protection of beauty required a physical or even violent defence.[19]

As it happened, Thomas had just ensured that he himself would be incapable of any form of physical defence for some time to come. On 2 January, descending the Shoulder of Mutton, he sprained his ankle so severely that he would be unable to put any weight on it for several weeks. It was not until 6 January that he was able to make it out of bed and into the deck chair that Helen had brought into the bedroom. The sprain would leave him immobile for the month, and inconvenienced for much longer, and for the time being would kick any thought of enlistment into touch. But for his poetry it would be a tremendous blessing.

Laid up in his bedroom in Yew Tree Cottage, Thomas began to tell his friends openly for the first time about the poetry he had started writing. 'I have even begun to write verse,' he told Jesse Berridge, 'but don't tell a soul, as if it is to be published at all it must be anonymously.' He dug out a selection of poems to send to Eleanor Farjeon, and invited her to keep any that she liked provided she made typed copies, for he was sending his only typescripts. By 7 January he was able to sit in his deck chair for most of the day with his foot up, and by 10 January was finally able to make it downstairs. But he could only hop, and was in a filthy temper. Under the low ceilings of the cottage, he penned a claustrophobic trimeter in tight rhyming couplets about his desire to be out under the open skies. 'While I, I know that trees | Under that lofty sky | Are weeds, fields mud, and I would arise and go far | To where the lilies are.' *Arise and go?* Yeats's 'Lake Isle of Innisfree' had not been far from his thoughts, but the more interesting influence within these lines was still to be felt: the resonating 'I, I' that Robert Frost would echo when he wrote 'The Road Not Taken'.[20]

Eleanor Farjeon was reading all of Thomas's verse by January. She wrote with some comments about Thomas's use of rhythm, to which he replied, 'If I am consciously doing anything I am trying to get rid of the last rags of rhetoric and formality which left my prose so often with a dead rhythm only,' adding, 'If I can be honest and am still bad at rhythm it will be because I am bad in rhythm.' A few days later Eleanor wrote again, this time about his use of rhyme. Once again Thomas responded with frank insight, 'I don't believe rhyme is at all a *bad* trouble. I use it now more often than not and always fancy I leave the rhymed pieces as easy as the rest, but tho I am so young a versifier I don't pretend to be sure.' The ankle may have curtailed his movements but had offered him an uninterrupted run at his poems, and the result had been a literary dam burst. Confined to the cottage, between 4 and 23 January, Thomas completed sixteen poems in twenty days.[21]

As Edward Thomas read back through his field notebooks on 8 January, he came across this entry from his train ride to Dymock on 24 June 1914.

A glorious day from 4.20 a.m. & at 10 tiers above tiers of white cloud with dirtiest grey bars above the sea of slate and dull brick by Battersea Pk – then at Oxford tiers of pure white with loose longer masses above and gaps of dark clear blue above haymaking and elms.

'Then we stopped at Adlestrop', the notebook had continued, and quickly it had suggested to Thomas the easy, wistful tone that would become his most loved and best remembered poem; but its opening lines had been anything but effortless.

> Yes I remember Adlestrop,
> At least the name. One afternoon
>   train
> The express ⌃ slowed down there and drew up
> Quite

He stopped and scored this out with a rapid repeated stroke, and underneath he started again, this time giving the poem its title and changing the variety of the train.

> Yes, I remember Adlestrop,
> At least the name. One afternoon
> Of heat The ~~steam~~ train slowed ~~down~~ and drew up
> There unexpectedly. 'Twas June.

He had reworked the third line and added a fourth, and from there the three remaining stanzas followed rapidly with just two minor corrections along the way. But he remained unsatisfied with the first stanza and made two further attempts at tightening it. Of course the train had to be 'express' if it was to pull up 'unexpectedly', he reasoned, though about this word he also had doubts and tried 'Against its custom' before he hit upon exactly the word he wanted: 'unwontedly'.

ADLESTROP

> Yes. I remember Adlestrop –
> The name, because one afternoon
> Of heat the express-train drew up there
> Unwontedly. It was late June.
>
> The steam hissed. Someone cleared his throat.
> No one left and no one came
> On the bare platform. What I saw
> Was Adlestrop – only the name
>
> And willows, willow-herb, and grass,
> And meadowsweet, and haycocks dry,
> No whit less still and lonely fair
> Than the high cloudlets in the sky.
>
> And for that minute a blackbird sang
> Close by, and round him, mistier,
> Farther and farther, all the birds
> Of Oxfordshire and Gloucestershire.

Of all the poems that Edward Thomas would leave behind, it is these sixteen lines of loose tetrameter that are perhaps hardest to put a finger on. What is it that has gotten so under the skin of readers over the years? This gently chimed poem, cherished among the nation's favourites, has none of the expressive rhythm that Thomas so championed in Frost, and none of his dramatic narrative. Perhaps it is something to do with the lazed, heat-filled atmosphere it evokes of that last summer before the war (its provenance a mere six weeks before the start of the conflict, its drafting less than six months later), or the inscrutable chorus of birdsong into which the poem dissolves. Most probably, it is not the pinpointing of any particular episode or event that stirs this poem to life, but something about the wordlessness of thought and memory, the power of recall, the notion that the senses are capable of remembrance, and that the mind can overcome things lost or misplaced to travel across space or time; what one of Thomas's greatest admirers, Ivor Gurney, would call, 'nebulously intangibly beautiful'. It would be published in the *New Statesman* three weeks after Edward Thomas's death.[22]

The month's outpouring of poetry had been extraordinary, but Thomas was keenly aware that these verses, however pleasing, were not a source of income, and as he looked over his finances for the month he realised that he had earned a sum total of two pounds in January. It came as a welcome relief when, on 24 February, he received a cheque from the *English Review* for £11 6s. 10d. He told John Freeman that he still wished to join Frost in America but wondered where the money might come from. And now he had in his pocket the literature on enlistment that he had collected from the National Service League.

It isn't glory that I want, but just to get rid of the thoughts I have had since I first felt I ought to do something, tho I never felt I could except under what seems a sort of alien compulsion. I hate all crowds. I hate uncertainty. So naturally I hate the idea of being in the army in any capacity.[23]

By the beginning of February, Frost's final travel arrangements were falling into place, but not Mervyn's, for whom an obstacle now arose. Having left his enquiries rather late, Frost discovered that, at fifteen, the boy was under-age by a year in the eyes of US immigration. Frost urged Thomas to make contact with the American Consulate in London. 'Say who you are and who I am that he is going with. Ask if he would better have a passport. Say he may be staying a matter of a year or two and leave it to the consul to mention ages if he likes to. Hurry this up.' A gloom descended over the Thomas household: they had depended upon Frost to know the particularities of US immigration, and now became anxious that at the eleventh hour he would disappoint Mervyn and leave the boy behind. Frost, meanwhile, was caught up in preparations for the journey home. On 5 February, the family moved out of the Gallows and into Oldfields in Ledington, and gave away their furniture in return for a week's board. The pull home to America away from the European war was stronger now than ever, Frost told Jack Haines. 'I can't help being glad I decided to use the protection of our flag.'[24]

At Steep, Thomas was still immobile, and continued dutifully typing his English anthology and speculating as to whether the cyclist corps might be the right place for him if he were to serve when he recovered. He wrote 'House and Man' (a poem that possibly provoked Frost's 'An Old Man's Winter Night'), but his ankle was too badly sprained to make one last journey to Dymock to see his friend depart. Frost had offered to put back their boat tickets if Thomas would return to Gloucestershire one last time, but Thomas was in no state to go, and Frost conceded that, 'we doubt if it would be wise to put off that evil day'. And so Frost came to Thomas, and at 10.15 on the morning of 6 February he and his family arrived in Hampshire to say their goodbyes. They stayed from Saturday until Tuesday morning, the poets sitting up late each evening in the cramped Yew Tree Cottage, talking into the small hours. So much had changed since they had first spoken this way a year ago. In Frost's words: 'Thomas and I had become so inseparable that we came to be looked on as some sort of literary Siamese twins in a literary scene, with a spiritual bond holding us together.' With the American's retreat home, that bond would now be tested to the full, in what must have been a private agony for Thomas. Frost had brought him inspiration and humour, kindness and sympathy and understanding; he had listened with patience to his complaints, he had encouraged him in his marriage and had guided his writing, roughed him up when called upon, and now Thomas would have to face all this by himself.[25]

After the Frosts departed, Thomas wrote a quiet, ruminative lyric in which he noticed the felling of a willow copse, appreciated only after it had gone:

> Strange it could have hidden so near!
> And now I see as I look
> That the small winding brook,
> A tributary's tributary, rises there.

On the morning of 11 February, the Thomases rose at six. Father and son said a strained goodbye, before the boy left with Helen, his travel documents still unresolved, to be reunited with the Frosts at Liverpool docks. Thomas wrote a hand-wringing poem for Mervyn that day:

> Parting today a double pain:
> First because it was parting; next
> Because the ill it ended vexed
> And mocked me from the Past again . . .

In fifteen years, Thomas had struggled to find a way to fully relate to his son. His own father had been pushily aspirational, and Edward would not make the same mistake with Mervyn; but he would make a different one, detaching himself to the point where his son was left uncertain of his father's feelings. 'It means the end of any chance of being anything to the boy,' Thomas told Eleanor. 'But I only hope I haven't been nothing to him for too long now.' Myfanwy, the youngest, felt it too, and commented once, 'For most of my life I have felt that he did not care for me.' Only Bronwen seemed to break through the barriers that he silently erected. She alone seemed capable of pulling him out of himself, whether through her delight in botany or her simple refusal to be down-trodden. It was to her that this uncollected lyric was written, inked into her schoolgirl autograph album, probably in 1914 or early 1915:

> This is the constellation of the Lyre:
> Its music cannot ever tire,
> For it is silent. No man need fear it:
> Unless he wants to, he will not hear it.

But starting that day Thomas tried in his letters to make manifest his love for Mervyn, through paper and ink in a way he had not managed in the flesh.[26]

Frost had not left time to make his other farewells personally, and sent hasty notes to Harold Monro, promising to return just as soon as he had made some money, and to F. S. Flint, thanking him for his introductions, leaving just enough time for a departing swing at Wilfrid Gibson ('You and I wont believe Gibsons is a better kind of poetry than mine,' he wrote to Sidney Cox. 'Solway Ford is one of his best. It is a good poem. But it is oh terribly made up'), and on 13 February he and his family stood with Mervyn on the gangway of the SS *St Paul* at Liverpool, preparing to board the ship that would take them home. He idled a few moments away chatting about his poetry to a ticket inspector who, reported Frost, urged him to stay in England 'till our greatness ripened a little more'. 'If I don't go now I wont go at all,' Frost had protested, and suggested playfully that if he stayed any longer he would become a British subject and might even take a run at the Poet Laureateship. The inspector, apparently an admirer of Robert Bridges, had thought that was more than enough of that and ushered the family aboard. The *St Paul* sailed for New York City under the cover of darkness, joining a convoy that was shepherded out into the Irish Sea by two naval destroyers. Among the flotilla was the *Lusitania*, a Cunard liner, that in only a few months' time would be sunk by a German U-boat, taking almost 1,200 lives. It would be the worst tragedy of the campaign at sea, and would begin to effect a change in public opinion that would lead to America entering the war.[27]

Helen would not have shared her husband's enthusiasm to send her son away with the two Americans of whom she had formed such a low opinion. For her eldest child at fifteen to be crossing the Atlantic in a time of war – and for an indefinite stay – could only have caused her distress, even if the plan was now for the family to follow him out when the conflict was over. She left with Myfanwy for a fortnight's break at Hatch, while Thomas took Bronwen into London, where his father was quarrelsome and his mother beleaguered. From Steep, he wrote a coded and ponderous lyric that he entitled 'Home', possibly alluding to the difficulties at Balham but possibly also reflecting his own peripatetic state of recent years. Steep had often been a suggestion as much as a lived reality, for him; latterly, at least, it had not been the site of conflict that it once was, but it had hardly been a place of happiness. Where was his home exactly? In Hampshire? In London? Or would it be overseas with Frost?

All the while, Thomas's restless conscience continued to needle him about the war. On 24 February he wrote of an owl's cry 'telling me plain what I escaped | And others could not': namely, enlistment. Eleanor, meanwhile, was by now sending out scores of Edward's poems to journals under his direction.

He asked her to use the pseudonym 'Edward Phillips', before changing his mind in favour of 'Edward Marendaz' from his mother's family, and then once again for the name that he was to stick with throughout his publishing of his poetry, 'Edward Eastaway', from his father's side. Thomas explained his desire for anonymity: 'I want to begin by doing without the advantages and disadvantages of being known,' he told John Freeman. 'I don't want to be asking for compliments from friends; also I don't feel at present that I could stand criticism.' When the poems were eventually returned by *Blackwood's Magazine* in March, Thomas took the news stoically. 'I suppose Blackwood just thought it looked very much like prose and was puzzled by the fact that it was got up like verse.' G. W. Blackwood had returned the pieces to Eleanor Farjeon, writing 'the poems are to me somewhat of a puzzle, and I do not think I could venture upon them. They are, however, exceedingly interesting, and I shall be very pleased indeed to consider anything else which Mr Eastaway may write at any time which he thinks likely to suit Maga.' What Thomas had received from *Blackwood's* was a note of encouragement, but he certainly was not relaying that to friends.[28]

The Atlantic crossing had been wretched: nine days of getting 'kicked about' in high seas, had brought seasickness and a vow by Robert Frost never to make the voyage again. Predictably, Mervyn's papers were not in order and for once Frost found himself in a situation of which he could not talk his way out. The boy was detained as an illegal alien and incarcerated at Ellis Island detention centre for the night. Frost had to ring around for help, and eventually connected with friends in New York City who were able to assist in the clearance of Mervyn's papers; but not before the boy had experienced life with, as Frost put it, 'the scum of the earth'. Elinor and the Frost children retired to a farm in Bethlehem, New Hampshire, where they would stay as paying guests until June, while Mervyn remained temporarily detained. It was not the triumphant return that Frost had hoped for, nor the arrival that Mervyn might have wished. 'The first sight of America was bad very bad and disposed us to sing Why did I cross the deep?' said Frost. But there was one piece of good news that awaited Frost when he stepped off the boat from England. On 20 February, while he was at sea, *North of Boston* had been published in New York City by Henry Holt and Company.[29]

Frost's journey may have been uncomfortable, but he and the family had at least arrived at their destination. On 28 February Rupert Brooke had set sail on a journey to the Dardanelles that he would not complete. His mood had been urgent and provocative. In January he had written to John Drinkwater in quarrelsome form from Dorset, where he was training with 'A' Company of the Hood Battalion, awaiting the orders that would take him towards Constantinople.

Not a bad place and time to die, Belgium, 1915? I want to kill my Prussian first. Better than coughing out a civilian soul amid bed-clothes and disinfectant and gulping medicines in 1950. The world'll be tame enough after the war, for those that see it. I had hopes that England'ld get on her legs again, achieve youth and merriment, and slough the things I loathe – capitalism and feminism and hermaphroditism and the rest. But on maturer consideration, pursued over muddy miles of Dorset, I think there'll not be much change. What there is for the better though. Certain sleepers have awoken in the heart. Come and die. It'll be great fun. And there's great health in the preparation. The theatre's no place, now.[30]

III

HIGH BEECH

1915–16

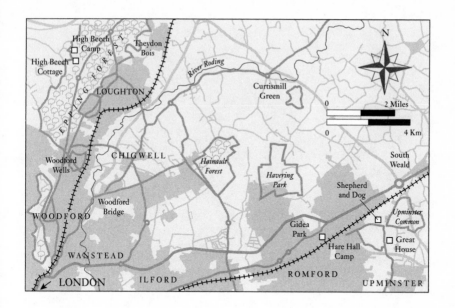

Spring

Snow lay on the ground in Steep late into February. Stoner Hill was locked in ice, and conditions for walking, had Thomas been capable of it, were treacherous. He was still lame, but now at least able to manage short distances. On 3 March Eleanor came for the night against the wishes of her mother, who believed that her daughter was caught in an unrequited relationship with Edward and that her visits could only cause her pain. But Eleanor came regardless, and encouraged Thomas out on a short walk. Mostly, when Thomas went walking, he took with him a stick to regulate his stride or aid an ascent. But now he needed one simply for balance as he eased himself back onto his feet after two months laid up. He took pride in making and seasoning his own sticks, and she recalled how his eye would scour the hedgerows and the tree roots as he walked, looking for an arm of ash or hazel or his favoured oak. When Eleanor left the next day, so did Thomas. Moving more freely now than at any time for two months, he took flight from Steep once again, to London and Coventry, returning to Helen after a week away.[1]

Consciously now, Thomas was examining the transition of his writing from prose into poetry, and he grasped each opportunity that came his way to discuss it. He told John Freeman, 'What I have done so far have been like the quintessences of the best parts of my prose books – not much sharper or more intense, but I hope a little: since the first take off they haven't been Frosty very much or so I imagine.' He was driven with a passion for writing that he had never experienced before. Some mornings Thomas could hardly wait to walk up the hill and light the fire in his study. His daily routine was now study–garden–study: rising at seven and climbing up to the Bee House, descending to Yew Tree Cottage at lunchtime, and returning to his study in the middle of the afternoon; bed at 11. He reached into his boyhood holidays in west Wales to write one of the comparatively few poems in which he drew on the Welsh countryside, relating a child's yearning (his brother's, he said cagily) for their mother. He wrote an accompanying poem which looked to his urban upbringing in London: once a place of suffocation for him, but now portrayed as a haven of sorts to the outsider. And in between these poems of Welsh country and English towns was sandwiched a short, unsettling lyric under whose arches the past and the future converged uneasily. He called it 'The Bridge', and wrote to John Freeman following a visit by his friend to Steep on 20 March: 'Do come down again and let us prove that we have some Englishness in common. You shan't label me Welsh whatever you do to escape my remarks.'[2]

His poems were reflecting the changing season, in particular the loosening of the frozen ground and the crops that Thomas was able now to sow in the garden of Yew Tree Cottage. He was trying out new forms when he could: short lyrics based on folk as well as verse metres, some of which struggled for effect. Meanwhile he continued to push Frost's poetry whenever he could, coaxing friends and nudging editors, but taking care to avoid the kind of divisive response that Pound had stirred up. He explained the delicacy of the situation to his friend Edward Garnett, a writer and critic who knew all about such sensitivities, having been instrumental in getting D. H. Lawrence's *Sons and Lovers* published in 1913. 'He had been at American editors 10 years in vain,' wrote Thomas:

But may I suggest it might damage him there if you rubbed the Americans' noses in their own dirt? I know he thought so. Most English reviewers were blinded by theories they had as to what poetry should look like. They did not see how true he was, and how pure in his own style. I think the Hired Man, the Wood Pile, the Black Cottage and one or two others – such as Home Burial – masterpieces.

But Thomas could not extend the same compliments to Frost's former neighbours in Gloucestershire. 'I've not dipped into New Numbers yet,' he admitted three months after publication of its final issue. 'Drinkwater is hopeless. Gibson, for me, almost equally so. Abercrombie, I fancy, applies the lash, and I wonder whether he always did. I used to think he was naturally a spirited steed. I am always anxious to like him.'[3]

Thomas had listened attentively to Frost's criticisms of his poems, and made adjustments in the light of his friend's comments, but he was altogether more resistant to the comments of others. Hudson and Farjeon had commented with little effect on Thomas's early verses, and now Edward Garnett would encounter the same. When Garnett responded to the selection given to him on 9 March, Thomas found the advice uncomfortable, and batted it back. He refused Garnett's suggestion to correct the last line of 'The Manor Farm' (W. H. Hudson had singled out the very same line for criticism) and let him know firmly that it was his favourite among the pieces sent. He refused to correct 'Tears' to make it, as Garnett had suggested, 'marketable'. He conceded faults elsewhere in the poems that he said he did not feel minded to correct, and even pointed out others that his friend had overlooked; Garnett must have wondered why he was asked for his comments in the first place. He had found Thomas's verse proximate, coarse and rhythmically untidy, and yet Thomas would seek his opinion once more, sending him what he called a further 'swamping' in April: 'You cannot imagine how eagerly I have run up this byeway and how anxious I am to be sure it is not a cul de sac.'[4]

Thomas shared his work with more of his friends to much the same effect. Vivian Locke Ellis, at whose house in East Grinstead he had spent his winters, told Thomas his rhythm was rough and not emphatic enough. Gordon Bottomley agreed that he was enslaved by his own prose rhythms. W. H. Davies took a quick look at a small unsigned selection and, to mutual embarrassment, pronounced confidently that this was unquestionably the work of Robert Frost. Thomas would be more careful in future about passing around his poems anonymously. Monro, Hudson, Garnett, Ellis, Bottomley, Davies: to a man, they had failed to see as Frost had seen the quality of their friend's work. Julian Thomas, Edward's youngest and closest brother, did at least appreciate the poems, and late in March read them out at home to their parents in Edward's absence, but the response there was hardly better. 'Father calls them pure piffle,' Julian recorded in his diary, 'and says no one will publish them.'[5]

That spring, Thomas wrote two poems that centred on the cold, unlovable house at Wick Green above Steep, but with money now so tight, Thomas reluctantly accepted what he dubbed a 'filthy job – a book on the Duke of Marlborough to be done in haste'. And done in haste it would be: six weeks of research, four weeks in the writing: some 75,000 words, up to 3,000 a day. Thomas loathed every minute of it: the mind-numbing research at the British Museum (he called this 'pap'), the weariness of the prose laid down at Steep ('undigested and useless') about a subject with whom he felt no affinity. 'The only good thing will be letting me deeper into the secret of how not to write.' As a publishing enterprise, it was at least mercifully quick: Chapman & Hall issued the book on 19 October 1915, a mere six months after Thomas had begun it. But it was an agony for Thomas. He had moved beyond prose now, and hated the chore of having to write to length. It would be the last prose book that he would produce and it was a relief to get back to writing lyric verse at Easter, among which was a penetrating quatrain that would typify the oblique way in which Thomas would write about the war.

IN MEMORIAM (EASTER, 1915)

The flowers left thick at nightfall in the wood
This Eastertide call into mind the men,
Now far from home, who, with their sweethearts, should
Have gathered them and will do never again.[6]

For such a short lyric it made for long and uncomfortable
reading, full of disruptive sense and quarrelsome syntax, awkward to read aloud due to rhythms that he tied trickily to what he
once praised in a review as 'thought moments' rather than those
that belong to metre or speech. Nowhere would the reader be
allowed to settle amid the careful knots that the poet had pulled
so tightly: the skilful way the word 'thick' swats across the first
line, knocking out what would otherwise be a neat line of iambic
pentameter; the way 'This Eastertide' surprises the sense in the
second; the clipped sub-clauses of the third line, each a set of
gates to slow, enclose and hold up the understanding; and the
final five words of the fourth line, quite deliberate in their stac-
cato shaking of the rhythm. Here, at the end, the stressed line
endings that have come before are dispensed with, and the effect
is hesitant, uncertain, irresolvable. There is no choice but to read
this poem over again, to go back to the start and refresh the eye, to
keep the lines turning on the tongue and in the mind, so that they
stay within the reader's thoughts as a memorial should. Nowhere
does the poem mention war, and yet it is a powerful war poem.[7]

The short, Eastertide lyrics had followed 'Lob', a much length-
ier piece that had attracted Frost's attention. 'The goodness is in
Lob,' Frost had written of Thomas's longest poem to date, and
perhaps his finest, thought Frost, written and worked over on 3
and 4 April 1915. It was his most confident performance yet: strid-
ing effortlessly across 150 lines of iambic pentameter and rhyming couplets, exploring English folklore and mythology through
an archetypal countryman who had appeared in many guises
throughout his prose and verse: mole-catcher, umbrella man,

watercress man, sage. But the model was real as well as creative, based upon someone Thomas met fishing on a canal bank during his childhood holidays in Wiltshire, David 'Dad' Uzzell. 'I called [him] Dad, in the Wiltshire style, almost from the first day. I remember him first as a stiff straight man, broad-shouldered and bushy bearded, holding his rod out and watching his float very intently.' Uzzell knew the names of the birds and could imitate their calls, and identify most of the wild flowers that he and the teenage Thomas encountered on their wanderings between Swindon and Wootton Bassett. He lived simply with his wife in a modest terrace in Swindon, taking his living partly from his catches in the river or the fields outside the town. 'Every man who was ever any good had a little apple-face man or woman like this somewhere not very far back in his pedigree,' wrote Thomas in his 1913 book *The Country*, someone who stood, like the badger of the coombe, as that most ancient of Britons. 'He has been in England as long as dove and daw.'[8]

'I like the first half of Lob best: it offers something more like action with the different people coming in and giving the tones of speech,' continued Frost. 'But the long paragraph is a feat. I never saw anything like you for English.' Gordon Bottomley responded warmly too, as did Eleanor Farjeon, but when Edward Garnett repeated his wish to see greater regularity in the verse, Thomas politely but firmly brushed his view aside. 'It would be the easiest thing in the world to clean it all up and trim it and have every line straightforward in sound and sense,' he replied, 'but it would not really improve it. I think you read too much with the eye perhaps.'[9]

Thomas had recovered sufficiently from his disappointment with Harold Monro to repeat his approach for publication. On 20 April he wrote once again to the Poetry Bookshop to say that he would very much like to bring out a small book of poems and that he would like Monro to be 'the publisher and keeper of the secret' – by which he meant the true identity of Edward Eastaway. He had sixty-one poems, ample for a sixty-four-page book, the preferred extent at the time. Fearing that Monro might ask about finance, Thomas made clear that he could not afford to subsidise the publication himself, but would send along a manuscript if the editor was interested. This time Monro was willing to take a look, and five days after his initial enquiry, Thomas packaged up a 'variety of verses' and posted them off to Devonshire Street.

I should like some to please you. Let me know if any do, but if any don't, please don't tell me what you *think* of them, – for this reason, that I do not care a button what anybody thinks of them but I am at the same time excessively thin skinned[.] I should have said I don't want to know what anyone thinks of them whether favourable or not. But I am anxious to know if anyone really *likes* them or some or one of them . . . Can you manage to return these before the end of the week?[10]

To be both thin skinned and not caring a button would be a tightrope that Thomas would find difficulty in walking. Monro did get back to Thomas before the week's end, but with a decision to turn down the manuscript for publication. Monro's response is sadly lost, but piecing together Thomas's comments it appears as though the editor felt there was a gulf between 'conception and execution', hinting that he felt the poems were not the authentic voice of a writer whose prose he had come to know so well. Thomas wrote back:

Many thanks for saying it. I am sorry because I feel utterly sure they are me. I expect obstacles and I get them. It was chiefly to save myself what I think unnecessary pain that I asked for no explanations. One blow was better. I assume the verses expressed nothing clearly that you care about, as that is the only ground for not liking written work. But don't let us talk about it.[11]

Thomas insisted that he was not at all influenced by the views of Monro or anyone else, though he conceded such responses took a certain readjustment. In truth, he felt let down by Monro's offhand rejection: it was the first he had experienced from a poetry publisher and it would leave a bitter taste; from that point on, Thomas cashed the contributors' payments that *Poetry and Drama* posted him, having worked for free until then. To Eleanor, he relayed only that he had sent Monro 'a lot of verses in hopes he would make a book of them. He won't. He doesn't like them at all.'[12]

Monro was not the only editor unwilling to take a chance on Edward Thomas. In the final two weeks of March alone, Eleanor sent out no fewer than thirteen of Thomas's poems to nine different journals: all were rejected. These journals – *The Nation*, *TLS*, *English Review*, *New Statesman* among them – were busy publications with a large postbag, and it is possible to see how an unknown, pseudonymous poet might have been overlooked. But Monro's postbag was not so overrun, and he knew the identity of the author and had (this time at least) taken the trouble to read the submission; so why might he have turned Thomas down?[13]

Edward Thomas's poems were unlike those of his Georgian peers. Their tone was more tentative and more complex than most of the period's poetry; they drew no special attention to themselves, and avoided showy sonnets or epic dramas and tended to resist the various formal symmetries of the time. The cadence of the speech rhythms and particularly of the 'thought moments' was strange to Georgian ears. The restlessness, the unresolved endings, the refusal to bow to nostalgia or to a moral convenience may have left contemporary readers unsatisfied, where today these are some of the very qualities that keep his work alive for modern readers. Thomas was a modern writer in still-modernising times, quite out of keeping with many Georgian sentiments. These lines on ecology, for example, sound eerily contemporary and contrast with Georgian ideas about preservation.

Men help to maintain the country as they think it should be. According to their tastes they destroy or they work to preserve rights of way:
while some blotch and blight the hills, others will have this hollow or
that summit made a possession of the people for ever, or they save old
houses or build new ones worthy to please the eyes of 1912 and 2012.[14]

Frost attempted to shed some kindly light on the poor
reception of Thomas's poems to date. 'You are a poet or you
are nothing. But you are not psychologist enough to know that
no one not come at in just the right way will ever recognize
you. *You* can't go to Garnett for yourself; *you* can't go to De
la Mare. I told you and I keep telling you. But as long as your
courage holds out you may as well go right ahead making a fool
of yourself. All brave men are fools.'[15]

Harold Monro would recognise his error in turning down the
poems of Edward Thomas. In November 1917 he hosted a tribute reading of Thomas's work at the Bookshop and so began
his amends. In 1920 he wrote to Helen to ask if he might take
on a collected edition of her husband's work. 'I wish I could
fall in with your suggestion,' wrote Helen, 'but I can't. I very
much wish that you had accepted the poems when Edward first
showed them to you: I remember well his hurt at your refusal.
But it can't be helped now, & it's man of you to acknowledge
your mistake . . . I can't help wishing that Edward's poems had
had the advantage that they would have had coming from the
Poetry Bookshop. But it's too late now.'[16]

On 18 April Rupert Brooke was aboard the *Grantully Castle*
anchored in the Aegean when a cutting from *The Times* reached
him. It carried the story of a rousing sermon given by the Dean
of St Paul's on Easter Sunday in which he concluded a reading
from Isaiah with Brooke's poem 'The Soldier'. The Dean had
commented from the pulpit that such 'enthusiasm of a pure
and elevated patriotism had never found a nobler expression', a

comment which *The Times* had reprinted along with the poem. A few days later, Brooke developed a swelling on his lip where a mosquito bite had become infected. He took to his bunk; pain flushed in his chest and back, while the abscess that had formed on his neck pumped the poisoned blood around his body. The battalion surgeon looked in on him with increasing frequency, transferring him to a French hospital ship anchored at Skyros, the *Duguay-Trouin*. On 22 April he was barely conscious, and on 23 April not at all. At 4.46 in the afternoon he died. When the *Grantully Castle* sailed for Gallipoli the next morning, it did so without Rupert Brooke's body. His friends had buried him in an olive grove on Skyros.[17]

Winston Churchill grasped the moment politically. 'He expected to die; he was willing to die for the dear England whose beauty and majesty he knew; and he advanced towards the brink in perfect serenity, with absolute conviction of the rightness of his country's cause, and a heart devoid of hate for fellow-men,' he wrote in *The Times*. 'He was all that one would wish England's noblest sons to be in days when no sacrifice but the most precious is acceptable.'[18]

'I was struck sad for Rupert. But he chose the right way,' Robert Frost wrote to Jack Haines in Gloucestershire. 'Your letter telling of his death came right on the heels of another from [J. C.] Smith saying how much the war had done to make him a better poet. The war saved him only to kill him.' In the other corner of the county, the grief among the *New Numbers* poets was palpable. 'O Eddie, it's too terrible! I cannot realize at all yet what it means,' said Gibson to Marsh, who in turn locked himself away at Greenway Cross for eight days to work on a prose tribute. Heartfelt, hopeless sentiments poured out in verse from Abercrombie, from Drinkwater and from Gibson. But the sharpest memoriam in verse had already been written, and came not from the Dymock Poets but from Brooke's long-standing companion, Frances Cornford, who in 1910 had characterised her friend as a young Apollo, 'Magnificently unprepared | For the long littleness of life'.[19]

Edward Thomas kept a cooler head, and made a typically canny assessment of his friend's literary standing in public. 'No poet of his age was so much esteemed or admired, or was watched more hopefully. His work could not be taken soberly, whether you like it or not. It was full of the thought, the aspiration, the indignation of youth.' It was simply the glamour and flashiness of Brooke's personal life that Thomas mistrusted, and he wrote revealingly (accusingly?) of Brooke 'dying conspicuously'. In private, Thomas was even more incisive, admitting to Frost that he had written the obituary on Brooke

not daring to say that those sonnets about him enlisting are probably not very personal but a nervous attempt to connect with himself the very widespread idea that self sacrifice is the highest self indulgence. You know. And I don't dispute it. Only I doubt if he knew it or would he have troubled to drag in the fact that enlisting cleared him of 'All the little emptiness of love'? Well, I daren't say so, not having enlisted or fought the keeper.

Were these sonnets, cherished by the public as expressions of the highest self-sacrifice, in fact to be understood in contradiction to the very values that won them fame? To have said so in print, at that moment, might have been more incendiary than Thomas wished to be, given the national mood; but it remains a profound loss to our understanding of Brooke that Thomas would never return to develop his thought.[20]

'Men never spoke ill of him,' said Thomas and nor would he. He knew the work to be immature – 'eloquent experiences of thoughts or fancies rather than pure poetry' he once said to Jack Haines – but it was the talent as yet unachieved in Brooke that made his passing such a loss to literature. When Frost pressed him for his assessment, Thomas said everything that needed to be said. 'I think he succeeded in being youthful and yet intelligible and interesting (not only pathologically) more than most poets since Shelley. But thought gave him (and me) indigestion. He couldn't mix his thought or the result of it with his feeling. He could only think about his feeling. Radically, I think he lacked power of expression. He was a rhetorician, dressing things up better than they needed. And I suspect he knew too well both what he was after and what he achieves.' Indeed he did; though Thomas had no way of knowing, Brooke had made his own assessment of the sonnets that won him fame: 'God they're in the rough, these five camp-children.'[21]

1914 and Other Poems was hurried into print in June 1915 and opened with the five sonnets that had made Brooke's name. Sidgwick & Jackson issued 1,000 copies in a hopeless underestimation of the book's appeal; they reprinted twice that month alone, three times in July and were in their tenth impression by November. Rupert Brooke's verse would sell a quarter of a million copies within a decade.

On 1 May RMS *Lusitania* embarked on her final voyage across the Atlantic, departing Pier 54 of New York harbour with almost two thousand passengers aboard. Five days later the liner's Captain, William Turner, received an intercept from the British Admiralty warning of U-boat activity in the area. He ordered a blackout and posted a double lookout on deck, but he did not zig-zag as liner captains were taught to do, nor did he increase speed in line with procedure. The *Lusitania* was thirty miles off the coast of the Old Head of Kinsale on 7 May when she crossed in front of *U-20*. At 14.10 a young lookout spotted a line of foam hurtling towards the ship's starboard side. The torpedo struck beneath the bridge; the liner went down in eighteen minutes. Only six of her forty-eight lifeboats were successfully lowered; some tipped as the crewmen lost their grip on the lowering-falls, spilling passengers into the sea, others overturned under the list of the ship or caught on the port-side rivets. Of the 1,198 deaths,

128 were Americans. The sinking had brought the first significant US casualties of the war, and sparked public outrage. 'I wonder if your papers made you realize that we are ready to fight over the Lusitania if Germany doesn't come to terms?' wrote Frost to Jack Haines. But America still had further to go before she was ready to enter the war, and did not feel sentimental over the invasion of Belgium as Britons did, Frost explained. 'No nation ever went to war from sentiment alone. I have said this before. We are out of this fight to stay out.'[22]

'The Lusitania seems to increase the distance between us,' wrote Thomas to Frost, still uncertain of which side of the Atlantic he would eventually find himself on.

> The war will have ended, many other things
> Have ended, maybe, that I can no more
> Foresee or more control than robin and wren.

Frost was the only person he could be 'idle' with, Thomas said, but the financial cost of emigrating seemed prohibitive and the uncertainty of employment intimidating. 'I could perhaps only risk it if I really made up my mind I would see editors as much as possible. I dread them as much as that keeper,' he told Frost. 'Like everything else that means an unusual and conscious step it looks impossible, like becoming a teacher or a soldier – I suppose I ought to write a long short story about a man who didn't enlist.'[23]

Summer

Zeppelins were coming to London, Thomas wrote to Frost on 1 June. The capital was bombed the night before and gripped now by the panic buying of gas masks. Air strikes were a new threat for the British people: they had begun along the east coast in January but had been sporadic and ineffectual; now the airships were coming for the cities, spreading terror as they went. Helen worried about her husband's visits to town, but Edward had not needed to travel to London since he began writing up *The Life of the Duke of Marlborough* in May. By 19 June, the book was finished. Thomas celebrated with a week's cycling that led him up to Jack Haines's house at Hucclecote in Gloucestershire, where he wrote a confessional lyric, opening:

> I built myself a house of glass:
> It took me years to make it:
> And I was proud. But now, alas,
> Would God someone would break it.

Thomas had found joy in childhood throwing stones 'over into the unknown depths of a great garden and hearing the glass-house break'. He longed for someone to break through the edifice that he had put around himself, an edifice designed, he said, to protect his humility. To Edward Garnett he explained that any 'superiority' that his friend detected was nothing more than a self-defence, prone to thickening into a 'callosity'. More than anything, he missed Frost's companionship, a feeling that was only deepened by his walks that week with Haines around Dymock, when the two men had talked about Frost as they strode. Frost alone among his friends had taken him by the scruff of the neck and urged better things from him: he had been the one man willing to throw stones, to 'kick' the nonsense out of him. Helen and Eleanor were too much in awe of Thomas – or feared too much his rebuke – to take on such a bullish role, but not Frost, who had urged Thomas not to judge himself with such harshness. 'I can't help it,' had been Thomas's response, 'but I can help personally-conducted tours to the recesses.' It was a new realisation from Thomas: that he might now be able to control his descent into the worst areas of his depression.[1]

Haines and Thomas climbed May Hill together that visit, though not to the crown of fir trees that ringed the summit where he had walked the previous summer with Frost. He began 'Words', a poem set on the great hillside: 'Out of us all | That make rhymes, | Will you choose | ... | Choose me, | You English words?' Everything now was revolving around Thomas's quarrel with himself: whether or not to write poetry, go to America, enlist. Money was tighter than ever. 'It is wretched to be willing to work, to think I know what I can do, and yet not to be sure of £150 a year,' he told Eleanor. 'If anybody said You go and join the Royal Garrison Artillery and they will give you a commission, I believe I should go next month.' Food prices were a quarter higher than when the war broke out, bread by as much as a half – 'and work so much more than 25% scarcer' – and he began to watch more jealously than before as the few remaining bursaries and grants passed him by, some of them given to his friends. 'De la Mare has got £100 a year now from the Civil List, and he was making £400 at least,' he complained to Frost. 'I was annoyed especially as I am told I have no chance myself as being too young and not as well known as many others who will be applying. Let me admit also that I felt they might have let me sign the petition as I have probably reviewed him more than anyone else. That is frank.' Thomas was beginning to lose patience with friends that he had spent years supporting in his reviews – de la Mare in particular, Davies to an extent – friends who showed no sign of returning the encouragement when it came to his own poetry, let alone petitioning on his behalf for a Civil List pension as he had done over the years for others.[2]

America had never seemed so certain, Eleanor Farjeon recalled. Thomas had gone so far as to prepare his mother for the news that he might emigrate. In those early weeks of June his mind seemed all but made up. 'I am thinking about America as my only chance (apart from Paradise),' he wrote to Frost on 14 June, and to Eleanor he said much the same, that 'America is a chance and that I see no other'. In his correspondence he used and reused this word 'chance', as if America were both an opportunity but also a lottery outside his control. Departure to the States would use up what savings he had (enough to last for only four months) and would, he felt certain, sever his ties with the English newspaper editors for good. It would also mean pulling Bronwen out of Bedales, her fees having been subsidised by Helen's occasional teaching there, so the gamble was substantial: was he prepared, he asked himself, to wager his savings 'and leave the rest to chance'? What guarantees did he have? None that he could see. Some people, he acknowledged, would let their faith guide them in their decision, but not Thomas, who was adamant that he was alone when it came to such matters. 'It all comes of not believing. I will leave nothing to chance *knowingly*.'[3]

Thomas's vacillation was now bordering on comic, and even Helen teased him with a precision of wit not lost upon him. He explained to Frost, 'These last few days I have been looking at 2 alternatives, trying to enlist or coming out to America. Helen points out that I could try America and then enlist if it failed, but not the other way around.' But secretly, Thomas admitted that the venture might not necessarily include Helen. 'We shall certainly not all go to America,' he confessed to Bottomley. 'I should go alone if other things fail.' Would he really cross the Atlantic without his wife and daughters now, after the difficulties that they were beginning to overcome in their relationships? And in a time of war? When he had no income with which to support them? What about that other crossing, of the English Channel to join British soldiers in France? Was the war the more realistic outcome? 'Frankly I do not want to go,' he confessed, 'but hardly a day passes without my thinking I should. With no call, the problem is endless.'[4]

But the problem was not endless, for a poem of Frost's had arrived which would dramatically force Thomas's hand.

THE ROAD NOT TAKEN

Two roads diverged in a yellow wood,
And sorry I could not travel both
And be one traveler, long I stood
And looked down one as far as I could
To where it bent in the undergrowth;

Then took the other, as just as fair,
And having perhaps the better claim,
Because it was grassy and wanted wear;
Though as for that the passing there
Had worn them really about the same,

And both that morning equally lay
In leaves no step had trodden black.
Oh, I kept the first for another day!
Yet knowing how way leads on to way,
I doubted if I should ever come back.

I shall be telling this with a sigh
Somewhere ages and ages hence:
Two roads diverged in a wood, and I –
I took the one less traveled by,
And that has made all the difference.[5]

Noble, charismatic, wise: in the years since its composition, 'The Road Not Taken' has been understood by some as an emblem of individual choice and self-reliance, a moral tale in which the traveller takes responsibility for their own destiny. But it was never intended to be read as such by Frost, who was well aware of the playful ironies contained within it, and would go on to warn audiences, 'You have to be careful of that one; it's a tricky poem – very tricky.' Frost knew that reading the poem as straight morality tale would pose a number of difficulties. For one: how can we evaluate the outcome of the road *not* taken? For another: had the poet chosen the road *more* travelled by, then that, presumably, would also have made all the difference. Choices might actually be equal, in other words, and Frost had set traps in the very heart of the poem intended to explode a more earnest reading. First he placed a mischievous admission about the wearing of the grass, that along each path 'the passing there | Had worn them really about the same', suggesting that neither was apparently more travelled by. And just in case the trap was missed he set another: 'both that morning equally lay | In leaves no step had trodden black', meaning that there was no discernible difference between the two paths at all. So when the poem culminates in a claim that he took the path less travelled by, it does so with its tongue in its cheek.[6]

'The Road Not Taken' is typical of Frost's skill with perspective and with mirrors: behind the neat, unfussy frontage is an experience of great depth and subtlety, and no small amount of wit. For the poem to appear wise to some and ironic to others is a credit to the sophisticated way in which Frost had become the poet 'for all sorts and kinds': no wonder it stands as such a beguiling poem in the minds of readers; no wonder it has been taken so much to heart. But the poem carried a more personal message besides, 'about a friend who had gone off to war', as he later recalled it, 'a person who, whichever road he went, would be sorry he didn't go the other'. That person was Edward Thomas.[7]

Begun, most likely, at the Gallows in the late autumn of 1914, the poem was set in the woods of Dymock where Frost and Thomas had walked that season and on which Frost now based his mischievous tribute. *Two roads diverged in a yellow wood*: the much celebrated opening line may itself have been intended as a homage to Thomas, who had opened a 1911 story, 'Three roads meet in the midst of a little green'. (Thomas made Eleanor Farjeon a gift of that story in 1913; it is not beyond possibility that he did the same for Frost.) Many were the occasions when Thomas would guide Frost on the promise of rare wild flowers or birds' eggs, only for the walk to conclude in self-reproach when the path Thomas chose bore no such wonders. Amused at Thomas's inability to satisfy himself, Frost chided him, 'No matter which road you take, you'll always sigh, and wish you'd taken another.' But to Thomas, it was not the least bit funny. It pricked at his confidence, at his sense of fraudulence, reminding him he was neither a true writer nor a true naturalist, cowardly in his lack of direction. And now the one man who understood his indecisiveness most astutely was mocking him for it.[8]

Thomas took the 'tease' badly. He felt the poem to be a rebuke for his own inability to choose between the pursuit of poetry and a career in prose – worse, at his indecisive attitude toward the war, so often expressed to Frost. And he retorted with a sting. 'It's all very well for you poets in a yellow wood to say you choose, but you don't,' he protested. 'If you do, ergo I am no poet. I didn't choose my sex yet I was simpler then. And so I can't leave off going in after myself tho' some day I may. I didn't know after I left you at Newent I was going to begin to write poetry.' Contrary to his understanding of the poem, Thomas was announcing himself as a fatalist, it was clear now. He did not believe in self-determination, or that the spirit could triumph over adversity; some things seemed unavoidable, inevitable. Had he *chosen* poetry he could not be a poet: as he had written in 'Words', it had in some sense to choose him. How free spirited his friend seemed in comparison. This American who tossed aside his teaching and sailed for England on a long-shot, knowing no one and without a place to go; who rode his literary fortunes and won his prize, then sailed again to make himself a new home. None of this was Thomas. 'It isn't in me.'⁹

It seems curious that Edward Thomas, the man who had understood Frost's writing better than anyone, could not see the poem for what it was. He puzzled at 'the simple words and unemphatic rhythms' which could not, he surmised, lead to great things. 'It staggered me to think that perhaps I had always missed what made poetry poetry if it was here,' he told the American. And he determinedly assured Frost that he had 'got the idea', when plainly he had not.¹⁰

Frost, a little stung, responded, 'Edward, Methinks you strikest too hard in so small a matter. A tap would have settled my poem. I wonder if it was because you were trying too much out of regard for me that you failed to see that the sigh was a mock sigh, hypocritical for the fun of the thing.' But Thomas saw no such fun: 'You have got me again over the Path not taken & no mistake. . . I doubt if you can get anybody to see the fun of the thing without showing them & advising them which kind of laugh they are to turn on.' Frost had already discovered as much on reading the poem before a college audience, where it was 'taken pretty seriously', he admitted, despite 'doing my best to make it obvious by my manner that I was fooling . . . Mea culpa.'¹¹

A strange but revealing exchange had occurred in which Thomas had exposed something deep within his poetry and his character. And what he had exposed was this: that choice was not, counter to his reading of Frost, an act of free will. Instead, some choices are prescribed, compelled, ingrained in circumstance or personality; some characters are 'called'.

He broke the news to Frost. 'Last week I had screwed myself up to the point of believing I should come out to America & lecture if anyone wanted me to. But I have altered my mind. I am going to enlist on Wednesday if the doctor will pass me.' Thomas made his will, granting Helen its sole execution. On

Saturday 10 July he rose early and walked up through the Ash-ford Hanger to his study where he drafted 'The Brook', in which the poet watched his daughter paddling in the stream, when a butterfly settled on a hot stone, 'as if I were the last of men | And he the first of insects to have earth | And sun together and know their worth.' Thomas had made the same allusion in his prose piece written about his walks with Frost in Dymock, 'This England', of the urgent need to connect – to understand and fight for – the value of the landscape around him. 'Something, I felt, had to be done before I could look again composedly at English landscape,' he wrote then, 'at the elms and poplars about the houses, at the purple-headed wood-betony with two pairs of dark leaves on a stiff stem, who stood sentinel among the grasses or bracken by hedge-side or wood's-edge. What he stood sen-tinel for I did not know, any more than what I had got to do.' Now, finally, he knew what he had to do. Thomas was passed fit, and the same week, he sat down to lunch with his confidante, Eleanor Farjeon, and informed her that he had enlisted in the Artists Rifles, and that he was glad; he did not know why, but he was glad. Only days before it seemed certain that he would emigrate to America to join Frost, as the two men had planned. And yet suddenly, everything was different. Eleanor would later describe how, in volunteering, the 'self-torment had gone out of him'. And Helen: 'I had known that the struggle going on in his spirit would end like this.'[12]

Thomas explained himself to Frost in a letter. 'To find myself living near you and not working for editors would be better than anything I ever did and better than I dare expect,' but he could not leave now, he said, not before he had taken the King's shilling: he would have to wait out the war. 'The best way out is always through,' Frost had written in *North of Boston*, and now Thomas echoed his friend's words as he explained his enlistment: 'It is not my idea of pleasure,' he admitted, 'but

I do want to go right through.' The pain in Thomas's letter was palpable. He wanted more than anything to keep alive the possibility that he might come to New England at some later time. 'There is no one to keep me here except my mother,' he confessed. And he told Frost of his first sonnet: 'A month or two [ago] I dreamt we were walking near Ledington but we lost one another in a strange place & I woke saying to myself "somehow someday I shall be here again" which I made the last line of some verses.'[13]

A DREAM

Over known fields with an old friend in dream
I walked, but came sudden to a strange stream.
Its dark waters were bursting out most bright
From a great mountain's heart into the light.
They ran a short course under the sun, then back
Into a pit they plunged, once more as black
As at their birth; and I stood thinking there
How white, had the day shone on them, they were,
Heaving and coiling. So by the roar and hiss
And by the mighty motion of the abyss
I was bemused, that I forgot my friend
And neither saw nor sought him till the end,
When I awoke from waters unto men
Saying: 'I shall be here some day again.'

The roar and hiss and the mighty motion of the abyss seemed unmistakably war torn, and amid the din his friend would be temporarily forgotten, neither seen nor sought until the episode was done. It had been the greatest friendship of his life, but it had been challenged first by a gamekeeper and now by the notion of a road not taken, and Thomas dreamed of forgetting his friend. Curious that he should choose this moment to explore a sonnet for the first time, a form frequently employed for love poetry, and one which he had long loathed. 'I have a dread of the sonnet,' he had written in 1902. 'It must contain 14 lines and a man must be a tremendous poet or a cold mathematician if he can accommodate his thoughts to such a condition. The result is – in my opinion – that many of the best sonnets are rhetoric only.' He wrote just seven, and a handful of double and treble sonnets; but here the form had fitted the moment exactly.[14]

Thomas's verse seemed naturally in tune with Frost in that week of his great decision. On 11 July he wrote the poem that Frost would describe as 'the loveliest of all', 'Aspens', after the whispering poplars on the crossroads at the Cricketers Inn, Steep; the next morning he wrote 'The Mill-Water', with its unmistakable tribute to Frost: 'The sound comes surging in upon the sense'. On 14 July Thomas took his army medical examination. He was seen along with six other men, stripped and measured together and made to hop around the room on each foot. He told the doctor nothing of the diabetes which he believed had begun to develop some time before 1914, and they did not spot it; he knew that had it been diagnosed it would have been grounds on which to reject him. And so he passed, and began the process of letting his friends know. At St George's Café that day, Edward Garnett was the first to receive the news, then Davies and Freeman. Jack Haines got the first letter, written that evening. 'I am enlisting. I passed the doctor today and go up on Monday to join the Artists Rifles and get turned (if possible) into an officer.' For Eleanor, he prepared a personal visit, calling at her mother's home on Fellows Road. 'I rose as he came into the room,' she wrote. 'He bent his head, and for the only time in our four years of friendship we kissed spontaneously. He sat down saying, "Well, I've joined up."' But to Helen, he broke the news by telegram, and left her alone in Steep with her despair: '"No, no no," was all I could say; "not that".'[15]

On the morning of 19 July Thomas reported to 17 Dukes Road, near London's Euston station, to be attested Private 4229 in the 28th Battalion, The London Regiment (Artists Rifles). He swore his oath. 'I, Philip Edward Thomas, swear by Almighty God, that I will be faithful and bear true allegiance to His Majesty King George the Fifth, His Heirs, and Successors, and that I will, as in duty bound, honestly and faithfully defend His Majesty, His Heirs, and Successors, in Person, Crown and Dignity, against all enemies, according to the conditions of my service.' To swear before a god in whom he did not have faith, to a monarchy he had been brought up to believe was imperialist, and to defend their Person, Crown and Dignity (not *People, Country* and *Culture*): what was he agreeing to?[16]

Thomas reported for physical drill at Regent's Park the next morning, six full hours of it, but it was hardly the start that he had been hoping for, as his new army boots pressed painfully at the still-sore tendon on his right foot and he had to be put on sick leave for the remainder of the week. 'Silly to be in uniform and useless,' he told Eleanor ahead of an appointment with the doctor. 'I only hope he won't give me leisure to think why I joined. Several people *have* asked me, but I could not answer yet.' To Bottomley he could offer only the haziest of explanations, pleading that it was not a desperate resolution, nor one with a particular purpose, 'but the natural culmination of a long series of moods and thoughts'. Laid up and out of action on his first week, Thomas spent the time writing poetry from his parents' house in Balham where he had been billeted, spending six hours 'perspiring' over ten lines. He began to look over his dreaded Marlborough proofs and, more pleasantly, spent the weekend catching up with friends in and around London. He wrote regularly to Helen, but did not return at the weekend to be with her in Steep. By now she had come to be glad of one thing at least: that there was to be no move to the States; she put her store instead in the hope that the war would be over long before Edward would be sent overseas. But at that moment his mind was tuned to confrontation, and he wrote eight lines of verse that seemed to serve as a call to arms:

COCK-CROW

Out of the wood of thoughts that grows by night
To be cut down by the sharp axe of light, –
Out of the night, two cocks together crow,
Cleaving the darkness with a silver blow:
And bright before my eyes twin trumpeters stand,
Heralds of splendour, one at either hand,
Each facing each as in a coat of arms:
The milkers lace their boots up at the farms.

'Here then ends reviewing & I suppose verses, for a time,' he told Gordon Bottomley. Indeed it did: it would be four months until Thomas felt prepared to face another poem.[17]

Robert Frost had received the news from Edward Thomas of his enlistment. If there had been so much as a whiff of cowardice over the incident with the gamekeeper then it had been most certainly dispelled. From the farm in Franconia, New Hampshire, where he had moved in April, Frost wrote to Thomas in heroic terms. 'I am within a hair of being precisely as sorry and as glad as you are. You are doing it for the self-same reason I shall hope to do it for if my time ever comes and I am brave enough, namely, because there seems nothing else for a man to do.' Thomas would have chuckled affectionately at Frost's bluff and rhetoric, which seemed more closely aligned to the Frontier spirit than anything he would experience in the Home Counties training camps; but he would have appreciated the sentiment well enough. He was quite untroubled by the notions of masculinity that could entangle Frost at times, though he would have greatly valued the camaraderie which Frost now offered him. 'You have let me follow your thought in almost every twist and turn toward this conclusion,' Frost wrote. 'I know pretty well how far down you have gone and how far off sideways. And I think the better of you for it all. Only the very bravest could come to the sacrifice in this way.'[18]

On Monday 26 July Thomas returned from sick leave to try again at army life. For the next two weeks he wondered if his tendon would hold up to the strain of daily drill, but hold up it did. Typhoid inoculations and poor sleeping left him feverish and weary by the week's end, however, and he was grateful when Vivian Locke Ellis offered to drive him from London to Steep and back in his new motor car on the weekend of 7–8 August; Mrs Ellis came too, and stayed on with Helen to offer her company. It was as much as Thomas could manage to walk gingerly up to the hilltop study with Bronwen, who chatted in her indefatigable way: did he have his uniform yet? what was the drill like? and a dozen other questions about his new life in the army.

Thomas's billeting at his parents' at Rusham Road, Balham was, predictably, causing strain and he anxiously awaited a transfer to camp. 'My father is so rampant in his cheery patriotism that I become pro German every evening,' he reported to Frost. 'We can never so beat the Germans that they will cease to remember their victories. Pom-pom.' The Defence of the Realm Act had been introduced days before, and anyone now speaking well of the enemy could expect a fine, even for a comment made at a private dinner party; Edward must have wondered wryly whether his father might be close to invoking it. Mercifully, he believed that he would be in the Artists Rifles camp at Epping Forest within the fortnight, and once there, expected three to four months of training before deployment. But this was guesswork, he admitted, for he had no sense of which regiment he might ultimately serve in or where his first commission might take him, and for the moment it did not much matter: 'one ceases to be curious'.[19]

By the fourth week he was recovered and beginning to enjoy life again. 'I am a real soldier now,' he told Frost on 10 August.

'I stand very nearly as straight as a lamp post and apparently get smaller every week in the waist and have to get new holes punched in my belt.' His day began at six each morning, polishing his buttons and belt, his boots and his badge, before leaving Balham and heading across London to Dukes Road for physical drill. He enjoyed the exercise: the running, the battlefield training, even the leap-frog that the recruits were put through daily; but he found the society strained, as he told Jack Haines. 'The drills and lectures and marches are quite interesting, but not the men – they are the worst yet, quite impossible to make friends of and everyday acquaintances, and mostly cockneys, business men, clerks etc.' The regiment was populated by those with intelligent newspaper opinions and an interest in clothes, he thought – public school, literary or professional men – in short, those quite like himself with whom he could not get along. 'It is a question now whether I should have been worse off say in the Welch Fusiliers with a mixture of clerks and shopmen and manual workers.'[20]

The Artists Rifles formed in the middle of the nineteenth century as a volunteer group of writers, painters, musicians and engravers; Minerva and Mars were their patrons. They founded their headquarters in Dukes Road in 1880, one of twenty-eight volunteer battalions that combined to form the London Regiment. Dante Gabriel Rossetti had served with the Artists, as had Algernon Swinburne and William Morris. Paul Nash saw service there during the Great War, as would Wilfred Owen. Eventually, recruitment was limited by recommendation from serving members ('they let in anybody now who will pay 25/- a year subscription', Thomas complained), but for the time being it was a popular choice among university and public school graduates, who were frequently considered such capable officers that they were poached by other army units or chosen to set up Officers Training Corps. In excess of 10,000 officers were commissioned during the war after training with the Artists Rifles; the Royal Artillery alone took nearly a thousand. But they suffered appalling casualties: some 6,000 of the 15,000 serving Artists were killed, wounded or posted missing or captive.[21]

As Thomas settled into life with the Artists, Edward Garnett had left for duty with the Ambulance Corps on the Italian Front. T. E. Hulme was returning injured from the Western Front, while John Masefield was serving as a hospital orderly and Ralph Hodgson in the anti-aircraft squadron patrolling the east coast of England. Abercrombie, Gibson and Drinkwater were in civilian clothes; Rupert Brooke was dead. Jack Haines reported he would go mad if he enlisted, but expected that he would have to anyway. Walter de la Mare was forty-two and would be beyond even the age limit for conscription when it was introduced in 1916. W. H. Davies and Gordon Bottomley were invalided. Harold Monro was 'in the country with his girl', said Thomas, apparently unaware of his efforts to enlist, while two other visitors to the Poetry Bookshop, Siegfried Sassoon and Robert Graves, were now serving in France. Wilfred Owen was still a civilian teacher, but he had now made his decision to enlist.[22]

Edward Thomas had felt that none of his friends besides Frost had seemed willing to help his poetry forward that summer, but Lascelles Abercrombie now would. He was prospecting for an anthology of contemporary verse that he was hoping to co-edit for Constable, and when Bottomley showed him the poems that Thomas had sent him, Abercrombie agreed at once that they should be included. *An Anthology of New Poetry* would come out in March 1917, a month before Thomas's death; it would be the only time that he saw a selection of his work in print. Across the Atlantic, Robert Frost was toasting news which testified to the new readership that he was winning. 'The Road Not Taken' appeared in the *Atlantic Monthly* in August 1915. But if he mentioned this to Thomas then that particular letter has gone astray.[23]

Autumn

As Edward Thomas walked through the streets of Balham with his daughter Bronwen, he began to feel the south London crowds pressing in on him. 'I stand it better with her,' he told Frost, 'but it is pretty bad – all the mean or villa streets that have filled the semi-rural places I knew 25 years ago.' It was a strange and strained existence he now lived: a thirty-seven-year-old man billeted with his parents, settled in neither army nor literary work, separated from his wife and children apart from the weekend reunions under the scrutiny of his father. But the training drills at least had become more adventurous: mapping on Hampstead Heath on 6 September, night operations on the 9th. Thomas was assigned guard duties – twenty-four hours on, twenty-four hours off – and given musket training, map-making lectures and a troop to march around the Heath weekly; 'It is all like being somebody else.' Tired from the drill work, numbed by the routine, Thomas felt his perspectives beginning to warp. 'The country is a little strange to me,' he confessed to Frost. 'It seems as if in my world there was no Autumn though they are picking hops in Kent. On Hampstead Heath the other day I watched the bees at the bramble flowers and green blackberries and they looked so unfamiliar and with a kind of ugliness, partly but not wholly due to the fact that the earth around was dirty London earth.' As if to restore some normality to his senses, he tried to coax these thoughts into blank verse in his head, but failed to finish them and the lines drifted out of reach. The transfer to camp could not come soon enough.[1]

On 17 September Thomas made the move that he had longed for, by train from Liverpool Street station out to High Beech

Camp near Loughton, Essex, on the fringe of Epping Forest. He was already familiar with the area's literary history (Alfred, Lord Tennyson had written 'In Memoriam' in the village at the same time that John Clare was at the neighbouring asylum), but he was less intimate with the countryside itself, and so had travelled up previously to acquaint himself with his new surroundings. Epping Forest he found a miniature paradise, crowded with oaks and beeches and bustling with wild flowers and deer, but the camp proved to be something quite else: noisy and draughty and ugly, he thought, badly arranged, dirty. It was also semi-deserted when he arrived, with half of the men on leave, and Thomas found himself hanging around restlessly, escaping for walks to nearby Loughton or Theydon Bois. He described the scene to Jack Haines. 'We are in huts, nearly a hundred of us in a big corrugated iron room formerly used for Sunday school treats etc to feed in. High Beech is a great pleasure resort, high in the middle of Epping Forest. The conditions are cramped and not over clean. The food is ill-cooked and ill-served, and has to be eaten in haste in a dark dirty room that the rain comes into. And the nights are cold.'[2]

Thomas did his best to settle in, in those first weeks at the end of September, but found the situation isolating and the routines stultifying. In fact, 'dismal' was the word Thomas used to describe his moods by the start of October. Whether it was the company or the discomfort or the solitude, he could not say, but he felt his spirits lowering once again. No one sought out his companionship in those early weeks, nor did he seek theirs: the Artists were not making a good impression. 'I suppose writers generally have been people who tasted far more things than they ever swallowed,' he wrote to Helen. There were exceptions, he continued: Shelley had been an activist, Tennyson a volunteer, 'And I –,' he wrote dryly, 'dig in the garden.' But worse than the company was the restriction on his movements, forbidding him to wander in Epping Forest or slip away back to London. It annoyed him to think that 'a foxhunting major' had the power to deny him leave on a whim. He could not take pleasure even in reading, as he explained to Walter de la Mare. 'I don't think about books or writing except on a sleepless night when I sometimes make a few lines and a half and don't bother to write them down.' The poems were slipping away from him in his fatigued state, and he was resentful of the aimless physical labour, digging channels in the heavy clay, spading it into the barrow, carting it away, all watched over by a bullying officer: 'The hardest work I ever did,' he told de la Mare, and a waste of time to boot, he felt, when that time might be better spent improving his leadership skills. 'Apparently any man who will stand up and get shot is useful however hurried his training,' he told Frost wearily, and shortly after that he succumbed to an injured knee that would lame him for two days. Finally, his despondency did tip into verse. 'Some day I shall think this a happy day, | And this mood by the name of melancholy | Shall no more blackened and obscured be,' he wrote gloomily, in the first poem he had written since enlisting in the summer. And his mood was not a bit improved to learn that his younger brother Reggie had enlisted with the Artists, and would soon be joining him at camp.[3]

Despite the cutbacks that publishers made in their commissioning they were at least honouring their existing commitments; indeed they were doing so expeditiously, noted Thomas, before conditions worsened. 'My books come streaming out,' he told Bottomley, as no fewer than three appeared at once: the dreaded *Life of the Duke of Marlborough* from Chapman and Hall at a pricey 10s. 6d., while Duckworth issued *Four-and-Twenty Blackbirds* at 2s. 6d. and Oxford University Press published the anthology he had edited, *This England*. The trio received 'friendly useless reviews', he told Frost, but included in *This England* were two poems by Thomas himself under the name of 'Edward Eastaway', which he had inserted at the eleventh hour after the publisher asked him to fill two blank pages that had arisen in the typesetting. 'Haymaking' and 'The Manor Farm' became the first publication of his poems in book form, and joined the 'House and Man' and 'Interval', which had recently appeared in his friend James Guthrie's *Root and Branch* magazine, as among the first of his poems to have been published anywhere. Edward Marsh, however, had decided against the inclusion of either Thomas or Frost in his second volume of *Georgian Poetry*, not caring for Thomas's verse and imposing a new rule to exclude overseas writers from consideration. *Georgian Poetry 1913–1915* would go through 19,000 copies in nineteen impressions, but Thomas could hardly have cared less. His letters were becoming less literary and more focussed upon army life and war. 'The air here is full of rumours. Some say we are all going to leave the camp in a week to make way for 300 young officers. There is a remote chance that they may try to turn me into an instructor of some kind. I am rather loth to entertain the idea, partly because now I have taken the step the only way to satisfy my vanity is to become an officer and go out.' If anything, Thomas had more interest in the welfare of his family now that he was forcibly parted from them. He saw Bronwen whenever he had leave for London, and kept in close touch with Helen over Myfanwy, and in his letters to Frost he asked frequently after Mervyn, who was temporarily lodging with the family in Franconia. Edward and Helen now hoped the boy would return to England in December to take up the schooling they had arranged for him in Coventry. At long last, Thomas expressed an interest in and anxiety for the well-being of his son.[4]

Temperatures in camp dipped regularly below freezing in November. Icy rain gave way to snow, four inches of it on the 15th. Thomas had been promoted to lance corporal, the second tier of non-commissioned officer ranking just above private, in charge of a dozen men for five days a week. His duties involved helping the men with their understanding of the lectures, and guiding them with the use of a compass and protractor to sketch the kind of topographic detail on their manoeuvres that could be put to military advantage; it was a good application of Thomas's eye for natural detail. Instructing the men was beginning to ease his long-standing fear of teaching, and he let Frost know that he would be better equipped to teach in an American summer school in future.[5]

When Helen wrote to say that she was suffering from influenza, Thomas took leave to look after her. It was to be a surprise, but the surprise backfired on him emotionally; he returned to find the house in a mess and Helen 'as much scared and surprised as pleased' to see him, and he felt the familiar depression overtake him. He descended to what he called 'the old level' that he had come to associate with Steep, and realised that his army work had been acting as a counterbalance to his spirits. 'Does one really get rid of things at all by steadily inhibiting them for a long time on end?' he asked Frost. 'Am I indulging in the pleasure of being someone else?' Thomas returned to London to find that he had been asked to report to a new camp not far from High Beech: Hare Hall, in Gidea Park, Romford.[6]

At Dukes Road, in Euston, where Edward Thomas had signed up, a new signatory had added his name to the Artists Rifles on 21 October. Wilfred Owen had failed in his bid for a university scholarship and had left England in 1914 to teach in France when the war had broken out. For another year he remained in France, nonchalant, he said, toward the horrors of the conflict despite having seen the mutilation at first hand on a visit to a war hospital. But by the summer of 1915 he was fully intent on enlisting, and returned to England that September to volunteer for the Artists Rifles. On 20 October he underwent his medical, receiving a typhoid injection that badly inflamed his arm, though not enough to prevent him taking his oath the next day, nor from attending a reading at the Poetry Bookshop that night. Owen had made visits to the Bookshop earlier in the year, but now over the next month he would become a regular caller, returning the following week when he listened to a gloomy recital by Harold Monro and exchanged a few words with the bookshop's owner. On 4 November 1915 Owen returned once more, this time in uniform. He remembered the sound of his new army boots clomping up the workshop stairs and the admiring looks of what he called the 'poetic ladies'; he recalled also the glance given to him by Monro, saddened to see yet another young poet enlisted. Owen had written only two dozen poems by then, and had just rented a room above a coffee house opposite the Bookshop at 5s. 6d. per week: 'a plain enough affair – candlelight – no bath'. But no sooner had he taken the room than he received his orders to report to Hare Hall training camp.[7]

Owen would get a chance to return when a week's instruction in London later that winter allowed him to take a room in the Poetry Bookshop itself. At the week's end, when Owen was packing for his return to camp, Harold Monro climbed the stairs to the attic rooms with the manuscript that Owen had given him. 'So we sit down,' Owen recorded excitedly, 'and I have the time of my life. For he was "very struck" with these sonnets. He went over things in detail and told me what was fresh and clever, and what was second-hand and banal; and what was Keatsian, and what "modern". He summed up their value as far above that of the Little Books of Georgian Verse.' Owen was a long way from the outpouring of verse that he would experience at Craiglockhart War Hospital on the outskirts of Edinburgh in the autumn of 1917. As Monro leafed through the poems, there was scant trace of the poet Owen would within two years become: it would take the savagery of the St Quentin trenches and the friendship of Siegfried Sassoon to instil that in him.[8]

On 15 November Wilfred Owen joined his company at Liverpool Street station and boarded the train that would take him to

Gidea Park. On the same station platform were Edward Thomas and his brother Reggie, entering Hare Hall on the very same day.

'No one much wants to go into camp in low country Essex only 12 miles from London, and in winter,' Thomas wrote to Frost, 'but they say it is a particularly good camp. The huts etc. were prepared for the Sportsman's Battalion and filled up at unusual expense by some of the rich members of the Battalion.' The camp was designed and built by the architects and engineers who served in it to hold 1,400 men in forty long huts, with a canteen, hospital and sergeants' mess: twelve companies in three battalions in all. 'All very nicely set out here,' Owen reported mildly, as he and Thomas settled in.[9]

'I wonder would you recognize me with hair cropped close and carrying a thin little swagger cane,' Thomas wrote to Frost, adding, 'I was never so well or in so balanced a mood'. And he wrote to his mother's sister in California in similar vein, telling her that he had enjoyed his training at almost every point, and had been shown nothing but kindness in camp. 'I really hope my turn will come and that I shall see what it really is and come out of it with my head and most of my limbs.'[10]

But if Thomas's spirits were buoyant, Frost's were not. Elinor's pregnancy had ended in miscarriage; in a reversal of form, it was the American who now wrote melancholically. 'I have reached the point this evening where no letter to or from you will take the place of seeing you. I am simply down on the floor kicking and thrashing with resentment against everything as it is. I like nothing, neither being here with you there and so hard to talk to nor being so ineffectual at my years to help myself or anyone else.' Frost doubted Thomas's revived spirits. In Dymock, they had felt able to run themselves down without reproach, but now Frost worried that an equilibrium might have become unbalanced. Behind his friend's reports of happiness, Frost suspected that there was a nihilism in Thomas that was fuelling his high spirits. Thomas had written that he did not look forward with any anxiety, but merely looked forward 'without a thought to something'. 'I don't want you to die,' Frost wrote. '(I confess I wanted you to face the possibility of death): I want you to come over here and begin all over the life we had in St Martin's Lane at Tyler's Green at White Leaved Dale and at Balham. Use should decide it for you. If you can be more useful living than dying I dont see that you have to go behind that. Dont be run away with by your nonsense.'[11]

Yet Thomas's moods were not quite as he presented them to his aunt or Frost. With others he was more variable, telling Eleanor that he continued to find companionship a problem, that he had always found communion difficult unless with someone like Frost. To Jack Haines he admitted that he knew his happiness might not lie in England: 'I can't see that there will be anything for me when the War is over, if I am alive and well, but to go to New Hampshire and start afresh.' But the routine was at least comfortable enough for him to find time once again to write verse. He was now wholly dependent upon Eleanor for typing and sent her two poems for putting into typescript. But he kept his writing entirely secret from his camp colleagues. His reservation is a matter of regret, for only a few huts away was Wilfred Owen, who likewise was keeping his early verses to himself. Had the two men declared their interest then they would surely have taken to one another's company. Thomas would have liked Owen for his gentle, unassuming presence, his passionate belief in the power of verse, his sharp intelligence and his knowledge of Wales. Owen would have flourished under Thomas's guidance, learned from his knowledge of literature and welcomed the kind of senior patronage that he would find in Siegfried Sassoon. Fifteen years the junior, it remains a tantalising thought that Owen might have learned about speech rhythms and sound-sense from Edward Thomas at such an impressionable age. Owen would go on to write some of the most graphic, shocking and energised poetry of the war, but who knows how it might have developed under Thomas's guiding eye. Owen was probably instructed in map-reading by Edward Thomas, but being at the time outside the professional literary world, he would not have recognised his tutor for the literary critic he was. It seems likely that two of the finest poets of the war may have seen each other or even spoken, before going about their army business none the wiser.[12]

Whatever the reason for the swings in Thomas's mood and for the differing reports that he gave, there may have been one new factor at play that he was largely concealing from his friends. In November, Thomas made a social call on a woman he had not seen in more than fifteen years. She lived only a few miles from Hare Hall Camp and was a poet and painter, trained at the Slade by Henry Tonks. She was a year younger than Thomas, beautiful, a mother of two; and she was desperately lonely. Her friendship with Edward would pose Helen Thomas a sterner test than was ever presented by Eleanor Farjeon. Her name was Edna Clarke Hall.

Winter

Great House, near Upminster Common, a few miles from Hare Hall Camp, was a red-brick Georgian farmhouse with tall chimneys and a large bay window which opened outward onto a wild overrun garden. The house was surrounded by so many trees that on first appearance it seemed to have grown out of a coppice. Elm floorboards were laid throughout, and the house was furnished by curiosities that the owner had acquired over the years: a Clementi piano rescued from a local tavern, a delicate pearwood writing desk. The house was home to William and Edna Clarke Hall, but more so to Edna, as her husband was very rarely at home.

Edna Clarke Hall had exhibited her watercolours annually with Vanessa Bell's Friday Club since 1910; in April 1914 a successful solo exhibition at the Chenil Gallery in Chelsea showed fifty-six works and grossed £147 in sales. Shortly after, she temporarily set aside her paints to spend the next two years on verse. Her life in Essex was lonely. William Clarke Hall was a barrister and campaigner for children's rights who spent lengthy weeks in his chambers at Gray's Inn, leaving his wife feeling isolated in their country house. The couple had two boys of their own, but Edna could not forgive her husband's decision to apply his energies to the children of his charity work, some of whom were foundlings, abandoned by prostitutes. William would return at the weekends with an orphan in tow, sometimes leaving Edna to care for the child when he returned to London the next week. For Edna, the longing and the hurt was intense. 'O why does a man engross [sic] his mind in this cause of prostitutes leaving his wife sick to the heart in loneliness,' she wrote in her journal.[1]

On a cold day in November 1915, Edna returned to Great House from London, where she had spent a restless night in a strange hotel, recalling a face 'young and sad and full of exquisite gentleness'. The face belonged to Edward Thomas, and on recalling him instantly, she said, 'the little room became sacred with his incense'. Edna and Edward met around the turn of the century, when even then it was apparent to both that her marriage seemed to lack understanding. Thomas used to visit her then in the company of a solicitor friend who would discuss law with William, leaving Edna and Edward to one another's company. '*They* are *there* –', said Edward flirtatiously, '*we are here* –'. Each recorded a physical awareness of the other, and Thomas went so far as to tell Edna that Helen had become one of her admirers after he described her beauty to his wife, 'though I will swear that I have not done you justice in my descriptions'. Helen saw Edna for herself in the autumn of 1900, and was intimidated, she told Edna, by her presence. 'You came unexpectedly and you had your arms full of autumn branches and I felt very shy of you because of your beauty and your sweetness, because you had so much that because of my love for Edward I hoped to have.' There was an ease and an intimacy about Thomas's manner with Edna in those turn-of-the-century days, and in 1900 he told her, 'I live – if living it may be called – by my writing, "literature" we call it in Fleet St. (*derived from "litter", as we say "a litter of pigs" or "he made an awful litter"*).'[2]

Fifteen years had passed before Edna's dream of Edward in the 'strange hotel' in 1915. Edna herself takes up the story of what happened next.

But that day when I returned home Willie greeted me with 'who do you think came here yesterday?' My mind said 'Edward Thomas' but my lips questioned 'who?' 'M.__ P. __'! answered Willie and though I would give him welcome my 'O really' was a flimsy disguise to the disappointment to that sense of inner certainty which the name had contradicted – and then came from Willie – 'who do you think came

with him?' I held my answer which this time came leaping to my lips
and well content to my 'tell me?' I heard the name from his

'Edward Thomas.'

And when he came again the next day I spoke of that – and he spoke
of the clay as we sat by the open fire with the window on either side.

Edna's journals are littered with the word 'clay'. It was a medium
she understood artistically, but its value here lies in the symbol
that she associated with Thomas, as she described him, 'he clay
if you will'. In her journal she wrote out his line from 'Wind and
Mist' – 'the clay first broke my heart and then my back' – before
setting to verse their meeting that November day.

> I spoke yesterday of that strange
> Heralding on your return that came to me
> You spoke to me of clay –
> Thus sitting quiet, my son upon my knee
> At open hearth where orchard wood did burn
> We met again with words spoke casually
> Of pshycie [sic] hours and heavy clay by turn
> Your words gave weight to what I had to say
> And mine did lightly penetrate your clay.[3]

Over his eight months stationed at Hare Hall Camp, Thomas
became a frequent caller, though how frequent neither he nor
Edna recorded. The two would walk together in the fields and
lanes surrounding the house, gathering fallen wood from the
orchard with which they would feed the open fire as they talked
of their arts of poetry and painting.

When in the barn studio he found a drawing of our road dipping down he
said that he had often prayed they would never be asked to march down
there because of the mystery it held for him, and then finding a water-
colour – trees and a woman and goat by the road side he was filled with
pleasure – 'I am glad you like that but why do you?' 'Because it is so *true.*'

Thomas standing a little apart wrote something. 'Are you still at
your mapping?' I asked. 'No' he said 'I was only making a note – it is a
bad habit I have.' and he smiled a little saying it.[4]

Thomas's gentle understanding of Edna's domestic plight, and their rangy, artistic conversations and shared interests, were a lifeline to Edna that winter of 1915. Throughout her journals she captured many of his characteristic, gentle touches.

There is a smile at the corner of those lips where pride with tenderness dwell – There is ease in the quiet manner and in the blue of those eyes like thoughts shy and perfect as a bird – elusive as the unknown bird he tells of in the earthly woodlands.

> O genius of Edward Thomas
> you are dearly loved –
> give me your flowers.[5]

As 1915 drew to a close, Thomas seemed changed. He was happier – at least at camp, though lonely and missing the friendship of Robert Frost. His work as a map instructor had brought him a new confidence in his abilities to teach and impart his skills, and the routine of army life had given him a structure within which he could contain the darker urges of his depression. But his hesitations about the war itself continued to surface: he questioned the motivation of the conflict, despised its jingoism and profiteering, and could not abide the brutish xenophobia that it engendered by 'the cross-eyed gents' who ran the newspapers. On 26 November he had jotted the first lines to a poem that would be his angriest response yet to the war; one month later, on Boxing Day 1915, he completed a draft in verse.

THIS IS NO CASE OF PETTY RIGHT OR WRONG

> This is no case of petty right or wrong
> That politicians or philosophers
> Can judge. I hate not Germans, nor grow hot
> With love of Englishmen, to please newspapers.
> Beside my hate for one fat patriot
> My hatred of the Kaiser is love true: –
> A kind of god he is, banging a gong.

But I have not to choose between the two,
Or between justice and injustice. Dinned
With war and argument I read no more
Than in the storm smoking along the wind
Athwart the wood. Two witches' cauldrons roar.
From one the weather shall rise clear and gay;
Out of the other an England beautiful
And like her mother that died yesterday.
Little I know or care if, being dull,
I shall miss something that historians
Can rake out of the ashes when perchance
The phoenix broods serene above their ken.
But with the best and meanest Englishmen
I am one in crying, God save England, lest
We lose what never slaves and cattle blessed.
The ages made her that made us from the dust:
She is all we know and live by, and we trust
She is good and must endure, loving her so:
And as we love ourselves we hate her foe.[6]

Mervyn arrived home from America on Sunday 19 December, but he had missed his connecting train to Steep and so missed his father, who had had to be back in Hare Hall for 9.15 that evening. Edward managed to get home the following week and spent time walking with his son. He told Eleanor, 'Mervyn met me and I hardly knew him,' – he found his son easier in temper, as he himself had become, and he wrote to Frost that they took pleasure in one another's company. For the first time in almost a year the family were all together: Helen, Bronwen, Myfanwy, Edward and Mervyn, each one pleased to be spending their Christmas together at Steep.[7]

On New Year's Day, Thomas got away from camp and up to London, but he had a quarrelsome day. He saw his father, and this time the simmering disagreements about the war broke out fully into the open. 'He made me very sick,' Thomas recounted to Frost. 'He treats me so that I have a feeling of shame that I am alive. I couldn't sleep after it. Nothing much happened. We argued about the war and he showed that his real feeling when he is not trying to be nice and comfortable is one of contempt. I know what contempt is and partly what I suffered was from the reminder that I had probably made Helen feel exactly the same.' Over the weeks that followed Thomas composed the only poem about his father that he would write, a scornful, poisonous verse dripping with animosity.

> I may come near loving you
> When you are dead
> And there is nothing to do
> And much to be said.

Edward would not see that day; his father died in 1920. It would be some time before Helen would release the poem for publication; when she did, Walter de la Mare queried the openness of its punctuation with the poetry editor of its publishing house, T. S. Eliot, who replied, 'I do not find the slight ambiguity unpleasing.'[8]

Thomas returned to camp more drearily than ever before following the row with his father. 'I shall recover, but it makes a difference and I am inclined not to see him again for a time.' He called on Monro at the Poetry Bookshop, but found the proprietor in cantankerous form, delighting in opinions that were given, believed Thomas, simply for the sake of self-assertion. 'It will be a good thing if I don't see Monro again,' said Thomas, who seemed to be turning from anyone he could. But there was at least one piece of news that pleased him from his visit to the Poetry Bookshop: Ralph Hodgson, he learned, with whom he had quarrelled about the war, had 'sent his love to me, so I am forgiven'.[9]

If the row with his father overshadowed Thomas's first week back at camp, a move to a new company did little to improve his mood. The fastidiousness of their morning parade was a daily irritant.

Although only a lance corporal, Thomas was the senior officer in the hut, which meant he had to take charge of its twenty men, organising cleaning duties, supervising mealtimes and calling the roll. He admitted to Eleanor that he was not really enjoying it and had been out of sorts since the row with his father. And to top it all, Thomas ran foul of the authorities after covering for one of his men, the artist Arnold Mason, and signing him present when he knew him to be stealing a few hours' extra leave; when Mason did not return until the next morning he and Thomas were each hauled up before the senior officers for 'serious talks', which Thomas suspected might impede his chances of a promotion to full corporal.[10]

Thomas began to draft 'Rain', set in the camp's Hut 51 but drawing heavily on that evening in 1911 when he was caught in the blackening downpour along the Icknield Way. Thomas had continually drawn upon his field notebooks to aid his memory, but on this occasion he had lifted his published prose.

RAIN

Rain, midnight rain, nothing but the wild rain
On this bleak hut, and solitude, and me
Remembering again that I shall die
And neither hear the rain nor give it thanks
For washing me cleaner than I have been
Since I was born into this solitude.
Blessed are the dead that the rain rains upon:
But here I pray that none whom once I loved
Is dying tonight or lying still awake
Solitary, listening to the rain,
Either in pain or thus in sympathy
Helpless among the living and the dead,
Like a cold water among broken reeds,
Myriads of broken reeds all still and stiff,
Like me who have no love which this wild rain
Has not dissolved except the love of death,

If love it be towards what is perfect and
Cannot, the tempest tells me, disappoint.[11]

Thomas was indeed denied his promotion to corporal in retribution for his misdemeanour with Arnold Mason. The episode
left him feeling inadequate, and not succeeding as he instinctively felt he should, while his teaching was bringing only mixed
results. When the call for officers came in that month Thomas
gave it serious consideration. 'I felt inclined to volunteer for
France when 300 were asked for last week, and I still hope we
may (all of us instructors) go if only for a time just to get me out
of this camp to a different kind of mind.' And coming home from
Hare Hall that weekend of 22 January, Thomas put to paper a
sixty-four-line poem that he had begun to turn over in his head
the week before, and which very clearly now pointed towards
the next step in his journey:

> Now all roads lead to France
> And heavy is the tread
> Of the living; but the dead
> Returning lightly dance:
>
> Whatever the road bring
> To me or take from me,
> They keep me company
> With their pattering,
>
> Crowding the solitude
> Of the loops over the downs,
> Hushing the roar of towns
> And their brief multitude.[12]

As the winter deepened, something began to change in the poetry
that Edward Thomas was writing. In January and February, and
then again in March and April, a string of poems mined, or struggled to mine, the subject of love. By the early spring there were
seven pieces, another by the middle of May. He had written lit-

tle love poetry among his first hundred poems, and those he did
compose were largely rhetorical or song-based verses that could
hardly be described as confessional. But there was something different in the tone of the pieces that winter and spring, something
concentrated, even wilful. Was he simply deepening the range
of his craft with the love lyric, or was he experiencing anguish
at his separation from home and Helen? Or was he touched by a
different proximity altogether: the return into his life of another
woman who had stirred something deep within him?

The first of these lyrics, 'The clouds that are so light', seemed
to speak knowingly of the interdependence of the observed and
the observer, the muse and poet: 'Away from your shadow on me
| Your beauty less would be'. It was a coquettish, even mysteri-
ous poem, which Edward sent to Helen, as was his habit, though
her questioning of it revealed that she had deemed it not to be a
piece about herself. Thomas was short tempered in his response.
'Fancy your thinking that I might have someone in view in those
verses beginning "The clouds that are so light",' he wrote. 'Fancy
your being pleased at the idea. Well, perhaps you wouldn't be, if
there really were someone, in which case I would hardly write
verses, I think.' The phrasing seemed peculiar, goading even, *if
there really were someone*: why say what there was no need to say,
why plant a seed of worry? Perhaps realising that he had over-
stepped the mark, Thomas tried a consolatory tone. 'Oh, you
needn't think of another lady. There would have to be 2 to make
a love affair and I am only one.' But this was still ambiguous:
was there then 'another lady'? Did 'one' of the '2' wish for a love
affair? Finally, Thomas struck a tone of reassurance. 'Nobody
but you would ever be likely to respond as I wished. I don't like
to think anybody but I could respond to you. If you turned to
anybody else I should come to an end immediately.' Helen took
huge comfort from the moments when Edward addressed her
with affection. To her it harked back to more romantic days
when the demand for love seemed mutual and dependent; it also

gave her hope that the time ahead would be a better one. But what had Thomas stirred up?[13]

On past experience alone Helen had cause to worry. Thomas had spent the winter of 1907–8 in Minsmere on the Suffolk coast, preparing his biography of Richard Jefferies, with a family for whom Helen had been a governess when she was courting Edward. Hope Webb had been a favourite of Helen's then, and now, aged eighteen, she had grown into an attractive girl, as Thomas reported to Bottomley at the time. 'I got very fond of a girl of 17 [sic] with two long plaits of dark brown hair & the richest grey eyes, very wild & shy, to whom I could not say 10 words, nor she to me . . . But I liked her for her perfect wild youthfulness & remoteness from myself & now I think of her every day in vain acquiescent dissatisfaction, & shall perhaps never see her again, & shall be sad to hear she ever likes anyone else even tho she will never like me.' Over the Christmas holidays that year, Edward and Hope had taken walks along the coast, collected pebbles and shells (and a human skull for Walter de la Mare that had rolled out of the crumbling cliff-top graveyard); he had settled in to tactful criticism of her teenage verses. 'I had the sharpest pains and pleasures of satisfaction, longing and - - - -' Thomas broke off a letter to de la Mare at the time. When Hope returned to school in January 1908, Thomas stayed on in Suffolk and lent her books and wrote her letters, and urged her to keep their wanderings secret. 'I have become so deeply corrupted,' he told a friend at the time. 'My wife and family are quite forgotten among these delights.' Thomas experienced a kind of fretful giddiness and could not concentrate on his book; he sent her his *Pocket Book of Poems and Songs for the Open Air* and felt what he referred to at the time as 'a strong unreasoning liking' for the girl. It was at this point that he shared his feelings quite matter-of-factly with Helen.[14]

Helen responded in a string of letters, with each one expressing more anxiety than the last. 'If I was the Webbs, I'd be proud to think that you loved Hope,' she wrote with initial restraint, 'for they might see with half an eye that you are not the sort to enter her room at night, or kiss her behind the door – unless she wanted you to. Well never mind sweetheart, perhaps she loves you – in her way, – she's reading Jefferies, that's something isn't it?' But the next day her tone had become more concerned. 'Hope's written again to you, and you to her I suppose. I wonder (I do really so please tell me, I'm quite serious) what you want her to develop into, or what you want "it" to develop into. You are fond of her, but you can't make her fond of you without making it difficult for her. Is it to be the friendship of a middle aged man, a man of letters etc. etc. and of a simple schoolgirl, the sort of idyllic affair that your biographers will dote on – a passionless, innocent, intimate, uncleish, loverish affair that makes one wish in reading the biography that "I" had been the girl. Is it to be that sort? Or is she meant to slip unconsciously into something more, with senti-ment in it, and heart openings, and in fact a love affair, or what? It puzzles me . . . Do tell me . . . I don't know if I'm any better for having written this letter, or if I'll cry myself to sleep.' Next Helen urged her husband to come to his senses: 'you will be care-ful won't you; she's so very young, so very ignorant, and you don't know her a bit, what she is at all, only that she's different from the others, dark haired and dark eyed'. And then Helen made a risky move: rather than repel Edward's feelings, she offered to bring them into their inner circle. 'I don't want anything else at all if you'll love me,' she wrote. 'I want you to love Hope if you'll love me, too. But I'm so different I don't see how you can.' What followed were a series of pounding love letters in which Helen stressed her understanding and his need for independence. 'The greatest thing I could do for you would be to slip away,' she had written on Valentine's Day 1908.[15]

Helen's departure would not be necessary. Thomas's exchanges with Hope were unsatisfying, as he knew they would be, for he understood full well that his interest in the girl was consolation against a depression that 'no doctor can cure me of'. Hope did not keep her own counsel, as Thomas had asked, but confided in her sister, who, knowing that Thomas was a married man and suspecting his intentions, passed chapter and verse onto her parents. Thomas was interviewed by her irate father, who demanded that no further contact with his daughter be had, and a humiliated Thomas bid his friends not to speak of it. Helen believed that Edward had taken a cruel pleasure in stoking her jealousy; but he had at least responded by inviting her to join him in Minsmere, which she did. The episode was concluded; Edward tried to curb his unkindness, Helen to improve the home life that she offered. She had handled the episode deftly: encouraging his sense of independence, understanding his desires, praising his attractiveness and appealing subtly to the impeccability of his morals. Five years later she would manage the arrival of Eleanor Farjeon in a similar way, bringing her into the inner circle and supervising the feelings of all involved; but she was not able to extend the same influence with the older, wiser and more beautiful Edna Clarke Hall.[16]

The friendship of Edward and Edna progressed delicately, without scandal and without causing pain to anyone else. Edna was captivated by the return into her life of her former friend; the private journals she kept after his death are teeming with rich, physical and sometimes intimate descriptions of Thomas. She wrote out in full or in part no fewer than fifteen of his poems in her journals, and many of her own besides, as she explained to him in a letter after his death.

Dear Edward, I fear it is your lot to bear upon your stalwart but ghostly shoulder the responsibility of many nerves and I must confess to you – so dear among the dead – that you have been an inspiration to me, and that many verses are written to you, but there are some *not* penned in your name – and it is these unnamed that may in the imagination of the few be yet so placed. I see you smile – you make no trouble of it? dear friend! then all is well.

Typical of Edna's many verses:

TO E. T.

Remote and still you stood a little space
With eyes scarce lowered 'gainst the rays that sought them
And warmly touched the lips that could have taught them
How beauty dwells in any sunlit place
And thus you stood the sunlight on your face.

But Thomas, in the next of the winter love poems, his first in February and among the most brutally honest of any in his collection, chose to make an announcement of a very different sort: a lyric which questioned his capacity to love at all, setting the grander claims of the love poets ('Those things that poets said') against his more muted personal experience.

For certainly not thus,
Then or thereafter, I
Loved ever. Between us
Decide, good Love, before I die.

Only, that once I loved
By this one argument
Is very plainly proved:
I loving not am different.

Who, if anyone, did Thomas now address? Was he working through his withdrawal from Helen or conveying a message to Edna that he was incapable of love? Or was he simply talking to nobody but himself? It seemed for whatever reason that in his verse he now felt the need to explore or explain himself romantically. And two days after the last poem, came another, this one untitled.

No one so much as you
Loves this my clay,
Or would lament as you
Its dying day.

You know me through and through
Though I have not told,
And though with what you know
You are not bold.

None ever was so fair
As I thought you:
Not a word can I bear
Spoken against you.

All that I ever did
For you seemed coarse
Compared with what I hid
Nor put in force.

My eyes scarce dare meet you
Lest they should prove
I but respond to you
And do not love.

We look and understand,
We cannot speak
Except in trifles and
Words the most weak.

For I at most accept
Your love, regretting
That is all: I have kept
Only a fretting

That I could not return
All that you gave
And could not ever burn
With the love you have,

Till sometimes it did seem
Better it were
Never to see you more
Than linger here

With only gratitude
Instead of love –

A pine in solitude
Cradling a dove.[17]

For the second time Helen found herself questioning the inspiration behind Edward's new poem. Thomas told her that these were verses to his mother, and it is not beyond possibility they might have begun that way in the mind of the author. Thomas was on sick leave and had been staying at Balham with his parents at the time, and the only surviving manuscript shows that he had struck out 'London' as the place of composition (replacing it with 'Going home on sick leave' to Steep); his mother may well have been in his thoughts then, not least because he had written the poisoned verses to his father only three days before. But by the conclusion of the poem the addressee seemed not to be a mother at all but a person to whom the 'I' was incapable of returning affection: a lover, in other words, or rather a former or potential lover; Helen, perhaps, whom he was heading home to see that day, or possibly there lies a clue planted knowingly or otherwise by its author – 'clay', which had already become a kind of codeword that he shared with Edna Clarke Hall.

The love poems he wrote in the winter of 1916 do not point neatly to one person; nor should it be assumed that their author was in love in order to have written them (he had stressed that he was not). In response to this last poem, Thomas had been at pains to tell Helen that he was in fact incapable of loving:

you know my usual belief is that I don't and can't love and haven't done for something near 20 years. You know too that you don't think my nature really compatible with love, being so clear and critical. You know how unlike I am to you, and you know that you love, so how can I?

He held no naive assumptions about the true subject of love poetry. In 1910 he had written:

Love-poetry, like all other lyric poetry, is in a sense unintentionally overheard, and only by accident and in part understood, since it is written not for any one, far less for the public, but for the understanding spirit that is in the air round about or in the sky or somewhere.

That 'understanding spirit' might well have been Thomas himself, for it seems likely that these poems were written as much in address to himself as ever they were to another person. Why give your lover a mere poem, Thomas wrote once, when the gift of love itself was on offer? 'The love-poem is not for the beloved, for it is not worthy, as it is the least thing that is given'. He understood that the most apparently intimate poem may be a performance. 'A poet writes always of his personal life,' said W. B. Yeats, but with a caveat: 'there is always phantasmagoria'. Thomas's poems are filled with a 'phantasmagoria' of fictive voices and imaginative episodes, and it would be an underestimation of his creative powers to read them as mere transcriptions of life events. Nevertheless, there were moments in his poetry when the distance between art and life seemed barely anything at all. 'I *am* the aspen,' Thomas wrote to Eleanor Farjeon when advising her how to understand his poem about the poplar trees beside the crossroads where he lived in Steep. And now yet another love poem followed on 14 February, Valentine's Day; the final stanza:

> She is to be kissed
> Only perhaps by me;
> She may be seeking
> Me and no other: she
> May not exist.

This, entitled 'The Unknown', is the most knowing and most playful of three February poems and may express most truly the flirtation with Edna: that it was to Thomas, and possibly to Edna, an unobtainable idea.[18]

Ever the martyr when it came to Edward's feelings, Helen said that she was glad that he had met Edna once again, that it was good for him to have someone there to talk to in the strange new life he had undertaken. The times at Great House refreshed him, she knew, and she welcomed anything and anyone who brought warmth to his life. But privately she agonised about the one quality that she knew she could not bring him: beauty. In that sense alone, Eleanor Farjeon had not been a threat to their marriage, and Hope Webb had been but a girl; but Edna Clarke Hall had a beauty that took their relationship out of Helen's hands, and it was a source of anguish for her. 'Why wasn't I beautiful to Edward?' Helen asked Edna in 1919. 'Oh I did so long for your beauty not to take it from him, not take but give, to have hair & eyes & mouth & that something else ... I remember you so clearly standing for all I longed to have to give him.'[19]

Snowstorms and gales battered Hare Hall Camp in February. Three inches of snow fell on the 26th alone. Thomas evaded the measles that were rife in the camp, but he could not elude the chill that was doing the rounds, and was signed off on convalescent leave for the first week in February. He spent it in Balham, writing 'The Ash Grove', sending drafts of six stanzas to Helen and of seven to Eleanor, before paring it down to just four. In the meantime, he had been at work on a war sonnet which fizzled with anti-religious anger toward a 'stone-deaf and stone-blind' God sitting aloft the rampage of conflict. But it was the love poems which had captured his attention that month, and it was telling of the vulnerability that had crept in between Helen and Edward that when, in February, he sent her the poem about his father with its hurtful finale 'But not so long as you live | Can I love you at all', Helen mistook them to be lines about herself. Once again, Thomas was called upon to reassure. 'Fancy your thinking those verses had anything to do with you,' he insisted. 'Fancy your thinking, too, that I should let you see them if they were. They are not to a woman at all. You know precisely all that I know of any woman I have cared a little for. They are as a matter of fact to father. So now, unless you choose to think I am deceiving you (which I don't think I ever did), you can be at ease again.'[20]

There was a pause of almost three weeks until Thomas wrote his next poem in early March, though that too was a love poem, 'Celandine':

> She found the celandines of February
> Always before us all. Her nature and name
> Were like those flowers, and now immediately
> For a short swift eternity back she came,
> Beautiful, happy, simply as when she wore
> Her brightest bloom among the winter hues
> Of all the world; and I was happy too,
> Seeing the blossoms and the maiden who
> Had seen them with me Februarys before,
> Bending to them as in and out she trod
> And laughed, with locks sweeping the mossy sod.

Thomas had a special affection for the yellow flower that he had seen each spring while walking through Ashford Hanger. It took to the damp, mossy banks there, and was to him every bit the messenger of spring, appearing most commonly in the first week of March, as it did now when he wrote this poem, though less commonly with the five petals that the flower in the poem bore.

> But this was a dream: the flowers were not true,
> Until I stooped to pluck from the grass there
> One of five petals and I smelt the juice
> Which made me sigh, remembering she was no more,
> Gone like a never perfectly recalled air.

Within the stream of love poems that Thomas was writing that winter and spring, two themes seemed to have emerged quite clearly now: his belief in his inability to love and the illusory quality of love itself.[21]

As February deepened the snow came heavily. It settled into a thick, dirty coverage that prevented all walking. Cold and hemmed in, Thomas was in gloomy form. He told Jack Haines that his *Four-and-Twenty Blackbirds* had been little reviewed; 'As to a book of my verses I can't think of it now. I am in no hurry and I hardly think there would be any buyers for Eastaway or Thomas. I shall remain Eastaway for a time yet.' There was no news of any likely deployment that might take him away from Essex, and in fact very little news of the war itself, about which the men in camp rarely liked to say too much.[22]

Germany had begun an offensive in Verdun, north-eastern France, on 21 February. It was a bombardment on a scale never before witnessed: more than a million shells rained in on that day alone on French trenches that were first blown apart, then lit up by flame-throwers and finally mopped up by storm troopers. A hole was punched in French lines three miles deep, though continued resistance would ensure that the battle would rage for a further ten months. It would be the longest single campaign of the war, costing a quarter of a million lives.

Spring

Since leaving England a year earlier, Frost had written to Thomas once a month or so, but the American's correspondence that winter had all but stopped and Thomas began a string of letters by highlighting the silence. 'It seems an age since I wrote and longer since I heard from you' (December); 'Again it is an immeasurable time since I heard from you' (January); 'I wish you would write' (January); 'What have I done that you shouldn't write to me for a month or more?' (February). Was there a problem, he wondered. Was Frost retreating in his friendship, sensing that Thomas's future in New England seemed uncertain? Finally, in February, Frost broke his silence and wrote to say that he had been detained delivering a talk for an audience in Lawrence, Massachusetts, but he said nothing of the poems that his friend had been sending. 'Your not mentioning them made me think I had missed fire,' wrote Thomas, 'I have written so many I suppose I am always missing fire.'[1]

Frost did indeed believe that Thomas's future looked uncertain. Once, the war had seemed a temporary interruption to his preparation for America, but now it began to fill his vision, deeper and further than before. 'You ask if I think it is going to be a long war,' Thomas told him. 'I don't think, but I do expect a lot of unexpected things and am not beginning really to look forward to any change. I hardly go beyond assuming that the war will end.' The inactivity was making Thomas restless. He could neither see an end to the conflict nor very clearly what his role in it would be. The camp measles, his chill, the numbing cold, a denied promotion and now the refusal of leave which meant he had to spend his thirty-eighth birthday in camp instead of at Steep. 'The long and short of it seems to be that I am what I was, in spite of my hopes last July,' he told Frost: the improvement in his spirit that had begun with his enlistment had reached a plateau. He continued to 'go in' on himself, as he had once put it to Frost, to ruminate and deflate. He managed at least to take walks around Epping Forest, sometimes in company, though usually alone, but found the countryside eerily quiet, the villages emptied of men, while those in camp simply waited and waited for orders. 'We don't know who or where or what we are.'[2]

If camp offered an artificial state, 'home' seemed a less and less authentic alternative. The word in itself sounded strange and strained, and Thomas sensed he was not alone in finding the captivity of camp something akin to an escape from family life. He wrote twenty-seven lines in which three men (possibly Thomas and the artists Paul Nash and John Wheatley) returned through the snow towards Hare Hall Camp, their 'home' and shelter for the time ahead: 'The word "home" raised a smile in us all three, | And one repeated it, smiling just so | That all knew what he meant and none would say.' Days later, he returned to the poem and added the final eight lines, in which thoughts of homesickness were dispelled: to admit as much would make life unendurable, 'else I should be | Another man, as often now I seem'.[3]

Thomas was feeling homeless and ill at ease with himself. He knew 'this captivity | Must somehow come to an end', but had no idea how to bring that about. The snow lingered into the first week of March, when conditions finally began to improve. 'The weather is changing at last. The snow has melted. The sun is very warm. The rooks in the camp trees are nesting. They wake us at 5.30.' Thomas recorded the 'thought moment' precisely in verse.

THAW

Over the land freckled with snow half-thawed
The speculating rooks at their nests cawed

And saw from elm-tops, delicate as flower of grass,
What we below could not see, Winter pass.

On 16 March he sat in the Shepherd and Dog public house, two
miles from camp, writing to Frost while Arnold Mason quietly
sketched him. News that his younger brother Reggie had been
made a full corporal ahead of him hardly lifted his mood. 'These
reminders that I am going to be passed over all the time don't
please me.' But Edward made full corporal himself at the end of
the month ('I wear 2 stripes or chevrons on my upper arm now
– not on the skin, but the sleeve'), and was working daily with
three other non-commissioned officers to teach the hundred-
strong company to read and make maps, lecturing twice a day to
thirty men at a time. He found himself getting ever more comfortable in his teaching, and told Eleanor that he wished for the
time being to continue in this role rather than seek any kind of
action abroad.[4]

Whatever the provenance of the winter love poems, the quartet
of pieces he wrote that spring were very certainly written for his
family. He once referred to them as 'household poems', one for
each of his children, and one for Helen.[5]

The first, the shortest and the sweetest of the quartet, was for
'my elder daughter', and drew upon the Essex places that he
would like to give her in return for the flowers that she brought
him. For Mervyn he would write a poem 'to my son' in which
reciprocity was more of a tussle. For 'my daughter the younger',
he had nothing to give her but 'Steep and her own world'. And
for Helen, 'I would give you back yourself, | ... And myself, too,
if I could find | Where it lay hidden and it proved kind.'[6]

On Easter Sunday from his hut at Hare Hall, Thomas drafted
an identical pair of twelve-line lyrics each of which hinted
at the passing of opportunity. One found two people walking,

believing that happiness had eluded them, or perhaps simply accepting the limits of their situation.

> When we two walked in Lent
> We imagined that happiness
> Was something different
> And this was something less.

It was a poem that balanced yearning with the solace that came from survival, knowing that each had been able to 'live free' at least in the memory of what had been shared. A second poem also drew upon walking.

LIKE THE TOUCH OF RAIN

> Like the touch of rain she was
> On a man's flesh and hair and eyes
> When the joy of walking thus
> Has taken him by surprise:
>
> With the love of the storm he burns,
> He sings, he laughs, well I know how,
> But forgets when he returns
> As I shall not forget her 'Go now.'

There for a moment the ink of the first draft ended, until Thomas returned later to add in pencil:

> Those two words shut a door
> Between me and the blessed rain
> That was never shut before
> And will not open again.

It would seem hasty or unwise to claim that any one person might have been the subject of this runic poem: Thomas himself had already made clear that even the most apparently intimate love poems might have taken more than one person (or even nobody at all) as their subject.

It is not only the present or past lover of one particular woman that can read and penetrate and enjoy love-poems, and this fact alone might show how vain it is to regard them as addressed merely to those whose names they may bear.

And yet the timing of both poems and their references to walking would fit with the way in which he spent his hours with Edna Clarke Hall in Essex. Lent had begun on 8 March that year, when Thomas was in camp two miles from Edna, and they may well have walked together then, picking celandines just as Thomas had written. Of course, there was nothing in the poems to suggest that it had to apply to *that* Lent of 1916, and the companion might equally well have been Helen, if indeed the poem was not a pure fiction. But the stirring of the physical senses – touch, flesh, hair, eyes – the burning with the love of the storm – these might well have been features of Thomas's attraction to Edna, and were all details mentioned by Edna in her journals; even if it is doubtful if the situation ended with a dismissal, 'go now'. Whatever the feelings that might have captivated him that spring, it would appear, at least in his verse, as if he were aware of having survived something or having scrambled to safer ground. Whether that threat had been intimacy or something quite different, it seemed now as May came that he really was preparing to 'go now': from the frustration of camp life in Essex to a further field.[7]

Thomas never mentioned Edna to Robert Frost: after the men's talks about marriage and responsibility in 1914 he almost certainly would not have chosen to confide any feelings he might have had. In 1908 he had made the mistake of telling his friends of Hope Webb, only to be roundly humiliated and having to instruct them, blushingly, 'Don't talk about this.' The relative absence of Edna's name in Thomas's correspondence is no surprise, especially when he was writing letters from camp that might very well have been prone to gossip or censorship. For Thomas, a private allure would have been enough: a companion, a muse, a subject of desire. He once wrote that the goal of love was not the possession of another person but the stimulation of desire for things both known and unknown: 'It is a desire of impossible things which the poet alternately assuages and rouses again by poetry.' This phantom love, if that is what it was – a world in which 'she may not exist', where 'flowers were not true', where dreams and clouds and shadows and storms leave us 'unillumined' or in 'helpless fretting' – this now, after happy months of flirtation and speculation, may have been coming to a close.[8]

Less than two years on from the experiment in semi-communal living in Gloucestershire, Dymock's poets were now scattered. Robert Frost was in America; Rupert Brooke in a grave in Skyros. Edward Thomas was in camp in Essex and John Drinkwater kept largely to Birmingham. Wilfrid Gibson had been rejected from army service on health grounds, and though he remained for the time being at the Old Nail-Shop in September he would leave for West Malvern. Lascelles Abercrombie had been rejected on the same grounds, but in March 1916 the founding and driving spirit of the Dymock Poets was preparing to leave the Gallows for good. Though his family would stay on in the cottage while he looked for a new home, he himself was preparing to move back north to the Mersey, where he was to undertake industrial work steel-testing in a munitions factory in Liverpool. With no poets at Little Iddens or Oldfields, and with Abercrombie now away from the Gallows, it was an unlikely time for a new poet to come calling in Dymock; but that is exactly what happened when a young writer and musician, dressed in his army khakis, wandered the parish lanes to find the poets he had heard about. At Ryton he met Catherine Abercrombie playing with her young boys in a field near the Gallows, and asked if she could direct him to the home of the poet Lascelles Abercrombie.

He was Ivor Gurney, and he would be wounded on Good Friday 1917 at Vermand south of Arras, three days before Thomas's death nearby. In 1918 he would begin setting to music the first of nineteen of Thomas's poems and would remain fascinated with his work in post-war years of deteriorating mental health. Helen would visit Gurney in Dartford Asylum after the war, bringing maps of Gloucestershire on which he would trace out the paths that Thomas and the Dymock poets had walked.[9]

But if the Dymock community had floundered, the Poetry Bookshop continued to flourish. Yeats gave his second reading on 11 April, held at the Passmore Edwards Settlement on Tavistock Square to accommodate the interest from an audience of more than three hundred. Monro had the good sense to publish 'The Farmer's Bride' by Charlotte Mew, and a debut from Robert Graves, though he squandered the chance to publish Siegfried Sassoon, and found that D. H. Lawrence and Robert Frost had existing contractual arrangements when he enquired after books from them. A second volume of *Georgian Poetry* had appeared from the Bookshop that winter, though Thomas thought little of it. 'The new man Ledwidge isn't any good, is he?' he had told Frost after thumbing it through. Francis Ledwidge was an Irish republican who had joined the British army because it stood between Ireland and a common enemy; but when British soldiers executed the leaders of the Easter Rising in Dublin that April, he became a desperately conflicted man. He drank heavily, reported late for duty and was court-martialled for insubordination. Ledwidge was killed by a German shell in 1917 while road-building on the Western Front, but the events in Dublin seemed curiously not to register with Thomas, who had been schooled in Irish Home Rule by his father. He seemed cut off now from external events, able to see little beyond camp life. The events of the Easter Rising might have had a profound effect on the life of Edward Thomas had he not already joined the army. On the day after the Rising, Prime Minister Asquith caved to pressure from David Lloyd George and on 26 April introduced universal military service.[10]

Nightingales surrounded the camp in May. The warm evenings opened into hot days, and Thomas found himself able to take more frequent walks, sometimes in the company of his fellow map-reading instructors, sometimes alone. He was finding the life comfortable enough to consider, seriously now, professional work within the military. A Welsh army job had come to light, Thomas told Eleanor Farjeon, to provide reportage ('"Eye-witness" stuff') for the newspapers, which he supposed he could do, if with a little reluctance 'and not to suit Welsh taste', though in the event, nothing would come of this. He wrote a quatrain, twinned with 'In Memoriam (Easter, 1915)', alike in almost every part of its syntax, 'The Cherry Trees', and a few days later, at Hare Hall Camp, a poem which appeared to trace the walks that Thomas might have taken in the woods around Great House, Edna's Essex home.[11]

IT RAINS

It rains, and nothing stirs within the fence
Anywhere through the orchard's untrodden, dense
Forest of parsley. The great diamonds
Of rain on the grassblades there is none to break,
Or the fallen petals further down to shake.

And I am nearly as happy as possible
To search the wilderness in vain though well,
To think of two walking, kissing there,
Drenched, yet forgetting the kisses of the rain:
Sad, too, to think that never, never again,

Unless alone, so happy shall I walk
In the rain. When I turn away, on its fine stalk
Twilight has fined to naught, the parsley flower
Figures, suspended still and ghostly white,
The past hovering as it revisits the light.

In only two of Thomas's 142 collected poems do people kiss, here and in 'The Unknown', written three months apart, both in Essex, with Helen away and Edna close by. It is reasonable to suppose both poems are fantasies, projections of ideals and desires; even so, the settings on which they were based would appear to be real enough. Edward and Edna did take walks in the rain through the orchard around Great House where they collected firewood. One entry from Edna's journal reads, 'A night under the orchard trees again which seems to restore me to curious energy'; another, already quoted, records Edna and Edward feeding the fire 'At open hearth where orchard wood did burn'. But there is little in Edna's journals to expressly suggest that a kiss might have taken place. So intensely does she linger over the minute detail of their glances and touches that an event as noteworthy as this would probably have been written up more than once. In only one poem does she hint that this might have happened, a sextet linked to Thomas by the finest of threads only: the sunlight in which she recorded seeing him for the last time. 'And in the sun stood you; | Your kiss took me to heaven!'[12]

It remains fanciful stuff; and yet, something had gotten beneath Thomas's skin. On 13–14 May he followed 'It rains' with a sonnet whose love-worn speaker pronounced, 'I had not found my goal', finishing, 'But thinking of your eyes, dear, I become | Dumb: for they flamed, and it was me they burned.' And travelling from Essex to Hampshire in June he wrote a lingering, even lascivious poem, more corporeal than before, in which eyes met eyes, and gazed on cheeks and hair, culminating in the uncharacteristic claim, 'I know your lust | Is love.' The months in Essex had produced eight or nine intimate poems, but whoever or whatever had been in his thoughts, those musings would now cease and his thoughts would turn toward the war.[13]

On 1 May Frost sent Thomas a new poem, set in familiar blank verse and featuring a wounded soldier invalided home to his grateful wife, knowing that the sooner the recovery the sooner the return to action. The poem was not based upon Thomas biographically, but the gentle domestic drama between the soldier and wife seemed sympathetically in tune with Thomas's life in Steep, even down to the wife's attention to the face and hands of her beloved, an obsession of Helen's.

NOT TO KEEP

They sent him back to her. The letter came
Saying . . . And she could have him. And before
She could be sure there was no hidden ill
Under the formal writing, he was in her sight,
Living. They gave him back to her alive –
How else? They are not known to send the dead –
And not disfigured visibly. His face?
His hands? She had to look, to ask,
'What is it, dear?' And she had given all
And still she had all – *they* had – they the lucky!
Wasn't she glad now? Everything seemed won,
And all the rest for them permissible ease.
She had to ask, 'What was it, dear?'
                                        'Enough,
Yet not enough. A bullet through and through.
High in the breast. Nothing but what good care
And medicine and rest, and you a week,
Can cure me of to go again.' The same
Grim giving to do over for them both.
She dared no more than ask him with her eyes
How was it with him for a second trial.
And with his eyes he asked her not to ask.
They had given him back to her, but not to keep.

'This last letter . . . with the poem "Not to Keep" mends all,' Thomas wrote to Frost. Though the letter has not survived, from the tone of the poem alone Thomas must have felt understood once more, no longer goaded by Frost, no longer belittled, but cared for, empathised with. The next day, Thomas wrote the poem that would most keenly express the value of the friendship with Frost that grew up in Gloucestershire that summer of 1914.

THE SUN USED TO SHINE

The sun used to shine while we two walked
Slowly together, paused and started
Again, and sometimes mused, sometimes talked
As either pleased, and cheerfully parted

Each night. We never disagreed
Which gate to rest on. The to be
And the late past we gave small heed.
We turned from men or poetry

To rumours of the war remote
Only till both stood disinclined
For aught but the yellow flavorous coat
Of an apple wasps had undermined;

Or a sentry of dark betonies,
The stateliest of small flowers on earth,
At the forest verge; or crocuses
Pale purple as if they had their birth

In sunless Hades fields. The war
Came back to mind with the moonrise
Which soldiers in the east afar
Beheld then. Nevertheless, our eyes

Could as well imagine the Crusades
Or Caesar's battles. Everything
To faintness like those rumours fades –
Like the brook's water glittering

Under the moonlight – like those walks
Now – like us two that took them, and
The fallen apples, all the talks
And silences – like memory's sand

When the tide covers it late or soon,
And other men through other flowers
In those fields under the same moon
Go talking and have easy hours.[14]

An ease had been restored to the friendship of Edward Thomas and Robert Frost. Frost shared his recollections on his anxiety of reaching forty, but Thomas was in resolute form. 'I find less to grumble at out loud than 10 years ago: I suppose I am more bent on making the best of what I have got instead of airing the fact that I deserve so much more.' Yet his visits to the theatre of late had made him feel old enough, at least as a writer. He had spent the afternoon of 20 May seeing a trio of plays by Brooke, Gibson and Bottomley, and found he had seen right through each piece, exposing the artificiality of the writing and the techniques employed; it was this that made him feel old, he told Frost. His literary friendships were receding for his new life at camp. Nobody recognised him now, he said. He had exchanged his tweeds for khaki, and acquaintances from his literary life had stood just a yard away from him at the theatre without a flicker of recognition. But two young artists in camp were becoming friends to Thomas in terms to which he could relate: a gifted young painter called Paul Nash was particularly skilled at finding birds' nests; another, John Wheatley (whose portrait of Thomas hangs in the National Gallery) was a 'perfect Welshman'. 'I am really lucky to have such a crowd of people always round & these 2 or 3 nearer,' he told Frost in a nod to his snowy walk back to camp with the men, 'you might guess from "Home" how much nearer'. There was a kindness about these men that extended into the senior ranks, he explained, and in particular their captain who hoped they would stay out of trouble, remember their Ps & Qs and generally do everything 'top-hole'. 'He is a kind huge man with no memory, very fond of the country. The other day in the fields he said "Company, attention! Oh, look at that rabbit."'[15]

Towards the end of May Thomas's ambivalence to a war overseas seemed as pronounced as ever. Life at camp was convivial enough for him to have been considering permanent positions, and until now he had no interest in serving abroad. Woken by the camp bugle, he wrote lines that were a conscious response to Brooke's now famous war sonnets and their corner of a foreign field. "'No one cares less than I, | Nobody knows but God, | Whether I am destined to lie | Under a foreign clod'". Nobody knew indeed, but Thomas himself was about to have a change of heart that would bring the foreign clod very much closer.[16]

The war was less than two years old – Thomas's own war almost a year – when he began a poem on 27 May with the working title of 'The Last Team'; by the time he had finished it, he had taken a step towards his decision to seek a commission on the front line. The poem he wrote may not have been a conventional war poem, but the war touched every part of it. It would be written into the storm and the fallen tree, into the missing man and in the mysterious lovers. It would bring together, as the war itself would, a confluence of class: labourer and poet, manual worker and man of leisure; archetypes and of course real men, who might meet again in France, where the furrow would become the trench.[17]

AS THE TEAM'S HEAD-BRASS

As the team's head-brass flashed out on the turn
The lovers disappeared into the wood.
I sat among the boughs of the fallen elm
That strewed an angle of the fallow, and
Watched the plough narrowing a yellow square
Of charlock. Every time the horses turned
Instead of treading me down, the ploughman leaned

Upon the handles to say or ask a word,
About the weather, next about the war.
Scraping the share he faced towards the wood,
And screwed along the furrow till the brass flashed
Once more.
                    The blizzard felled the elm whose crest
I sat in, by a woodpecker's round hole,
The ploughman said. 'When will they take it away?'
'When the war's over.' So the talk began –
One minute and an interval of ten,
A minute more and the same interval.
'Have you been out?' 'No.' 'And don't want to, perhaps?'
'If I could only come back again, I should.
I could spare an arm. I shouldn't want to lose
A leg. If I should lose my head, why, so,
I should want nothing more.... Have many gone
From here?' 'Yes.' 'Many lost?' 'Yes: a good few.
Only two teams work on the farm this year.
One of my mates is dead. The second day
In France they killed him. It was back in March,
The very night of the blizzard, too. Now if
He had stayed here we should have moved the tree.'
'And I should not have sat here. Everything
Would have been different. For it would have been
Another world.' 'Ay, and a better, though
If we could see all all might seem good.' Then
The lovers came out of the wood again:
The horses started and for the last time
I watched the clods crumble and topple over
After the ploughshare and the stumbling team.[18]

'If we could see all', Thomas had written, 'all might seem good.'
This skilfully awkward, monosyllabic line, with its mirrored
'all's turning to face one another in its middle, was arguably the
most revealing 'thought moment' that Edward Thomas had written. The speaker idling on his elm tree had appeared unmoved
by the war when the poem began. He had been flip when the

ploughman had asked if he had been out to France, adopting a tone of Shakespearean foolery over the loss of limbs. But in the ellipsis he had understood something invaluable, and realised what was wrong with the scene in which he sat: that the world he enjoyed was contingent upon those who were willing to fight for it. It was somewhere around this time, said Eleanor Farjeon, that she pressed him on precisely why he chose to enlist. Thomas was said to pause, bend down to scoop a handful of soil from around his shoe, and say, 'Literally, for this.'[19]

If we could see all, then we could know the consequence and the value of our actions and so choose which paths to take. Thomas had agreed as much with the young soldier he met on the train the day he collected his enlistment papers: the difference between people was that some strained harder than others to foresee what they could of it. Many of Thomas's poems are about moments that cannot be seen or chosen. Poets in their yellow wood might claim to choose but not Thomas: his roads were not of his making and do not yield up their destination readily.

Within eight weeks of writing this poem, Thomas had committed himself to service overseas. He recorded the moment in a letter to Frost, on 28 July 1916.

A new step I have taken makes a good moment for writing. I offered myself for Artillery and today I was accepted, which means I shall go very soon to an Artillery School and be out in France or who knows where in a few months. After months of panic and uncertainty I feel much happier again except that I don't take easily to the trigonometry needed for artillery calculations. I have done very nearly all that I could do here in the way of teaching, lecturing, and taking charge of men in and out of doors. My old acquaintances were mostly moving out. The speeding up of things left no chance of enjoying the walks we used to have. So I had to go.

In writing 'As the team's head-brass' he had made his decision to seek a commission at the front, and now it seemed possible to find the war in much that he wrote: the bugle call was echoed in the calls of moorhens, tall reeds resembled the criss-cross of bayonets, the eyes that had looked tenderly were now turned towards the battlefield. His mind was made up.

> I'm bound away for ever,
> Away somewhere, away for ever.[20]

Summer

Thomas knew little about the artillery work for which he applied that June. He would require a precise knowledge of trigonometry in order to prepare the necessary calculations of angle, depth and velocity that the heavy siege guns would need to knock out German trenches. It took him some weeks to convince the authorities of his capabilities, though to a friend he put the application more simply: 'I am delighted with the idea of change'. From the Civil List he learned that he was not to receive a pension but a single grant of £300 to aid his writing; the news of missing out on an annual income could only have increased his sense of living day by day: 'the only certain thing is that the unexpected will happen,' he told Frost.[1]

Thomas's relief that the two men were corresponding again was palpable; he told Haines, 'Frost by the way has begun to send me letters again and some verses, very good ones. He is cheerful again, and not yet easy. The War preys on him, and he can't be feeling quite at home.' Frost must have forgiven his old friend for his outburst over 'The Road Not Taken' to send his poems across the sea once more, and they met only praise from Thomas, 'An Old Man's Winter Night', 'Out, Out –' and 'Encounter' among them.[2]

Thomas fell sick with an indeterminate illness again in June. His health was a regular concern now: he was highly susceptible to chills, colds and infections in the cheek-by-jowl life at camp. His immune system may have been weakened by the diabetes from which he was convinced he was suffering. According to his friend Jesse Berridge, Thomas was obsessed with a story he had heard that sufferers grew so hungry that they ate earth, and not without cause: sufferers were often starved as part of their treatment. Insulin was not medically available until 1921, and without a carefully regulated diet sufferers risked the onset of coma. But Thomas had refused to declare his illness to the army authorities; he ate the same food in camp as everyone else and seemed quite indifferent to the danger his diet might pose, and while weight loss in camp was not uncommon due to the plain fare and physical regime, it could also be a symptom of the illness. He had already told Frost that he was having to get new holes punched in his belt, so much was he shrinking in the waist; by 1916, photographs would picture him looking wiry and gaunt. He never suffered a serious episode (which may suggest Type I diabetes), and kept his suspicions almost entirely to himself, and with good reason, said Gordon Bottomley, for had Thomas declared his illness he would not have been sent to the front.[3]

Thomas's poems that summer reflected his desire to apply himself:

> But now that there is something I could use
> My youth and strength for, I deny the age,
> The care and weakness that I know – refuse
> To admit I am unworthy of the wage
> Paid to a man who gives up eyes and breath
> For what can neither ask nor heed his death.

Eleanor described the sentiment within these lines as 'sick', but Thomas defended them, saying, 'I thought it was more than a shade heroic.' And the 'shades' were certainly darker now. But by the month's end he had penned a poem that beckoned its reader into the echoing forest that lay at the end of 'The Green Roads', a fragment of woodland six miles from his camp. He said that he could not imagine a wilder, quieter place than this; but the poem bore a sinister undercurrent of stolen memories and forgetting, of nettle towers and dead oak trees, the white feathers of a plucked goose. Thomas's meditative and formal powers had rarely been in a state of fuller accomplishment, nor his subject matter darker or more strange.[4]

On 24 June an Allied bombardment began nearby the River Somme in north-eastern France; the explosions were so ground-shaking that windows reverberated in London 160 miles away. The assault would last for a week on a scale so destructive that by the time the artillery had finished pounding German lines, the infantry should have been able to push unopposed into the space evacuated by the Germans. Or at least that was the hope. But the German trenches were dug far deeper than had been allowed for, and when thirteen divisions of the British army went over the top on 1 July, the enemy machine guns rose from their dugouts and mowed them down in their thousands: 19,000 British soldiers were killed and twice that number were wounded. It would be the costliest day the British army had ever known. In Franconia, Robert Frost monitored events from afar. 'I believe the forward movement has come,' he told Haines. 'They are off, and my heart's with them with all the love I bear England.' But the forward movement came at unprecedented cost. By November, the Somme campaign had floundered in the French mud with 420,000 British losses; three to every two Germans. The scale of the devastation would produce a reassessment of training and of tactics in the British army; but it would do something else besides: it would alter the initial mood of patriotism among the ranks for ever. The optimistic war that Rupert Brooke and others had cheered would now give way to a harrowing out-pouring of verse from the men who had witnessed the horror of the slaughter.[5]

Robert Graves found himself in reserve north of Mametz Wood at the Somme that month. On 20 July his Royal Welch regiment were entrenched on a ridge beside a churchyard in Bazentin-le-Petit when the German bombardment came in. A fragment of shell punctured Graves's back beneath his shoulder blade and passed out through his chest, inches from his heart. He was ferried to a dressing station outside Mametz Wood where his death was announced to his colonel; his parents were informed and an obituary printed in *The Times*. But he had not died, and on 5 August *The Times* printed a correction that he was in fact recovering from his wounds in London's Highgate hospital. He would return to France briefly in 1917, but nerve damage largely kept him from further action at the front.[6]

Godwin Baynes had been in the comparative safety of a base hospital in Etaples, on the north-west French coast, when the Battle of the Somme began; but he would get much closer to the action. By August he was at the front, and was knocked down and bruised by a German shell at Delville Wood where he also caught trench fever. He was invalided to the Isle of Wight on 4 September and spent the remainder of the year there at Osborne House Convalescent Home for Officers, recovering from what on his army form was listed as 'debility', most likely shell-shock. It was a moment that turned out to save his life: the doctors that were sent to replace him were all killed when their hospital was bombed.[7]

Edward Thomas was clearing out his study at Steep that first day of the Somme offensive. With her husband fighting abroad, Mrs Lupton had asked Thomas to empty the Bee House in the garden of Wick Green so that she could take it back for her own use. For seven years it had been where Thomas worked and was the place where nearly all of his poetry had been written. 'I never thought it could happen,' he told John Freeman, of an ousting that would, as it turned out, be a severing of the final significant tie for Thomas in Hampshire. With Bronwen at school in London and Mervyn preparing to start an apprenticeship in the bus works at Walthamstow, Yew Tree Cottage was more spacious than it had been when they moved in the summer of 1913, though not spacious enough to accommodate a study or his many books, and once again Thomas prepared to sell off his stock to anyone who would take it. More importantly, Helen was now anxious and isolated. She wanted to move to Walthamstow, to make a home there for Mervyn which would also bring her nearer to Hare Hall Camp. Steep had lost its hold upon them all.[8]

Thomas had had two poems included in the arts journal *Form*: 'Lob' and 'Words', printed under the name Edward Eastaway. It was the third publication to have issued his work, although all had come either through personal connections or under his own editorship. By contrast, that July alone Frost had poems published in three separate journals, among them the harrowing 'Out, Out –' in *McClure's*, based on an incident in Bethlehem, New Hampshire, in 1910, when a family friend, a boy of sixteen, died following an accident involving a sawing machine. Frost had earned around £200 from poetry publications since leaving England, but for Thomas seeing his own poems in print was still something new, and yet he was not impressed by *Form*, which had run late by several months and seemed to him 'an ugly tasteless mess'. But James Guthrie was about to issue Thomas's first single-authored selection, *Six Poems*, which rolled off his Flansham press from 1916 in an elegant edition limited to one hundred copies. By now, Thomas had enough poems to fill two books of verse, and he began to turn his mind to exactly that: to seeing a volume of his poetry published.[9]

In London on 15 August he met Roger Ingpen, a brother-in-law of Walter de la Mare, whom he knew from his childhood days in Wandsworth. Ingpen had once brought Thomas a contract for *Richard Jefferies*, and was now running a modest London imprint called Selwyn and Blount ('I believe he is both Selwyn and Blount', wrote Thomas). Not since his disappointment with the Poetry Bookshop had Thomas approached a publisher, but when Ingpen asked to see a manuscript Thomas readily agreed. Over the next two weeks, from his parents' house in Balham,

Thomas prepared a typescript. He had finished 131 poems to date, and with eighteen of those reserved for the anthology that Abercrombie was preparing, Thomas was left with the task of omitting about half of the pieces he had written. By the start of September he had made his preliminary selection. He had not yet written the poem he would place first; but he knew exactly where he wished the book to finish, with 'Words', the poem he had composed after visiting May Hill with Jack Haines the day they spoke about Robert Frost. The final verse:

> Let me sometimes dance
> With you,
> Or climb
> Or stand perchance
> In ecstasy,
> Fixed and free
> In a rhyme,
> As poets do.[10]

It had been just over a year since Thomas enlisted and he told Frost that, 'I don't believe I often had as good times as I have had, one way and another, these past 13 months.' He wrote eight stanzas that seemed firmly to set the passing seasons behind him. The falling of the apples that August reminded him of the previous summer when the war began 'To turn young men to dung'; and in what might conceivably have been an enigmatic parting reference to Edna Clarke Hall, he wrote of a time 'when the lost one was here'.[11]

Thomas's departure would be a hard blow for Edna, who would sink into a terrible depression in the years to come. In Edward she had found a relationship of a kind that she believed she could never have with her husband: one that was careful, artistic and loving. It was sunset when she said her goodbye.

These eyes looked upon him, and may not do so again
These ears heard his voice, and may not do so again
This hand has touched his, and may not do so again
Yet with eyes of my new knowledge would I look upon him . . . I
would again mark the gentleness and resolution of the contours of that
face that had so haunted my imagination as I saw it last in light of the
setting sun – he standing before me silent and unaware.[12]

Robert Frost replied to Thomas's news of his transfer to the
artillery. 'My whole nature simply leaps at times to cross the
ocean to see you for one good talk,' he wrote, though he knew
that he might not find Thomas if he did. Thomas had explained
that he might 'go out' at any moment: 'This waiting troubles me.
I really want to be out.' And so Frost left open the offer that he
hoped might still one day be taken up. 'What's mine is yours,'
he wrote. 'Here are a house and forty odd acres of land you can
think of as a home and a refuge when your war is over. We shall
be waiting for you.'[13]

At Steep, Thomas lit a bonfire as he had once before and
burned papers and letters, and those books that he had been
unable to sell; the fire burned so hot that the embers smouldered
for days. On 25 August he reported for duty at Handel Street, in
Bloomsbury; he was now an Officer Cadet in the Royal Artillery.

Autumn

The Thomases were a family dispersed that autumn. Edward was stationed in Bloomsbury by day; by evening, billeted back at his parents in Balham. Mervyn was in Walthamstow and Bronwen with Helen's sister in Chiswick, while six-year-old Myfanwy stayed on at Yew Tree Cottage with John Freeman's family, who had now assumed the lease. Helen had taken advantage of the childminding and escaped to the Lake District with her sister for a few days' walking, but Edward was not best pleased to find the organisation of the house move left to him: 'Helen runs away so comfortably from affairs,' he grumbled to Frost. Thomas was in particularly nihilistic form. 'I am rather impatient to go out and be shot at,' he continued. 'That is all I want, to do something if I am discovered to be any use,' he wrote, having at last discovered that 'something' which he could use his 'youth and strength for'. The future seemed more unknowable than ever, he wrote, and hard to take quite seriously let alone depend upon. 'I have been saying to myself lately that I don't really care a fig what happens. But perhaps I do. – I am cut off. All the anchors are up. I have no friends now.'[1]

Edward Thomas sat in the sunlight of Brunswick Square in the grounds of the Foundling Hospital that September, watching the children play beneath the great London planes of Coram's Fields. Talk among the cadets was about anything but the war, and he wrote now that it formed a seal around them and him, of silence and of secrets that might only be broken with his death. The daily rhythm was his only guiding drive, not love or country but the modest pleasures in such moments as he experienced watching the children in Brunswick Square. Many times in the past Thomas had imagined a world without him in it, or thought about the effect his absence might have on others, and now he asked himself the question in verse:

> What will they do when I am gone? It is plain
> That they will do without me as the rain
> Can do without the flowers and the grass . . .

In the spring Thomas had complained mildly to Frost that 'nobody recognises me now'; at the time he had shrugged it off, but in the poem he wrote now he was pained to find that those who knew him had passed him in the street without recognition: 'I was naught to them. I turned about | To see them disappearing carelessly'. It was typical of Thomas to turn such a casual or benign episode into an assumed lack of self-worth, when in truth any one of his friends would have delighted at the encounter; instead, he wondered what would happen if he took away that friendship.[2]

Thomas was in a bleak mood: run down physically and with an infected hand, and possibly suffering from a lack of balance in his blood sugars. He told Frost, 'I am still poor and feeble and it is very nearly all I can do to keep on with the work here, tho it is not hard physically.' Not for the first time, Frost chuckled at the self-pity he detected in Thomas, and was certain it was time to kick some nonsense out of him once again. 'I began to think our positions were reversed –', he replied cheerily, 'you had got well-minded from having plunged into things and I had got soul-sick from having plunged out of them. Your letter shows you can still undertalk me when you like. A little vaccination and a little cold and you are down where it makes me dizzy to look in after you. You are so good at black talk that I believe your record will stand unbroken for years to come. It's as if somebody should do the hundred yards in five seconds flat.' Frost was the only one ever able to send up Edward Thomas successfully, but for a moment he laid his mischief aside. 'I'm afraid Englishmen aren't liking Americans very much now,' he continued. 'Should I dare go back to England at this moment? I often long to.' But

Thomas only smiled at the suggestion of Frost's return, 'It is one of the impossiblest things,' he wrote.[3]

By the third week of September, Thomas had sent off his type-script of poems to Roger Ingpen at Selwyn and Blount, and had received the orders that would take him gratefully out of London, to the Royal Artillery Barracks in Trowbridge, Wiltshire. There, he found that his weekends were his own, and delighted in two days' walking through the fields to Dillybrook Farm and to Bradford on Avon along the route he had cycled for *In Pursuit of Spring*. The camp was set up in tents, rather than the huts he had come to know in Essex, and he welcomed the chance to see the night sky once more, to be outdoors and to make new acquaintances. The barracks' trumpeter announced everything from reveille to lights out on a cracked horn and with no real proficiency, but Thomas found he did not mind.

THE TRUMPET

Rise up, rise up,
And, as the trumpet blowing
Chases the dreams of men,
As the dawn glowing
The stars that left unlit
The land and water,
Rise up and scatter
The dew that covers
The print of last night's lovers –
Scatter it, scatter it!

While you are listening
To the clear horn,
Forget, men, everything
On this earth newborn,
Except that it is lovelier
Than any mysteries.
Open your eyes to the air

That has washed the eyes of the stars
Through all the dewy night:
Up with the light,
To the old wars;
Arise, arise![4]

Thomas's experience of the war was very different from that of the other soldier poets. Where Sassoon, Graves and others had rushed to enlist and then recoiled at the horror of their experience of the conflict, Thomas's war seemed to be running in reverse. Initially unmoved and unsympathetic, fervently anti-nationalist, the longer the war went on the more committed he appeared, ever keener to seek action at the front, and writing the conflict into his verses with increasing verve. But his attitude to the conflict essentially did not change, and even this apparently front-footed poem did not abandon its guile or its irony. It was a mark of Thomas's accomplishment as a poet that he could now set his form and his content in opposition: the form, strident, galloping, heroic, offering no room for detour or for doubt, as clear and assured as the bugle call itself, but the content suggesting other tones – the dark stars that failed to illuminate the earth below, the hounding of dreams, the need to disperse the impression of the lovers in the dew, the cry to forget the newborn life for a loyalty to older wars.

Thomas had written the poem he would place first in his collection, and yet in composing he did his best to conceal that it was a poem at all. The verses were scribbled down amid the arithmetic calculations that Thomas was making about the trajectory of shells, disguising it as prose with a code to distinguish the line breaks. 'You see I have written it with only capitals to mark the lines,' he told Eleanor, 'because people are all around me and I don't want them to know.' As she observed, the paper bore testament to how hard self-consciousness died in Thomas: he did not mind poets knowing he was a soldier, but he would not allow soldiers to learn he was a poet.[5]

*

Helen moved into a cottage in the village of High Beech on 8 October. It seemed a bitter-sweet irony that all the while that Edward had been in camp there Helen had lived in Steep, and now she moved to Essex two months after he had moved out. The setting was picturesque, as Thomas told Elinor Frost: high on a hill alone beside seven or eight miles of forest, amid small ponds and wide glades and 'oaks, hornbeams, beeches, bracken, hollies, and some heather'. But the cottage itself was squalid: a semi-detached nurseryman's house, 'ugly, cold and inconvenient', remembered Helen, 'dismal and poorly-planned', said Eleanor. Edward could not get leave on the weekend that Helen moved her possessions and she was left supervising hired help whom she suspected to be drunk. But together, Helen and the children made the best of it and soon Helen was keeping Leghorn chickens and netting crops to keep out rabbits. And it was only seven miles from Mervyn's work, to which he cycled in the dark at six each morning while owls were still about the roads.[6]

On 20 October Thomas sent Helen a set of the verses which he was preparing for Selwyn and Blount with an instruction to forward them by registered post to Frost in Franconia, having first made a careful copy of the contents so that he could replicate them at a later date. 'Don't send to Frost before I tell you that the thing is settled,' he urged, but the typescript never arrived in New England, and was believed to be lost at sea. Thomas himself was restless for news, and when Selwyn and Blount had not replied after a month, he wrote to Roger Ingpen to ask him to come to a decision. Late in November he received the news he wanted. 'I have an anthology[,] an upcoming volume of verses at last,' he told Jack Haines. 'The publisher is fixed – Selwyn and Blount. Frost is getting a duplicate to offer an American publisher. It has just gone.' And he had decided on a title for the volume. 'The book is to be simply "Poems",' he wrote to Bottomley, 'unless the publisher prefers "Lob & other Poems" or "The Trumpet & other

Poems"'. He had been given only sixty-four pages by Selwyn and Blount but that was plenty, he said, 'I find I can get a lot into 64 pp.' Indeed he could: sixty-four poems, in fact.[7]

Poems was assembled from two typewriters – Thomas's in part but mostly Eleanor's – and a title page emblazoned in Thomas's own hand: 'Poems by Edward Eastaway'. The copies were drawn from typescripts that were not always the most recent drafts, and so required him to make one or two minor corrections: an added or amended word to the last lines of 'The Manor Farm' and 'The Green Roads', changes to articles in 'As the team's head-brass', and in 'Haymaking' a last-minute switch to have the reformer William Cobbett replace the poet William Cowper. 'November Sky' became 'November', and elsewhere Thomas gave no fewer than twenty-three poems their titles for the first time, now that he could put off that moment no longer. He carefully marked the folios to correspond with the contents page, where he made only small alterations to the running order, shuffling 'Lights Out' down to the third-last poem to stress its importance to the collection. 'The Trumpet', his ironic bugle call, would be first; 'The Sign-Post' from his indecisive traveller, second; 'Words', would remain the book's finale.[8]

'I just arranged my book in the nick of time,' Thomas told Frost on 29 November. 'For a letter came today warning me to expect a call to my "new unit". Which means probably going straight to a battery and not to any final school.' He told Frost that Roger Ingpen would wait to hear from him directly before passing the typescript for press, which spoke volumes about the store Thomas set in Frost's word.[9]

Frost, meanwhile, had seen his work in four journals that past month in the run-up to the publication of his latest book. In the early winter of 1916 *Mountain Interval* became Frost's third collection in little over three years. It was published by Henry Holt in New York, so becoming Frost's first original American edition. The poems in the book were leaner than those in *North of Boston*, frequently in blank verse, skilfully balancing neat dramatic dialogues against shorter lyrics. The collection opened with 'The Road Not Taken', typeset in italics to suggest a governing tone for the book, as was the concluding poem, 'The Sound of the Trees', ensuring that the collection was bookended by two of the poems from Ryton. In between, it moved through pieces that had been written before his time in England (such as 'An Old Man's Winter Night', 'Hyla Brook'), and those written after ('A Time to Talk', 'Out, Out –' and 'Snow'), and a fair showing of the pieces he had written or published in Beaconsfield ('A Patch of Old Snow' and 'Birches') or Gloucestershire ('Pea Brush', 'Putting in the Seed' and 'The Cow in Apple Time'). Thomas was no longer reviewing, and even if he had been Frost no longer would have needed his help. His reputation was growing so powerfully that he was offered a professorial position at Amherst College within a month of publication; from a single semester's teaching he would make around double the annual salary that Thomas had made in his best days as a hack.[10]

Frost meditated on the upcoming American presidential elections that would return Woodrow Wilson to office by the narrowest of margins. Wilson had campaigned as the man who had successfully kept the country out of the war; now America was only months away from joining it. But Frost told Thomas he had 'stopped asseverating' from his safe-house across the Atlantic. As an American, he said, he did not believe he should enlist, but the very least he could do was not to attempt to empathise with those taking greater risks than he.

You rather shut me up by enlisting. Talk is almost too cheap when all your friends are facing bullets. I don't believe I ought to enlist (since I am of course an American), but if I can't enlist, at least I refuse to talk sympathy beyond a certain point.

Instead, he concentrated once again on an attempt to lure Thomas to America, this time with the suggestion of a three-week lecture tour. 'Does that sound so very unmilitary?' asked Frost. 'They ought to consider that you were literary before you were military.' But Thomas's attentions were almost entirely military. 'I might very well be in France before Christmas,' he replied. 'I hope so.' When a room-mate, the actor Granville Barker, left for duties on Coast Defence, Thomas told Eleanor, 'I suppose his friends have urged his country not to risk his life. I hope I shall always be as eager to risk mine as I have been these last few months.' In fact Thomas was also on the move, to Wanstrow in Somerset for a week's further training, where he was billeted with a squad of forty men for lectures and practical work by day (walks and writing by night) before being granted ten days of leave. On 20 November he travelled to Lancashire to see his old friend Gordon Bottomley in Silverdale. Bottomley recalled Thomas's composure, and the sense of ease and contentedness that had now come over him: 'a happy, tranquillising presence, with a steadfast, gentle outlook on new dangers and old troubles'. Thomas sang bawdy army songs with a quiet mischief that Bottomley found very funny, and the two men watched a storm coming in over the mountains 'painted by the wild air' of the Kirkstone Pass; it was magnificent, and Thomas told Bottomley that he was a fortunate man. *Fortunate*, said Bottomley, surprised, with *his* life of disability? Yes, replied Thomas, fortunate because no one, even in ill health, could deserve so much.[11]

Thomas returned from Silverdale to High Beech, where Eleanor Farjeon came to stay. She found him in the very opposite of the mood described by Gordon Bottomley: restless, waspish, argumentative, out of sorts, making no disguise of the fact that life in camp was more of a home to him than the little cottage. Eleanor watched him chop the wood stack, knowing that he would not be burning it with his family that winter.[12]

On 23 November Thomas had been given a commission as second lieutenant, Royal Garrison Artillery (Special Reserve), making the call to France imminent. From Trowbridge, he wrote 'Lights Out', a poem that he said 'sums up what I have often thought at that call'; though no reader could mistake its deeper undercurrent.[13]

LIGHTS OUT

I have come to the borders of sleep,
The unfathomable deep
Forest where all must lose
Their way, however straight,
Or winding, soon or late;
They cannot choose.

Many a road and track
That, since the dawn's first crack,
Up to the forest brink,
Deceived the travellers
Suddenly now blurs,
And in they sink.

Here love ends,
Despair, ambition ends,
All pleasure and all trouble,
Although most sweet or bitter,
Here ends in sleep that is sweeter
Than tasks most noble.

There is not any book
Or face of dearest look
That I would not turn from now
To go into the unknown
I must enter and leave alone
I know not how.

The tall forest towers;
Its cloudy foliage lowers
Ahead, shelf above shelf;
Its silence I hear and obey
That I may lose my way
And myself.[14]

Winter

On 3 December Thomas transferred to Lydd, on the south coast of Kent, to complete the last sections of his training. There the Royal Artillery had their barracks in a camp that became known to the locals as 'Tin Town' for the cheap metal huts the army had erected. Lydd camp was a bare place even in good weather, but in winter it was desolate. Soon the wind and hail belted over the flats, chilling the shingle and caking the long rows of low huts in salt. It was blustery and bustling: two or three battalions a week passing through on their way to Codford in Wiltshire, the mustering point for their departure to France. But Thomas was glad of the setting, and appreciated the shingle flats, and the medieval village with its church tower commanding the marshes in all directions. And he was comforted to recognise at least one familiar face among the men who had been assigned to his hut.[1]

On 5 December the conciliatory Herbert Asquith had resigned as prime minster, replaced two days later by David Lloyd George. Robert Frost for one was pleased. 'Lloyd George is the great man and he belongs where he now takes his place,' he wrote, and he sent Thomas an unconvincing Shakespearean sonnet, 'Suggested by Talk of Peace at This Time', which, 'from a quiet place apart' in Franconia, hesitantly bid France onward until Truth be saved and Hell thwarted. The poem was neither published nor collected by Frost, though Thomas recognised the good intentions behind its hesitation to command others to do what the poet himself would not. But the politicians had no such hesitation. On 12 December Germany attempted to consolidate her gains by offering a 'Peace Note' via the Vatican. The

Note promised proposals that would 'serve as the basis for the restoration of a lasting peace', and for a week the Allies waited for a clarification. None was forthcoming, and on 19 December Lloyd George used his first prime ministerial address to kick the offering into the gutter. 'To enter, on the invitation of Germany, proclaiming herself victorious, without any knowledge of the proposals she proposes to make, into a conference is to put our heads into a noose with the rope end in the hands of Germany,' he pronounced. 'We shall put our trust rather in an unbroken army than in broken faith.' David Lloyd George, the man who once walked to Westminster every morning with Philip Henry Thomas, had committed Britain to a continuation of the conflict, ensuring that Edward Thomas would see the front.[2]

'This is only to tell you just a few facts,' Thomas wrote to Eleanor Farjeon on 7 December. 'One is that they asked for volunteers to go straight out to Batteries in France and I made sure of it by volunteering. Don't let Helen know.' Thomas seemed fully absorbed in army life now; his letters to Helen were businesslike, informing her of the latest chances of his going to France, and telling her not to begin to grumble if he were denied leave at Christmas, before signing off with a distant 'I hope all is well'. There was little else for him to say in those loitering weeks in Lydd, other than that he had surprised himself as an acting commander by 'not making too bad a hash of it'.[3]

By mid-December, *Poems* was almost 'fixed up'. 'One or two pieces' might have to be cut for length, thought Thomas, though in fact the publishers managed to retain them all. He expected not to see the proofs himself, and asked John Freeman and Eleanor Farjeon to supervise their production on his behalf. Mentally, he was tidying loose ends in preparation for France, and he told both Frost and Farjeon that he had put away his childish things. He now knew he would be posted to 244 Siege Battery: a captain, a lieutenant and five second lieutenants (of which he was one), and a company of around 150 men – a motley rabble in the words of their commanding officer, 'semi-trained and ill-disciplined, and quite unfit for active service'.[4]

On 22 December a camp order was issued forbidding week-end leave that extended into Christmas. Thomas let Helen know the disappointing news that this last Christmas before France would be spent apart. He could be posted at any time now, he told her, and to any place, adding that if she were to hear of anyone wanting to give him a Christmas present he could do with any of the following: an oilskin overcoat, arctic socks (two sizes too small for wearing inside his army boots), a periscope, a pocket sextant. To Helen the news was devastating: it made a thumping noise in her head. But then something happened that Helen could think of only as a 'miracle': the army changed its mind. Leave was granted after all, and Edward was able to go to High Beech. Helen and the children sang songs in delight; and if that were not enough, she received an unexpected gift of £20 from a fund to writers administered by Wilfrid and Viola Meynell, and travelled into London to buy supplies for the family and a small Christmas tree for Myfanwy, who would go pale with surprise when she came into the room to find it on Christmas Day. Mervyn and Bronwen went down the lane to wait for their daddy, while Helen returned to prepare a turkey with Myfanwy. The approach of Edward's footsteps had been muffled by the snow, but the call of his 'Coo-ee' from the lane was unmistakable. He was 'so very glad' to be home.[5]

On 29 December, having returned to Lydd, Thomas wrote to Myfanwy telling her about the poem 'Out in the Dark' written on an evening over Christmas in which she had not wanted to enter the sitting room because it was gloomy. He told her that they were to shoot with real guns for the first time, and that France seemed ever closer. 'I do hope peace won't come just yet. I should not know what to do, especially if it came before I had really been a solider. I wonder if you want peace, and if you can remember when there was no war.' And then he sympathised with her visit to town to have a bad tooth taken out. 'I hope you don't dislike the dentist who took it away.' It was a care and kindness that Thomas would show more of in the weeks ahead.[6]

On 23 December Wilfrid Gibson left England for a tour of the United States. (Thomas to Frost: 'You have borrowed Gibson from us. Pray don't trouble to return him unless empty.') He was the last of the Dymock poets to leave Gloucestershire. British soldiers had been drafted into the parish to help with hay-baling; children picked wool where it had snagged on the hedgerows and barbed wire for the war effort. German prisoners of war worked in the fields of Dymock in 1917, turning potatoes in the fields. Peggy Carless was a telegram girl for the Greenway Post Office. When a message was received she was sent out on her bicycle to deliver it. It was a job she had loved until then, riding the gentle lanes on her red bicycle, but now the telegrams she carried to families that she had grown up with told of the death of their sons. Over a hundred of Dymock's men left to fight; a third did not return.[7]

New Year's Day broke sunny and bright over Lydd. The rattle of practice fire had become as routine to the men as it had to the wildlife. Sixteen rounds of ammunition cracked no more than twenty yards from where Thomas was standing, and it deafened him for a moment only. A hundred yards further off, sheep barely scattered at the sound and a thrush continued to sing from a gorse bush. The men were getting to know the heavy weaponry with which they would be working; guns that weighed up to four and a half tons and took a team of a dozen draught horses to pull. A six-inch howitzer fired from Trafalgar Square could reach Crystal Palace six miles away; a sixty-pound field gun could fire a shrapnel or lyddite shell two miles further still, as far as Epping Forest.[8]

On the weekend of 6–7 January, Thomas was at High Beech for the last time before he left for France. Friends arrived to say their goodbyes. Eleanor Farjeon was among them, and received her instructions to work with John Freeman in supervising Edward's typescript through the press. At the top of the stairs, Farjeon and Thomas kissed goodnight. 'Strong as it was,' she wrote, 'and for me so very deep, our friendship had remained undemonstrative from beginning to end.' She left on 9 January, while Helen cooked and Edward bathed Myfanwy in an old zinc tub in front of the open fire and sang the folk songs she so loved to hear:

> O Father, Father come build me a boat
> That on the ocean I may float
> And every flagship I chance to meet
> I will enquire for my William Sweet
> For a maid a maid I shall never be
> Till apples grow on an orange tree.

He read stories to Bronwen and studied maps with Mervyn and told each of them to be always kind to their mother while he was away. But between Edward and Helen the kindness was not so easily manageable. Helen remembered his sharpness and her provocation. He was terse as he reminded her about their life assurance and other documents he thought she might one day need, and they bickered about trivialities, Helen wanting a bookshelf put up on a wall that Edward said was too rotten to support it. The last day he might have had with Helen he spent in London instead. He had a dental check, lunch with Harry Hooton and invited his literary friends to present themselves, at St George's Café; in the event only two came, Roger Ingpen and W. H. Davies, and after Ingpen left, Davies and Thomas strolled up Charing Cross Road together in silence, the mood awkward even between these two oldest of friends. Thomas returned to High Beech and to Helen. With his luggage standing in the hall the enormity of the situation seemed too much to speak of. He pressed upon her the need, should he not return, for hired help to dig in the potatoes, and when that failed to ease the tension took out his prismatic compass and showed her how to take a bearing from it; when she cried he closed the casing and put the instrument away. Helen could no longer rein back her desperation and felt engulfed by an uncontrollable grief of a kind that would plague her in the years ahead. She would recount his tenderness in that moment. She wrote of his gentle ability to soothe and steady her, to give her both the emotional and the physical reassurance for which she so longed. He read to her and carried her to the bedroom in his greatcoat. 'Helen, Helen, Helen,' he had said, 'Remember that, whatever happens, all is well between us for ever and ever.' When the morning came, she stood at the gate and watched him disappear into the mist and snow. Edward for his part recorded nothing of the details, only this entry in his diary: 'Said goodbye to Helen, Mervyn and Baba.'[9]

Bronwen travelled with Edward into London and on to his parents' house at Balham. Each of Edward's five brothers came to dinner that night; next morning he said goodbye to them all and to Bronwen and returned to Lydd, where in his diary he scribbled a cluttered and probably unfinished poem of twelve lines regarding the hope behind the gloom of parting.

> The sorrow of true love is a great sorrow
> And true love parting blackens a bright morrow:
> Yet almost they equal joys, since their despair
> Is but hope blinded by its tears, and clear
> Above the storm the heavens wait to be seen.[10]

There was still some snow lying on the Kentish roads when Thomas wrote to his son from Lydd to wish him a happy birthday for the 15th: he sent the boy a book on slide-rulers, and said that he hoped to be home for the next one. He wrote to Helen to say that, for intelligence reasons, he would be able to tell her little of his whereabouts once in France and so outlined for her a code with which he might evade the censor. 'If I am at the Somme I shall say "I am pleased with my situation". If I am at Ypres I shall say "I am *fairly* pleased with my situation". If I am at Havre or somewhere far back in reserve, which may happen at first, I shall say "We are as safe as at Lydd".' He was dawdling in camp, waiting for the call to go to Codford, the final staging post before France, and told Frost that he was 'impatient to go'.[11]

On 15 January Thomas left Lydd beneath light snow and red sun and reached Codford on Salisbury Plain under cover of darkness. The camp where he was to be billeted for the next two weeks was bitterly cold and conditions were poor: though there was electric light and an open fire, the huts had bare boards and there was no officers' mess, leaving the men to club together to buy whatever they needed. It was here that the final mobilisation would take place: guns and stores were collected for transport, while final provisions were issued to the men: gas respirators, tin hats, field dressings. But spirits were high as the men marched through a frosty, clear, following day to Wylye, Stockton, Sherrington, singing as they went. These were days of light snow at night and hard frosts by morning and walks at dusk. Thomas considered little beyond what he would take to France. He had the works of Shakespeare, the Book of Common Prayer and Laurence Sterne's *Sentimental Journey* (he had smiled to overhear an officer at Ashford station asking for the poetry of Ella Wheeler Wilcox): 'It will probably be all I want,' he told Eleanor, though from Helen he asked for a few more home comforts: socks, waistcoat and slippers. Beyond that, he kept more intimate feelings at bay and even seemed remote as he signed off a letter to his mother, 'Yours ever Edward Thomas'.[12]

Thick snow descended in mid-January; Eleanor recalled that it held back the spring until April. At Codford, the camp locked in against the bitter cold for its final fortnight of training. Thomas gave lectures on map-reading and learned to ride a motor cycle; in the post came a cake from his mother and a volume of Shakespeare's Sonnets from Helen. 'No church parade for me,' Thomas noted in his diary for Sunday 21 January, and chose instead to walk for thirteen miles along iced roads and over frozen grass to Barford St Martin and Netherhampton, where he had lunch with the family of Henry Newbolt. He noted the ivied ash trees, the freezing drizzle, the view over the Downs, and a family of poachers that he stopped to watch roasting their catch over a slow wood fire. The next morning at 10.30 he made the last of his personal visits, to see Jack Haines in Gloucester. He told Haines that he had taken to composing his poems in the early hours when it was too dark to read, before committing them to paper in daylight. They sat up into the early hours 'gossiping about Frost' and Haines gave Thomas the one book he had hoped to take to France more than any other, Frost's *Mountain Interval*. When Haines toasted his good future, Thomas smiled and said 'no one could tell what future was good future'.[13]

Though a poet and a botanist, it was in his capacity as a solicitor that Haines sat down with Thomas that weekend, having drawn up by hand a Memorandum of Agreement with Selwyn and Blount for Thomas's *Poems*. The clauses were familiar to Thomas; he had signed contracts for thirty books of his own and many besides that he had edited; but this would be the last. The six clauses were simple and standard. The work would be produced at the publisher's expense, indemnified by the author who would offer them English language rights throughout the world. In return, the publisher would pay Thomas a royalty of ten per cent on the published price after 250 copies, and fifteen per cent should the edition reprint its initial 500 copies; but the fact that the publishers would withhold payment on the first 250 copies meant that, in effect, Thomas would contribute £4 7s. 6d. to the expense of the book. All other sums from sales in any other territories – be they books, printed sheets or serial – would be equally divided between the author and the publisher. If the print run of 525 sold through, Thomas stood to earn £4 16s. 3d.[14]

On 23 January, on the train back from Gloucester, Thomas read the whole of *Mountain Interval* except for one piece, the long poem 'Snow', which he kept back for another time. 'They are very good,' he told Eleanor, 'though never better or different from "North of Boston".' To Frost he wrote affectionately, 'I did admire, but much more it was getting close to you again that the reading meant. Probably it is that makes me more homesick than I have been for some time. Homesick or something.' Thomas missed the plain-speaking companionship that Frost had given him; he missed being able to be simply himself. He had heard girls in the train talk heartlessly of how 'facing realities' would be the making of so-and-so; but 'so-and-so can't face more than he was born to, I expect: nor I,' he wrote. 'So that I worry less and less about that gamekeeper.' His fatalism was on full display. The incident with the gamekeeper and the quarrel over 'The Road Not Taken': each had been instrumental in demonstrating what he understood as the inevitability of certain forces in life. By this, he did not mean preordination or destiny or any of the terms a church might appropriate, but something to do with the elemental conditions embedded in the natural world: the coursing of water, the power of wind, the gravity of rain – something pagan and ancient, as he once explained, 'When gods were young | This wind was old.' For so long, he had been plagued by indeterminacy, but the war was an irresistible force that overtook the uncertainty in Thomas, and for a moment he sounded more Frost-like than Frost. 'It is always better to do a thing than to "imagine" what it would be like to do it,' he wrote. 'Someday we can discuss the difference – that is if you have imagined [it] at all.'[15]

In the final days at Codford he walked as much as he could, too far in fact, for trailing over the frosty Downs under a clear new moon, his new boots began to chafe his ankles and cause abrasions that would dog him throughout his time in France. As he rested his sore heels, he learned that the guns would ship out to France on 27 January, the battery embarking two days later. The loading of lorries began in earnest, attaching the guns to the four-wheel drives in biting, easterly winds. The rawness of his ankles was such that it kept him awake in the cold nights, and prevented him from walking far enough by day to fully warm up.

With two days to go before embarkation, Saturday broke with the sighting of a fox in the frost, and 'the sun like a bright coin between the knuckles of opposite hills'. A telegram had come to say that Myfanwy was staying with Arthur Ransome's wife Ivy at Hatch, which told him all that he needed to know of how things had gotten on top of Helen in his absence from Essex; in the time to come, she would place young Baba with friends while wrestling with her grief for Edward. Hatch was only thirteen miles from Codford, and Thomas swapped his boots for a colleague's and set off to see his daughter. Warm fires and cold ice for his feet awaited him at the Ransomes', where he spent the night. He mentioned nothing of it to Helen in his letters, only the journey back on Sunday, which he made through freezing rain on a hired bicycle in order to save his blistered feet. For once, he followed a sentimental path, returning along the hedgeless roads that previously he had taken with Mervyn towards the house of the man who had formally opened the Poetry Bookshop, Henry Newbolt. It must have seemed such a long time ago that he had attended that opening of the Devonshire Street shop, gossiping about the literary world, of commissions and reviews, of new poets and of the squabbles of the poetry fraternity that seemed so minor now. How many things had changed for him since he chatted in that bookshop, unaware that the greatest friend he would ever have stood only a few feet away. That friendship, the birth of his own verse and the outbreak of war had led him here, to an isolated lane in a frozen dusk, on the last evening he would experience in England.[16]

IV

ARRAS

1917

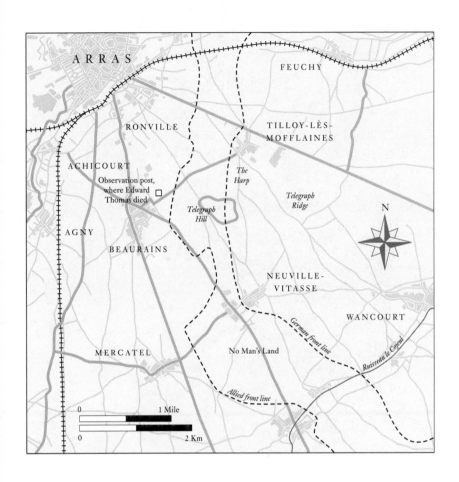

ARRAS

FEUCHY

RONVILLE

TILLOY-LÈS-
MOFFLAINES

ACHICOURT

Observation post,
where Edward
Thomas died.

The
Harp

Telegraph
Ridge

Telegraph
Hill

N

AGNY

BEAURAINS

NEUVILLE-
VITASSE

WANCOURT

German front line

Ruisseau le Cojeul

MERCATEL

No Man's Land

Allied front line

0   1 Mile

0   2 Km

Winter – Spring

The men of 244 Siege Battery rose in the winter cold at five o'clock; by half past six they were marching from Codford through the frost, singing 'Pack Up Your Troubles' in the darkness. Edward Thomas said to hear the men sing the rotten song with such gusto brought a tear to his eye. The train to Southampton was perishingly cold, but delivered them to the docks by half past nine that morning. The rest of the day would be spent waiting for dusk to fall so that they could sail under cover of darkness. Thomas sat in the South Western Hotel, listening to the sea captains talking of sailing routes to Australia, and writing to Helen as he would now do systematically – mostly, some five letters a week for the next two months. At seven o'clock that evening, they sailed on the *Mona's Queen*. It was 'a tumbling crossing' he noted, but the arrival at Le Havre at four the next morning was restful and unforgettable. Tall pale houses lit the quay. At sunrise they marched through fields full of cotton bales and falling snow. They arrived at camp at 9.45 a.m.; Thomas wrapped himself tightly in blankets from the officers' mess to stave off the worst of the chill. His single duty that day was the censoring of letters, which would be his almost daily activity from now on; for one so reticent in his own correspondence, he always encouraged his men not to be shy of familiar comments in theirs. He wrote to Eleanor Farjeon to ask after the progress of his book proofs and to make sure that she had not omitted the dedication, TO ROBERT FROST. He barely felt like reading, and was sure that writing verse was an impossibility. 'No more goodbyes now,' he told Eleanor. 'I shall begin to look ahead perhaps, if I ever do look ahead again. Long it is since I did so.' And to Helen, he wrote this: 'What do you think of "Armed Men in Tears" as the title of my next book?' Neither Edward nor Helen could have thought much of it as a title, but then he did not suppose it could be. For the question was in fact a code: Edward was letting Helen know that he thought he was on his way to Armentières, 200 miles north on the French–Belgian border.[1]

The battery spent almost a week in Le Havre. Thomas took the opportunity to purchase some soft low-topped boots in order to ease his chafed ankles, and on 4 February the orders came to leave the port and begin the move up to the front. For two hours the men were held at the station; singing broke out along the platform and some men joked 'All tickets' as they were boarded thirty-five to a carriage. For the next two days the train crawled through the snow-filled countryside of Picardy: first Buchy, then Alaincourt, then Amiens, arriving at Doullens at sunset. All the while, the clanking of the train was accompanied by the sound of the guns that seemed to draw ever closer.[2]

Spirits among the officers were good. Thomas cooked dinner for the six of them (the CO rarely joined them for dinner), while the talk was light and silly, and he wrote to Helen of 'a very merry evening'. Many evenings would pass off this way: with wine, cooking and cheese, and the mess gramophone lifting tunes into the night air. 'We six are a rum company', he told Frost, amid an atmosphere that more closely resembled a superior class of picnic than an outpost seven miles from enemy lines. Thomas even had a manservant assigned to lay his dining table, collect his firewood, wash and darn his clothes. 'Very good, sir,' he would say, and, 'You gentlemen have to put up with the same as us,' and 'It's the same for everyone.' Sometimes it took the heavy firing through the nights to remind them just where they really were.[3]

For a week the battery moved up unhurriedly through snowy roads and frozen fields. Thomas would scout ahead in one of the advance lorries looking for a farmhouse or a barn in which

to billet the men, noting, as he travelled, the details of his surroundings: the crookedness of a farmyard, a crumbling dovecote,
an 'enemy plane like pale moth beautiful among shrapnel bursts'.
He relayed the atmosphere to Eleanor: 'We have crept slowly,
uncomfortably, but to me amusingly up to our fighting position,
often cold, never certain of the next 24 hours, picknicking, pigging it, and arrived at last yesterday afternoon. We officers are in
a farmhouse alongside a main road leading to a cathedral town 2
miles off. We are warm but have no other luxuries. We are part
of the target of the German artillery 3 miles or so to the east of
us; their shellholes are common behind us and the shells rattle
our windows frequently, while friendly batteries shoot over our
heads.' The cathedral town was Arras, capital of the Nord-Pas-
de-Calais region, a citadel with a once-fine cathedral square that
had narrowly avoided capture by the Germans in the autumn of
1914. Thomas had billeted his men there on a road to the south of
the city on 9 February. The next day, with little fuss, he recorded
in his diary, 'One dead man under railway bridge', so neat and
still in his sacking that Thomas at first did not realise he was
dead.[4]

Each morning, Thomas's duty was to identify an observation
post from which he might survey the placement and the condition of the German lines, and so determine the tactical situation
of his own battery. Many of the best posts had long since been
demolished by shell-fire: the church towers and chimneys of the
surrounding villages, even the tall poplars so characteristic of
the landscape; now the slightest ridge might be a valuable rampart, but by definition these areas had very little in the way of
cover. Thomas was never more exposed than in his work looking out from the observation posts; a head too long poked above
the rise or a glint from the sun on his field glasses might be all
a sniper needed to lock on. Not a living thing came into view
on the first day of his observation, only a 'snowy broken land
with posts and wires and dead trees' and a shadow-line where

he knew the German trench to be. But he told his parents that he was 'privately pleased' to have completed what he called 'his first day of the real thing'.[5]

By 11 February, the battery had settled into positions outside Arras, a mile from German lines. Snow lay thick on the ground in all directions, and silenced everything but the guns. It was desolate, beautiful, cold; white fields rolled into no-man's-land. The first death was reported in the sister battery and someone put on a recording of Gounod's 'Ave Maria'; it rang out over the snow and brought everyone to a standstill.[6]

A thaw came and exposed the year's first grass. Thomas watched hare and wild duck in the field south-east of the guns, but nowhere on the rolling hills did he see sheep or cattle, only barbed wire and the occasional telephone pole rising out of the snow. Here and there the ground was pocked with shell holes and all around villages lay in ruins, mostly abandoned, with only the most hardened inhabitants remaining. Thomas read the volume of Shakespeare's Sonnets that Helen had given him, but mostly he did not feel much like reading. 'Of course I can't write,' he told de la Mare, 'but then I don't want to or think about it.' No letters had yet arrived for the battery and men's moods were occasionally tetchy: his captain barked at him. 'You get on with your sonnets.' 'Awful fug,' thought Thomas.[7]

When finally the letters did come through, Thomas learned from Eleanor that the proofs for *Poems* had arrived from Selwyn and Blount and that they had corrected some minor slips. 'My proofs sound as if they would be perfect,' he wrote back. In fact the proofs were less than perfect. The compositor had been careless, centring the poems unevenly, separating some by two lines, others by one, and stretching the turned lines artificially to meet the right-hand margin as if they were prose. The thin leading beneath the titles lent the page a mean, cramped look. In short, it was a mess.[8]

*

Thomas was seconded to the headquarters of the Heavy Artillery Group on 21 February, three miles from his battery. His skills in map reading were much needed at HQ to help assemble the reconnaissance photographs that the aeroplanes were bringing back, and for the next two weeks he would be loaned out from his battery, working on minor intelligence scraps, dispatches, administrating and answering telephones. Rather than enjoying the outdoors as he had with the 244th, he was now stuck inside the inner workings of the army, and Thomas was not pleased. 'Am I to stay on here and do nothing but have cold feet', he asked in his diary, adding, 'No thrushes, but chaffinches say "Chink" in the chestnut tree in the garden.' He puzzled at the lack of thrushes more than he did the deployment of the guns, and the fact that he had not heard a blackbird since his arrival in France.[9]

'You know that life is in so strange that I am only half myself,' he wrote to Frost on 23 February, 'and the half that knows England and you is obediently asleep for a time. Do you believe me? It seems I have sent it to sleep to make the life endurable – more than endurable, really enjoyable in a way.' Thomas had struggled to reconnect to Frost since leaving England. He said that he had read the remaining poem in *Mountain Interval*, 'Snow', and liked it, comparing it to Horace, but that was all the literary conversation he would manage. Rarely as he looked out over no-man's-land from his observation post did he think of human suffering; the German line was just 2,000 yards away but in his diary, he wrote: 'The shelling must have slaughtered many jackdaws but has made home for many more.' A few days later, 'Chaffinches and partridges, moles working on surface', adding, 'Does a mole ever get hit by a shell?' He had still seen only one dead body, and recorded only one Allied fatality. He had supervised the digging of the trenches, though the cold weather had largely spared him and his men the terrible mud. He had done 'a little firing', he told Bottomley, but essentially had not yet been fired at in return. He knew that must surely change. 'Why do Huns not retaliate on Arras guns?' he wrote on 24 February. 'Some day this will be one of the hottest places this side of Hell, if it is this side.' That evening, the officers took a long dinner: hors d'oeuvres, roast mutton, Christmas pudding, whisky, coffee, Maraschino chocolates; *Peer Gynt* played on the gramophone. Walking back to Arras in the dark, owls hunted on the Dainville road.[10]

Edward Thomas came under fire for the first time on 26 February. He had gone to Achicourt to inspect whether a gun position was visible to the Germans: it must have been, for machine-gun bullets whistled overhead accompanied by four shell bursts 150 yards away. Thomas wrote to Helen that the experience had made him feel 'shy', and yet eager to carry on as far as possible as though nothing had happened. 'This makes the heart beat but no more than if I were going to pay a call on a stranger,' he wrote. 'I try to console myself by reflecting that you cannot escape either by running or by standing still. There is no safe place and consequently why worry? And I don't worry.' But German fire was only the half of his danger that day. Returning back from Achicourt toward his siege battery, Thomas had just walked clear of the muzzle of his own eighteen-pounder when it opened up. 'I was within 3 yards of being shot by one of our own guns,' he told Bottomley; 'The order comes to fire and they fire,' to Helen, 'damn them.' It was not all Grieg and poetry, he now had to admit.[11]

He had professed his happiness to Frost, but he adopted no such disguise with Helen. The lack of exercise and the excess of food and perhaps his recent exposure to artillery were making him downcast. He asked after Mervyn, wondering whether the boy might join an Officer Training Corps, and then he paused, 'But I am depressed', he wrote:

it becomes harder for me to think about things at home and somehow, although this life does not absorb me, I think, yet, I can't think of anything else. I don't hanker after anything I don't miss anything. I am not even conscious of waiting. I am just quietly in exile, a sort of half or quarter man – at Romford I was half or *three* quarter man. Only sometimes I hear things I really care for, far off as if at the end of a telephone.

And he added, 'The fact is it is a sort of interval in reality, a protracted railway waiting room. Yet of course not always merely that.'[12]

For the next week, Edward Thomas continued his secondment to Group HQ three miles from his battery. He recorded 'idle cold hours indoors', sitting up late for dispatches and stifling tempers, while artillery fire rattled constantly through the streets where the operations were situated. 'I am fed up with sitting on my arse doing nothing that anybody couldn't do better,' he wrote furtively. His thirty-ninth birthday came and went without any post. 'I still don't hear from you,' he wrote to Frost, and relayed to his friend the recent skirmishes; how enemy planes were chased off with salvos of anti-aircraft fire, only to be followed by a barrage of German artillery as the planes reported back on positions. But at least the whistle of the raining shells told them all that it was not gas coming in. Thomas wrote that he no longer wanted anything consciously, 'except, I suppose, the end'. His moods had been dampening for days; he told Frost,

I hear my book is coming out soon. Did the duplicate verses ever reach you? You have never said so. But don't think I mind. I should like to be a poet, just as I should like to live, but I know as much about my chances in either case, and I don't really trouble about either. Only I want to come back more or less complete.[13]

No sooner had Thomas mailed this off than another came in the post: Helen had forwarded a letter she had received from

Frost, who had written to her believing it the quickest way to get news to him. 'I have found a publisher for his poems in America,' Frost declared. On the strength of the poems that had gotten through to Frost, he had convinced Holt of the merits of his friend's work, and to their credit Holt showed none of the caution that had marked their acquisition of Frost: they agreed to follow Selwyn and Blount and issue Thomas's *Poems* on their side of the Atlantic. It was extraordinary news: the poet who had come so recently to his trade and who had met with one rejection after another from English editors was, with a little help from his friends, to have his debut published in both Britain and America. Frost offered to write a foreword for the book if Thomas were willing to 'throw off' his pseudonym and publish under his own name.[14]

'So you did find a publisher after all. I have just heard,' Thomas replied. And that was it: no thank you, no euphoria, and only a passing mention in his diary. 'Yesterday was cold and raw and I became very depressed and solitary by the evening,' he continued in his letter to Frost. 'Very soon, I expect to have no time or room left for depression.' The snow had set in once more, and there was nothing to see but the snow itself, nothing to hear but artillery. Occasionally he saw children in the devastated villages 'too poor or too helpless' to leave, he told his friend, 'but I probably am not going to describe any more except to make a living'. It was a telling comment for Thomas to make. In January he had written something tiny but of equal importance to Helen: 'Please put these letters in my drawer.' It seemed he intended to use his letters and his diary to write about the war after his return; his enlistment was something he intended to survive and the re-emergence of his gloom expressed not a death wish but a growing recognition that he might not live.[15]

'I can't *feel* that my chances of escape are very good,' he wrote to Walter de la Mare, who had just returned from his lecture tour of the States where he had met a reluctant Frost. This was the final letter that Thomas would write to his old friend, and it would be plaintive. In purple pencil, in a cramped and urgent hand, he described the cold and the dirt and the fatigue and the uncertainty.

We might see the apple blossom but I doubt that. Nobody is very hopeful. I think myself that things may go on at this rate for more than a year. The rate may be changed, but not if the Hun can help it, and his retirement looks very inconvenient in every way. I wish you had said more about Frost. One is absolutely friendless here . . . You say it would be good if we could have a talk, but, you know, I fancy it would not do to have a real friend out here.[16]

At an exposed crossroads on the outskirts of Arras known as the 'Windy Corner', Thomas surveyed his most dangerous observation so far. There stood one of the few factory chimneys that had not been destroyed by shelling: two hundred feet high, it promised a key vantage point from which to observe the German lines; but it was horribly vulnerable and had been hit three times already by small fire, loosening parts of the brickwork. From reconnaissance, Thomas knew that iron rings inside the chimney served as a ladder, and that one of the rings was loose, but he did not know which one. Worse still, the funnel tapered, so that in climbing the inside of the chimney he would hang further out over the ground below with each rung he ascended. He tested the first rings and began to climb. A shell exploded close by and shook the chimney. Then another and another. Thomas's nerve failed him. 'It was impossible and I knew it,' he explained to Frost. 'As a matter of fact I had no light and no information about the method of getting up so that all the screwing up I had given myself would in any case have been futile. It was just another experience like the gamekeeper.'[17]

The incident with the keeper haunted him until the very end.

*

The following day was calm: the first thrush appeared, and from the orchard that was his billet Thomas watched a ploughman take his team of horses up and down the misty field; each time they climbed the ridge they came into view of German artillery, but not a shot was fired. The night brought heavy bombardment. Thomas had barely slept for the pounding; when he did, he dreamed almost for the first time since leaving England. In his dream he was at home again, but as he told Helen in a letter, 'I was a sort of visitor and I could not stay to tea.' It was a very feeble dream, he told her, but in his mind it clearly signified something more: 'You must not convince yourself you are merely waiting, you know.'[18]

On 20 March Thomas started out at four in the morning through the darkness toward the observation posts at Ronville. The trench where he would begin his observation was stiff with cold until the rain fell and loosened it into a terrible slurry. 'You have often heard of the mud out here, haven't you? Well, I have been in it. It is what you have heard. You nearly pull your leg off, and often your boot off, at each step in the worst places – the stiff soft clay sucks around the boot at each step.'[19]

A few hundred yards to the west of their position lay the strategic promontory of Telegraph Hill, overlooking the Allies along a ridge that linked it to the German lines. 'Telegraph hill quiet as if only rabbits lived there,' he recorded in his diary, but two German snipers lay patiently in wait for the slightest movement by an unwary infantryman. With his keen eyesight, he had already spotted them and would stay out of their sights that day, but he felt terribly exposed. The fact that for once he left his diary at camp, 'in case', as he put it, spoke of the danger he was prepared for. The first shelling went south into Beaurains, but it turned slowly northward to his position at Ronville. In came the fire – 'horrible flap of 5.9 a little along the trench' – all day, all night. He slept leaning against the trench wall, in a cold, wet and seemingly endless night. He was finally relieved at eight o'clock the next morning, returning to billet as engineers were repairing the roads; the shell holes had filled with water and blood. He fell into an exhausted sleep that afternoon and did not wake until morning.[20]

'Nobody quite knows what is happening and whether it is really altogether favourable or not,' he wrote to a friend. The battery was still stationed in the orchard outside Arras, and still they waited for the order to move up. His senses seemed sharply alive, exaggerated even, after his terrible night in the trench. His diary records: 'Beautiful was Arras yesterday coming down from Beaurains and seeing Town Hall ruin white in sun like a thick smoke beginning to curl. Sprinkle of snow today in sun.' That evening, the gramophone played Chopin's 'Berceuse'. For a second time, Thomas watched the plough going up over the crest towards Beaurains; once again, the German artillery let the farmer alone.[21]

'Isn't it wonderful how some men get hit and some don't,' he wrote to Mervyn. 'But it is the same with trees and houses, so that I don't see why it makes some people "believe in God".' But belief did have its virtues, he told his son. 'It is a good thing to believe. I think brave people all believe something and I daresay they are not so likely to be killed as those who don't believe and are not so brave.' And he mentioned Mervyn's new bicycle that his son had told him about: could he buy the old one from him on his return? Might Mervyn oil it for him and hang it on the kitchen wall at High Beech? 'I should like to ride out to Jesse's with you in the summer.'[22]

Thomas rose early on 24 March and set out for Beaurains, a devastated village on the lip of the front line. He had observed this 'ghastly' place many times from a distance, but now that he saw it up close it was, he said, a true vision of Hell. Never did he imagine it would be so bad. The broken brick and stone walls had formed 'dunes' of rubble throughout the pulverised village; the trees were splintered and snapped and torn; only the tomb-stones in the graveyard still stood: they were all the evidence that a church had once stood there. Overhead, a British plane went down in a hail of flaming fragments. Thomas was pleased to retreat to what was to be the battery's new position: an ash copse in an old chalk quarry where hazel and birch had taken root, between the villages of Agny and Achicourt. He rested his back against the mossy chalk and watched a rabbit which had refused to be driven out. He marvelled at the animals' ability to survive. The chalk soils reminded him of the Froxfield plateau, just as the broken stone of Beaurains village had put him in mind of his old Steep cottage.[23]

The battery moved up on the 26th. The Service Corps lorries arrived to transport the equipment up to the chalk pit, leav-ing the men to make the journey on foot through the night. The darkness covered the troops' movement, and by daylight no shell-fire had come into the copse. Thomas supervised the bending and cutting of the birches which lay in their battery's line of fire, and for a few brief moments he and another offi-cer looked for primroses. These were 'pleasant and even merry hours and moments', he noted, in particular for the kindness between the men, sharing their provisions from home, among them the Fortnum and Mason package that Eleanor had sent out. 'I keep feeling that I should enjoy it more if I knew I would survive it.'[24]

A new zero-line was established, and the battery began to dig in in earnest. 'Death looms, but however it comes it is unex-pected, whether from appendicitis or bullet,' he wrote to his youngest brother. 'I have suffered more from January to March in other years than this.'[25]

*

Heavy snow fell on 2 April. 'Things are closely impending now and will have happened before you get this and you will know all about them, so I will not try to tell you what they are, especially as I could not get them past the censor,' he told Frost. 'And I hear nothing of you – yet you are no more like an American in a book than you were 2½ years ago. You are among the unchanged things that I can not or dare not think of except in flashes.' These would be the final words that Thomas wrote to Frost.[26]

On 4 April Helen Thomas wrote from High Beech to her dear friend Janet Hooton.

I'm getting on all right tho' this terrible winter will stand out in my memory as a sort of nightmare. The intense cold and the long dark days in this strange place, and then on January 11th that terrible parting, not knowing when we should see each other again; knowing nothing but that for each of us it was so terrible that I did not know one could live through such agony ... That awful fear is always clutching at my heart, but I put it away time after time, and keep at my work and think of his home-coming.[27]

On Good Friday, Edward Thomas read over a clipping that Gordon Bottomley had sent him. *An Anthology of New Poetry*, co-edited by Lascelles Abercrombie, had been published in February, carrying eighteen of Thomas's poems under the name of Edward Eastaway. A review in the *Times Literary Supplement* had singled out his contribution. 'He is a real poet, with the truth in him.' A second, in the *New Statesman*, claimed to know (but did not reveal) the author's true identity: 'His poems are better than his prose, good though some of this has been. There are not enough of them here to give one an exact notion of his power and his limitations. But "The Wood", "Aspens", "The Brook", "Wind and Mist", and "For These" would, by themselves, be enough to show that he is worth fifty Frosts.'[28]

Robert Frost said this: 'His poetry is so very brave – so

unconsciously brave. He didn't think of it for a moment as war poetry, though that is what it is. It ought to be called Roads to France.'[29]

Good Friday was the day that the United States entered the war.

On the weekend of 7–8 April the heavy guns of 244 Siege Battery stood wheel to wheel on the sunken road before the quarry that ran parallel to the front.

Saturday April 7 or 8 – Arras

Dearest

Here I am in my valise on the floor of my dugout writing before sleeping. The artillery is like a stormy tide breaking on the shores of the full moon that rides high and clear among white cirrus clouds . . . Hardly anything came near the O.P. or even the village. I simply watched the shells changing the landscape. The pretty village among trees that I first saw two weeks ago is now just ruins among violated stark tree trunks. But the sun shone and larks and partridge and magpies and hedgesparrows made love and the trench was being made passable for the wounded that will be harvested in a day or two. Either the Bosh is beaten or he is going to surprise us . . . One officer has to be at the O.P. every day and every other night. So it will be all work now till further notice – days of ten times the ordinary work too. So goodnight and I hope you sleep no worse than I do . . .

Sunday. I slept jolly well and now it is sunshine and wind and we are in for a long day and I must post this when I can.

All and always yours Edwy[30]

Edward Thomas spent the day before he died under particularly heavy bombardment. The shell that fell two yards from where he stood should have killed him, but instead it was a rare dud. Back at billet, the men teased him on his lucky escape; someone remarked that a fellow with Thomas's luck should be safe wherever he went.

Myfanwy Thomas was embroidering a wild duck onto a postcard to send to her daddy when the telegraph boy drew up outside the house. Helen read the message in silence, while he waited for her reply. 'No answer,' she eventually said.[31]

Thomas's commanding officer wrote, 'We buried him in a little military cemetery a few hundred yards from the battery, the exact spot will be notified to you by the parson. As we stood by his grave the sun came and the guns round seemed to stop firing for a short time.'[32]

On the last pages of his war diary, Edward Thomas wrote, 'I never understood quite what was meant by God', and in pencil the following three lines,

> Where any turn may lead to Heaven
> Or any corner may hide Hell
> Roads shining like river up hill after rain.[33]

Robert Frost wrote to Helen in condolence. 'I want to see him to tell him something. I want to tell him, what I think he liked to hear from me, that he was a poet.'[34]

Helen lived for fifty years following Edward's death; she never remarried. The memoirs that she wrote of their life together would be cherished by readers, though little loved by Edward's friends at the time. Robert Frost for one railed against them. He thought Helen had made Edward look ridiculous in his innocence, emasculated in an 'undressing to the public'. Robert and Helen never reconciled their differences; in later years he removed a dedication to her from his *Selected Poems*.[1]

Mervyn was seventeen when his father died. They never overcame what he called the 'unhappy strangeness' between them. He had been unable to relate to his father's literary life, but through his apprenticeship they had begun to find a language they could share based on engineering or the servicing of an army motorbike. Mervyn would qualify as a draughtsman and would work as a technical editor and motor journalist; he served with the Kent Rifle Regiment in 1918 and with the REME Corps in the Middle East during the Second World War.[2]

Bronwen's adult life was marked by tragedy: she lost three husbands and suffered poor health, and though she trained to be a dress designer she never made a profession for herself. Myfanwy stayed with her aunt during Helen's long period of illness that followed Edward's death; she became a teacher after the Second World War. Both daughters brought up children through periods of absent fathers.

Robert Frost would face tragedy of his own. In 1938 Elinor died, and without the woman that he had loved from his school days, he became grief stricken. His son Carol shot himself shortly after; he was the fourth child that Robert had buried. But Frost's poetry prospered. He won a Pulitzer prize for his fourth book of poems, the homely named *New Hampshire*, and sold a million poetry books in his lifetime; he spoke at the inauguration of President Kennedy. He wrote poems that touched upon Thomas and the war; a copy of *Mountain Interval* was among Edward's personal effects.[3]

Within a month of Thomas's death, Siegfried Sassoon and Wilfred Owen had both been invalided back to England. Sassoon had taken a sniper's bullet in the chest at Arras; that summer he would write a letter of 'wilful defiance', published in *The Times*, in which he accused the British government of deliberately prolonging the war. It took an intervention by Robert Graves to prevent a court-martial. Sassoon was dispatched to the care of W. H. R. Rivers at Craiglockhart War Hospital, where he met Owen suffering from shell-shock. Together they would write some of the most powerful poetry of the war before returning to action, Sassoon surviving his ordeal, Owen not.

Ezra Pound was furious at the way he thought Britain had served up her young men to slaughter: 'For an old bitch gone in the teeth, | For a botched civilization'. He moved to Italy where his anti-American and anti-Semitic broadcasts for Radio Rome saw him arraigned for treason by the United States; Frost was among the writers who secured his release from a Washington mental asylum in 1958. Richard Aldington fought in and survived the conflict; T. E. Hulme was not so fortunate. T. S. Eliot was unsuccessful in his attempt to serve in the United States Navy.[4]

Thomas's agent, Charles Francis Cazenove, died after a short illness in 1915; Godwin Baynes moved to Zurich to study under Carl Jung.

Eleanor Farjeon became a leading author of children's books. Edna Clarke Hall returned to painting and exhibited widely in the 1920s and 30s; she lived to be one hundred.

Walter de la Mare was saddened to discover that Thomas felt

let down by his friends. 'E. T. was probably feeling bitterly isolated,' Edward Garnett explained to him in 1920, 'I don't think
I gauged the extent of this, myself, till later on.' De la Mare
penned an affecting tribute: 'You would have grieved – 'twixt joy
and fear – | To know how my small loving son | Had wept for
you, my dear.'⁵

Wilfrid Wilson Gibson published the most widely read book
of war poetry by a non-combatant, but his popularity would
not endure. In 1934 he wrote to Frost to say, 'I am one of those
unlucky writers whose books have predeceased him'; he did not
write a single line of verse for the final twelve years of his life.
Ivor Gurney died in an asylum in Dartford in 1937; John Drinkwater died that year too. W. H. Davies married after the war; it
was said that he conducted the ceremony in near panic.⁶

Lascelles Abercrombie came to see his life's work as 'unre-
alized ambition', and would reflect ruefully, 'I have lived in
Gloucestershire, and I have known what it is to have Wilfrid
Gibson and Robert Frost for my neighbours; and John
Drinkwater, Rupert Brooke, Edward Thomas, Will Davies, Bob
Trevelyan, Arthur Ransome have drunk my cider and talkt [sic]
in my garden. I make no cider now, and I have no garden. But
once I lived in Gloucestershire.'⁷

Georgian Poetry sold close to 70,000 copies across five volumes,
but the poets it published began to distance themselves from it
after the war. By the time the last in the series appeared in 1922
it had outstayed its welcome, and was meekly swept aside by the
force of the new, modernising literature. T. S. Eliot's *The Waste
Land* and James Joyce's *Ulysses* were published that year, and
seemed infinitely more attuned to the disruptive and disturbing new world in which readers found themselves – what Eliot
in 1923 called, 'the immense panorama of futility and anarchy
which is contemporary history'. The truths and reliabilities of
the old order had foundered in the war: nine million young men

had gone to their graves in adherence to them. The Georgians would be all but forgotten in the decade ahead. The lease at the Poetry Bookshop expired in 1926, and Harold Monro moved to new premises opposite the British Museum. The original atmosphere never quite transferred, and when Monro died in 1932, the shop struggled on for three years before finally closing its doors.[8]

Poems, by Edward Thomas, was published in London by Selwyn and Blount in October 1917, and by Holt in New York City four months later. Some, like W. H. Hudson, held to their opinions that Thomas's poetic gift 'was rather a small one'. But F. R. Leavis wrote in 1932 that it was a body of work of 'a very rare order'. W. H. Auden and C. Day Lewis said that Thomas was a poet they had 'little or no hope of ever equalling'. Dylan Thomas believed he had grown to be loved by so very many that we could hardly think of a time when he was not alive: 'It is as though we had always known his poems, and were only waiting for him to write them.' In preparing the *Oxford Book of Twentieth Century English Verse*, Philip Larkin would permit Edward Thomas as many poems as T. S. Eliot. Ted Hughes would put it most clearly of anyone. 'He is the father of us all.'[9]

Acknowledgements

I am indebted to the Estate of Edward Thomas for permission to reproduce unpublished and copyrighted materials. 'Iris by Night', 'The Road Not Taken' and 'Not to Keep', The Poetry of Robert Frost, edited by Edward Connery Latham, © 1969 Henry Holt and Co.; reprinted by permission of Henry Holt and Co., LLC. Robert Frost letters to Edward Thomas from Selected Letters of Robert Frost, edited by Lawrance Thompson, © Lawrance Thompson and Henry Holt and Co; reprinted by permission of Henry Holt and Co., LLC.

I am grateful to the following institutions and individuals: Art Workers Guild (Monica Grose Hodge); Battersea Library, Wandsworth Heritage Service (Jane Allen, Felix Lancashire and Ruth MacLeod); Bodleian Library, Oxford (Colin Harris); British Postal Museum and Archive (Claire Woodforde); Cardiff University Library, Edward Thomas Collection (Alison Harvey and Peter Keelan); Dartmouth College, Rauner Special Collections Library (Andrea Bartelstein); Durham University Library, Claude Collier Abbott Collection (Mike Harkness); Fleet Architects (Richard Henson); Foundling Museum (Shelley Mullane); Gloucester Archives (Mick Heath); Imperial War Museum (Tony Richards and Alan Wakefield); Lincoln College Library, Oxford (Andrew Mussell); Met Office (Mark Beswick, Sandy Berridge); National Library of Wales, Aberystwyth (Martin Robson-Riley); New York Public Library, Berg Collection (Steve Crook); State University of New York, University at Buffalo, Poetry Collection, Lockwood Memorial Library (James Maynard); University of British Columbia Library, Norman Colbeck Collection (Katherine Kalsbeek); University of Gloucestershire, Dymock Poets Archive (Lorna Scott); University of Texas at Austin, Harry Ransom Center (Molly Schwartzburg).

My thanks to Maggie Fergusson, Paula Johnson and Tom Ponsonby (also to James Meek) for a Royal Society of Literature Jerwood Award for Non-Fiction, and to the following publications: *A Winter*

Garland 2006 (Wordsworth Trust, 2006), *Branch Lines: Edward Thomas and Contemporary Poetry* (ed. Guy Cuthbertson and Lucy Newlyn, Enitharmon 2007); *Edward Thomas Fellowship Newsletter* (ed. Richard Emeny); *Dymock Poets and Friends* (ed. Jeff Cooper).

My special gratitude to Richard Emeny for his insight and advice, and to those who have aided me at the Edward Thomas Fellowship, in particular Chris Brown, Liz Emeny, Anne Harvey, Edward C. Thomas, Colin Thornton, Stephen Turner and Rosemary Vellender; at the Friends of the Dymock Poets especially Jeff Cooper, Linda Hart (and The Butterfly) and Roy Palmer; to Barbara Davis, Jean Eversham and Bob May in Dymock, to Kirsten and Paul Westaway and Goliath at Gamage Hall Farm, where some of this book was written; to Pippa Bush and Robert Moreland; to Jonathan Barker, Bill Barnett, Diana Baynes Jansen, Sabina ffrench Blake, Roland Chambers, Ron Costley, John Haffenden, Andrew Motion, Juliet Nicolson, Richard Purver, Keith Sands and Alison Thomas.

Thank you to Neil Belton and to Kate Murray-Browne at Fabers for their expertise and passion, to Rachel Alexander, Kate Burton and Alex Holroyd, and to Shona Andrew, Robert Brown, Eleanor Crow, Patrick Fox, Hannah Griffiths, Paul Keegan, Gemma Lovett, Sarah Savitt and Kate Ward also. To Polly Clark, Antony Dunn, Clare Pollard and Owen Sheers.

My personal thanks to Mum and to Simon, and to Claire, James and Beowulf.

In suggesting amendments for this paperback edition, I am grateful to Jeff Cooper, Julia Copus, Robert Gomme, Linda Hart, John Jurica, Andrew Stevenson and Frances Whistler.

Notes on Sources

In researching Edward Thomas I have drawn only upon primary sources, though I would like to acknowledge below those titles which informed my reading or might be of interest to readers wishing to know more. Some of the primary sources I have seen have been examined by others before me, and inevitably I have made links that I went on to discover had already been made; in no way do I intend to be disrespectful to other researchers, and where their work has consciously informed mine I have acknowledged it to be the case. No writer on Thomas can be unaware of the contribution made to our reading of the poems by two scholars in particular: Edna Longley, whose *Poems and Last Poems* was published by Collins in 1973 (wholly revised as *The Annotated Collected Poems*, Tarset: Bloodaxe, 2008), and R. George Thomas, whose edition of *Collected Poems* was published by Oxford University Press in 1978 (reissued as *Collected Poems and War Diary*, London: Faber & Faber, 2004); both editors offer extensive original notes on the poems. William Cooke's research with the manuscripts also deserves special mention (*Edward Thomas: A Critical Biography*, London: Faber & Faber, 1970), while Matthew Spencer's work on the letters of Thomas and Frost has been invaluable in the preparation of this book.

Selections of Edward Thomas's prose can be found in Roland Gant (ed.), *The Prose of Edward Thomas* (London: Falcon Press, 1948) and *Edward Thomas on the Countryside* (London: Faber & Faber, 1977), and Edna Longley (ed.), *A Language Not to Be Betrayed: Selected Prose* (Manchester: Carcanet, 1981), which also contains a selection of Thomas's reviews, as does Richard Emeny (ed.), *Edward Thomas on the Georgians* (Cheltenham: Cyder Press, 2004) and Trevor Johnson (ed.), *Edward Thomas on Thomas Hardy* (Cheltenham: Cyder Press, 2002). For bibliographic information I have consulted Robert P. Eckert, *Edward Thomas: A Biography and a Bibliography* (London: Dent, 1937), Richard Emeny, *Edward Thomas 1878–1917: Towards a Complete Checklist of His Publica-*

tions (ed. Jeff Cooper, Blackburn: White Sheep Press, 2004) and John Buchan, 'A Bibliography of Philip Edward Thomas, 1878–1917' (private collection, 2005). Students of Thomas's work might also like to know of Judy Kendall's edited volume *Edward Thomas's Poets* (Manchester: Carcanet, 2007) and of Guy Cuthbertson and Lucy Newlyn's forthcoming series of *Prose Writings* (Oxford University Press).

Memoirs by Eleanor Farjeon and Helen Thomas merit special mention. *Edward Thomas: the Last Four Years* is an invaluable account of Eleanor's friendship with Thomas; written forty years after events, it understandably contains some factual inconsistencies as well as a number of transcription and dating errors, and where my text departs from the published text it is because I have followed the original letters in Battersea Library (though I have included page numbers from the memoir for readers familiar with the work). Helen Thomas's *As it Was* and *World Without End* (collected in *Under Storm's Wing*) are a moving account of her life with Edward, written to help her come to terms with her grief; yet as Myfanwy Thomas acknowledged, the works contained 'a fictional licence' (notably, the book's much-praised honeymoon sequence), and though they offer a moving insight into the marriage their perspective is also a partial and in places distorted one and I have been cautious in drawing upon them in depth here. Nevertheless I recommend both of these works to readers seeking a personal account of Thomas's life.

There exist a number of critical and biographical works not cited in my sources, chief among them: H. Coombes, *Edward Thomas* (London: Chatto & Windus, 1956), Jan Marsh, *Edward Thomas: A Poet for his Country* (London: Elek, 1978) and Stan Smith, *Edward Thomas*, Faber Student Guides (London: Faber & Faber, 1986).

In researching Robert Frost and others I have consulted many sources, both primary and secondary (see bibliography below), but the following deserve special and grateful acknowledgement. Two books on Robert Frost's English years by Lesley Lee Frances and John Walsh have been particularly valuable, while Lawrance Thompson's three-volume biography of Frost has been a frequent point of consultation.

The best introduction to the work of the Dymock Poets remains Linda Hart's *Once They Lived in Gloucestershire: A Dymock Poets Anthology* (Lechlade: Green Branch, 1995); Sean Street's *The Dymock Poets*

(Bridgend: Seren, 1994) provides a critical account and many valuable articles can be found in *Dymock Poets and Friends* (ed. Jeff Cooper) and the *Edward Thomas Fellowship Newsletter* (ed. Richard Emeny and Guy Cuthbertson). For local history, I have consulted Jennifer Davies, *Safe in Print: Memories of Donnington, Ryton and Broomsgreen* (published privately, 1994), George Dudfield, *Mud on My Boots: A View of Dymock Life 1909 to 1930* (Ledbury: published privately, 1988) and J. E. Gethyn-Jones, *Dymock Down the Ages* (published privately, 1959, 1966). Robert H. Ross, *The Georgian Revolt: Rise and Fall of a Poetical Ideal, 1910–22* (Carbondale: Southern Illinois University Press, 1965) provides a fine overview of the era. In addition to works on the Poetry Bookshop by Joy Grant and Dominic Hibberd, I have drawn on J. Howard Woolmer, *The Poetry Bookshop 1912–1935: A Bibliography* (Revere, Penn.: Woolmer Brotherson, 1988).

My background reading on the war includes Correlli Barnett, *The Great War* (London: Park Lane Press, 1979 and BBC, 2003), Cyril Falls, *Military Operations: France and Belgium, 1917* (London: Macmillan, 1940), Edward Gleichen, *Chronology of the Great War*, 3 vols (London: Constable, 1918–20), Michael Howard, *The First World War* (Oxford: Oxford University Press, 2002), Hew Strachan, *The First World War* (London: Simon & Schuster, 2003) and A. J. P. Taylor, *English History, 1914–45* (Oxford: Clarendon Press, 1965).

I – ARCHIVE SOURCES

Berg	Berg Collection, New York Public Library
BL	British Library
Bod.	Bodleian Library, University of Oxford
DCL	Dartmouth College Library, Hanover, New Hampshire
DPA	Dymock Poets Archive, University of Gloucestershire
DUL	Claude Collier Abbott Collection, Durham University Library
ETC	Edward Thomas Collection, Cardiff University Library
FF	Faber & Faber
GA	Gloucestershire Archives
IWM	Imperial War Museum
LCL	Lincoln College Library, University of Oxford
LML	Lockwood Memorial Library, State University of New York at Buffalo

NA	National Archives, Kew
NLW	National Library of Wales, University of Aberystwyth
UBC	Norman Colbeck Collection, University of British Columbia, Vancouver
UTA	Harry Ransom Center, University of Texas at Austin
WHS	Wandsworth Heritage Services, Battersea Library

Diaries, Notebooks, Manuscripts and Typescripts

ADW	A. Duncan Williams transcript, 1908–09 (Bod. MS Eng. misc. c. 501)
BL 44990	autograph of 62 poems, 24 Dec. 1914–24 May 1915 (BL Add. Mss. 44990)
diary	Edward Thomas's diary, 12 Dec. 1900–20 Oct. 1901 (NLW 22900B), 13 Sept. 1902–13 June 1904 (NLW 22902B), 1908 (NLW 22907B), 1915 (NLW 22912B)
Don d. 28	notebook of 67 fair copies, 25 June 1915–24 Dec. 1916 (Bod. MS Don. d. 28)
ECH	Edna Clarke Hall, journals and papers: four uncatalogued journals (here called ECH$_{1-4}$) Aug. 1917–23 July 1923, and a notebook of fair copies (poems) (private hands)
FNB	Field Note Books (Berg)
JT	typescript of 23 poems, once owned by Julian Thomas, Dec. 1914– (NLW 23077C)
JWH	John Wilton Haines papers: 'Edward Thomas by J. W. Haines', GA (D10828/4/11) and 'E.T. 22 Jan. 1917', (GA D10828/4/4)
LML MS	notebook of 5 poems, 16 Nov.–7 Dec. 1914 (LML)
M$_{1-2}$	Mervyn Thomas, two notebooks of 27 poems, 14 Dec. 1914–4 May 1915 (NLW 22920A) and 27 poems, 4 March 1916–5 July 1916 (NLW 22921A)
MET	typescript of 17 poems, once owned by Mary Elizabeth Thomas (BL)
PTS	*Poems* (printer's) typescript (Bod. MS Eng. poet. d. 214)
RLW	Memories of Edward Thomas Collected by Rowland L. Watson, ETC (DPA)
WD	Edward Thomas's War Diary, private collection

II – PERIODICALS AND BROADSHEETS

Academy
American Literature (AL)
Atlantic Monthly (AM)
The Athenaeum
The Bookman
Clapham Observer (CO)
Claremont Quarterly (CQ)
The Criterion
Daily Chronicle (DC)
Daily Express (DE)
Daily Mirror (DM)
Daily News (DN)
The Dial
Dymock Poets and Friends (DPF)
Daily Telegraph (DT)
English Review (ER)
Edward Thomas Fellowship Newsletter
  (ETFN)
Everyman
Form
Guardian
Morning Post (MP)

The Nation
New Age (NA)
New Freewoman (NF)
New Numbers (NN)
New Statesman (NS)
New Weekly (NW)
New York Times (NYT)
Newsweek
Observer
Poetry (Chicago) *(PC)*
Poetry and Drama (PD)
Poetry Review (PR)
Poetry Wales (PW)
Root and Branch (RB)
The Spectator
The Times
Times Literary Supplement (TLS)
T.P.'s Weekly (TPW)
Virginia Quarterly Review (VQR)
Westminster Gazette (WG)
Week's Survey (WS)
Yale Review (YR)

III – PUBLISHED WORKS BY EDWARD THOMAS

ACP *Annotated Collected Poems* (ed. Edna Longley), Tarset: Bloodaxe, 2008
ACS *Algernon Charles Swinburne: A Critical Study*, London: Martin Secker,
     1912
BW   *Beautiful Wales*, London: A. & C. Black, 1905
CET *The Childhood of Edward Thomas: A Fragment of Autobiography*, Lon-
     don: Faber & Faber, 1938
Country *The Country*, London: B. T. Batsford, 1913
CP1920   *Collected Poems*, London: Selwyn and Blount, 1920
CP1928   *Collected Poems*, London: Ingpen and Grant, 1928
CP1949   *Collected Poems*, London: Faber and Faber, 1949
CP1978   *Collected Poems* (ed. R. George Thomas) Oxford: Clarendon, 1978
CS   *Celtic Stories*, Oxford: Clarendon, 1911

FIL	*The Flowers I Love: A Series of Twenty-Four Drawings in Colour* (ed.), London: T. C. & E. C. Jack, 1916
FIP	*Feminine Influence on the Poets*, London: Martin Secker, 1910
FTB	*Four-and-Twenty Blackbirds*, London: Duckworth 1915
GB	*George Borrow*, London: Chapman & Hall, 1912
HE	*The Heart of England*, London: J. M. Dent, 1906
HGLM	*The Happy-Go-Lucky Morgans*, London: Duckworth, 1913
HS	*Horae Solitariae*, London: Duckworth, 1902
IPS	*In Pursuit of Spring*, London: Thomas Nelson, 1914
IW	*The Icknield Way*, London: Constable, 1913
Keats	*Keats*, London: T. C. & E. C. Jack, 1916
LDM	*The Life of the Duke of Marlborough*, London: Chapman & Hall, 1915
LH	*Lafcadio Hearn*, London: Constable, 1912
LP	*Last Poems*, London: Selwyn and Blount, 1918
LPE	*A Literary Pilgrim in England*, London: Methuen, 1917
LS	*The Last Sheaf*, London: Cape, 1928
LT	*Light and Twilight*, London: Duckworth, 1911
MM	*Maurice Maeterlinck*, London: Methuen, 1911
NT	*Norse Tales*, Oxford: Clarendon, 1912
Oxford	*Oxford*, London: A. & C. Black, 1903
PB	*The Pocket Book of Poems and Songs for the Open Air* (ed.), London: E. Grant Richards, 1907
Poems	*Poems*, London: Selwyn and Blount, 1917
RJ	*Richard Jefferies*, London: Hutchinson, 1909
SC	*The South Country*, London: J. M. Dent, 1909
SP	*Six Poems*, Flansham: Pear Tree Press, 1916
TE	*This England: An Anthology from Her Writers* (ed.), London: Oxford University Press, 1915
WL	*The Woodland Life*, London: William Blackwood and Sons, 1897
WP	*Walter Pater: A Critical Study*, London: Martin Secker, 1913

IV – CORRESPONDENCE

Letters from Edward Thomas

–ADW	A. Duncan Williams, IWM; *Poems* (facsimile edn.), London: Imperial War Museum, 1997
–CB	Clifford Bax, UTA; *Selected Letters* (ed. R. George Thomas), Oxford: Oxford University Press, 1995

–CFC   Charles Francis Cazenove, DUL

–EB   Emily Bottomley, ETC; *Letters to Gordon Bottomley* (ed. R. George Thomas), London: Oxford University Press, 1968

–ECH   Edna Clarke Hall, Berg

–EF   Eleanor Farjeon, WHS; Farjeon

–EG   Edward Garnett, UTA; *Letters to Edward Garnett*, Edinburgh: Tragara, 1981

–EWF   Elinor White Frost, *Elected Friends: Robert Frost and Edward Thomas to one another* (ed. Matthew Spencer), New York: Handsel, 2003

–GB   Gordon Bottomley, ETC; *Letters to Gordon Bottomley* (ed. R. George Thomas), London: Oxford University Press, 1968

–HEMT Helen Elizabeth Myfanwy Thomas, ETC

–HH   Harry Hooton, Colbeck Collection, University of British Columbia, Vancouver; Moore, *Selected Letters* (ed. R. George Thomas), London: Oxford University Press, 1995, R. George Thomas

–HM   Harold Monro, LML; *Poetry Wales*, XIII, 4 (Spring 1978), 43–70

–HT   Helen Thomas, ETC; *Letters to Helen* (ed. R. George Thomas), Manchester: Carcanet, 2000

–IMacA Ian MacAlister, WHS

–JB   Jesse Berridge, NLW; *Letters of Edward Thomas to Jesse Berridge* (ed. Anthony Berridge), London: Enitharmon, 1983

–JF   John Freeman, Berg, typescript in WHS

–JH   Janet Hooton, ETC; *Letters to Helen* (ed. R. George Thomas), Manchester: Carcanet, 2000

–JT   Julian Thomas, ETC; *Selected Letters* (ed. R. George Thomas), Oxford: Oxford University Press, 1995

–JWH   John Wilton Haines, GA

–MET   Mary Elizabeth Thomas, ETC

–MPT   Mervyn Philip Thomas, ETC

–MT   Margaret Townsend, Bod. MS Eng. Lett. d. 281

–PHT   Philip Henry Thomas, ETC; *Letters to Helen* (ed. R. George Thomas), Manchester: Carcanet, 2000

–RF   Robert Frost, DCL; *Elected Friends: Robert Frost and Edward Thomas to one another* (ed. Matthew Spencer), New York: Handsel, 2003

–RMBT Rachel Mary Bronwen Thomas, ETC

–WdlM   Walter de la Mare, Bod. MS Eng. Lett. c. 376

–WHH   W. H. Hudson, private collection; *ETFN*, LII (Aug. 2004), *Selected Letters* (ed. R. George Thomas), Oxford: Oxford University Press, 1995

Other Correspondence

CFC– Charles Francis Cazenove to Edward Thomas (ET), DUL

DHL– D. H. Lawrence to Edward Marsh (EM), *The Letters of D. H. Lawrence*, vol. II, *June 1913–October 1916* (ed. G. Zytaruk and J. T. Boulton), Cambridge: Cambridge University Press, 1981

EG– Edward Garnett to Walter de la Mare (WdlM), Whistler

EM– Edward Marsh to Rupert Brooke (RB), Hassall, *Edward Marsh*

EP– Ezra Pound to Alice Corbin Henderson (ACH), Harriet Monroe, *Poetry* (Chicago) (*PC*), *Letters of Ezra Pound 1907–1941* (ed. D. D. Paige), London: Faber & Faber, 1950

EWF– Elinor White Frost to Margaret Bartlett (MB), Leona White Harvey (LWH), *Selected Letters of Robert Frost* (ed. Lawrance Thompson), New York: Holt, Rinehart and Winston, 1964

FH– Florence Holt to Robert Frost (RF), *Selected Letters of Robert Frost* (ed. Lawrance Thompson), New York: Holt, Rinehart and Winston, 1964

FL– Franklin Lushington to Helen Thomas (HT), ETC, WHS

GG– Geraldine Gibson to John Wilton Haines (JWH), DPA

GWB– G. W. Blackwood to Eleanor Farjeon (EF), *Letters to Edward Garnett*, Edinburgh: Tragara, 1981

HJ– Henry James to Mrs Humphry Ward (HW), *The Letters of Henry James* (ed. Percy Lubbock), vol. II, London: Macmillan, 1920

HT– Helen Thomas to Edna Clarke Hall (ECH), private collection; Edward Thomas (ET), ETC (NLW), *Letters to Helen* (ed. R. George Thomas), Manchester: Carcanet, 2000; Janet Hooton (JH), ETC, *Under Storm's Wing*; Harold Monro (HM), LML, *Poetry Wales*, XIII, 4 (Spring 1978)

IG– Ivor Gurney to Marion Scott (MS), *Collected Letters of Ivor Gurney* (ed. R. K. R. Thornton), Manchester: Carcanet, 1991

JWH– John Wilton Haines to Robert P. Eckert (RPE), Bod. MS Eng. Lett. c. 281

LA– Lascelles Abercrombie to Edward Marsh (EM), Berg, DPA; John Wilton Haines (JWH), GA

MPT– Mervyn Philip Thomas to Edward Thomas (ET), ETC

RB– Rupert Brooke to Edward Thomas (ET), *Letters of Rupert Brooke* (ed. Geoffrey Keynes), London: Faber & Faber, 1968 (*Letters*); Eileen Wellesley (EW), *Letters*; Harold Monro (HM) [King's College Library, Cambridge], Hibberd, *Harold Monro*; John Drinkwater (JD), *Letters*; Jacques Raverat (JR), *Letters*; Ka Cox (KC), Hassall,

Rupert Brooke; Leonard Bacon (LB), *Letters*; Noel Olivier (NO), *Song of Love: The Letters of Rupert Brooke and Noel Olivier* (ed. Pippa Harris), London: Bloomsbury, 1991; Russell Loines (RL), *Letters*; Ruth Mary Brooke (RMB), *Letters*; Walter de la Mare (WdlM), Whistler; Wilfrid Wilson Gibson, (WWG) *Letters*

RF–   Robert Frost to Edward Garnett (EG), *Selected Letters of Robert Frost* (ed. Lawrance Thompson), New York: Holt, Rinehart and Winston, 1964 (*Selected Letters*); Ernest Jewell (EJ), Sergeant, *The Trial by Existence*, New York: Holt, Rinehart and Winston, 1960; Ernest Silver (ES), *Selected Letters*; Edward Thomas (ET), Berg, ETC, *Elected Friends: Robert Frost and Edward Thomas to one another* (ed. Matthew Spencer), New York: Handsel, 2003 (*Elected Friends*); F. S. Flint (FSF), UTA, Lawrance Thompson, *Robert Frost: The Early Years, 1874–1915*, New York: Holt, Rinehart and Winston, 1966, Walsh; Gertrude McQuesten (GMcQ), Boston University Library, Walsh; Grace Walcott Conkling (GWC), *Poetry Wales*, XIII, 4 (Spring 1978); Harold Monro (HM), *Selected Letters*; Harold Roy Brennan (HRB), *American Literature*, LIX, 1 (March 1987), 117; Helen Thomas (HT), DCL, *Elected Friends*; John T. Bartlett (JTB), *Selected Letters*; John Wilton Haines (JWH), private collection, *Selected Letters*; Lascelles Abercrombie (LA), *Selected Letters*; Louis Untermeyer (LU), *Letters of Robert Frost to Louis Untermeyer* (ed. Untermeyer), New York: Holt, Rinehart and Winston, 1963; R. P. T. Coffin (RPTC), *Selected Letters*; Sidney Cox (SC), *Selected Letters*; Susan Hayes Ward (SHW), *Selected Letters*; Thomas B. Mosher (TBM), *Selected Letters*; Wilbur E. Rowell (WER), *Selected Letters*

RH–   Ralph Hodgson to Robert Frost (RF), DCL, *Selected Letters of Robert Frost* (ed. Lawrance Thompson), New York: Holt, Rinehart and Winston, 1964

RMBT– Rachel Mary Bronwen Thomas to Edward Thomas (ET), ETC

TSE–   T. S. Eliot to Conrad Aiken (CA), Eleanor Hinkley (EH), *Letters of T. S. Eliot*, vol. I, *1898–1922* (ed. Valerie Eliot and Hugh Haughton), revised edn, London: Faber & Faber, 2009; Miss Grenside (MG), FF, Rdlm163

WBY– W. B. Yeats to Lady Gregory (LG), *Letters of W. B. Yeats* (ed. Allen Wade), London: Rupert Hart-Davis, 1954

WHH– W. H. Hudson to Edward Garnett (EG), *Letters from W. H. Hudson to Edward Garnett*, London: Dent, 1925, *153 Letters from W. H. Hudson* (ed. Edward Garnett), London: Nonesuch Press, 1923

WO– Wilfred Owen to Susan Owen (SO), *Collected Letters of Wilfred Owen* (ed. Harold Owen and John Bell), London: Oxford University Press, 1967

WWG– Wilfrid Wilson Gibson to Edward Marsh (EM), Berg; Robert Frost (RF), DCL

V – ADDITIONAL WORKS CITED

Abercrombie, Catherine, 'Memoirs of a Poet's Wife', *The Listener*, 15 Nov. 1956

Abercrombie, Lascelles, *The Poems of Lascelles Abercrombie*, London: Oxford University Press, 1930

Abercrombie, Lascelles and R. C. Trevelyan (eds.), *An Annual of New Poetry*, London: Constable, 1917

Aiken, Conrad, *Ushant: An Essay*, New York: Duell, Sloan and Pearce, 1952

Baynes Jansen, Diana, *Jung's Apprentice: A Biography of Helton Godwin Baynes*, Einsiedeln: Daimon Verlag, 2003

Berridge, Jesse, 'Edward: A Memoir', *Letters of Edward Thomas to Jesse Berridge* (ed. Anthony Berridge), London: Enitharmon, 1983

Blunden, Edmund, 'Poetry of the Present Reign', *John O'London's Weekly*, 27 April 1935

Bottomley, Gordon, 'A Note on Edward Thomas', *Welsh Review*, IV, 3 (Sept. 1945), 166–78

Brooke, Rupert, *Poems*, London: Sidgwick and Jackson, 1911

———, *1914 and Other Poems*, London: Sidgwick and Jackson, 1915

Browne, Maurice, *Recollections of Rupert Brooke*, Chicago: Alexander Greene, 1927

Carlyle, Thomas, *On Heroes, Hero-Worship and the Heroic in History*, London: James Fraser, 1841

Carpenter, Humphrey, *A Serious Character: A Life of Ezra Pound*, London: Faber & Faber, 1988

Cornford, Frances, *Poems*, London: Priory, 1910

Crane, Joan St C., *Robert Frost: A Descriptive Catalogue of Books and Manuscripts in the Clifton Waller Barrett Library, University of Virginia*, Charlottesville: Virginia University Press, 1974

Davies, Jennifer, *Safe in Print: Memories of Donnington, Ryton and Broomsgreen*, published privately, 1994

Davies, W. H., *The Autobiography of a Super-Tramp*, London: Jonathan Cape, 1908

———, *Later Days*, London: Jonathan Cape, 1925

Davies, W. H. et al., *In Memoriam: Edward Thomas*, London: Moreland Press, 1919

Day Lewis, C., 'The Poetry of Edward Thomas', *Essays by Divers Hands* (Transactions of the Royal Society of Literature of the United Kingdom), XXVIII (1956)

De la Mare, Walter, *Motley and Other Poems*, London: Constable, 1918

del Re, Arundel, 'Georgian Reminiscences', *Studies in English Literature*, English Seminar, University of Tokyo, 1932, 1934

Drinkwater, John, *Olton Pools*, London: Sidgwick and Jackson, 1917

——, *Loyalties*, London: Sidgwick and Jackson, 1919

——, *Discovery: Being the Second Book of an Autobiography, 1897–1913*, London: Ernest Benn, 1932

Dudfield, George, *Mud on My Boots: A View of Dymock Life 1909 to 1930*, Ledbury: published privately, 1988

Ede, H. S., *A Life of Gaudier-Brzeska*, London: Heinemann, 1930

Egremont, Max, *Siegfried Sassoon: A Biography*, London: Picador, 2005

Eliot, T. S., 'Verse Pleasant and Unpleasant', *The Egoist*, March 1918

——, *Poetry Speaks: A Twentieth-Century Anthology Read by the Poets* (cassette recording), ed. Peter Orr, Argo, 1982

——, *The Waste Land: A Facsimile and Transcript of the Original Drafts including the Annotations of Ezra Pound* (ed. Valerie Eliot), London: Faber & Faber, 1971

English Catalogue of Books, London: The Publishers' Circular, 1914–25

Farjeon, Eleanor, *Edward Thomas: The Last Four Years*, London: Oxford University Press, 1958

Fast Beat My Heart: Edward Thomas and Family at Steep (audiobook), Edward Thomas Fellowship, 2008

Feld, Rose C., 'Robert Frost Relieves His Mind', *New York Times Book Review*, 21 Oct. 1923

Fletcher, John Gould, *Life is My Song*, New York: Farrar and Rinehart, 1937

Ford, Ford Madox, *Return to Yesterday*, London: Gollancz, 1931

Francis, Lesley Lee, *The Frost Family's Adventure in Poetry: Sheer Morning Gladness at the Brim*, Columbia: Missouri University Press, 1994

Francis, Robert, *Robert Frost: A Time to Talk*, London: Robson, 1973

Frost, Lesley, *New Hampshire's Child: The Derry Journals of Lesley Frost* (ed. Arnold Grade and Lawrance Thompson), New York: SUNY Press, 1969

Frost, Robert, *A Boy's Will*, London: David Nutt, 1913

——, *North of Boston*, London: David Nutt, 1914

——, *Mountain Interval*, New York: Henry Holt, 1916

Frost, Robert, *New Hampshire*, New York: Henry Holt, 1921

———, *Collected Poems*, New York: Henry Holt, 1930

———, *A Further Range*, New York: Henry Holt 1936

———, *Family Letters of Robert and Elinor Frost* (ed. Arnold Grade), Albany: SUNY Press, 1972

———, *Notebooks of Robert Frost* (ed. Robert Faggen), Cambridge, Mass.: Harvard University Press, 2006

———, *Collected Prose of Robert Frost* (ed. Mark Richardson), Cambridge, Mass.: Harvard University Press, 2007

Gallup, Donald, *A Bibliography of Ezra Pound*, London: Rupert Hart-Davis, 1969

Garnett, David, *The Golden Echo*, London: Chatto & Windus, 1953

Gawsworth, John, *Ten Contemporaries: Notes Towards Their Definitive Bibliography*, London: Ernest Benn, 1932

Gethyn-Jones, J. E., *Dymock Down the Ages*, revised edition, privately printed at Gloucester by Albert E. Smith (Printers) Ltd, 1966

Gibson, Ashley, *Postscript to Adventure*, London: J. M. Dent, 1930

Gibson, Wilfrid Wilson, *Battle*, London: Elkin Mathews, 1915

——— *Friends*, London: Elkin Mathews, 1916

——— *The Golden Room and Other Poems*, London: Macmillan, 1928

Gleichen, Edward Lord, *Chronology of the Great War*, 3 vols, London: Constable, 1918–20

Goldring, Douglas, *South Lodge: Reminiscences of Violet Hunt, Ford Madox Ford, and the English Review Circle*, London: Constable, 1943

Grant, Joy, *Harold Monro and the Poetry Bookshop*, London: Routledge and Kegan Paul, 1967

Graves, Robert, *Goodbye to All That*, London: Jonathan Cape, 1929; revised edn., London: Cassell, 1957

Graves, Robert and Laura Riding, *A Survey of Modernist Poetry*, London: Heinemann, 1927

———, *The Common Asphodel: Collected Essays on Poetry, 1922–1949*, London: Hamish Hamilton, 1949

Haines, John Wilton, 'The Dymock Poets', *Gloucestershire Countryside*, I, 9 (Oct. 1933), 131–3

Harvey, Anne (ed.), *Adlestrop Revisited: An Anthology Inspired by Edward Thomas's Poem*, Stroud: Sutton, 1999

Hassall, Christopher, *Edward Marsh: A Biography*, London: Longman, 1959

———, *Rupert Brooke: A Biography*, London: Faber & Faber, 1964

Hibberd, Dominic, *Harold Monro: Poet of the Age*, Basingstoke: Palgrave, 2001

————, *Wilfred Owen: A New Biography*, London: Weidenfeld and Nicolson, 2002

Hodgson, Ralph, *Poets Remembered*, Cleveland, Ohio: Rowfant Club, 1967

Jefferies, Richard, *The Gamekeeper at Home* (1878) and *The Amateur Poacher* (1879), Oxford: Oxford University Press, 1978

Jepson, Edgar, *Memories of an Edwardian and Neo-Georgian*, London: Secker, 1938

Keynes, Geoffrey, *A Bibliography of Rupert Brooke*, London: Rupert Hart-Davis, 1959

Larkin, Philip (ed.), *The Oxford Book of Twentieth Century English Verse*, Oxford: Clarendon, 1973

Lathem, Edward Connery (ed.), *Interviews with Robert Frost*, New York: Holt, 1966

Lawrence, D. H., 'The Georgian Renaissance', *Rhythm*, II (March 1913)

Leavis, F. R., *New Bearings in English Poetry*, London: Chatto & Windus, 1932/ Peregrine, 1963

Lowell, Amy, 'A Letter from London, 28 Aug. 1914', *Little Review*, I (Sept. 1914)

Marsh, Edward (ed.), *Georgian Poetry 1911–1912*, London: Poetry Bookshop, 1912

Masefield, John, *The Everlasting Mercy*, London: Sidgwick and Jackson, 1911

Mertins, Louis, *Life and Walks-Talking*, Norman: Oklahoma University Press, 1965

Monro, Harold, *Some Contemporary Poets*, London: Leonard Parsons, 1920

Moore, John, *The Life and Letters of Edward Thomas*, London: Heinemann, 1939

Motion, Andrew, *The Poetry of Edward Thomas*, London: Routledge & Kegan Paul, 1980

Nevinson, H. W., *Changes and Chances*, London: Nisbet & Co., 1923

Newham-David, Lieut.-Col., *Dinners and Diners: Where and How to Dine in London*, London: Grant Richards, 1899

Norman, Charles, *Ezra Pound*, London: Macmillan, 1960

Patry, Rose I., *Practical Handbook on Elocution*, London: Swan Sonnenshein, 1909

Pound, Ezra (ed.), *Des Imagistes: An Anthology*, London: Poetry Bookshop, 1914

————, *Lustra*, London: Elkin Mathews, 1916

————, *Hugh Selwyn Mauberley*, London: Ovid, 1920

————, *Literary Essays* (ed. T. S. Eliot), London: Faber & Faber, 1954

Reeves, Maud Pember, *Round About a Pound a Week*, London: G. Bell & Sons Ltd, 1913

Sassoon, Siegfried, *Siegfried's Journey 1916–1920*, London: Faber & Faber, 1945

Sergeant, Elizabeth Shepley, *Robert Frost: The Trial by Existence*, New York: Holt, Rinehart and Winston, 1960

Severn, Mark (Major Franklin Lushington), *The Gambardier*, London: Ernest Benn, 1930

Sitwell, Sir Osbert, *Laughter in the Next Room*, London: Macmillan, 1949

Sokol, B. J., 'The Publication of Robert Frost's First Books: Triumph and Fiasco', *Book Collector*, XXVI, 2 (Summer 1977), 228–40

Stock, Noel, *The Life of Ezra Pound*, London: Routledge & Kegan Paul, 1970

Stonesifer, Richard J., *W. H. Davies: A Critical Biography*, London: Jonathan Cape, 1963

Sutton, William (ed.), *Newdick's Season of Frost: An Interrupted Biography of Robert Frost*, Albany: SUNY Press, 1976

Taylor, A. J. P., *English History, 1914–45*, Oxford: Clarendon Press, 1965

Thomas, Alison, *Portraits of Women: Gwen John and Her Forgotten Contemporaries*, Cambridge: Polity, 1994

Thomas, Dylan, *On the Air with Dylan Thomas: The Broadcasts* (ed. Ralph Maud), New York: New Directions, 1992

Thomas, Helen, *Under Storm's Wing*, Manchester: Carcanet, 1988

Thomas, Myfanwy, *One of These Fine Days: Memoirs*, Manchester: Carcanet, 1982

Thomas, R. George, *Edward Thomas: A Portrait*, Oxford: Clarendon, 1985

Thompson, Lawrance, *Robert Frost: The Early Years, 1874–1915*, New York: Holt, Rinehart and Winston, 1966

————, *Robert Frost: The Years of Triumph, 1915–1938*, New York: Holt, Rinehart and Winston, 1970

Thompson, Lawrance and R. H. Winnick, *Robert Frost: The Later Years, 1938–1963*, New York: Holt, Rinehart and Winston, 1976

Tomalin, Ruth, *W. H. Hudson: A Biography*, London: Faber & Faber, 1982

Voices and Visions: Robert Frost (videotape), Annenberg/CPB Collection, New York Center for Visual History, 1988

Walsh, John Evangelist, *Into My Own: The English Years of Robert Frost*, New York: Grove Weidenfeld, 1988

Whistler, Theresa, *The Life of Walter de la Mare*, London: Gerald Duckworth, 1993

Whiteman, W. M., *The Edward Thomas Country*, Southampton: Paul Cave, 1978/1988

Yeats, W. B., *The Wild Swans at Coole*, London: Macmillan, 1919

————, *Essays and Introductions*, New York: Macmillan, 1961

Notes

I – STEEP

WINTER 1913

1. 35 Devonshire Street, Bloomsbury WC (now renamed 34–5 Boswell Street); Monro, *PR*, I, II (Nov. 1912), 498.
2. Browne, 37; also Sitwell, 35; del Re, 38; Grant, 61–5.
3. Sergeant, 105, 101.
4. Gaudier-Brzeska in Ede, 131; RB–HM, 11 June 1913, 126.
5. Sassoon in Hassall, *Rupert Brooke*, 451; Austin, 'Jameson's Raid', *The Times*, 11 Jan. 1896; EP–PC, 22 Oct. 1913, 13; HJ–HW, 24 Oct. 1912, 273–6; Lawrence, xvii–xx.
6. *TLS*, 11 Nov. 1920, 729; Brooke, 'A Channel Passage', *Poems*, 49; *TLS*, 29 Aug. 1912, 337; Masefield, 2–3.
7. Blunden, III; Monro, 23.
8. Monro, *PD*, II, 6 (June 1914), 180.
9. A. K. Sabin in Grant, 93.
10. Aldington in Carpenter, 178; Graves and Riding, 118–19; *WP*, 215–16; Eliot, 'Verse Pleasant and Unpleasant', 43–4; *Country*, 55.
11. Marsh, v.
12. Flint, *PC*, I, 6 (March 1913), 199; Pound, *Literary Essays*, 3; Pound, *PR*, I, 2 (Feb. 1912); Pound, 'In a Station of the Metro', *PC*, II, I (April 1913), 12, and *Lustra*, 45 in variant form.
13. Ford, 419; RF–FSF, 21 Jan. 1913, Thompson, *Early Years*, 408; RF–EG, 29 April 1917, 217.
14. See ET–EB, Nov. 1912, 225; see ET–HM, 3 Jan. 1913, 54; Thomas Seccomb, *TLS*, 16 April 1917; Walter de la Mare, *WG*, 28 April 1917.
15. See *GB*, *LH*, *ACS*, *NT*, *IW*, *Country*, *HGLM*.
16. See Ashley Gibson, 10; see Hodgson in RLW, 59; see Bottomley, 168; see ECH, c. March 1919; see Walter de la Mare, *CP1920*; see Farjeon, 24; see JWH, 'Edward Thomas by J. W. Haines', 5; see Helen Thomas, 21–2; see Catherine Abercrombie.
17. See ET diary, 2 May 1901: 'I brood too much for suicide; the thought to kill

myself kills itself by intensity. How many sedentary people do commit suicide?'; see ET–GB, 5 Dec. 1912, 225–6; ET–JB, 14 Feb. 1913, 70.

18. Helen Thomas, 143.

19. ET, loose notes, 9 Oct. 1907, in R. George Thomas, 141.

20. 'The Attempt', *LT*, 160–73; Helen Thomas, 113–14; ET diary, 29 Nov. 1908: 'Up, 7. Reading. After tried to shoot myself. Evening reading. Read Marlowe. To bed, 11.'

21. ET–GB, 6 Nov. 1908, 174–5.

22. See *WL*.

23. ET–HH, *c*.1898, Moore, 41.

24. Nevinson, 195.

25. 117 Atheldene Road, Earlsfield, London SW (2 Nov. 1900–12 Feb. 1901), see *HS*, 103–5; 7 Nightingale Parade, Nightingale Lane, Balham, London SW (12 Feb. 1901–Oct. 1901); Rose Acre, Bearsted, nr Maidstone, Kent (9 Oct. 1901–March 1903); see ET–JB, 6 May 1902, 29; Helen Thomas, 90–1; HT–JH, 7 June 1902.

26. Irene McArthur in RLW.

27. See *Oxford*; Ivy Cottage, The Green, Bearsted, nr Maidstone, Kent (March 1903–Feb. 1904); diary, 27 Oct. 1903; Helen Thomas, 99, 101; HT–ET, 10 Dec. 1903, 23.

28. Elses Farm, The Weald, nr Sevenoaks, Kent (May 1904–26 Oct. 1906); Helen Thomas, 103.

29. ET–JB, 8 Aug. 1905, 47; ET–GB, 30 June 1905, 87, and 24 Jan. 1906, 103; see 'Hawthornden', *LT*, 120–1.

30. Frost in Mertins, 135.

31. Helen Thomas, 42, 96.

32. ET–GB, 19 July 1908, 165; ET–HH, Dec. 1911, *Selected Letters*, 68–9; WHH–EG, 12 Nov. 1911, 118.

33. ET–GB, 21 May 1908, 163.

34. 30 Victoria Park Square, behind the Bethnal Green Museum (now Museum of Childhood).

35. ET–GB, 18 April 1912, 221.

36. Baynes Jansen, 137.

37. ET–GB, 26 Dec. 1906, 129.

38. Frost in Sergeant, 89.

39. See Frost, *Collected Prose*, 35–73; see Frost in Mertins, 102; Lesley Frost, quoted in D. Tatham, *A Poet Recognized: Notes about Robert Frost's First Trip to England*, privately printed, 1969, 9–10, reproduced in Walsh, 30–1.

40. RF–JTB, *c*.5 Nov. 1912, 99; RF–SHW, 15 Sept. 1912, 52; *Voices and Visions*.

41. See Farjeon, 88.

42. See Thompson, *Early Years*, 504–5n; see Sergeant, 7.

43. See Thompson, *Early Years*, 308–9, 340.

44. Sergeant, 71; RF–SHW, 4 Nov. 1907, 41, and 19 Dec. 1911, 43; Jack Haines in Mertins, 131; *Voices and Visions*; RF–EJ, 6 May 1913, 108.

45. See ET, 'Wind and Mist', 1 April 1915, Abercrombie and Trevelyan, 42–4 and *LP*, 41–3; 'The Combe', 30 Dec. 1914, *Poems*, 19; *SC*, 148–9; 'The Path', 26 March 1915, *Poems*, 18.

46. See ET, 'When first', July or Oct. 1916, *Poems*, 22–3; Berryfield Cottage, Ashford Chase Estate, Steep (26 Oct. 1906–18 Dec. 1909); ET–GB, 15 March 1910, 199; Wick Green, Froxfield (18 Dec. 1909–22 July 1913); see ET, 'The New House', 19 March 1915, Abercrombie and Trevelyan, 41, *LP*, 34, 'Wind and Mist', *LP*, 41–3.

47. ET–EF, 10 Jan. 1913, 5.

48. ET, *DC*, 14 Jan. 1913; ET–HM, 26 Dec. 1911, 52; ET, *The Bookman*, March 1913; ET–HM, 15 Jan. 1913, 55; Newbolt, *PD*, I, 1 (March 1913), 46.

49. ET–HM, 23 Nov. 1911, 50; ET, *PD*, I, 1 (March 1913), 33–42.

50. ET–EF, 5 Dec. 1913, 46.

51. ET, 'How I Began', *LS*, 15–20; *HGLM*; *CET*.

52. 10 Upper Lansdowne Road North, Lambeth, SW (now renamed, 14 Lansdowne Gardens) (1878–80).

53. *CO*, 24 Dec. 1920; *CET*, 17.

54. See ET–PHT, undated [1899], 11; ET, 'I may come near loving you', 8 Feb. 1916, *CP1949*, 189.

55. *CET*, 18–19.

56. *CET*, 19; ET–EF, ?mid-June 1913, 13; Helen Thomas, 28; *CET*, 19.

57. 49 Wakehurst Road, Wandsworth, London SW (1880–8); 61 Shelgate Road, Wandsworth, London SW (1888–97).

58. *CET*, 44.

59. *CET*, 32–3.

60. *CET*, 103, 105, 115.

61. *CET*, 143–4.

62. *CET*, 26.

SPRING 1913

1. *IW*, 91.

2. *IW*, 137, 142.

3. *IW*, vi; *Athenaeum*, 26 April 1913, 454–5.

4. *IW*, 280–3.

5. ET–HM [Feb. 1913], 55, and 24 Feb. 1913, 56; Monro, *PD*, I, 1 (March 1913), 7; Patry, 221; RB–NO, 12 Feb. 1913, 243.

6. ET, *PD*, I, 1 (March 1913), 53–6.

7. ET, *DC*, 5 March 1909; ET, *DC*, 12 July 1902.

8. ET, *WS*, 18 June 1904; ET, *DC*, 1 Jan. 1907; ET, *WS*, 18 June 1904.

9. Frost, 'In England', Thompson, *Early Years*, 396; Sergeant, 97; RF–SHW, 13 May 1913, 73.

10. Frost in Mertins, 107; Frost in Robert Francis, 16; RF–LA, 21 Sept. 1915, 193.

11. Sergeant, 102; Thompson, *Early Years*, 411; EP–ACH, March 1913, 14; EP–PC, March 1913, 16.

12. See Pound, 'How I Began', *TPW*, 6 June 1913; Pound, *Paris Review*, 28 (1962); WBY–LG, 1909, 543; Yeats, 'A Song', *Wild Swans at Coole*, 22; Pound, *Paris Review*, 28 (1962); Pound, *PC*, I, 4 (Jan. 1913), 125; WBY–LG, 1 and 3 Jan. 1913 quoted in Carpenter, 192; Pound, 'The Later Years', *PC*, IV, 2 (May 1914), 65; Carpenter, 172.

13. RF–JTB, *c.*4 April 1913, 71; Goldring, 49.

14. EWF–MB, *c.*3 July 1914, 78; RF–TBM, 15 June 1913, 74.

15. Frost, Milton Academy, Massachusetts, 17 May 1935; Frost in Sergeant, 106; Frost interviewed by Richard Poirier, 'The Art of Poetry No. 2', *Paris Review*, 24 (Summer–Fall 1960), 16; RF–TBM, 24 Oct. 1913, 96.

16. ET–GB, 1 May 1909, 185; ET, *DC*, 7 June 1909; ET, *ER*, June 1909.

17. Jepson, 140–1.

18. ET–GB, 12 June 1909, 187; ET, *DC*, 23 Nov. 1909.

19. ET–GB, 14 Dec. 1909, 197.

20. Pound in Stonesifer, 239.

21. *IPS*, 44.

22. *IPS*, 119, 124–7.

23. *IPS*, 141.

24. *IPS*, 219–20.

25. Wordsworth, 'Anecdote for Fathers'; *IPS*, 282.

26. ET–JB, 3 May 1914, 74.

27. ET–GB, 7 May 1913, 228; see ET–JB *c.*25 July 1913; ET–EF, ?31 Oct. 1913; Farjeon, 43.

28. RF–JTB, *c.*4 April 1913, 70; *Athenaeum*, 5 April 1913, 379; *TLS*, 10 April 1913, 155; Ezra Pound, *PC*, II, 2 (May 1913), 72–4, and *NF*, I, 9 (Sept. 1913).

29. RF–SHW, 13 May 1913, 73.

30. RB–ET, *c.*15 May 1913, 459.

31. *MP*, 11 Dec. 1911; *NA*, 18 Jan. 1912; *TLS*, Dublin *Express* in Hassall, *Rupert Brooke*, 535–7; ET, *DC*, 9 April 1912.

SUMMER 1913

1. Helen Thomas, 142; see ET–GB, mid-June 1913, 229–30; see ET–HT, 23 June 1913, 68–70.
2. ET–EF [?midsummer 1913], 13.
3. ET–CFC, 14 Sept. 1912; CFC–ET, 16 Sept. 1912; ET–CFC, 18 June 1913; ET–CFC, 10 Nov. 1913.
4. RF–JTB, 6 Aug. 1913, 88; RF–TBM, 17 July 1913, 84; see RF–SHW, 4 Dec. 1894, 25 and RF–SHW, 8 July 1896, 27; RF–JTB, 4 July 1913, 79–80.
5. See Farjeon, 90.
6. RF–JTB, 4 July 1913, 80–1.
7. Frost, *Collected Prose*, 116.
8. Carlyle, 135; RF–RPTC, 24 Feb. 1938, 461; RF–SC, 19 Jan. 1914, 107–8; RF–TBM, 17 July 1913, 83.
9. See RF–FSF, 16 July 1913, UTA in Walsh, 125.
10. See Thompson, *Early Years*, 598n; Lesley Frost, II, 2; Lathem, 109; Frost, 'Birches', *AM*, Aug. 1915, and *Mountain Interval*, 29–30.
11. Frost interview with Cecil Day Lewis, BBC, 13 Sept. 1957, *CQ*, Spring 1958; Frost in Feld, 2; Frost, 'The Figure a Poem Makes', *Collected Prose*, 132.
12. See Frost, *Notebooks*; see Thompson, *Early Years*, 597; Frost, *Newsweek*, 11 Feb. 1963, 90–1.
13. Arundel del Re, 'Georgian Poets', New Zealand Broadcasting Service talk cited in Grant, 78; ET–JB [early June 1913], 71; ET–GB, 2 Aug. 1913, 230; HT–JH, 6 Aug. 1913, 200.
14. Farjeon, 24–7.
15. WWG–RF, 4 Aug. 1913, DCL, Walsh, 156; DHL–EM, 17 Dec. 1913, 119–20; RF–GMcQ [early Dec. 1913], 157; see Gibson, 'The First Meeting', in Thompson, *Early Years*, 439.
16. ET, *DC*, 15 Dec. 1902; *MM*, 28; ET, *DC*, 18 April 1908.
17. ET, *DC*, 9 March 1912.
18. See WWG–EM, 14 and 23 Jan. 1913; Bridges and Marsh see Hassall, *Edward Marsh*, 208.

AUTUMN 1913

1. ET–CFC, 9 Sept. 1913; ET in Farjeon, 12.
2. See Farjeon, 30; ET, 'Insomnia', *LS*, 39–43.
3. ET–WdlM, 'Sunday' [?7 Sept. 1913], 220v–221r; ET–WHH, 18 March 1915, 11.
4. ET, 'Notes mainly out of doors', IV, 28 April 1896, ETC, *CP1978*, 455–6.

5. *BW*, 82–3; Bottomley, 173; ET–GB, 30 June 1905, 87; ET–GB, 14 May 1907, 140.

6. See Thompson, *Early Years*, 441; RH–RF, 14 Sept. 1913, 92; RH–RF [*c*.1–5 Oct. 1913], DCL.

7. ET–HH, 24 Sept. 1913, *Selected Letters*, 86; ET–EF [post dated, 5 Oct. 1913], 37.

8. ET–WdlM, 6 Oct. 1913, 209r–v; ET–WdlM, [post dated, 6 Oct. 1913], 211r.

9. St George's Café, 37 St Martin's Lane, London; Frost in Mertins, 114; Ashley Gibson, 2; see Newham-David, 93; see Hodgson, 16; ADW, 1–22; ET–RF, 4 Nov. 1916, 156.

10. Farjeon, 41.

11. See ET–GB, 26 Aug. 1910, 207; see Moore, 137, 79.

12. *WP*, 220.

13. Virginia Woolf, *TLS*, Oct. 1917; A. H. Anderson, *Observer*, 25 Nov. 1917; ET–EF [*c*. Oct. 1913], 41, and 'Friday' [poss. 31 Oct. 1913], 43; see Helen Thomas, 137.

14. ET–IMacA, 18 Dec. 1913; RMBT–ET, 9 Nov. 1913; see *Keats*.

15. See *CS*; ET–CFC, 30 Nov. 1913; ET–CFC, 14 Nov. 1913; see *FTB*.

16. *HGLM*, 1; WHH–EG, *153 Letters*, 94.

17. F. T. Marinetti, *PD*, I, 3 (Sept. 1913), 263; Aldington, *NF*, I, 12 (Dec. 1913), 226; Harold Monro, *PD*, I, 3 (Sept. 1913), 262.

18. RF–JTB, *c*.5 Nov. 1913, 98; RF–ES, 8 Dec. 1913, 103.

WINTER 1913/14

1. ET–EF, 5 Dec. 1913, 46.

2. See Davies, *Autobiography*, 162; see Ashley Gibson, 49–50; Helen Thomas, 217.

3. ET, *DC*, 21 Oct. 1905; ADW, 11.

4. Stidulph's Cottage, Egg Pie Lane, The Weald; see ADW, 11; 14 Great Russell Street, Bloomsbury WC (1916–22); see also Hodgson, 14–15.

5. Frost's annotated copy of *PD*, I, 4 (Dec. 1913), 421, enc. RF–JTB, *c*.15 Dec. 1913, 105; RF–SC, 18 May 1914; 123; see Helen Thomas, 220; see Davies *Later Days*, 50.

6. See *PD*, I, 4 (Dec. 1913); RF–JTB, *c*.15 Dec. 1913, 105; ET, 'Reviewing: An Unskilled Labour', *PD*, II, 5 (March 1914), 37; ET–JB, 27 April 1902, 27; ET–JB, 7 Nov. 1902, 37; ET–HM, 19 July 1911, 48–9; ET–JWH, 15 July 1915; ET, 'I never saw that land before', 5 May 1916, *LP*, 9.

7. ET–EF, 5 Dec. 1913, 46, and 8 Dec. 1913, 47–8.

8. ET–CFC, 18 Dec. 1913; ET–IMacA, 18 Dec. 1913.

9. Farjeon, 52–3.

10. ET–EF, 26 Dec. 1913, 53.

11. ET–RF, 17 Dec. 1913, 3.

12. WWG to EM, 7 Nov. 1913; Frost in Mertins, 117; RF–GMcQ, Dec. 1913 in Walsh, 157–8.

II – DYMOCK

WINTER 1914

1. RB–RMB, 21 July 1913, 484.

2. RB–WWG, 23 July 1913, 486–7.

3. *NN*, I, 1 (Feb. 1914): Gibson, 'Bloodybush Edge'; Brooke, 'Sonnet', 'A Memory', 'One Day', 'Mutability'; Abercrombie, 'The Olympians'; Drinkwater, 'The Poet to His Mistress', 'The New Miracle', 'The Boundaries', 'A Town Window', 'Memory'; GG–JWH, 12 Jan. 1914.

4. HM, *PD*, II, 6 (June 1914), 178–9; WdlM, *TLS*, 19 March 1914; ET, *NW*, 21 March 1914, also *DC*, 19 April 1914.

5. Haines.

6. See RB–KC, 13 June 1914, 449; ET–GB, 4 April 1917, 283.

7. WWG–EM, 12 Dec. 1912; EM–RB, 18 Aug. 1913, 242; RB–RL, 6 July 1914, 598; Catherine Abercrombie; Lascelles Abercrombie in Gawsworth; Gibson, 'Trees', *Friends*, 19.

8. ET–GB, 12 Oct. 1909, 195; LA–EM, 5 Sept. 1914.

9. ET, *DC*, 29 Feb. 1908; ET, *DC*, 28 Dec. 1911; ET *DC*, 28 Dec. 1911; ET, *DC*, 9 Aug. 1911; ET, *DC*, 10 Jan. 1913; RF–TBM, 139; ET–GB, 28 Dec. 1914, 241.

10. 11 Luxemburg Gardens, Hammersmith, London; see ET–EF, 26 Jan. 1914, 59; see ET–RF, 30 Jan. 1914, 6; see ET–EF [Feb. 1914], 60; see ET–CB, 19 Feb. 1914, 90.

11. Frost in Mertins, 135.

12. ET–RF, 19 Feb. 1914, 7; *PC*, III, 5 (Feb. 1914), 169–71; ET–RF, 24 Feb. 1914, 8.

13. See ET–GB, 30 June 1905, 87; ET–CFC, 23 Feb. 1914, Bod. MS Eng. Lett. d. 281.

SPRING 1914

1. See Farjeon, 61–2.

2. RF–SC, 26 March 1914, 121.

3. See Frost, 'The Fear', 'A Hundred Collars', *PD*, I, 4 (Dec. 1913), 406–15; RF–SC, 26 March 1914, 121; see Sergeant, 146; RF–WER, 26 March 1914, 120.

4. Little Iddens, Ledington (*c.*3 April–Sept. 1914); see RF–SC, 18 May 1914, 124; see EFW–LWH, *c.* 20 June 1914, 126; *Voices and Visions*; RF–SC, 26 March 1914, 121.

5. See ET, 'This England', *The Nation*, 7 Nov. 1914, 170–1, *LS*, 216–17; see Far-jeon, 89; see RF–JWH, 17 July 1915, 183; RF–JWH [*c.*1 July 1914], 128.

6. See Farjeon, 69; see FNB 74; RF–SC, 18 May 1914, 124.

7. See FNB 74; see ET–EF, 28 April 1914, 69; see ET, 'This England', *LS*, 215; RF–JWH, 20 Jan. 1921, 263.

8. ET–GB, 22 May 1914, 233.

9. RF–SC, 18 May 1914, 123; RF–SC, [17 Sept. 1914], 136; RF–SC, 18 May 1914, 123.

10. Frost, 'A Romantic Chasm', *Collected Prose*, 158; RF–SC, 18 May 1914, 124; EWF–LWH [*c.*20 June 1914], 126.

11. RF–ES, 23 Feb. 1914, 118.

12. Reeves, 19.

13. See Farjeon, 66, 71.

14. See, ET–EF, 16 May 1914, 73.

15. See Frost, 'Preface to an Expanded *North of Boston*', *Collected Prose*, 196.

16. Frost, *North of Boston*, x; Frost in Feld, 2.

17. Frost, 'The Pasture', *North of Boston*, vii; RF–JTB, *c.*5 Nov. 1913, 98.

18. ET–RF, 19 May 1914, 9–10; RF–SC, Dec. 1914, 140; *WP*, 103; *FIP*, 293.

19. *DC*, 27 Aug. 1901; *The Bookman*, Oct. 1907; *LH*, 48; *ACS*, 174.

20. *WP*, 104, 218, 210.

21. ET–GB, 22 March 1912, 220; ET–RF, 19 May 1914, 10–11; RF–HRB, 19 Dec. 1925, *AL*, 59, 1 (March 1987), 117.

22. ET–CFC, 4 April 1912.

23. *TLS*, 28 May 1914, 262; RF–LU, 14 Nov. 1916, 45.

SUMMER 1914

1. ET–RF, 6 June 1914, 12; ET–GB, 29 May 1914, 234; ET–RF, 6 June 1914, 12.

2. ET–RF [10 June 1914], 14 (as 'possibly July 1, 1914').

3. ET–EF, 20 June 1914, 75; ET–HT, 17 June 1914, 73.

4. Bottomley, 175.

5. *NYT*, 24 June 1914; ET–EF [24 June 1914], 76.

6. FNB 75, 24 June 1914; for a detailed investigation into this journey see Harvey, 1–22.

7. ET–GB, 27 June 1914, 235; Gibson, 'The Golden Room', *AM*, Feb. 1926, and *Golden Room*, 172.

8. ET–GB, 27 June 1914, 235; ET–GB, 7 July 1914, 236; see Frost in Sergeant, 105, and Fletcher, 72; Eliot, *Waste Land*, 98; EP–PC, 12 Oct. 1915, 64; Pound in Carpenter, 179; ET–GB, 22 May 1914, 233; see Jeff Cooper, *DPF*, 7 (2008), 32–9 for Abercrombie and Pound.

9. See *LPE, FIL*; ET–GB, 7 July 1914, 236; ET–EF, 17 July 1914, 79.

10. ET, *The Bookman*, July 1914; ET, *DC*, 16 Dec. 1911; Drinkwater, 'Daffodils', *Olton Pools*, 27; Catherine Abercrombie; ET–GB, 6 Nov. 1915, 256.

11. A. K. Sabin in Grant, 81; Lowell, 6; Arundel del Re, 'The Poetry Bookshop', BBC talk 1962, in Grant, 81 (some versions of this story assign the heckler as Amy Lowell herself).

12. Abercrombie, *The Nation*, 13 June 1914, 423; RF–JWH [late June or early July 1914]; Gibson, *The Bookman*, July 1914; RF–FSF, 24 Aug. 1916; see Walsh, 172–7.

13. ET, *DN*, 22 July 1914.

14. ET, *ER*, Aug. 1914, 142–3.

15. ET, *NW*, 8 Aug. 1914, 249.

16. RF–GWC, 28 June 1921, 22–3.

17. ET–EF, 2 Aug. 1914, 81.

18. See Thompson and Winnick, 241.

19. See Hibberd, *Harold Monro*, 147.

20. RB in Hassall, *Rupert Brooke*, 457.

21. See Baynes Jansen, 97.

22. See Egremont, 63.

23. See WO–SO, 25 May 1917, 464.

24. *DM*, 4 Aug. 1914; *DT*, 4 Aug. 1914; *The Times*, 4 Aug. 1914; *DE*, 5 Aug. 1914; *DT*, 5 Aug. 1914; *Guardian*, 5 Aug. 1914.

25. See ET, 'This is no case of petty right or wrong', 26 Dec. 1915, *LP*, 77; ET–MT, 23 Nov. 1914, *CP1978*, 406.

26. See Helen Thomas, 229.

27. ET, 'It's a Long, Long Way', *ER*, Dec. 1914, 85–92, *LS*, 140; WWG–EM, 23 Aug. 1914; see Helen Thomas, 230.

28. See FNB 78, 19 Aug. 1914; see ET, 'This England', *LS*, 216–17.

29. See ET, 'The sun used to shine', 22 May 1916, *Poems*, 47–8.

30. Frost, 'Iris by Night', *VQR*, April 1936, *A Further Range*, 81–2; ET–EF, 22 May 1915, 141.

31. See Helen Thomas, 228–30; ET–EF, 14 Aug. 1914, 83; ET–JF, 14 Aug. 1914; see ET–EF, 14 Aug. 1914, 83.

32. See Farjeon, 90–5.

33. FNB 77, 26 Aug. 1914.

34. CFC–ET, 26 Aug. 1914.

35. RF–SC, 20 Aug. 1914, 131.

36. *English Catalogue of Books*, 1914, 1919; LA–EM, 5 Sept. 1914; ET–GB, 3 Sept. 1914, 238; see WWG–EM, 18 Nov. 1914.

37. Brooke, 'An Unusual Young Man', *NS*, 23 Aug. 1914, 638–40; RB–EW, 15–17 Aug. 1914, 608.

38. RB–EW, 15–17 Aug. 1914, 608.

39. See ET–GB, 3 Sept. 1914, 238; ET–WdlM, 30 Aug. 1914, 239. *Blast*, a new journal produced by Wyndham Lewis and Ezra Pound, had been launched in London in June 1914.

40. ADW, 8; *BW*, v; ET, 'Addenda to Autobiography', Berg; notebook, 31 Aug. 1899, UBC); ET–IMacA, 30 Aug. 1900, *Selected Letters*, 16; see ET, 'Home', *LP*, 39; see *SC*, 7.

41. ET–JB, 3 Sept. 1914, 74.

AUTUMN 1914

1. MPT–ET [*c.*3 Sept. 1914].

2. See ET–EF, 13 Sept. 1914, 96, and ET–GB, 21 Sept. 1914, 239; see ET–GB, 17 March 1904, 53.

3. ET, 'Tipperary', *ER*, Oct. 1914, *LS*, 113–34.

4. ET, 'It's a Long, Long Way', *ER*, Dec. 1914, *LS*, 135–49.

5. ET, 'England', *ER*, Oct. 1914, *LS*, 98; *HE*, 194; *LS*, 104–5; ET, 'England', *ER*, Oct. 1914; *LS*, 111.

6. RB–RL, 6 July 1914, 597; see Drinkwater, *Discovery*, 213; see EM–RB, 18 Aug. 1913, 242–3; WWG–EM, 9 March 1914 (see also 22 Dec. 1913 and 22 March 1914); DHL–EM, 24 May 1914, 176–7; ET–GB, 21 Sept. 1914, 239; RF–JWH, 21 Sept. 1914.

7. ET–JB, 3 Sept. 1914, 74. see ET–GB, 3 Sept. 1914, 238;. ET–EF, 4 Sept. 1914, 95; ET–EF, 13 Sept. 1914, 96.

8. FH–RF, 7 Aug. 1914, 131; Holt–Nutt letters, 2 and 12 Sept. 1914 in Frost, *Selected Letters*, 133–4.

9. TSE–EH, 8 Sept. 1914, 60.

10. Aiken, 258; Eliot, *Poetry Speaks*; Conrad Aiken to Joy Grant, 31 Oct. 1962 in Grant, 102; for a questioning of Aiken's account of events see Hibberd, *Harold Monro*, 153–4.

11. ET–EF, 21 Oct. 1914, 101; EP, *The Criterion*, XI (July 1932), 583; TSE–CA, 30 Sept. 1914, 64; TSE–EH, 14 Oct. 1914, 66–7.

12. ET–EF, 21 Oct. 1914, 101; ET–CFC, 16 Oct. 1914 (and CFC–ET of same date); ET–CFC, 10 Dec. 1914; FNB 79, Oct.–Dec. 1914.

13. ET–RF, 31 Oct. 1914, 29–30.

14. RB–JR, 24 Sept. 1914, 619; RB–LB, 11 Nov. 1914, 632; Monro, 'Personal Recollections of Rupert Brooke', *Everyman*, 24 July 1930, 803; Brooke, 'The Soldier', *NN*, I, 4 (Dec. 1914), 169, *1914 and Other Poems*, 15; RB–WdlM, 20 Nov. 1914, 238; RB–LB, 11 Nov. 1914, 633.

15. ET–HM [*c.* late Oct. 1914], 61. ET–GB, 30 Jan. 1915, 243; see Whistler, 238 for possible further encounter.

16. ET–WHH, 26 Nov. 1914; *Selected Letters*, 101.

17. Newdick notes of conversation with Frost, 26 July 1936 in Sutton, 298.

18. Ted Hill, *Voices and Visions*; Hill, interview with Rev. Reg Legge, Dymock 1982, private collection.

19. LA–JWH, 1 Dec. 1914.

20. LA–JWH, 4 Dec. 1914.

21. See Thompson, *Early Years*, 468.

22. RF–HM, Dec. 1914, 142.

23. RF–JWH, 2 April 1915.

24. See FNB 79, 27 Nov. 1914.

25. Myfanwy Thomas in Helen Thomas, 14; RF–GWC, 28 June 1921, 23; ET, 'An Old Song', *LP*, 69.

26. Frost in Mertins, 117; see RF–LA, 21 Sept. 1915, 193.

27. Frost in Newdick, Sutton, 298.

28. RF–GWC, 28 June 1921, 23; see Farjeon, 56.

WINTER 1914/15

1. ET–RF, 19 May 1914, 10.

2. FNB 79, facing 2 Nov. 1914 (reprinted in *CP1978*, 374); ET, 'The White Horse', LML (*CP1978*, 435–6, with variants).

3. ET, 'Up in the Wind', LML (*CP1978*, 437–41, for a differing transcription).

4. ET, 'Up in the Wind', 3 Dec. 1914, *CP1920*, 87.

5. FNB 79, 1 Dec. 1914 (*CP1978*, 379–80); ET, 'November', 4 Dec. 1914, *Poems*, 51; ET–EG, 13 March 1915, 25; ET–RF, 15 Dec. 1914, 38.

6. RF–HRB, 19 Dec. 1925, 117; *IPS*, 178; ET, 'March', 5 Dec. 1914, *LP*, 35.

7. ET–GB, 6 April 1910, 201.

8. FNB 79, 11 Nov. 1914 (*CP1978*, 381); ET, 'Old Man's Beard', 17 Nov. 1914, LML (*CP1978*, 443–4, for a differing transcription); ET, 'Old Man', 6 Dec. 1914, *LP*, 13.

9. ET, 'The Signpost', 7 Dec. 1914, *Poems*, 9.

10. FNB 79, *c.* Dec. 1914.

11. ET–RF, 15 Dec. 1914, 39.

12. RF–SHW, 10 Feb. 1912, 45.

13. ET–IMacA, in Moore, 172; *SC*, 73; *IW*, 137; ET, 'The Pilgrim', *LS*, 52.

14. ET–HM, 15 Dec. 1914, 63.

15. ET–EF, 26 Dec. 1914, 105; ET, 'The Manor Farm', 24 Dec. 1914, *Poems*, 12; Frost, 'Mending Wall', *North of Boston*, 11; ET–WHH, *Selected Letters*, 108.

16. ET, 'An Old Song', 25 Dec. 1914, *LP*, 69.

17. ET–EF [*c.*22 Dec. 1914], 104.

18. CFC–ET, 3 Dec. 1914; Frost–Graves meeting recorded by Robert Graves, 'The Truest Poet', *Sunday Times*, 3 Feb. 1963, 11 in Thompson, *Early Years*, 472; RF–SC, 14 Dec. 1914, 138–9; ET–RF, 15 Dec. 1914, 39.

19. ET, 'The New Year', 1 Jan. 1915, *LP*, 84; 'The Source', 4 Jan. 1915, Abercrombie and Trevelyan, 56, *LP*, 61; 'The Penny Whistle', 5 Jan. 1915, *Poems*, 59; see 'Tears', 8 Jan. 1915, 10–11.

20. ET–JB, 6 Jan. 1915, 76; see ET–EF, 6 Jan. 1915, 109; ET, 'The Lofty Sky', 10 Jan. 1915, *RB*, II, 2 (Dec. 1917), 32, *LP*, 45–6.

21. ET–EF, 10 and 16 Jan. 1915, 110–11.

22. FNB 75, 24 June 1914; BL Add. Mss. 44990; ET, 'Adlestrop', 8 Jan. 1915, *NS*, 28 April 1917, 87, *Poems*, 40–1; see *The Bookworm*, BBC1, 13 Oct. 1995; IG–MS, Nov. 1917, 375.

23. ET–JF, 21 Jan. 1915.

24. RF–ET, *c.*1 Feb. 1915, 42; RF–JWH [*c.*2 Feb. 1915].

25. ET, 'House and Man', 3–4 Feb. 1915, *RB*, I, 4 (*c.*1915), 59, *LP*, 90 ('It was dark with forest boughs | That brushed the walls and made the mossy tiles'); Frost, 'An Old Man's Winter Night', *Mountain Interval*, 14 ('All out-of-doors looked darkly in at him | Through the thin frost, almost in separate stars, | That gathers on the pane in empty rooms'): RF–JWH, *c.*10 Feb. 1915; Frost in Mertins, 136.

26. ET, 'Parting', 11 Feb. 1915, *LP*, 57; ET–EF, 24 Jan. 1915, 114; Myfanwy Thomas, 42; ET, 'This is the constellation of the Lyre', ETC.

27. See RF–HM and RF–FSF, both *c.*13 Feb. 1915, 152; RF–SC, 2 Feb. 1915, 151; RF–LA, 15 March 1915, 157.

28. ET, 'The Owl', 24 Feb. 1915, *Poems*, 12–13; ET–JF, 21 Feb. 1915; ET–EF, 12 March 1915, 124; GWB–EF, 6 March 1915, 34n.

29. RF–LA, 15 March 1915, 157; RF–Frost children [Feb. 1915], in Frost, *Family Letters*, 3; RF–JWH, 14 March 1915.

30. RB–JD, 18–25 Jan. 1915, 655.

III – HIGH BEECH

SPRING 1915

1. See Farjeon, 121–2.

2. ET–JF, 8 March 1915; see ET–EF, 25 March 1915, Farjeon, 127–8; ET, 'The Child on the Cliffs', 11 March 1915, *LP*, 53; 'Good-night', 16 March 1915, *LP*, 54; 'The Bridge', 12 March 1915, *NS*, 28 April 1917, 87, *Poems*, 30; ET–JF, 23 March 1915.

3. See ET, 'Will you come?', 25 March 1915, *Poems*, 14; 'The Wasp Trap', 27 March 1915, *LP*, 55; 'A Tale', 28–31 March 1915, *LP*, 56; ET–EG, 17 March 1915, 27; ET–JF, 8 March 1915.

4. ET–EG, 13 March 1915, 25.

5. See ET–RF, 3 May 1915, 52; see ET–EF, 4 May 1915, 133; see ET–RF, 15 May 1915, 54; see Stonesifer, 116; see Tomalin, 213; Julian Thomas, diary entry 23 March 1915 in *CP1978*, 409–10.

6. ET–EF, 5 April 1915, 128; see diary 1915 for daily progress on *LDM*; ET–RF, 22 April 1915, 47; ET, 'In Memoriam (Easter 1915)', 6 April 1915, *Poems*, 26.

7. ET, *DC*, 18 Sept. 1902, see Motion, 61.

8. RF–ET, 17 April 1915, 43; see ET, 'Lob', 3–4 April 1915, *Poems*, 30–5; *CET*, 129–30; see Helen Thomas, 46–52; *Country*, 9.

9. RF–ET, 17 April 1915, 43; ET–EG, *c.* April 1915, 29.

10. See ET–HM, 20 April 1915, 64; ET–HM, 25 April 1915, 65.

11. See ET–RF, 15 May 1915, 54; ET–HM [*c.* May 1915], 65–6.

12. ET, 1915 diary, 41v; ET–EF, 4 May 1915, 133.

13. ET, 1915 diary, 2v.

14. *Country*, 59.

15. RF–ET, 17 April 1915, 43.

16. HT–HM [*c.*1920], 67.

17. *The Times*, 5 April 1915; see Hassall, *Rupert Brooke*, 502.

18. Churchill, *The Times*, 26 April 1915.

19. RF–JWH, 15 May 1915; WWG–EM, 'Saturday' [?late April 1915]; see Abercrombie, 'R. B.', *Poems*, 15; Drinkwater, 'Rupert Brooke', *Loyalties*, 26; Gibson ['The Going'], 'Rupert Brooke', *Friends*, 7, 11–13; Cornford, 'Youth', 5.

20. ET, 'Rupert Brooke', *ER*, June 1915; ET–RF, 14 June 1915, 61 (as '13 June 1915').

21. ET–RF, 3 May 1915, 51; ET–JWH, 5 May 1915; ET–RF, 19 Oct. 1916, 153–4; Hassall, *Rupert Brooke*, 481.

22. RF–JWH, 15 May 1915.

23. ET–RF, 15 May 1915; ET, 'Fifty Faggots', *NS*, 28 April 1917, 87, *Poems*, 26; ET–RF, 23 May 1915, 57.

SUMMER 1915

1. See ET–RF, 31 May 1915, 59 (as '1 June 1915'); ET, 'I built myself a house of glass', 25 June 1915, *LP*, 16; *CET*, 53; ET–EG, 24 June 1915, *ETFN*, 52 (Aug. 2004), 16 (*ACP*, 242); see ET–RF [10 June 1914], 15 (as 'probably July 1, 1914'); ET–EF, 18 June 1915, 147.
2. ET, 'Words', 26–28 June 1914, *Poems*, 61–3; ET–EF, post dated 8 June 1915, 146; see Hansard, HC Deb., 22 April 1915, 71, 378; ET–RF, 14 June 1915, 62 (as '13 June 1915'); ET–RF, 28 June 1915, 74 (probably 29 June, diary, 28v).
3. ET–RF, 14 June 1915, 63 (as '13 June 1915'); ET–EF, post dated 18 June 1915, 147; ET–RF, 15 June 1915, 67.
4. ET–RF, 18 June 1915, 69; ET–GB, 30 June 1915, 251; ET–RF, 15 June 1915, 66.
5. Frost, 'The Road Not Taken', *AM*, Aug. 1915, *Mountain Interval*, 9.
6. Frost at Bread Loaf Writers' Conference, 26 Aug. 1961, in Thompson, *Years of Triumph*, 546.
7. Frost at Bread Loaf Writers' Conference, 23 Aug. 1953 in Thompson, *Years of Triumph*, 546.
8. ET, 'The Stile', *LT*, 46; see Farjeon, 40; Frost, in reminiscence, 16 Aug. 1947 in Thompson, *Years of Triumph*, 88.
9. ET–RF, 14 June 1915, 63–4 (as '13 June 1915'); ET–RF, 22 July 1915, 82.
10. EF–RF, 14 June 1915, 62 (as '13 June 1915').
11. RF–ET, 26 June 1915, 70; ET–RF, 11 July 1915, 78; RF–ET, 26 June 1915, 70.
12. ET–RF, 11 July 1915, 78; ET, 'The Brook', 10 July 1915, Abercrombie and Trevelyan, 59, *LP*, 85; ET, 'This England', *LS*, 221; Farjeon, 152; Helen Thomas, 153.
13. ET–RF, 22 July 1915, 82; Frost, 'A Servant to Servants', *North of Boston*, 66; ET–RF, 22 July 1915, 82–3.
14. ET, 'A Dream', *c.* 8 July 1915, *LP*, 22, see FNB 80 after 23 May 1915 and after 2 June 1915 for dream and early draft; ET–JB, 7 Nov. 1902, 36.
15. RF–ET, 31 July 1915, 87 (cf. ECH₁: 'I become aware of the loveliness of "Aspens". I am not among those men "who like a different tree."' [30 March–2 April 1919]; ET, 'Aspens', 11 July 1915, Abercrombie and Trevelyan, 49, *LP*, 68; 'The Mill-Water', *LP*, 20; see Bottomley, 177; ET–JWH [14 July 1915]; Farjeon, 152; Helen Thomas, 153.
16. ET, Attestation form, 19 July 1915, NA.
17. ET–EF, 20 July 1915, 152–3; ET–GB, 21 July 1915, 253; see ET, 'Digging', 21 July 1915, *LP*, 18, and ET–EF, 21 July 1915, 153; ET, 'Cock-Crow', 23 July 1915, 61; ET–GB, 15 July 1915, 252 (as '14 July 1915').

18. RF–ET, 31 July 1915, 86.

19. ET–RF, ?10 Aug. 1915, 89 (as '9.viii.15'); ET–RF, 21 Aug. 1915, 91.

20. ET–RF, ?10 Aug. 1915, 88 (as '9.viii.15'); ET–JWH, 28 Aug. 1915; ET–RF, 28 Aug. 1915, 93.

21. ET–RF, 28 Aug. 1915, 93; Artists Rifles Association figures.

22. ET–RF, 21 Aug. 1915, 91.

23. Frost, 'The Road Not Taken', *AM*, Aug. 1916, *Mountain Interval*, 9.

AUTUMN 1915

1. ET–RF, 5 Sept. 1915, 96; ET–RF, 3 Sept. 1915, 95.

2. See ET–EF [30 Sept. 1915], 166; ET–JWH, 28 Sept. 1915.

3. ET–RF, 4 Oct. 1915, 97; ET–HT, 11 Oct. 1915, NLW (*ACP* 262); ET–RF, 4 Oct. 1915, 98; ET–WdlM [*c*.5 Oct. 1915]; ET–RF, 5 Oct. 1915, 99; ET, 'October', 15–16 Oct. 1915, *Poems*, 48–9.

4. ET–GB, 6 Nov. 1915, 256; ET–RF, 6 Nov. 1915, 103–4; ET, *TE*, 111–12; *RB*, I, 4 (*c*.1915), 59–60; ET–RF, 12 Oct. 1915, 101.

5. See ET–RF, 12 Nov. 1915, 105.

6. ET–RF, 13 Nov. 1915, 107.

7. WO–SO, 26 Oct. 1915, 361; WO–SO [?31 Oct. 1915], 365 (as '[2 November 1915]').

8. See WO–SO, post dated 28 Feb. 1916, 382; WO–SO [?4 March 1916], 383–4.

9. ET–RF, 12 Nov. 1915, 105; WO–SO [post dated 15 Nov. 1915], 366.

10. ET–RF, 13 Nov. 1915, 107; ET–MT, 21 Nov. 1915, 84.

11. RF–ET, 23 Nov. 1915, 108–9; ET–RF, 12 Nov. 1915, 106; RF–ET, 23 Nov. 1915, 108–9.

12. See ET–EF, post dated 18 Nov. 1915, 170; ET–JWH, 20 Nov. 1915.

WINTER 1915/16

1. See Alison Thomas, 115–16; ECH₂ [21–30 May 1919].

2. ECH₂ [*c*.16–24 Sept. 1919]; ET–ECH, *c*.16 Nov. 1900; HT–ECH, 24 Feb. 1919; ET–ECH, *c*.16 Nov. 1900, Berg.

3. ECH₂ [*c*.1–19 Jan. 1920].

4. ECH₂, 21 May 1919.

5. ECH₁ [15–21 March 1919].

6. ET–GB, 11 Feb. 1916; see FNB 80, 26 Nov. 1915 ('This is no case of little right or wrong'); ET, 'This is no case of petty right or wrong', 26 Dec. 1915, *SP*, 9; *LP*, 77.

7. ET–EF [post dated 30 Dec. 1915], 178.

8. ET–RF, 2 Jan. 1916, 115; ET, 'I may come near loving you', 8 Feb. 1916, *CP1949*, 189; TSE–MG, 30 May 1949.

9. ET–RF, 2 Jan. 1916, 114–15.

10. ET–EF [post dated 7 Jan. 1916], 180; ET–EF [15 Jan. 1916], 'probably July 21', 205; ET–RF, 16 Jan. 1916, 116.

11. ET, 'Rain', 7 Jan. 1916, *Poems*, 54–5.

12. ET–RF, 30 Jan. 1916, 119; ET, 'Roads', 22 Jan. 1916, Abercrombie and Trevelyan, 53–5, *LP*, 74–6.

13. ET, 'The clouds that are so light', 15 Jan. 1916, *Poems*, 36; ET–HT, *c.*24 Jan. 1916, LCL (*CP1978*, 408–9).

14. ET–GB, 7 Feb. 1908, 156; ET–WdlM, 19 Feb. 1908, 32r; ET–HH, 18 and 28 Jan. 1908, UBC.

15. HT–ET, 18, 19 Jan. and 5, 13 and 14 Feb. 1908.

16. ET–GB, 26 Feb. 1908, 156; ET–HH, 7 March 1908, UBC.

17. ECH$_4$; ECH$_3$ [19 Jan.–16 Feb. 1920]; ET, 'Those things that poets said', 9 Feb. 1916, *LP*, 66; ET, 'No one so much as you', 11 Feb. 1916, *CP1928*, 192–3.

18. ET–HT, 24 Feb. 1916, 81; *FIP*, 76; Yeats, *Essays and Introductions*, 509; ET, 'The Unknown', 14 Feb. 1916, Abercrombie and Trevelyan, 45–6, *LP*, 28–9.

19. HT–ECH, 12 Dec. 1919.

20. ET, 'February Afternoon', 7–8 Feb. 1916, *LP*, 17; ET–HT, 24 Feb. 1916, 81.

21. ET, 'Celandine', 4 March 1916, *LP*, 11.

22. ET–JWH, 24 Feb. 1916.

SPRING 1916

1. ET–RF, 6 Dec. 1915, 2 and 16 Jan. 1916, 21 Feb. 1916, 111–21; ET–RF, 5 March 1916, 123.

2. ET–RF, 5 March 1916, 123–5.

3. ET, '"Home"', 7–10 March 1915, *Poems*, 55–6.

4. ET–RF, 16 March 1916, 126; ET, 'Thaw', 10 March 1916, *Poems*, 16; ET–RF, 16 March 1916, 128; ET–RF, 21 May 1916, 133.

5. ET–GB, 24 April 1916, 266.

6. ET, 'If I should ever by chance', 29 March–6 April 1916, *Poems*, 19; 'If I were to own', 1–7 April 1916, *Poems*, 20–1; 'What shall I give?', 2–8 April 1916, *Poems*, 20; 'And you, Helen', 9 April 1916, 21–2.

7. ET, 'When we two walked', 23 April–1 May 1916, *Poems*, 25; 'Like the touch of rain', 23–30 April 1916, M$_2$, *Poems*, 17–18; *FIP*, 76–7.

8. ET–HH, 7 March 1908, UBC; see ET–GB, 20 Dec. 1915, 258; *FIP*, 91.

9. See Catherine Abercrombie; see Helen Thomas, 239–41.

10. ET–RF, 6 Dec. 1915, 112.

11. ET–EF, 8 May 1916, 195.

12. ET, 'It Rains', 11–13 May 1916, *Poems*, 28; ECH₂ [5–8 Sept. 1919]; ECH₃ [1–19 Jan. 1920]; ECH, 'The Kiss', ECH poems.

13. ET, 'Some eyes condemn', 13–14 May 1916, 36–7; 'After you speak', 3 June 1916, *Poems*, 24.

14. Frost, 'Not to Keep', *YR*, Jan. 1917, *New Hampshire*, 97; ET–RF, 21 May 1916, 131. ET, 'The sun used to shine', 22 May 1916, *Poems*, 47–8.

15. ET–RF, 21 May 1916, 131–2.

16. ET, 'No one cares less than I', 25–26 May 1916, *LP*, 73.

17. ET–EF, 4 June 1916, 144 (wrongly sequenced as '4 June 1915').

18. ET, 'As the team's head-brass', 27 May 1916, *Poems*, 15–16.

19. Farjeon, 154.

20. ET–RF, 28 July 1916, 230; ET, 'Bright clouds', 4–5 June 1916, *Poems*, 35–6; 'Early one morning', 8–11 June 1916, *Poems*, 27–8.

SUMMER 1916

1. ET–JB, 12 June 1916, 80; ET–RF, 10 June 1916, 138.

2. ET–JWH, 13 June 1916.

3. See Berridge, 89; see Bottomley, 177; see ET–RF, 10 Aug. 1915, 88 (as '9 Aug. 1915').

4. ET, 'There was a time', 23 June 1916, *LP*, 71; ET–EF, 28 June 1916, 201–2.

5. RF–JWH, 4 July 1916, 205.

6. See Graves, 181–7; *The Times*, 5 Aug. 1915.

7. See Baynes Jansen, 104.

8. ET–JF, July 1916.

9. ET, 'Lob', 'Words', *Form*, I, 1, April 1916, 33–4; see Thompson, *Early Years*, 566–7; see RF–ET, 15 Aug. 1916, 141; ET–GB, 30 July 1916, 269; ET, *SP*: 'Sedge-Warblers', 'This is no case of petty right or wrong', 'Aspens', 'A Private', 'Cock-Crow', 'Beauty'.

10. ET–EWF, 27 Nov. 1916, 163.

11. ET–RF, 15 Aug. 1916, 145; ET, 'Gone, gone again', *c.*26–7 Aug. 1916, *NS*, 28 April 1917, 87, *Poems*, 46–7.

12. ECH₁ [30 March–2 April 1919].

13. RF–ET, 15 Aug. 1916, 142; ET–RF, 15 Aug. 1915, 144.

AUTUMN 1916

1. ET–RF, 9 Sept. 1916, 147; ET, 'There was a time', 23 June 1916, *LP*, 71.

2. See ET, 'That girl's clear eyes', 10 Sept. 1916, *LP*, 59; 'What will they do?', 15 Sept. 1916, *LP*, 25; ET–RF, 21 May 1916, 132.

3. ET–EF, 9 Sept. 1916, 146; RF–ET, 28 Sept. 1916, 150; ET–RF, 29 Nov. 1916, 164.

4. ET, 'The Trumpet', c.26–8 Sept. 1916, *Poems*, 9.

5. ET–EF [probably 27 Sept. 1916], 219, where it appears out of sequence; see Farjeon, 218.

6. ET–EWF, 27 Nov. 1916, 163; Helen Thomas, 162; Farjeon, 229; see ET–RF, 29 Nov. 1916, 165.

7. ET–HT, 20 Oct. 1916; ET–JWH, 29 Nov. 1916; ET–RF, 29 Nov. 1916, 165; ET–GB, c.1 Dec. 1916, 275.

8. PTS.

9. ET–RF, 29 Nov. 1916, 164; see ET–RF, 12 Jan. 1917, 172.

10. Frost, 'The Gum-Gatherer', *Independent*, Oct. 1916; 'The Bonfire', *Severn Arts*, Nov. 1916; 'An Encounter', *AM*, Nov. 1916; 'Snow', *PC*, IX, 2 (Nov. 1916); all collected in *Mountain Interval*.

11. RF–ET, 6 Nov. 1916, 158; ET–RF, 24 Nov. 1916, 160; ET–EF, 6 Nov. 1916, 218; Bottomley, 177–8.

12. See Farjeon, 229.

13. Official military record detailing confirmation of officer commission, 23 Nov. 1916, NA; ET–EF, 6 Nov. 1916, 218.

14. ET, 'Lights Out', Nov. 1916, *Poems*, 59–60.

WINTER 1916/17

1. See Severn, 115.

2. RF–ET, 7 Dec. 1916, 166–7; ET–RF, 31 Dec. 1916, 170; Lloyd George, *The Times*, 20 Dec. 1916.

3. ET–EF, 7 Dec. 1916, 231; ET–HT, 12 and 29 Dec. 1916.

4. ET–RF, 16 Dec. 1916, 169; see ET–EF, 16 Dec. 1916, 235; Severn, 119.

5. See ET–HT, 22 Dec. 1916; see Helen Thomas, 163–5; ET–EF, 27 Dec. 1916, 237.

6. ET–HEMT, 29 Dec. 1916.

7. ET–RF, 22 Jan. 1917, 173; see Dudfield, 12; see Jennifer Davies, 9; see Gethyn-Jones, 142.

8. See ET–HT, 1 Jan. 1917; see Severn, 12–17.

9. Farjeon, 241; Myfanwy Thomas in *Fast Beat My Heart*; W. H. Davies, *Voices*, 1919, in Stonesifer, 116; Helen Thomas, 167–73; WD, IV.

10. ET, 'The sorrow of true love', 13 Jan. 1917, WD, 15r.

11. ET–MPT, 12 Jan. 1917; ET–HT, 14 Jan. 1917; ET–RF, 12 Jan. 1917, 172.

12. See WD, 2r; see ET–HT, 15 Jan. 1917; see Severn, 115; see ET–HT, 20 Jan. 1917; ET–EF, 17 Jan. 1917, 242; see ET–HT, 17 Jan. 1917; ET–MET, 17 Jan. 1917.

13. Farjeon, 243; WD, 3v; JWH, 'E.T. 22 Jan. 1917'.

14. Bod. MS Eng. Lett. c. 281.

15. ET–EF, 25 Jan. 1917, 244; ET, 'The Mountain Chapel', Dec. 1914, *LP*, 62–3; ET–RF, 22 Jan. 1917, 173–4.

16. WD, 4v; ET–HT, 28 Jan. 1917.

IV – ARRAS

WINTER–SPRING 1917

1. WD, 29 Jan. 1917, 5r; ET–EF, 31 Jan. 1917, 247; Farjeon, 247.

2. WD, 4 Feb. 1917, 6r.

3. ET–HT, 7 Feb. 1917; ET–RF, 11 Feb. 1917, 178; WD, 8 Feb. 1917, 6v.

4. WD, 8 Feb. 1917, 6v; ET–EF, 10 Feb. 1917, 247; WD, 9 Feb. 1917, 7r.

5. WD, 9 Feb. 1917, 7r; ET–MET/PHT, 10 Feb. 1917, *Selected Letters*, 136.

6. See WD, 12 Feb. 1917, 7r.

7. ET–WdlM, 14 Feb. 1917; WD, 13 Feb. 1917, 7v.

8. ET–EF, 21 Feb. 1917, 251.

9. WD, 22 Feb. 1917, 8v.

10. ET–RF, 23 Feb. 1917, 179–80; WD, 23 Feb. 1917, 9r; WD, 25 Feb. 1917, 9r; ET–GB, 26 Feb. 1917, 277; WD, 24 Feb. 1917, 9r.

11. ET–HT, 27 Feb. 1917, *Selected Letters*, 142; ET–GB, 26 Feb. 1917, 277; ET–HT, 27 Feb. 1917.

12. ET–HT, 27 Feb. 1917, *Selected Letters*, 142–3.

13. WD, 9 March 1917, 10v; ET–RF, 6 March 1917, 182.

14. RF–HT, 6 Feb. 1917, 211.

15. ET–RF, 9 March 1917, 183–4 (as '8 March 1917'); ET–HT, 27 Jan. 1917.

16. ET–WdlM, 9 March 1917, 300r–301r.

17. See ET–MPT, 23 March 1917; see WD, 15 March 1917, 11v; ET–RF, 2 April 1917, 186–7.

18. ET–HT, 17 March 1917, 85–7.

19. ET–EF, 22 March 1917, 257.

20. WD, 20 March 1917, 12r.

21. ET–ADW, 22 March 1917; WD, 22 March 1917, 12v.

22. ET–MPT, 23 March 1917.

23. See ET–HT, 24 March 1917, 88.

24. ET–EF, 27 March 1917, 258.

25. ET–JT, 30 March 1917, 156.

26. ET–RF, 2 April 1917, 186–8.

27. HT–JH, 4 April 1917, 203–4.

28. *TLS*, 29 March 1917, 151; J. C. Squire ('Solomon Eagle'), *NS*, 31 March 1917, 617.

29. RF–EG, 29 April 1917, 217.

30. ET–HT, 7–8 April 1917, 96.

31. Helen Thomas, 300.

32. FL–HT, 10 April 1917.

33. WD, 14v; lines loose in WD.

34. RF–HT, 27 April 1917, 216.

*

1. RF–SC, 11 Oct. 1928, 351; see JWH–RPE, 22 Feb. 1934, 'In common with many of E.T.'s intimate friends, and certainly with some of the Thomas family, I was a good deal upset by Helen's two books when they were published.'

2. Mervyn Thomas in RLW, 16.

3. See Sokol, 228; see Frost, 'War Thoughts at Home' [Jan. 1918], *VQR*, Fall 2006, 113, 'To E.T.', *YR*, April 1920, *New Hampshires*, 83, 'A Soldier', *McCalls*, May 1927, *Collected Poems*; see Inventory of personal effects, 4 May 1917, NA.

4. Pound, *Hugh Selwyn Mauberley*, 13.

5. EG–WdlM, 29 April 1920, 230; de la Mare, 'To E. T.: 1917', *Motley*, 55.

6. See Gibson, *Battle*; WWG–RF, 3 Jan. 1934, DCL, Lesley Lee Francis, 190; Conrad Aiken in Stonesifer, 137.

7. Lascelles Abercrombie, v; Abercrombie in Gawsworth, 20–1.

8. Eliot, 'Ulysses, Order, and Myth', *The Dial*, 75 (Nov. 1923), 480–3; 38 Great Russell Street, London WC.

9. W. H. Hudson [1919] in Tomalin, 213; Leavis, 64; Day Lewis, 75; see Larkin; Dylan Thomas, 208; Ted Hughes speaking at Westminster Abbey, 11 Nov. 1985.

Index